D1154427

AUTHORS OF THE IMPOSSIBLE

AUTHORS OF THE IMPOSSIBLE

The Paranormal and the Sacred

JEFFREY J. KRIPAL

THE UNIVERSITY OF CHICAGO PRESS
CHICAGO AND LONDON

JEFFREY J. KRIPAL is the J. Newton Rayzor Professor of Religious Studies and chair of the Department of Religious Studies at Rice University. He is the author of several books, most recently of *Esalen: America and the Religion of No Religion*.

The University of Chicago Press, Chicago 60637
The University of Chicago Press, Ltd., London

Printed in the United States of America

19 18 17 16 15 14 13 12 11 10   1 2 3 4 5

ISBN-13: 978-0-226-45386-6 (cloth)
ISBN-10: 0-226-45386-3 (cloth)

Frontispiece: *Ailleurs* (circa 1960) by Arthur-Maria Rener (1912–91), Vallee private collection, hanging over the Vallee-Hynek parapsychological library. Used with permission.

Library of Congress Cataloging-in-Publication Data

Kripal, Jeffrey John, 1962–
Authors of the impossible : the paranormal and the sacred / Jeffrey J. Kripal.
p. cm.
Includes bibliographical references and index.
ISBN-13: 978-0-226-45386-6 (cloth : alk. paper)
ISBN-10: 0-226-45386-3 (cloth : alk. paper) 1. Parapsychology—History. 2. Religion—Psychic aspects. 3. Myers, Frederic William Henry, 1843–1901. 4. Society for Psychical Research (Great Britain) 5. Fort, Charles, 1874–1932. I. Title.
BF1028 .K75 2010
130—dc22

2009029969

♾ The paper used in this publication meets the minimum requirements of the American National Standard for Information Sciences—Permanence of Paper for Printed Library Materials, ANSI Z39.48-1992.

for David

for taking many chances on an aspiring author of the impossible who has tried his best not to become an impossible author

Read a book, or look at a picture. The composer has taken a wild talent that nobody else in the world believed in; a thing that came and went and flouted and deceived him; maybe starved him; almost ruined him—and has put that damn thing to work.

—CHARLES FORT, *Wild Talents*

DIMENSIONS

ACKNOWLEDGMENTS

> All things cut an umbilical cord only to clutch a breast.
> —CHARLES FORT, *The Book of the Damned*

Professionally speaking, one's intellectual and personal debts are inscribed in one's footnotes, but such secreted allusions seldom carry the full force of all those connections of person, place, and project that make a work of scholarship finally "pop" into view. Nor, alas, do long lists of names on an acknowledgments page. So I will try to write sentences here, and keep things short and to the point, which is to say, to the person.

The book is dedicated to T. David Brent, the editor of all six of my Chicago monographs (the sixth still coming to be). I do not underestimate, and I cannot overestimate, what David and the press's support have meant to me over the years, both those of the past and those spread out into the future (for publishing books is very much about the future). I mean every word of the dedication, and then some.

Michael Murphy and the Esalen Institute's Center for Theory and Research have generously supported an annual symposia series that I conceived and subsequently direct on the paranormal and popular culture in Big Sur each May. The latter is part of Esalen's Sursem research group on postmortem survival, of which I am deeply honored to be a part. Much of the talent of these two symposia series, and particularly Sursem, is represented in the pages that follow. Of special note are Stephen Braude, Adam Crabtree, Edward Kelly, Emily Williams Kelly, Dean Radin, Russell Targ, and Charles Tart.

Two of my four authors of the impossible, Jacques Vallee and Bertrand Méheust, also deserve special mention. Jacques went out of his way to welcome me into the inner sanctum of his home and library, shared with me many unpublished materials and secret stories, and responded to my thoughts about his work with helpful criticism and further insight. Bertrand was gracious and patient with an American English speaker struggling through thousands of pages of his erudite French. He even went so far as to declare what were clear translation errors on my part philosophical insights. This was very flattering. And very funny. I've fixed those errors. The reader can draw his or her own conclusion about what that means. I have also laughed a great deal with Bertrand, mostly in Big Sur, where he was once attacked by the dreaded black Spider-Man. That was very funny too. I deny everything.

I must also mention Victoria Nelson, whose work in *The Secret Life of Puppets* (Harvard, 2001) played a special role in the inspiration—it is really more of an uncanny haunting—for this book. Vicki has been a constant source of support, advice, and mind-bogglingly detailed editorial help. She also helped introduce me to other academics and professional writers more or less secretly working on such matters. One of the main goals of the present work is to help create a safe, or at least a safer, intellectual space within the humanities and the arts so that such writers working "off the page" can come back "on the page" and enlighten us about the deeper dialectics of consciousness and culture.

In terms of the Fort materials, I must thank Jim Steinmeyer, Fort's recent talented biographer. Fort is a veritable ocean in which one can easily get lost and drown. Jim's biography came at a crucial time for me and showed me my own way through the waves and fishes. The following individuals have also played key roles in one way or another: Kelly Bulkeley, who generously described (or compassionately lied about) my treatment of the neuroscientific materials as "just right"; Brenda Denzler, who taught me about the history of ufology and the professional costs involved in such anomalous interests; David Hufford, who taught me that materialism and rationalism are not the same thing, at all; Chad Pevateaux, my graduate student who has accomplished innumerable source-checking, editing, and indexing tasks for me with his usual Derridean verve and Blakean grace; and Jody Radzik, whose nondual experiences have long functioned for me as a kind of living mirror in which I can catch a fleeting glimpse of my own X. Thank you all.

Finally, I must thank Scott Jones of XL Films. XL Films has optioned this book for a feature documentary now in process. Scott showed great enthusiasm for the cinematic potentials of my thought and is presently teaching me that the paranormal mysteries of reading and writing extend into the acts of viewing and seeing as well. We are back to Plato's Cave and those shadows of social, historical, and religious truth projected on the cave wall now called a theater screen. Happily, there is also a way out of the cavelike theatre, always, of course, through that back door and sticky floor behind the projector.

Only spilled soda pop and bad carpet block our way out now . . .

An Impossible Opening

THE MAGICAL POLITICS OF BOBBY KENNEDY

> A dear friend, a great scientist, now dead, used to tease me by saying that because politics is the art of the possible, it appeals only to second-rate minds. The *first*-raters, he claimed, were only interested in the *impossible*.
>
> —ARTHUR C. CLARKE, *The Fountain of Paradise*

An opening is a beginning, but it is also a hole.

I want to open with a story that could not have possibly happened, which happened. I have chosen this story carefully. It is neither abstract nor distant to me. I know the central visionary well and can vouch for his complete integrity and honesty. I have absolutely no doubt that this event happened to this individual as described below. What it, and countless other stories like it, *mean* is quite another matter. Which is why I wrote this book.

I will suggest no adequate explanation for this impossible possibility. The simple truth is that I do not have one. Nor, I suspect, do you, or anyone else for that matter, other than, of course, the professional debunker, whose ideological denials boil down to the claim that such things never happened or, if they did, that they are just "anecdotes" unworthy of our serious attention and careful thought. Such mock rationalisms, such defense mechanisms, such cowardly refusals to think before the abyss will win nothing here but my own mocking laughter. Each of us, after all, is just such an irreducible, unrepeatable, unquantifiable Anecdote.

I begin with an impossibility, then, not to pretend some knowledge that I do not possess (like the debunkers or the believers), but to provoke and perform our own almost total ignorance and, more positively, to call us out of our rationalist denials into a more spacious and generous Imagination. I am not after easy rational solutions, much less "beliefs" in this or that cultural mythology. I am after liberating confusions. I am after the Impossible.

Adam is a friend, a colleague, a former Benedictine monk, an accomplished academic author, and a practicing psychotherapist. In 1968, he was living in Toronto, Canada. A little after 3:00 a.m. on June 5th, he suddenly awoke—instantly and completely. Here is what he wrote when I asked him for a full and precise account of what happened next:

> I couldn't figure out what was happening. As far as I knew there had been no noise, I felt no pain or discomfort. I turned on the light and, not knowing what else to do, reached for the transistor radio beside my bed. I flicked the "on" switch. I did not know what local station I had tuned to during the day, but, being the middle of the night and the AM band subject to those strange late-night bounces, now a distant station had supplanted the local one. It was a California station. The radio voice, a newsman of some sort, was asking Robert Kennedy a question [he was fresh off a victory in the California presidential primary election and was passing through a hotel kitchen on his way to a press conference]. The newscaster was walking with Kennedy and his entourage. As I listened, I heard sounds of mayhem. When the newsman was able to get his wits together, he said, with uncontrollable emotion, that Kennedy had just been shot. I was stunned. I could hardly believe what I was hearing. For the next hour or so I remained glued to this distant station, listening as the bits and pieces of news were put together to construct a picture of what had happened, and finally hearing the sad word of Kennedy's death, some time later.[1]

The emotional effect of all of this on Adam was as immediate and as dramatic as his sudden awakening in the middle of the night: "I was devastated. I was an admirer of Kennedy and impressed by his campaign. I had seen him the previous fall at the Exhibition Grounds in Toronto where he had attended a football game and had even shaken his hand as he left the area." The experience would not leave him, would not let him go:

> Later, when I reflected on what happened to me in those few minutes that night, I began to realize that something truly extraordinary had occurred—for several reasons: (1) I had never before (and have never since) gone instantaneously from a sound sleep to total wakefulness; (2) the fact that when I reached for the radio it was tuned to a position on the dial that would give me that particular California station; and (3) the fact that the events of the assassination occurred within five minutes of my sudden awakening. Was this coincidence? I simply could not bring myself to accept that explanation. Could it have been some kind of ESP, some kind of telepathic communication from Kennedy picked up perhaps at random? At first sight that may seem possible. But a little thought showed me that this explanation was not adequate. Events had to happen in my room in precisely the right way for this to occur, and there is no way that telepathy could have arranged them. Even if, as some might believe, a telepathic communication could have awakened me in that strange way, the telepathic explanation could not account for the physical state of things that was needed for the event to occur as it did, nor could it account for the crucial timing of my movements over those first few minutes after awakening. By that, I mean that it could not account for my radio being set at the very frequency at which the broadcast would occur, and it could not account for the fact that I turned on the radio at precisely the moment when the event was being broadcast. Besides, there are many other things I could have done instead when suddenly awakened, such as getting up to see that everything was all right in the house or getting a drink, but in fact I immediately reached over and turned on that fatefully tuned radio.

And there was more:

> For years I could not understand why, even given the paranormal dimensions of this experience, it was me to whom it happened. Then in the early 1980s I had occasion to study the traditional magico-spiritual system of the Hawaiian Islands, called "Huna." In his exposition of this fascinating doctrine, Max Freedom Long described the Huna belief that when people have some kind

> of meaningful contact with each other, a "sticky thread" comes into existence that connects the two and continues to connect them wherever they go for the whole of their lives. Without going into the implications of this belief, I would just like to say that when I read this I suddenly remembered that night in 1968, but also, and especially, my handshake with Robert Kennedy. I recalled that handshake very vividly. That day I was, of course, very moved to be shaking the hand of a man who so greatly impressed me. But something else, something very odd also affected me. It was how his hand felt. It was a strange impression that I could not get out of my mind at the time. Without realizing it, when I reached out toward Kennedy, I had expected to feel a warm moist hand, and what I felt instead really puzzled me. He hand was very dry, almost like leather. I was taken aback by the feeling, because it was so different from what I was expecting. Now, as I read Long's words about those "sticky threads," that contact with Kennedy's hand came back vividly to me. Viewing the experience in terms of the Huna view of the world, for the first time some bit of light seemed to be cast on the "Why me?" question. A vibrant thread of connection was there, and it was along that thread that the events of June 5, 1968, were strung. Even though questions remained, and even though this new insight did not remove the mystery of the event, I seemed to feel a little more understanding of one of the most extraordinary experiences of my life.

For what it is worth, Adam was not alone in his nightly vision. Alan Vaughan, the writer who would coauthor *Dream Telepathy* (1973) with Montague Ullman and Stanley Krippner, identified sixty-one precognitive dreams in his own journals (the researcher as researched), including two he wrote down on May 25, 1968, that he felt indicated Robert Kennedy's life was at risk. Vaughan wrote Krippner a detailed letter about them.[2] Kennedy was shot a week later.

Welcome to the art of the impossible.

Introduction

OFF THE PAGE

> The literature of *fantasy* and the fantastic, especially in science fiction, is much in demand, but we still do not know its intimate relationship with the different occult traditions. The underground vogue of Hesse's *Journey to the East* (1951) in the fifties anticipated the occult revival of the late sixties. But who will interpret for us the amazing success of . . . *2001[: A Space Odyssey]*? I am merely asking the question.
> —MIRCEA ELIADE, "The Occult and the Modern World"

> People like us, who believe in physics, know that the distinction between past, present, and future is only a stubbornly persistent illusion.
> —ALBERT EINSTEIN

This book began as another book, *The Secret Life of a Superpower*. There I explore some of the esoteric currents of American popular culture, particularly as these are narrated and illustrated in the superhero comic book, a pop mythology with some surprisingly intimate ties to the histories of occultism, psychical research, and related paranormal phenomena. In *The Secret Life of a Superpower*, I am especially interested in the manner in which certain seemingly universal human experiences—out-of-body flight, magical influence, telepathic communication, secret forms of identity, altered states of consciousness and energy—occupy a rather curious place in our present Western culture. Whereas such marvels are vociferously denied (or simply ignored) in the halls of academic respectability, they are enthusiastically embraced in contemporary fiction, film, and fantasy. We are obviously fascinated by such things and will pay billions of dollars for their special display, and yet we will not talk about them, not at least in any serious and sustained professional way. Popular culture is our mysticism. The public realm is our esoteric realm. The paranormal is our secret in plain sight. Weird.

As I read into the background literature of these modern mythologies, I found myself confronting the histories of Western esotericism, animal magnetism, psychical research, science fiction, and the UFO phenomenon (the latter, it turns out, has been especially influential on the superhero via science fiction). In the process, I began encountering a few select authors whose power of expression, humor, and unfettered freedom of speculative thought simply stunned me. There were many reasons for my sense of surprise. What shocked me the most, however, was the fact that these authors, through decades of extensive data collection, classification, and theorizing (that is, through a kind of natural history of the supernormal), had arrived at some basic metaphysical conclusions that were eerily similar, if not actually identical, to those that grounded the fantasy literature of the superhero comics. So, for example, the American psychoanalyst Jules Eisenbud came to the conclusion through his research on the psychokinetic abilities of Ted Serios (who could mentally imprint detailed images on photographic film under carefully controlled conditions) that, "man has in fact within him vast untapped powers that hitherto have been accorded him only in the magic world of the primitive, in the secret fantasies of childhood, and in fairy tales and legend."[1] This struck me as, well, *impossible*.

What also surprised me was the fact that I had never heard of these authors, that after over twenty-five years of studying comparative mystical literature professionally, I had never *once* encountered another scholar mentioning, much less engaging, three of the four writers whom I came to admire so. The British classicist and psychical researcher Frederic Myers was the exception to this rule, but even he was not much of an exception. Everyone in the field reads the American psychologist and philosopher

William James. But who reads James's close friend and intimate collaborator on the other side of the ocean? Who in the study of religion seriously engages Myers's massive and endlessly fascinating *Human Personality and Its Survival of Bodily Death*? A few for sure, but only a few.[2] The situation is much more dramatic for our second author of the impossible, Charles Fort, whom only a few radical folklorists appear to have read; or our third and fourth, Jacques Vallee and Bertrand Méheust, whom almost no one in the field has heard of, much less read. I hadn't anyway. My conclusion was a simple one: Myers, Fort, Vallee, and Méheust are not part of the scholarly canon that has come to define what is possible to be reasonably thought and comparatively imagined in the professional study of religion.

This latter realization both fascinated and upset me. It was as if my profession had somehow intentionally steered me away from such writers and thoughts. I do not, of course, attribute any personal intention here. I am not accusing anyone of anything. Nor do I wish to pretend that the four authors under discussion here somehow solve the problems other scholars have inadequately addressed. The truth is that I have deep reservations about the objectivist epistemologies that control much of psychical research to this day, and I think some of Fort's ideas are simply nuts (but, to his humorous credit, so did he). I do now suspect, however, that the study of religion as a discipline, as a structure of thought, *as a field of possibility*, has severely limited itself precisely to the extent that it has followed Western culture on this particular point, that is, to the extent that the discipline constantly encounters robust paranormal phenomena in its data—the stuff is *everywhere*—and then refuses to talk about such things in any truly serious and sustained way. The paranormal is our secret in plain sight too. Weird.

Definitions and Broken Lineages

It does not have to be this way.

It has not always been this way.

A few historical observations and opening definitions are in order here. The expression *psychic* goes back to nineteenth-century uses. It was probably first coined as "Psychic Force" by Serjeant Cox in an 1871 letter to the renowned English chemist William Crookes, who subsequently did more than anyone to bring this Psychic Force into the English language through a series of remarkable experiments and reports in the early 1870s on the observable effects that mediums like Daniel Dunglas Home had on inert objects and human bodies (including Home's own, which Crookes noted appeared visibly "drained" after employing the Psychic Force). Despite intense professional opposition and censorship, Crookes never retracted either the results of his experiments with Home or his firm conviction that "there exists a Force exercised by intelligence differing from the ordinary intelligence common to mortals."[3] In the wake of Crookes's brave new physics, the London Society for Psychical Research adopted the slightly longer adjective *psychical* as an unsatisfactory but workable descriptor for its own scientific pursuits. The S.P.R., as it came to be known, was founded in the winter of 1882 by a few close colleagues at Cambridge University. An American branch was founded three years later, in 1885, with William James of Harvard University as one of its key founding figures and certainly the most eloquent and sophisticated proponent of "psychical research" on this side of the Atlantic. In short, the terms *psychic* and *psychical* possess elite intellectual roots and were born in the professional academy.

The language of the *paranormal* arises a bit later. It originates in the early decades of the twentieth century as a way of referring to physical or quasi-physical events, often of an outrageous or impossible nature (think floating tables, materializing objects or "apports," and ectoplasm), that were believed to be controlled by as yet unknown physical, that is, natural laws. The term, however, was clearly connected to the earlier American and British Spiritualist movements and so quickly took on more religious connotations as well, often of a highly heterodox nature.

In order to counter such unwanted connotations (and the fraud that often accompanied their theatrical display), the terminology of *psi* was introduced by British psychologist Robert Thouless in 1942 as a neutral scientific term designed to replace the more loaded terms of the psychical, the paranormal, and the occult. The same term was meant to code or point to what was thought to be the underlying unitary nature of the disparate telepathic, precognitive, and psychokinetic phenomena. J. B. Rhine took this domesticating and unifying process further and adopted *parapsychology* as the preferred term for the field. Rhine operationalized psychical research at Duke University in the late 1930s, '40s, '50s, and '60s through controlled laboratory conditions and careful statistical analyses.

I have much admiration for the intellectual courage and pioneering spirit of parapsychologists and the numerous thinkers who have critically analyzed this data and drawn out its philosophical implications without regard for the very real professional costs and taboos that still surround the subject. I am neither a scientist nor a philosopher, however. I am a historian of religions. Consequently, what I am attempting in the pages that follow has little to do with the scientific protocols and statistical methods of the parapsychological lab and everything to do with the textual, narrative, and ethnographic methods of the early British and American psychical researchers. In the process, I hope to resurrect and re-theorize two terms, the psychical and the paranormal.

For the sake of what follows, I am defining the psychical as *the sacred in transit from a traditional religious register into a modern scientific one*. This transit is especially easy to see when we set, as we will in chapter 1, the psychical and its related notions (the imaginal, the supernormal, and the telepathic) alongside two other eminently modern terms, both of which took form at roughly the same time but that do not generally carry explicitly scientific connotations: the mystical and the spiritual. Along these same lines, I am defining the paranormal as *the sacred in transit from the religious and scientific registers into a parascientific or "science mysticism" register*. Basically, in the paranormal, *both* the faith of religion *and* the reason of science drop away, and a kind of super-imagination appears on the horizon of thought. As a consequence, the paranormal becomes a living story or, better, a mythology. Things also get wilder. Way wilder.

Both definitions, obviously, employ a shared third term that needs to be defined immediately as well: the *sacred*. By the sacred, I mean what the German theologian and historian of religions Rudolf Otto meant, that is, a particular structure of human consciousness that corresponds to a palpable presence, energy, or power encountered in the environment. Otto captured this sacred sixth sense, at once subject and object, in a famous Latin sound bite: the sacred is the *mysterium tremendum et fascinans*, that is, the mystical (*mysterium*) as both fucking scary (*tremendum*) and utterly fascinating (*fascinans*). The sacred (minus the fucking part) was a key concept in both the German and French streams of critical theory, particularly in thinkers like Otto, Emile Durkheim, and Joachim Wach, after which the Romanian historian of religions Mircea Eliade made it central to his own work at the University of Chicago in the 1960s, '70s, and early '80s. For a variety of reasons, most of them boiling down to some form of implicit materialism, the category has become taboo today. But the subject of the paranormal invokes it again, and in full force. We are back to terror and bedazzlement.

Unlike the sacred, neither the psychical nor the paranormal has survived in any active form within the professional study of religion. Neither, for example, merits its own entry in Mircea Eliade's *Encyclopedia of Religion*, and this despite the fact that "Psychical Research" merited a balanced three-page essay in James Hasting's classic *Encyclopaedia of Religion and Ethics* ninety years ago.[4] The author, moreover, was none other than James Leuba, a very prominent psychologist of the time with a penchant for bold reductionistic readings of religious phenomena ranging from conversion to mysticism. Leuba in fact ends his entry with the subject of my first chapter, the London Society for Psychical Research (the S.P.R.), and some comments expressive of that special combination of Enlightenment rationalism and Romantic imagination that characterized the period just before his, the period that gave birth to both modern psychology and the study of religion. Here is how Leuba concludes his entry:

> If, after thirty-four years of activity, many of the mysteries which the S.P.R. set out to explore are still unfathomed, much has, nevertheless, been explained. Thus the mischief which mystery works upon credulous humanity has been decreased. . . . But the greatest accomplishment to record is the approximate demonstration that, under circumstances still mostly unknown, men may gain knowledge by other than the usual means, perhaps by direct communication between brains (telepathy) at practically any earthly distance from each other. This dark opening is indeed portentous. It may at any time lead to discoveries which will dwarf into insignificance any of the previous achievements of science.[5]

Leuba's startling words about a "dark opening" still apparently open, still seemingly possible in 1918, is a clear reminder that we have inherited a certain forgetting. It would do us well to try to remember that which we have forgotten in order better to understand that the possible can be construed quite otherwise than it is at the moment, that that which is impossible can become possible. Let us, then, remember for just a moment, and this in just three fields of inquiry: philosophy, anthropology, and psychology.

Consider first the history of Western philosophy. As the classicist E. R. Dodds (who had read and absorbed his fellow classicist Frederic Myers) points out with respect to "Supernormal Phenomena in Classical Antiquity," the philosophical and historiographical conundrums of precognition were already fully recognized in the ancient world:

> The paradox of the situation was recognized in antiquity: Aristotle opens his discussion of the subject with the remark that it is difficult either to ignore the evidence or to believe it. Ostensible precognitions formed part of the accepted matter of history: the pages of nearly all ancient historians, from Herodotus to Ammianus Marcellinus, are full of omens, oracles, or precognitive dreams or visions. Yet how can an event in an as yet non-existent future casually determine

> an event in the present? This was already for Cicero, and even for his credulous brother, Quintus, the *magnus quaestio*, as it still is today.[6]

There is a funny story here that is quite relevant to our discussion of broken lineages. Fritz Graf, a contemporary classics scholar of epigraphy and Greek religion, remembers meeting Dodds in the mid-1970s at his home in Oxford in order to present the esteemed historian with his own newly minted dissertation on Orpheus and Eleusis, both widely considered to be distant historical origin-points of our modern term "mysticism." Dodds thanked Graf for his book, but then immediately added: "But I have no interest anymore in Greek religion. I am only interested in paranormal phenomena."[7]

If we jump from the classical world into the modern one, Dodd's *magnus quaestio* or "great question" with respect to the ancient materials hardly goes away, although it certainly becomes more questionable. In his *Dreams of a Spirit-Seer*, Immanuel Kant grappled, sarcastically but deeply, with Emanuel Swedenborg's seeming noumenal powers, which included one famous scene on June 19, 1759, when the spirit-seer saw a Stockholm fire, the advance of which he accurately described to a garden party in Göteborg, Sweden, as the fire raged three hundred miles away, stopping just three doors down from his own home.[8] A bit later, Hegel wrote appreciatively on animal magnetism, extrasensory perception, and a kind of World Soul, all key components of his astonishing vision of a kind of cosmic Mind or absolute Spirit (*Geist*) coming into fuller and fuller consciousness through history, culture, religion, philosophy, and, now, Hegel and his deep readers.[9]

Similarly, Schopenhauer engaged reports of the incredible powers of intention and mind-over-matter to fashion his own philosophy of Will. Throughout *The World as Will and Representation* (1818), the philosopher invokes Hindu, Buddhist, and Christian mystical sources in order to explain how all things are one in their essence, that is, in the occult force of a cosmic Will out of which all things ineluctably arise and into which they ineluctably disappear. Later, in *The Will in Nature* (1836), he turned to the subjects of animal magnetism and magic to find further support for his metaphysical doctrines. Here he explains, following Kant, that space and time are purely phenomenal. They are constructs or categories of our minds, not features of the world as it is in itself. Space and time are, to borrow Einstein's language in our opening epigraph, "stubbornly persistent illusions." Accordingly, the common transcendence of space and time one encounters in clairvoyance and precognition (the latter which

Schopenhauer himself experienced) are hardly illusory. Quite the contrary, they witness to the world as it really is. What is in fact illusory are our common everyday perceptions, which can only show us the real as it is mediated to us through our senses and mental categories.[10]

Such philosophical streams have recently been revived and renewed by the analytic philosopher Stephen E. Braude, who as a graduate student and self-described arrogant hardnosed materialist witnessed a table lift off the floor and communicate tapping messages to him and two friends during an impromptu séance session. "Now I won't mince words," Braude writes. "What happened that afternoon scared the hell out of me. For three hours I observed my own table tilt up and down, without visible assistance." The scholarly result? Nothing, until he got tenure ("I may be crazy, but I'm not stupid").[11] Since then he has written five especially provocative books, all of which orbit around the questions posed by that floating, tapping table and his intuitive suspicion that it was the three of them who controlled the table with still unknown, unconscious, unacknowledged powers.[12] Eisenbud's "vast untapped powers" come to life in the living room.

Similar moments could easily be located among the anthropologists. In *The Making of Religion* (1899), Andrew Lang put early anthropology into dialogue with the then cutting-edge categories of psychical research in order to plumb the speculative origins of various phenomena within the history of religions (magical influence, possession, and divinatory practices, to name just a few) and to ask whether "a transcendental region of human faculty," a "region X," might not exist. He also studied scrying (crystal gazing) among Scottish female seers and was especially fond of collecting ghost stories from around the world. It was this kind of field research and comparative collecting that led him finally to conclude that magical beliefs are not groundless superstitious or gross examples of bad thinking left over from a prescientific age, which is exactly what his most prestigious peers thought, but rather, that "[m]an may have faculties which savages recognize, and which physical science does not recognize. Man may be surrounded by agencies which savages exaggerate, and which science disregards altogether, and these faculties and agencies may point to an element of truth which is often cast aside as a survival of superstition." In Lang's mind, in other words, "certain obscure facts are, or may be, at the bottom of many folklore beliefs." Here he gave the fascinating example of a correspondent from India who had witnessed some anomalous lights at dusk in a Darjeeling garden, where the servants shared matter-of-fact descriptions of a race of "little men" (we'll return to those anomalous lights and humanoids soon enough). In essence, Lang was advancing a theory of the origins of religion in which those origins were grounded in empirical psychical phenomena that were subsequently exaggerated and embellished in folklore and myth. The idea of the soul, for example, he reasoned, did not come about through mistaken interpretations of dreams (which is what his mentor, Edward Tylor, had famously argued), but from real-world veridical experiences akin to those that the S.P.R. had recently labeled instances of "telepathy." Of the latter phenomenon, he confessed in his 1911 presidential address to the same society, "I am wholly convinced."[13]

A half century later, the Italian anthropologist Ernesto De Martino went so far as to claim that the data of ethnography and folklore, and now of psychical research, strongly suggest "the paradox of a *culturally-conditioned* nature, and all its embarrassing implications." Reality, De Martino realized, appears to behave differently within different linguistic codes. Magic, the mind's ability to affect the material world through acts of attention and intention, he went on to suggest, really and truly plays "a role in history."[14] A bit later, Edith Turner wrote of her encounter with spirits and experience of psychical abilities, and Margaret Mead wrote appreciatively on psychical matters, encouraging her intellectual peers to study even the most extraordinary examples of this literature, including the data emerging from the then still secret "remote viewing" or psychical espionage programs of the U.S. military.[15] More impressively still, Michael Winkelman demonstrated a striking "correspondence between parapsychological research findings and anthropological reports of magical phenomena" toward the thesis that real-life spontaneous magical experiences have their deepest (that is, ontological) basis not in social processes or logical mistakes (which, again, is what has traditionally been argued), but in extreme emotional states, largely unconscious primary process thinking, and "innate universal human potentials closely associated with psi abilities." These, he wrote, are "human capacities, still little understood, for affecting the world in a manner which is beyond our current understanding of the laws of nature."[16] In other words, magical powers are real.

The psychology of religion displays the same submerged patterns again. Pierre Janet, the pioneering French psychologist whose work deeply influenced a young Sigmund Freud, discovered, in the words of historian Alex Owen, "what magicians have traditionally claimed—that it is possible to hypnotize a subject from a distance." He also realized, correctly, that hypnotism replicated the earlier phenomena of Mesmerism (which in fact were much more robust and impressive), and he wrote his minor thesis on Bacon and the alchemists.[17] William James worked for years with a very convincing trance medium named Leonora Piper, puzzled over the possibility of postmortem survival, and wrote extensively on psychical matters.[18] C. G. Jung wrote his dissertation on occult phenomena (with his cousin as medium no less), attended séances for another thirty years, experienced paranormal events throughout his life (including in Freud's presence), and even produced a gnostic text out of a kind of "haunting," his famous *Septes Sermones ad Mortuos* or *Seven Sermons to the Dead*.[19]

Jung was also famously fascinated by the implications of quantum physics for understanding paranormal phenomena. Indeed, he even forged his category of synchronicity out of his correspondence with one of his patients, the pioneering quantum physicist Wolfgang Pauli. What is more (way more), Pauli was well known among his physics colleagues for a rather unique mind-to-matter effect. In the words of George Gamow, the "Pauli Effect" boiled down to the strange fact that an "apparatus would fall, break, shatter or burn when he merely walked into a laboratory."[20] This was such a common occurrence that when laboratory equipment failed or broke, the experimenters would ask if Pauli was in town.

So too with Sigmund Freud. Freud's close colleague Wilhelm Stekel published an entire book on telepathic dreams in 1921. Although originally dismissive, Freud became convinced that there was a kernel of truth in such occult phenomena. He publicly acknowledged this in a 1925 essay and wrote six essays in all on the subject of telepathy or "thought transference" (*Gedankenübertragung*), which he considered to be the "rational core" of occultism. And why not? Had not dreams, another classical occult subject, proven to possess meaning in his own system of thought; indeed, had not dreams, themselves closely tied to psychical phenomena, helped *found* his thought?[21] But if telepathy were now admitted and allowed to inform psychoanalytic theory, then what? Where would such a line of thought lead, or more importantly, where would it *end*? Freud's colleague and biographer Ernest Jones was concerned that such a development would end in "the essential claim of the occultists," namely, "that mental processes can be independent of the human body."[22]

For his part, Freud could finally not bring himself to allow such dangerous things into public debate. Hence he counseled Sandor Ferenczi not to relate his telepathic researches to the Hamburg Congress of 1925 with these telling words: "By it you would be throwing a bomb into the psychoanalytical house which would be certain to explode."[23] In other words, such matters are probably true on some level, but they must be denied for the sake of intellectual consensus and the stable future of a young, and still vulnerable, movement. By 1927, however, Freud appears to have moved away from even this hidden recognition. He was growing more skeptical and more ambivalent. Interestingly, he was also growing more ambivalent about a key psychoanalytic capacity, *Einfühlung*, "empathy" or "feeling into." In a letter to Ferenczi, Freud described seeing a certain "mystical character" in this well-documented but poorly understood analytic ability to fathom a patient's unconscious with one's own unconscious processes, and he could see no easy way to distinguish it from telepathy.[24]

This is hardly surprising and essentially correct, since the core themes of "resemblance," "sympathy," and especially "rapport" had long been central to magical, mesmeric, and magnetic practice before Freud came on the scene. Little wonder, then, that the lore of psychoanalysis is *filled* with moments of profound empathy that amount to instances of telepathy. After reading one of my essays on the subject, for example, one contemporary analyst contacted me and told me the story of a female patient of hers. As the patient began to talk, the analyst felt a sharp stabbing pain in her lower left ribcage. The patient then proceeded to tell her about how her father had stabbed her when she was a young girl, in the lower left ribcage.

And such paranormal moments continue down to the present day. In 2007, the impossible story of a prominent American analyst by the name of Elizabeth Lloyd Mayer was published (Mayer had died the year before). After her daughter's rare harp was stolen in the Bay Area in 1991 and she had exhausted all the normal police channels, Mayer, in desperation, took a friend's advice and called a dowser or psychic seer in Fayetteville, Arkansas. Using a map of the Bay Area, Harold McCoy told Mayer over the phone the precise location of the house where the stolen harp was located, in Oakland it turned out: "the second house on the right on D____ Street, just off L____ Avenue." After recovering the harp, Mayer found herself now missing something else, her sense of objective reality: "the harp was in the back of my station-wagon and I drove off. Twenty-five minutes later, as I turned into my driveway, I had the thought, *This changes everything*."[25]

Indeed, it did. The remotely viewed harp, after all, strongly suggested that consciousness is not bound to the brain or the body, as Mayer had assumed it to be. This, of course, was the same thing that bothered Ernest Jones so about those dreaded "occultists." It took a long professional quest into the history of psychical research, cold war remote viewing, and quantum physics in order to arrive at a tentative, and now public, thesis about the reality of what Mayer calls, with a phrase that can only be called a gross understatement, "extraordinary knowing."[26] She also organized, with Carol Gilligan, a long-standing series of popular panels on anomalous phenomena in the analytic session for the annual meeting of the American Psychoanalytic Association—the return, no doubt, of Freud's repressed insights into the mystical and telepathic nature of profound analytic empathy. The panels were hugely popular as they became the arena for stories like that of the analyst who was precognitively "stabbed" in the ribcage.

And the fields of philosophy, anthropology, and psychology are just the beginning. We could easily go on for dozens, for *hundreds*, of pages demonstrating how these questions lay at the very center of Western intellectual and cultural life. We could trace their pathways through numerous Nobel scientists, with physicists showing a particular fondness for the subject. We could then chart a similar lineage through major modern artists, including painters like Piet Mondrian and Wassily Kandinsky. The latter's *The Spiritual in Art*, for example, is clearly indebted to the "Thought Forms" of Theosophy and the philosophy of Rudolf Steiner.

And this is before we even get to modern literature, with authors like Edgar Allan Poe, Margaret Fuller, Sir Edward Bulwer-Lytton, Victor Hugo, Jules Verne, Mark Twain, Arthur Conan Doyle, Lewis Carroll, W. B. Yeats, Henry Miller, Philip K. Dick, Arthur C. Clarke, Stephen King, and Michael Crichton all writing explicitly about their spiritualist, psychical, paranormal, and occult interests and experiences. Such occult experiences were hardly tangential to such authors. They were integral components of the creative process. Hence Bruce Mills has recently written about the mesmeric and magnetic currents that played such an important role in the creation of a distinctly American literature in the middle of the nineteenth century, and Alex Owen has written about "the symbiotic relationship among vitalism, occultism, and advanced literary ideas" in turn-of-the-century Britain.[27] The accomplished occultist W. B. Yeats, whose magical name was *Demon Est Deus Inversus* or "The Devil is God in Reverse" (they just called him "Demon"), might have been an extreme case, but he was hardly alone when he confessed to John O'Leary in a letter that the "mystical life is the centre of all that I do and all that I think and all that I write."[28]

Finally, we could also show—and will show in chapter 4—how the metaphysical shock of the early psychical data was subsequently resisted, tamed, and safely transformed by the buffer or "stop zones" of later intellectual movements from psychoanalysis and psychiatry to surrealism and Derridean deconstructionism, each of which dealt with the paranormal, but only at a distance and in order to keep it at bay. Even Derrida, after all, wrote an essay called "Telepathy" and famously remarked in *Specters of Marx* that "There has never been a scholar who really, and as scholar, deals with ghosts. . . . There has never been a scholar who, as such, does not believe in the sharp distinction between the real and the unreal, the actual and the inactual, the living and the non-living."[29]

Derrida was wrong about that, as we will soon see. For now, though, it is enough to point out how little this intellectual history appears in contemporary theory. It is enough to pretend with Derrida that "there has never been a scholar who really, and as scholar, deals with ghosts."

Restoring a Lineage

Perhaps nowhere, however, is this proverbial fear of ghosts more apparent, and more poignant, than in the study of religion, that *locus classicus* of the paranormal. So whereas, for example, a figure like Rudolf Otto displayed a profound sensibility for the numinous as the eerie, the sacred at once alluring and terrifying, and insisted on the epistemological necessity of such a sensibility to study the sacred in any truly adequate fashion, today those ghostly sensibilities are continuously ridiculed as naive and self-serving, as if real scholarship can only proceed by denying the reality of that which it claims to study. Hence Edith Turner's reflections on witnessing a spirit emerge from a sick body in Zambia and her subsequent experiences of ESP, all almost completely incomprehensible before what she calls the "religious frigidity" of academics.[30]

And so that ancient "taboo against contact with supernatural forces are with us still," parapsychologist George Hansen observes with respect to the academy, "though in veiled form." This should not surprise us, Hansen goes on to suggest, for although taboos have always been violated "in order to release magical power," there is a real cost for such transgressive acts. "Society would be partly deconstructed in the process."[31] Hence the taboo, still very much in place in the academy, against any serious engagement with the paranormal.

Anthropologically speaking, however, "releasing magical power" is very much akin to "being culturally creative," so it is perhaps not too surprising to find, once again, some of the strongest occult interests in a founding thinker, which are then later denied, actively demonized, or just politely overlooked. From his youth, the Romanian historian of religions Mircea Eliade was deeply interested in esoteric thinkers and occult matters. This is already patently obvious in his "Folklore as an Instrument of Knowledge," an early essay (1937) in which he argues, more or less exactly like Andrew Lang had done, for the empirical or experiential reality of folkloric beliefs and psychical phenomena.[32] Behind at least some of these "miraculous" stories, Eliade argued, lays a series of actual concrete human experiences, which are then exaggerated and mythologized by the religious imagination. Eliade thus explores the critical literature on such things as levitation in Catholic hagiography and Indian yoga and the "fluid" link said to exist between an object and its previous owner assumed in various magical rituals and psychical practices (hence "contagious magic," the magical use of relics, and "psychometry" or the psychical perception of persons via their possessions). As a way of concluding the essay, Eliade takes the historicists to task for claiming faithfulness to the historical documents, until of course these documents violate their own positivistic and materialistic worldviews. Then they simply ignore them or brush their data aside as "primitive," "mistaken," and so on. Now the dismissing word in vogue is "anecdotal."

It appears that Eliade's convictions here flowed out of his own personal experience of such matters and date back to around 1928, when, "as a student, I went to study Yoga and Tantra with S. N. Dasgupta at Calcutta University," he tells us in an essay on "The Occult and the Modern World."[33] As he once explained in another context, these dissertation researches and early experiments with yoga taught him "the reality of experiences that cause us to 'step out of time' and 'out of space.'"[34] Since he doubted that he would be able to describe in "scientific prose"[35] the nature of such experiences, he would later "camouflage" them in his literary writings, and particularly in the novella *The Secret of Doctor Honigberger*, which he explicitly identifies as a species of *littérature fantastique*. Eliade explains all of this in his interview with Claude-Henri Roquet:

> In describing Zerlendi's Yoga exercises in *The Secret of Doctor Honigberger*, I included certain pieces of information, drawn from my own experiences, that I omitted from my books on Yoga. At the same time, however, I added other, inaccurate touches, precisely in order to camouflage the true data. . . . [The reader] would then be led to conclude that all the rest is invented—imaginary—too, which isn't the case.[36]

In other words, exactly as he had argued with respect to the empirical paranormal core of traditional folklore, Eliade was now hiding his own paranormal experiences in his literary creations. This then sets up a certain paradoxical structure for the reader: "some descriptions," he explained, "correspond to real experiences, but others reflect more directly yogic folklore," hence "the reader has no means to decide whether the 'reality' is hidden in the 'fiction,' or the other way around, because both processes are intermingled." Again, exactly as he had earlier argued with respect to folklore as "an instrument of knowledge," he seriously suggests that "such types of literary creativity may also constitute authentic instruments of knowledge," in the sense that the literature of the fantastic may "disclose some dimensions of reality that are inaccessible to other intellectual approaches."[37] In other words, literary theory, and in particular the literature of the fantastic, was one of Eliade's preferred modes of interpreting the "parallel worlds" of the history of religions.

Eliade was not always so forthcoming about the experiential core of his writing, however. One hundred pages further into the Roquet interview, the subject of De Martino's magical anthropology—whereby the experience of nature literally changes as a culture evolves—came up. When Roquet asks Eliade, point-blank, whether what Eliade himself had just called "transhuman experiences that we are forced to accept as facts" had happened to him, Eliade gives the following reply: "I hesitate to answer that."[38]

Also relevant here is Eliade's 1974 Freud Memorial Lecture, in which he turned to the "occult explosion" among the American youth culture erupting all around him and connected the paranormal to fantastic literature and Freud's discovery of the Unconscious (which Eliade liked to capitalize). After providing his listeners and readers with succinct modern histories of *esotericism* and *occultism*, two comparative categories that work as "umbrella terms" to gather together extremely diverse sets of practices and traditions, Eliade discussed these traditions' profound influence on early modern European literature and described their scholarly revival in the works of figures like Gershom Scholem on Kabbalah, Henri Corbin on Sufi mysticism, Antoine Faivre on Western esotericism, and his own work on Yoga, Tantra, and shamanism (the latter three subjects were all key to the American youth culture, he rightly notes). In each scholarly case, Eliade pointed out, the contemporary scholarship took up historical phenomena judged to be pure nonsense, if not veritable black magic, and "abundantly proved their theoretical coherence and their great psychological interest."[39] The interpretive power of Freud's psychoanalysis is one of his primary models here, for "Freud substantiated the gnoseologic values of the products of fantasy, which until then were considered meaningless or opaque." Once Freud articulated the Unconscious, "the immense number of imaginary universes reflected in literary creations disclosed a deeper, and secret, significance, quite independent of the artistic value of the respective works."[40]

One can hardly ask for a better introduction to the present project on the psychical and the paranormal. Hence my opening Eliade epigraph from the very last lines of the same Freudian lecture. Whether or not Eliade was "merely asking the question" about the religious meaning of science fiction and the occult dimensions of popular culture (I doubt this very much), I am certainly trying to offer his question a series of possible answers in the pages that follow. And it is certainly my intention—or at least my impossible wish—to take up phenomena judged by many of my peers to be pure nonsense and establish both their theoretical coherence and their psychological interest.

Eliade founded a certain intellectual lineage at the University of Chicago, a lineage in which I was trained in the 1980s and early '90s under his successor, Wendy Doniger, herself more than adept at negotiating mind-boggling metaphysical terrain.[41] This same lineage, as diverse and as contentious as any healthy intellectual community, has occasionally displayed a quite serious engagement with the paranormal. Nowhere is this more apparent and obvious than in Eliade's fellow Romanian and Chicago colleague Ioan Couliano. Couliano's lifelong interest in magical and gnostic matters was reflected in a rich personal occult life.[42] Together at Chicago in the early '80s, the two men studied what they were calling "cultural fashions" (their code for what I am calling the paranormal in popular culture), and particularly the mysticism of science literature that turned to quantum physics for a theoretical base for a new modern mysticism. Couliano was inspired by this bold comparative literature and by like-minded elite intellectuals, like the Yale literary critic Harold Bloom, who was a fan of Couliano's and who has written openly about his own gnostic experiences of a transcendent Self separate from the ego and beyond the reach of the orthodox religions. Couliano was clearly moving toward a fusion of quantum physics and the history of religions before he was murdered in a toilet stall one sad spring day in 1991.[43]

Such an attempted fusion of the sciences and the humanities is particularly apparent in Couliano's study of gnosticism, that strange and largely ignored book, *The Tree of Gnosis*. In the introduction to this text, Couliano asks the following crucial question: If we are now living in an Einsteinian space-time continuum determined by three extended dimensions and a fourth of time, the intimate participation of consciousness in the material world, and the metaphysical identity of energy and matter, themselves likely continuously created by utterly bizarre quantum processes that more or less destroy any stable notions of linear causality, time, locality, and independent existence, why are we still writing history as if we only inhabited a simple three-dimensional cosmos, lived in a neat linear time, and existed as so many disconnected billiard balls in a world of Newtonian causality, collisions, and reactions? If the world is so utterly bizarre, why do we pretend it is so simple? And if we now know that the universe is most certainly *not* a three-dimensional box or two-dimensional pool table, why do we keep writing history as if it were? Why, in other words, cannot we reimagine history (and hence ourselves) "outside the box" and "off the page" of what Max Weber so powerfully called the iron cage of modern rationalism, order, and routinization?

Good questions. Couliano tried to bring us up to speed through his historical method of morphodynamics. I will not go into the details here, mostly because I don't understand them (apparently I'm still in the box), but it is worth noting that Couliano's morphodynamic history writing is essentially about taking seriously the possibilities that religious systems function as archetypal forms (*morpho-*) that exist in a dimension outside the four of space-time, and that these can and do interact (*dynamic*) historically within the four dimensions of our perceived world in ways that appear strange and random but in fact are structurally organized and essentially meaningful.[44]

To explain such altered states of history, Couliano turned to Edwin Abbot (1838–1926), that imaginative British theologian whom Albert Einstein had previously invoked in order to explain his own theory of general relativity and its mind-blowing image of the universe as the hypersurface of a hypersphere (don't ask; I don't get it either). In his *Flatland: A Romance of Many Dimensions* (1883), written and illustrated under the humorous penname of "A Square," Abbot introduced the idea of the Flatlanders, two-dimensional beings who can only experience the intervention of a third dimension as hopelessly confusing or inexplicable, that is, as "miraculous." Couliano invokes the same Flatland to describe how the history of religions can be imagined as "a sequential interaction of multiple systems of thought." He explains:

> Let us suppose a two-dimensional world, like an infinitely thin sheet of paper, in which completely flat beings live. Imagine further that this film would let a solid object pass through it without the film breaking. Now let us indeed move a solid object through it, for instance a fork. What would a two dimensional inhabitant of Flatland *see*? S/he would see a disparate set of phenomena: first four rounding lines, recognized as being circles, without connection between them, corresponding to the four prongs of the fork; then a line whose size varies incessantly, corresponding to the base and handle of the fork; eventually the line

> will disappear from sight. Obviously, the fork would appear to the Flatlander as a sequence of disparate phenomena in time. One more dimension is needed in order to perceive it as a single solid.[45]

So too with systems of thought, which exist in their own logical dimension: "They interact with history at every moment, and the chronological sequence they form is a sort of sequential puzzle, like the four prongs of the fork viewed from the perspective of the Flatlander." What Couliano proposes, then, is that we begin to study history as a similar interaction, that we "study systems of thought in their own dimension" and "recognize the fork for what it is: an object coming *from outside* and crossing our space in an apparently disconnected way, in which there is a hidden logic which we can only reveal *if we are able to move out of our space*."[46] In other words, we cannot properly interpret religious systems and their appearance in time because we assume that the three (or four) dimensions we routinely experience exhaust the possible, when in fact we live in a universe of multiple dimensions to whose astonishing complexity and "strangeness" the history of religions, and particularly the history of gnosticism and mysticism, gives abundant witness.

Not surprisingly, Ioan Couliano was ignored. The implications of what he was trying to say are simply too deep and disturbing to the neat rational lines of modernity and the normally linear modes of writing history. He shattered our little box. He wrote "off the page," outside our Flatland.

I do not claim to know whether Ioan's particular model of a gnostic history of religions is an accurate or even a plausible one. That is not my point here. What I do know—and this *is* my point—is that any ordinary history of religions that relies exclusively on textual-critical, social-scientific, or political analyses (from Foucauldian constructionism and postcolonial theory to philology and materialist cognitive science) is woefully inadequate to the task of understanding and interpreting the paranormal, particularly when we get to ideas and experiences, as we will soon enough, surrounding the hyperdimensionality of UFOs and the possibility that these are fundamentally religious phenomena, "fishermen," if you will, from another dimension baiting and occasionally hooking us from above the four-dimensional waters of space-time.

An author like Ioan Couliano may be correct about the general solution to the metaphysical conundrums that this history of religions presents us. He might also be wrong. But at least he recognized the problem of the paranormal as something that will have to be central to any future and truly adequate history of religions. At least he was willing to think outside the iron cage and off the two-dimensional page of our present Flatland rationalisms.[47]

Authors of the Impossible: The Paranormal as Meaning

Authors of the Impossible is an attempted recovery of precisely this kind of thinking "off the page." Such a project is based on the wager that new theory lies hidden in the anomalous, that the paranormal appears in order to mock and shock us out of our present normal thinking. Seen in this way, psychical and paranormal phenomena become the still unacknowledged, unassimilated Other of modern thought, the still unrealized future of theory, the fleeting signs of a consciousness not yet become a culture.

This is hardly an easy claim to advance within our present order of knowledge and the possibilities it dictates for us. Paranormal phenomena, after all, dramatically violate those firm epistemological boundaries that, since Descartes, have increasingly divided up our university departments (and our social reality) into things pertaining to matter and objective reality (the sciences) and things pertaining to human experience and subjective reality (the humanities). Our scientific worldview has progressed, moreover, with the assumption more or less intact that it is the former objective reality that is really real, not the latter subjective . . . well, whatever *that* is.

Paranormal phenomena, however, bring the subjective component back in, and with a vengeance—the return of the repressed in all its fury. Whatever they are, it is clear that such events cannot be understood without reference to consciousness *and* the material world: Wolfgang is in town and the laboratory instruments fizzle and fry; the physical location of Elizabeth's harp is pegged by a mind over a thousand miles away; my analyst colleague feels a sharp stabbing physical pain in relationship to an emotional story she has not yet heard; and so on. Such events are thus not just casually, occasionally, or anecdotally anomalous. They are structurally and cognitively anomalous.

The Harvard psychiatrist John E. Mack put the matter as eloquently as anyone in an interview with *Nova* when he commented on how the physical phenomena of abduction reports violate our present epistemology and worldview: "we have a kind of either/or mentality. It's either literally physical, or it's in the spiritual other realm, the unseen realm. What we seem to have no place for—or we have lost the place for—are phenomena that can begin in the unseen realm, and cross over and manifest and show up in our literal physical world." Mack concluded what many thoughtful observers of such ufological matters have concluded, namely, that, taken alone, the framework of modern science is simply insufficient here. Rather, "multidisciplinary studies combing physics with comparative religion and spirituality are needed to further consider how the interdimensional bridging properties of the abduction phenomenon might work."[48]

Combining physics and comparative religion, of course, is exactly what Ioan Couliano attempted in his critique of the Flatland of the field. But how should we now proceed? How at least to begin to address this seeming "interdimensional bridging"?

As a humble way of beginning, we might say that the psychical and the paranormal appear in that space where the humanities and the sciences meet beyond both, where mind and matter, subjectivity and objectivity merge in ways that can only violate and offend our present order of knowledge and possibility. Accordingly, to approach such phenomena as subjective things, as "anecdotes" or "coincidences," as interesting internal states that have no real connection to the external physical world of objects and events is to seriously misunderstand them. Similarly, however, to approach such phenomena as objective, quantifiable, replicable things "out there" is inevitably to miss them, or to just barely see them.

This, I would suggest, is why the necessarily objectifying nature of the scientific method can pick up the slightest examples of something like psi in the controlled laboratory, but must miss all the most robust paranormal ones in the real world of human experience. I have heard contemporary parapsychologists joke about what J. B. Rhine really accomplished at Duke University by operationalizing psychical research and insisting on controlled laboratory conditions and statistical approaches: he figured out how to suppress psi and finally make it go away. Bored sophomores staring at abstract shapes on playing cards is no way to elicit psychical phenomena.

But love and trauma are. Consider what we will encounter below as the classic case of telepathic dreams announcing the death of a loved one. Such dreams are not objects behaving properly in an ordered mechanistic way for the sake of a laboratory experiment. They are *communications* transmitting *meaning* to *subjects* for the sake of some sort of profound *emotional need*. They are not about data; they are about love. Obviously, though, when the object becomes a subject and brain matter begins to express meaning, we are no longer in the realm of the natural sciences. We are in the realm of the humanities and hermeneutics, that is, we are in the realm of *meaning* and the Hermes-like or Hermetic art of *interpretation*.

My goal in the pages that follow is not to demean or deride the sciences (quite the contrary, I will end with them), nor to arrive at some false sense of rational or religious certainty—I possess neither—but to expand the imaginative possibilities of contemporary theory through a certain authorization of the Impossible. I am not asking us to know more. I am asking us to imagine more. This ability to imagine more is precisely what defines an "author of the impossible" for me. I intend this key title-expression in at least three senses.

In the first and simplest sense, I intend to state the obvious, namely, that these are authors who write about seemingly impossible things: think telepathy, teleportation, precognition, and UFOs. In the second sense, I intend to suggest that these are authors who make these impossible things possible through their writing practices. They do not simply write about the impossible. They give us plausible reasons to consider the impossible possible. They thus both author and author-ize it. In truth, they are authors of the (im)possible. Finally, in the third and deepest sense, I intend to suggest that the writing practices of authors of the impossible are intimately related to the paranormal itself, and this to the extent that paranormal phenomena are, in the end, like the act of interpretive writing itself, primarily semiotic or textual processes.

This is why "automatic *writing*" played such an important role in the history of psychical phenomena and why we still speak of "psychical *readings*." That is, after all, exactly what they are. There is another way to say this. Although paranormal phenomena certainly involve material processes, they are finally organized around *signs* and *meaning*. To use the technical terms, they are semiotic and hermeneutical phenomena. Which is to say that they seem to function as representations or signs to decipher and interpret, not just movements of matter to measure and quantify. This is my central point to which I will return again and again: *paranormal phenomena are semiotic or hermeneutical phenomena in the sense that they signal, symbolize, or speak across a "gap" between the conscious, socialized ego and an unconscious or superconscious field*. It is this gap between two orders of consciousness (what I will call the "fantastic structure of the Mind-brain" in my conclusion) that demands interpretation and makes any attempt to interpret such events literally look foolish and silly. We thus ignore this gap and the call to interpret signs across different orders of consciousness at great peril.

We might also say that such paranormal phenomena are not dualistic or intentional experiences at all, that is, they are not about a stable "subject" experiencing a definite "object." They are about the irruption of meaning in the physical world via the radical collapse of the subject-object structure itself. They are not simply physical events. They are also *meaning events*.[49] Jung's category of synchronicity, for example, is all about what we could easily and accurately call meaning events, that is, a moment in space and time where and when the physical world becomes a text to be read out and interpreted, where and when the event is structured not by causal networks of matter but by symbolic references producing meaning. If, however, paranormal phenomena are meaning events that work and look a great deal like texts, then it follows that texts can also work and look a great deal like paranormal phenomena. Writing and reading, that is, can replicate and realize paranormal processes, just as paranormal processes can replicate and realize textual processes. *This* is what I finally mean by the phrase "authors of the impossible." It is also what I am trying to effect with *this* text.

So look out.

Two more warnings before we begin. First, do not misread me here. I do not "believe" all the tales I will tell you in the pages that follow, however convinced I may sound in this or that passage. Indeed, as a professional scholar of religion, I consider it my job *not* to believe, and I take that professional commitment very seriously. Which is not to say, at all, that I discount these stories as unimportant, as simply fabricated or completely false. I do not. What I am trying to do is recreate for the reader what the field researcher calls "unbounded paranormal conditions," that is, a place in space and time, in this case a text recreated and realized in your mind, where—to speak very precisely now—really, really weird shit happens.

Second, I hope it goes without saying that I offer my hermeneutical model of the paranormal only as a contribution to the larger project of studying such phenomena, certainly not as any final or complete solution to these anomalous events. I am as baffled as anyone by this material, and I offer no rational or religious certainties here, only intuitive hunches and possible directions. The simple truth is that we simply don't know what is going on here. I would go further. With our present rules of engagement, that is, with our present reigning materialist methodologies, faith commitments, objectivist scientisms, and absolute cultural relativisms, we *cannot* know. So I suppose I am also after those rules of engagement. I want a new game.

The Fantastic Narrative of Western Occulture: The Paranormal as Story

Central to my attempted revival and re-theorization of the psychical and the paranormal is the notion that both categories are often wrapped up with profound narrative dimensions, that psychical and paranormal events are, on some level at least, very much about *story*. One might say that paranormal phenomena possess *mythical* dimensions. One might also say that they display dramatic *literary* features, as long as one defines that literary nature in a precise and careful way. But if paranormal events sometimes appear as if they were part of a larger living literature, just what kind of literature is it? If we are being written, in just what kind of story do we find ourselves? My own answer to this question is crystallized in a single phrase: *the fantastic narrative of Western occulture*. A bit of explanation is in order here.

I adopt the notion of a *fantastic narrative* from the Bulgarian literary critic Tzvetan Todorov. My specific employment of the category of *occulture* draws its inspiration from the work of the American historian of British occultism Alex Owen, the British historian of contemporary alternative religion Christopher Partridge, and the American literary critic and writer Victoria Nelson. The theoretical background of such an experiment goes like this.

Occultism, from the Latin *occultus* for "hidden" or "secret," is a broad umbrella term that scholars use to discuss a wide variety of ideas, beliefs, and practices—everything from alchemical speculations, astrology, and tarot reading, to crystal gazing, magical practices, and various psychical and spiritualist phenomena. Things are not quite as random as they seem, however. Owen points out that this otherwise confusing diversity is underpinned and organized by a single overarching idea, namely, "that reality as we are taught to understand it accounts for only a fraction of the ultimate reality which lies just beyond our immediate senses."[50] Historically speaking, the term also carried connotations of "a secret spiritual tradition that could be accessed only by an initiated elite," that "there is a hidden body of revelatory knowledge, part of a secret tradition that has been preserved and transmitted over the ages by an enlightened illuminati." Early modern occultists, moreover, also tended to believe that, "they were living in momentous times, witnessing the demise of the old world and the beginning of the new," that they were working toward "the establishment of a spiritually enlightened new age."[51]

On one level at least, they were quite right about this, as they inhabited a historical space that witnessed the birth of modernity. Occultism, in other words, is an eminently modern movement that arose into cultural prominence at the very end of the nineteenth century and was deeply engaged with the cutting-edge intellectual movements of the time, from the French decadent movement to psychiatry, psychoanalysis, psychical research, and surrealism. Owen convincingly demonstrates that there was a particularly "close connection between occultism and innovative approaches to the study of the mind."[52] Indeed, she places occultism and its double engagement with both secular science and individual mystical and magical experience at the very heart of contemporary debates about the nature, scope, and possibilities of consciousness itself. It is *precisely* this doubleness, at once rational and mystical, logical and mythical, that defines the occult for Owen. In her own words: "it is the crucial alignment of rational consciousness with the apparently irrational world of the myth-creating unconscious that produces the powerful experience of the occult 'real.'"[53] This is why, in Gauri Viswanathan's reading now, "occult knowledge is built on storytelling, which occult practices treat as a form of revelatory experience." What we have, then, is essentially "a shift in register from belief to imagination," which in turn played a major role in initiating the secularizing processes that created modern culture.[54] The point here is a quite radical one, namely, that, far from being an irrational escape or a collection of nonsensical superstitions, the occult "was itself intrinsic to the making of the modern at the turn of the century."[55]

Owen focused her work on the end of the nineteenth century and the beginning of the twentieth century. In his two-volume study, *The Re-Enchantment of the West*, Partridge makes a similar argument with respect to the final decades of the twentieth century, that is, the decades just behind us now. More specifically, he introduces the category of occulture in order to study the interface between popular Western culture and alternative religious movements and, more specifically, to name that reservoir of "often *hidden*, *rejected* and *oppositional* beliefs and practices associated with esotericism, theosophy, mysticism, New Age, Paganism, and a range of other subcultural beliefs and practices."[56] Occulture for Partridge, then, is that dark, nocturnal, fertile side of Western culture without which the public elite culture cannot be fully understood and out of which any number of popular cultural movements have sprung, usually in direct or indirect opposition to the reigning public and elite orthodoxies.

Particularly important here is what we might call the comparative practices of popular culture, which, it turns out, are often just as radical—indeed, often more so—than those of elite scholars, whose disciplined intellectual practices often end up disciplining them right back into the established order of things, where they can get and keep a job. Popular comparative practices work differently. They often appear exaggerated or outrageous. They are. This is how they escape the various social, political, and intellectual censors of their own social surround—by being serious by not being serious. Essentially, popular culture "flies low," well under the radar.

It is also worth underlining the fact that Partridge's central notion of reenchantment requires for both its logic and energy an earlier and equally profound disenchantment. Occulture is not a matter of naive belief, much less of orthodox faith. It is only possible after a robust and radical criticism of "religion." Like Owen's occultism, then, Partridge's occulture is a very modern phenomenon that has already incorporated the secular and the scientific. Which is not to say that occulture is entirely secular. Far from it. The category of occulture implies that there is a sacred dimension to secularization, that Western culture is not becoming less religious, but *differently* religious. Occulture, then, represents a dialectic, a "confluence of secularization and sacralization," not a final victory of one process over the other.[57]

I want to take up Partridge's key notion of occulture and develop it in my own directions in the pages that follow. More specifically, I want to suggest that the experience of reality—a "reality posit," as the cultural psychologist Richard Shweder has put it—is produced from the dialectical dance of consciousness and culture, always on a particular historical and material stage.[58] As Mind and the neurobiological hardware of the human brain are "cultivated" in different social, religious, and linguistic frames, the experience of reality shifts and changes accordingly. Reality itself—or so I am assuming—does not change, but what is generally possible and impossible to experience as real does appear to change from culture to culture, as each culture actualizes different potentials of human consciousness and energy. Such a dialectical model, I should stress, is both universalistic and relativistic at the same time. There is radical Sameness. And there is radical Difference. And neither can be sacrificed to the other.

In this model, the human being can be thought of as a kind of living musical instrument born into the world capable of playing any tune, any language, any belief system. Each culture, each historical period, each religious system, each family, however, will privilege only certain keys and will downplay, deny, or simply ignore others. Consider the research on human language acquisition. An infant, *any* infant, is born capable of speaking any language on the planet, but as the infant develops, the brain synapses and vocal abilities quickly lock onto a specific set of language skills until it is very difficult to learn other speech patterns. By the age of six or so, the brain is now wired for a specific language, by thirteen or so a specific culture and worldview. The universal musical instrument has become a very particular and local one.

It is within this same dialectical context that I understand occulture as a kind of public meeting place of spirit and matter, as the place where Consciousness *both* occults or hides itself in material and symbolic forms *and* allows itself to be seen, "as if in a mirror," so that it can be cultivated and shaped into definite, but always relative, forms. Occulture, then, both conceals and reveals. Its popular and elite expressions—from a ten-cent superhero comic book to this book—should not be taken literally. Ever. But neither should they be dismissed as meaningless or unimportant. They, after all, reflect and refract some of the deepest dimensions of the real.

The provocative work of Owen and Partridge can be fruitfully read alongside Victoria Nelson's *The Secret Life of Puppets*, a beautiful study of the Neoplatonic, gnostic, or Hermetic "soul" of Western culture as temporarily repressed and demonized. Here Nelson gives us a brilliant study of the modern demonization of the soul as puppet, robot, or cyborg and the bracketing (really repressing) of the deeper questions of human consciousness within contemporary intellectual culture. In the process, she examines what we too will encounter below, that is, the imaginative exile of Spirit into the furthest reaches of "outer space," from where, of course, it returns to haunt us as the Alien.

For Nelson, this demonization and subsequent alienation is born of an exaggerated and unbalanced scientism, a one-sided Aristotelianism that she sees us now moving beyond before a balancing Platonic resurgence. It is not about one or the other, though. It is about both. It is about *balance*. Western intellectual, spiritual, and cultural life, at their best and most creative anyway, work through a delicate balancing act between this Aristotelianism (read: rationalism) and this Platonism (read: mysticism). The pendulum has been swinging right, toward Aristotle, for about three hundred years now. It has now reached its rationalist zenith and is beginning to swing back left, toward Plato. Which is not to say, at all, that Western culture will somehow become irrational and unscientific again, that we suddenly won't need Aristotle or science any longer. This vast centuries-long process is ultimately about balance, about wisdom. It is also about making the unconscious conscious, about realizing and living our own secret life:

> The new sensibility does not threaten a regression from rationality to superstition; rather, it allows for expansion beyond the one-sided worldview that scientism has provided us over the last three hundred years. We should never forget how utterly unsophisticated the tenets of eighteenth-century rationalism have left us, believers and unbelievers alike, in that complex arena we blithely dub "spiritual." Even as we see all too clearly the kitsch of much New Age religiosity and fear the rigidity of rising fundamentalism, we remain alarmingly blind to our own unconscious tendencies in this same direction. Our conventional secular bias whispers to us that the ideas we see naively articulated on the cinema screen (ideas as blasphemous to secular humanists as they are to the religious orthodox), if they are to be taken seriously at all, signal a backward

> slide into religious oppression and intolerance. What our perspective does not allow us to recognize is the positive and enduring dimension of such ideas when they are consciously articulated in our culture. We forget that Western culture is equally about Platonism and Aristotelianism, idealism and empiricism, *gnosis* and *episteme*, and that for most of this culture's history one or the other has been conspicuously dominant—and dedicated to stamping the other out.[59]

Such a Platonic balancing or mystical revival, of course, cannot enter the house of elite culture directly. Its kitsch clothes and tastes in movies are too easily rebuffed, demeaned, belittled, and shamed by the scientistic and pious doorkeepers. So it walks around the house and comes in the back door, through the imaginative products of popular culture and the inexorable mechanisms of market capitalism (if elite intellectuals and orthodox religious leaders don't buy this stuff, almost everyone else does, literally). In our own time, Nelson argues, this back-door *gnosis* arises out of the "sub-Zeitgeist" of science fiction, superhero comic books, fantasy, and especially film.

This material is fundamentally gnostic or, better, Hermetic for Nelson, which is to say that it is very much about a cosmic form of consciousness that participates in the material world but also transcends and overflows that world. The Hermetic or gnostic soul, then, is someone who seeks a liberation from the limitations of an illusory world, who, like Neo in *The Matrix*, "takes the red pill" and discovers virtually limitless human powers within an unreal virtual reality. There is a dark side, a very dark side, however, to Neo's awakening. Basically, he discovers that his body is being used as a human battery to power a world ruled by aliens who deceive their human harvest by implanting a virtual-reality existence in their wired-up brains.

Things are not always this dark, of course. A gentler model can be found in the character of Truman in *The Truman Show*, who realizes, with more than a little anger, that he has been living his entire life in a television reality show, in essence, on a stage set. At the end of the movie, he sails out into the fake lake, discovers "a door in the sky," and walks through it. Whether disturbing or touching, demonic or divine, by consuming such "art forms of the fantastic," Nelson suggests, "we as nonbelievers allow ourselves, unconsciously, to believe."[60] We fly under the radar, perhaps even under our own radar.

Nowhere is this truer than in the ultramodern genre of science fiction, a genre closely allied with the fantastic. To take just one example that Nelson treats and that bears directly on my present methods, consider the iconic figure of Philip K. Dick, the American sci-fi writer who claimed to have been "resynthesized" by a pink laser beam emanating from a vast supercosmic consciousness he called VALIS, for "Vast Active Living Intelligence System." Valis was no abstract literary conceit for Dick. Nor was the Pink Light. Both were autobiographical facts for him of immense significance. Literally. This, after all, was a Light that beamed the noetic energies of *entire books* into him and hid itself in and as the material-virtual world.

Dick's biographer, Lawrence Sutin, is very clear that Dick's later work flowed out of the author's metaphysical encounters with this superbeing or Sci-Fi Spirit. Dick's encounter with Valis took place in the late winter of 1974. Hence Dick's constant elliptical reference to "2-3-74," that is, February and March of 1974. During this period of time, Dick, in Victoria Nelson's words now, "had the overpowering sensation of being 'resynthesized' by an entity he called 'the Programmer.'"[61] He also called this entity Zebra, for its ability to hide in the world, and Brahman, for its omnipresence and mystical nature. Here is how Dick himself described it:

> At the moment in which I was resynthesized, I was aware perceptually—which is to say aware in an external way—of his presence . . . It resembled plasmic energy. It had colors. It moved fast, collecting and dispersing. But what it was, what he was—I am not sure, even now, except I can tell you that he had simulated normal objects and their processes so as to copy them and in such an artful way as to make himself invisible within them.[62]

And this is before we even get to Dick's fascination with quantum physics and synchronicity, manifested in such moments as when he met a woman on Christmas Day of 1970 whose name, age, relationships, and life resembled in uncanny detail a "fictional" character he had written earlier that year in *Flow My Tears, the Policeman Said*.[63] Or his story about how he once diagnosed his young son's otherwise invisible internal hernia while listening to the Beatles' "Strawberry Fields Forever" after the pink beams of Valis zapped him. The surgery that was scheduled after Dick's diagnosis was professionally confirmed potentially saved the boy's life.

Dick explicitly identified this cosmic consciousness with the teachings of early Christian gnosticism and wrote *eight thousand pages* of interpretation in his private journals—known to his fans as the *Exegesis*—in order to explain it to himself. Not that he ever explained it. His ruthlessly honest interpretations ranged widely, from the possibility that he was being deluded (by what or who it was not at all clear) to the conviction that Valis was metaphysically related to his beloved fraternal twin sister, who had died shortly after they were both born. Sutin puts the matter in a way that bears directly on my own uses of the fantastic as the hermeneutical key to the paranormal:

> For all the subsequent confusion he sowed, Phil never really doubted that the visions and auditions of February–March 1974 (2-3-74) and after had fundamentally changed his life.
>
> Whether or not they were *real* was another question. As usual. In seeking an answer, Phil hovered in a binary flutter:
>
> Doubt. That he might have deceived himself, or that It—whatever It was—had deceived him.
>
> Joy. That the universe might just contain a meaning that had eluded him all through his life and work.
>
> The dialectic lies at the heart of the eight-year *Exegesis* . . . and of *Valis*. . . . In fact, the 2-3-74 experiences resemble nothing so much as a wayward cosmic plot from a Phil Dick SF novel—which is hardly surprising, given who the experiencer was. . . .
>
> Indeterminacy is the central characteristic of 2-3-74.
>
> And how fitting that is. Mystical experiences are almost always in keeping with the tradition of the mystic. Julian of Norwich, a Catholic, perceived "great drops of blood" running down from a crown of thorns. Milarepa, a Tibetan Buddhist, visualized his guru surrounded by multifold Buddhas on lotus seats of wisdom.
>
> Phil adhered to no single faith. The one tradition indubitably his was SF—which exalts "What IF?" above all.
>
> In 2-3-74, all the "What Ifs?" were rolled up into one.
>
> As *Valis* proved, it was, say whatever else you will, a great idea for a novel.[64]

Which is all to say that Phil Dick wrote out of that fundamental hesitation, that both-and, that real-unreal place that is the surest mark of the fantastic. Here is how *he* put it: "My God, my life—which is to say my 2-74/3-74 experience—is exactly like the plot of any one of ten of my novels or stories. Even down to the fake memories & identity. I'm a protagonist from one of PKD's books . . ."[65]

And us?

It would be easy, of course, to assert that a sci-fi author like Dick is not "really" religious, that he is pretending a revelation that he does not in fact possess, that his vast *Exegesis* was the result of temporal lobe epilepsy and a subsequent paranoia and hypergraphia.[66] It would be much more interesting and altogether more historical, though, to admit that what we now call "religion" is closer to what we now call "fiction" than anyone is willing to admit, that living mythology has *always* followed along the tracks of whatever science was available at the time, and that there are no good intellectual reasons (as opposed to ideological or religious ones) to distinguish whatever was speaking through Dick's gnostic systems from whatever was speaking through the systems of the early Christian and Jewish gnostic authors.

Hence Nelson's precise (and, in my mind, correct) invocation of the Platonic realm to describe Dick's Valis, "a meta-organism identical in all its features to Plotinus's World Soul."[67] Compared to Nelson's historically nuanced religious reading, an easy phrase like "temporal lobe epilepsy" offers little, as such neurological events could be the necessary biological condition or neurological opening, as opposed to the materialist cause, for such spiritual inrushes (much more on this in my conclusion). Besides, the early Christian and Jewish authors had temporal lobes too. Why deem one set of firing lobes revelatory and the other solipsistic? What *is* the difference?

I do not see a difference. And because I myself experienced something similar, if far less dramatic, many years ago, I happen to think that Dick's gnostic corpus carries its own genuine truths about the human condition and the fantastic nature of consciousness.[68] Put a bit differently, for both intellectual and mystical reasons, I am unable to draw any sharp distinctions between the "real," the "religious," and the "fictional." Hence this book on reading the paranormal writing us.

With Tzvetan Todorov, moreover, I want to suggest that it is *precisely* through this experiential irruption and this subsequent inability to decide what is real and what is fictional within a text (or a life) that the fantastic as the Impossible sparks and inspires. Indeed, Todorov defines the fantastic as "a break in the acknowledged order, an irruption of the inadmissible within the changeless everyday legality."[69] Todorov, that is, defines fantastic literature in terms of the anomalous. More precisely, he defines it in terms of a certain irreducible indeterminacy:

> The person who experiences the [fantastic] event must opt for one of two possible solutions: either he is the victim of an illusion of the senses, of a product of the imagination—and laws of the world then remain what they are; or else the event has indeed taken place, it is an integral part of reality—but then his reality is controlled by laws unknown to us. . . . The fantastic occupies the duration of this uncertainty. Once we choose one answer or the other, we leave the fantastic for a neighboring genre, the uncanny or the marvelous.[70]

It is *the reader's hesitation*, then, between a natural, reductive, or fictive reading and a supernatural, occult, or realist reading that constitutes the first and most important condition of the fantastic. The fantastic thus implies, in Todorov's words now, "not only the existence of an uncanny event, which provokes a hesitation in the reader and the hero; but also *a kind of reading*"[71]—a kind of reading that cannot finally decide on a natural or supernatural conclusion.

This comes very close to Owen's "crucial alignment of rational consciousness with the apparently irrational world of the myth-creating unconscious" that produces in turn "the powerful experience of the occult 'real.'" This is also, I would suggest, a surprisingly precise description of the existential situation of the modern study of religion, taken as a whole now rather than as this or that part. Hence the present set of chapters on the fantastic narrative of Western occulture and the authorization of the Impossible within four extraordinary authors.

By Mrs F. W. H. Myers.

Frederic W. H. Myers

one

THE BOOK AS SÉANCE

Frederic Myers and the London Society for Psychical Research

> Now, my theory is that the Supernatural is the Impossible, and that what is called supernatural is only a something in the laws of nature of which we have been hitherto ignorant.
> —EDWARD BULWER-LYTTON, "The Haunted and the Haunters," 1859

> My history has been that of a soul struggling into the conviction of its own existence.
> —FREDERIC MYERS, *Fragments of Inner Life*

The American horror and science-fiction writer Stephen King has written about his occult understanding of the creative writing process as an archaeological event through which one discovers and digs up a preexisting story, which he compares to a dinosaur skeleton buried in the ground. More extraordinarily still, he considers the craft of writing as a form of effective telepathy whereby one's mental state comes to transcend not only space but also time through the magical medium of the published text. A published story, for King, is a narrative state of mind "caught" in a text and waiting to be precisely reactivated—word for word—two, ten, even twenty years later down the space-time continuum.[1] Writing and reading stories for Stephen King, in other words, mimic or replicate paranormal processes.

King may or may not have been aware that it was the British classicist and psychical researcher Frederic W. H. Myers (1843–1901) who first coined and theorized the term *telepathy*, in 1882, and that Myers opened his autobiographical essay, "Fragments of Inner Life," with convictions very similar to King's own. For Myers, however, the book is not so much a telepathically communicated story designed to entertain future generations as a collective séance offered to inspire present readers and guide them toward their individual roles in the evolution of human consciousness. This is how he puts it in his very first sentences, intentionally published only after he died and so quite consciously spoken beyond the grave:

> I believe that we live after earthly death; and that some of those who read these posthumous confidences may be among my companions in an unseen world. It is for this reason that I now address them. I wish to attract their attention and sympathy; I wish to lead men and women of like interests but of higher nature than my own to regard me as a friend whose companionship they will seek when they too have made their journey to the unknown home.

Myers also happened to believe, as he immediately explains to his readers in his next lines, that there exists a kind of cosmic record or "photograph" of all that is thought and felt, and that therefore his own whole past "will probably lie open to those with whom I have to do."[2] Here he is drawing on the precognitive and clairvoyant data of early psychical research, which can indeed suggest as much, particularly when it is read through the writings of one of Myers's most beloved classical authors, Plato.

As explained in texts like the *Phaedo*—whose study "at sixteen effected upon me a kind of conversion,"[3] Myers explains—Plato taught that when the soul learns some profound truth, it is not creating or constructing this truth but in fact remembering something it already knew in a preexistent life. This is what the Greek philosopher called *anamnesis*, that is, learning-as-remembrance. Similarly, Myers thought that certain forms of knowledge—mathematical, geometric, and poetic knowledge in particular—preexist their human discovery in this other realm, and that such knowledge can be "brought down" into the world through the birth of a particularly gifted soul or genius. We are back to Stephen King's dinosaur-stories, "buried in the ground" and awaiting a sufficiently sensitive writer to discover and re-express them in a roar.

These are impossible convictions. But precisely as such, they witness admirably to what I have called a hermeneutical model of the paranormal, that is, they witness to the power of words and texts to encode human memories in some stable personalized form and help effect psychical communications of various sorts. It is difficult to overestimate what these convictions in the book-as-séance meant for Frederic Myers, or for anyone who attempts to read him deeply now, since, as we shall soon see, it is these textlike "chains of memory" that constitute one aspect of the personality and provide some of the most suggestive signs of its survival of bodily death. On one level at least, the human personality for Frederic Myers is an evolving story written into and read out of the cosmos over and over again within what he calls a "progressive immortality." Read and written thus, we are all occult novels composed by forces both entirely beyond us and well within us. As a One that is also Two, we author ourselves, *and* we are authored. We live in the possible, but we are lived by the Impossible.

As the reference to Plato makes clear, there is something very old about such convictions. There is also something radically new. Committed to the very new perspective of evolution, Myers at least believed that, "[w]e are still in the first moment of man's awakening intelligence; we are merely opening our eyes upon the universe around us."[4] As for the cultural wars over religion and science of his time, whose long-burning embers Darwin had fanned into a mighty flame, Myers was quick to point out that the argument against the survival of the soul was barely a generation old when he was writing, and that the evidence for survival a mere decade.[5] Clearly, it was the newness of it all that impressed Frederic Myers.

When Myers penned "Fragments of Inner Life," then, he chose to emphasize the same radical break with the past that we have come to see as one of the essential features of modernity. There could be no turning back now. A threshold was crossed. We were living in a New World. Accordingly, he turned to the discovery of America as an especially apt metaphor for the discovery of new psychical and spiritual truths. And this was no innocent metaphor. It came with an edge. He thus diplomatically confessed his admiration for Christ, but he also noted that Christ's pioneering work, like the Norsemen's discovery of America, grows more and more distant with each passing year and is, in the end, simply impossible to trace accurately in the waves of the ever-shifting sea of time. "A new discovery is needed," he noted, not by any single Columbus this time, but by "the whole set and strain of humanity." Such a systematic inquiry, Myers insisted, "must be in the first instance a scientific, and only in the second instance a religious one."[6] It is precisely here, in this transit of the sacred out of a traditional religious register and into a new scientific one, in this bold claim of a genuinely new spiritual discovery that can only be had by disciplined research and study, that "the psychical" rises on the horizon of Western thought.

The psychical rose into prominence at a particular moment in Western intellectual history, a moment when Darwinism, materialism, and agnosticism (a word newly coined by "Darwin's bulldog," Thomas Huxley, to capture and advance the spirit of the new era) were becoming increasingly dominant, when the universe was looking more and more indifferent to human concerns with each new discovery and every passing year. Science was conquering all, and it did not look good for the believer. Nor had it for quite some time. Ruskin put it well when, already in 1851, he expressed his own waning faith: "If only the geologists would let me alone, I could do very well, but those dreadful hammers! I hear the clink of them at the end of every cadence of the Bible verses."[7] By 1877, W. H. Mallock was even more sanguine: "It is said that in tropical forests one can almost hear the vegetation growing," he wrote. "One may almost say that with us one can hear faith decaying."[8]

There were, of course, different responses to such mournful sounds in the air. Some individuals embraced reason's science and rejected completely the now defunct and unbelievable claims of faith. Others embraced the claims of faith and chose to reject the science, or at least those parts of it that could not be reconciled with their particular belief system. There was a third option, however, a *tertium quid*, as its proponents often referred to it in the Latin they all could still read.[9] Emily Williams Kelly points out that Myers had been schooled in the mid-nineteenth-century liberalism of John Stuart Mill, who had argued that new knowledge is created by avoiding the extremes and taking truths from both sides of an honest argument. In this liberal spirit, he put the matter this way: "something is gained if, having started with the preconception that 'all which is not A is B,' we have come to the conclusion that our own subject-matter is neither A nor B, but X."[10] This was the X-option that, as Myers once put it in less Latin and more humor, has "fallen between two stools."[11]

Myers, in other words, belonged to a group of elite intellectuals who refused to be dogmatic about *either* their religion *or* their science. Put less metaphorically, they embraced science as a method that could throw new light on old religious questions. They attempted to work through the polarities of reason and faith toward what they thought of as a new and hopeful "science of religion." By such a shocking combination of words (and it *was* shocking), these Cambridge friends did not mean what their much more famous contemporary Max Müller meant by the same phrase over at Oxford, that is, they did not understand religious systems as comparable languages whose family organizations, grammatical structures, and devolving histories of literalization could be speculatively traced through time (whereby, for example, the ancient awe before the sun became the worship of a literal, personalized sun-god).

What they meant by a science of religion was a fully rational and fundamentally comparative exercise of collecting, organizing, and analyzing experiential data that could not be fully explained by either the theological categories of the churches or the reductive methods of the sciences. In other words, they did not equate rationalism with materialism. And here the reported experiences were the key: collected and compared in astonishing numbers, these constituted the researchers' experiments and functioned as the base of their empiricism.

By a science of religion, then, they did not intend a method that would necessarily reduce the religion to the science (although it just might). But neither did they intend a way of doing things that would somehow "respect" religion or protect it from the powerful gaze and hard questions of the new scientific method. Rather, what they intended was a still future method that would move beyond both materialistic science and dogmatic religion into real answers to ancient metaphysical questions that had never really been convincingly answered. As Myers put it, "I wish to debate the matter on the ground of experiments and observations such as are appealed to in other inquiries for definite objective proof."[12] In other words, belief was irrelevant. What mattered now was evidence—empirical, experiential evidence.

Both their Enlightenment hostility to traditional religion and their Romantic openness to religious experience are worth emphasizing here. On one page, for example, an author like Myers could write of "how much dogmatic rubbish" even the best minds of earlier centuries were clouded by, and then two pages later approach the pious subject of Prayer (which he capitalized) with "the need of a definition which shall be in some sense spiritual without being definitely theological" (HP 2:307, 309).[13] Such passages constitute more strong evidence that the modern popular distinction between the "religious" and the "spiritual" is by no means a recent invention, but in fact reaches at least as far back as the middle of the nineteenth century, that is, to the birth of modern science.[14]

Such passages also signal that categories like the psychical, the occult, and the paranormal should be studied alongside and contrasted to their cousin-categories of the spiritual and the mystical. All five categories, after all, are eminently modern constructions witnessing to the same broad individuation processes of Western society whereby religion is increasingly "psychologized," that is, identified as a psychological *experience* not bound by traditional religious authority. These five terms, however, use different methods, focus on different sorts of reports, and so do different cultural work. Most simply put, whereas the categories of the mystical and the spiritual selectively return to historical religious sources for the creative construction of what amounts to a new religious vision (a perennial philosophy, a comparative theology, and so on), the categories of the psychical, the occult, and the paranormal attempt to move out of the religious register, advancing instead strong scientific or parascientific claims and connotations. This book is concerned with the latter processes, not the former.

Although Myers was certainly deeply influenced by the history of Western mysticism, particularly in its Platonic and Neoplatonic origins, and although he employs the terms "mystical" and "mysticism" in various ways throughout his corpus, his work is also best located in the latter streams of method and thought.[15] Hence he can suggest that at least some mystical and occult events are both empirically real *and* entirely consistent with natural, though as yet unexplained, laws or patterns.

This both-and position is especially clear in a fascinating exchange Myers had with Lord Acton on how to write history after the discoveries of psychical research, especially the history of "miraculous" occurrences common in hagiography, church records, and the general history of religions. Myers counseled Acton to advance a historiography that would take such "impossible" events as real possibilities, all the while being very wary of pious exaggeration, fraud, and institutional religious motives.[16] In this, he followed earlier theorists of Mesmerism and animal magnetism, who had similarly turned to scientific language (hence the expression "animal *magnetism*") to explain the new forms of healing and psychical energy with which they were experimenting and advanced a historiography called "psychofolklore." By the latter neologism, they intended a new method of understanding the history of religions whereby the religious past (the *folklore* part) was read anew in the critical but sympathetic light of psychical research (the *psycho* part). It was a kind of "believing back," if you will, a kind of future of the past.

A good example of this new super naturalism or psychofolklore is Myers's treatment of the famous miracles of Lourdes. Listen:

> It is *not* true, a thousand times it is *not* true, that a bottle of water from a spring near which a girl saw a hallucinatory figure will by miraculous virtue heal a Turk

> in Constantinople; but it *is* true that on some influx from the unseen world,—an influence dimly adumbrated in that Virgin figure and that sanctified spring,—depends the life and energy of this world every day. (HP 1:215)

Obviously, Myers and his colleagues were not out to celebrate the Virgin's virtues, nor were they interested in privileging any other specific mythological expression of the cosmic influx, be it the Catholic's or the Muslim's. They were after a comparative model of the human psyche that could make some sense of these events' specific occurrences and dynamics under whatever cultural and historical guise they were expressed. Beyond A and B, there is an X.

Precisely because they recognized the gap that existed—that *always* exists—between the myth or symbol and that which is symbolized (the Virgin vs. the cosmic influx), they recognized that this new knowledge could never settle with mere descriptive accuracy of this or that religious experience, much less with speculative accounts of a particular religion's historical or social development. The Virgin and the spring were never enough. An adequately robust theory of religion would have to go much deeper than mere description or ordinary history, and it could *never* be bound by the believer's perspective. Nor, however, could it be bound by a scientistic perspective that conflated rationalism and materialism. It would have to be about the real questions, the metaphysical questions. The double nature of the human being, or what they preferred to call "the human personality," as it split in two in the process of dying would come to play the central role in this quest. In our own contemporary terms, we might say that they were after a comparative model of extreme religious experiences, the latter catalyzed mostly by traumatic dissociative events, with death being privileged as the ultimate, most complete, and truly universal dissociative event.[17]

Obviously, these were not minor questions. They were quite literally life-and-death issues. Accordingly, as these authors approached what they thought might be the first glimmers of a real answer, as the impossible began to look possible, a real excitement began to shimmer between their lines. And why not? A new metaphysical America was appearing on the horizon of their impossible thought. They were about to discover a New World.

After Life

Frederic W. H. Myers was the son of Frederic Myers, who was a pastor, and Susan Myers (born Susan Harriet), who loved poetry and nature.[18] He was born on February 6, 1843, in Keswick, Cumberland. He spent his childhood in a parsonage, which he remembers as a veritable paradise.

The boy's first existential crisis revolved around finding a mole crushed by a carriage wheel when he was five or six. It wasn't quite the little creature's death, however, that shocked the boy so. It was his mother's calm assurance that the thing had no soul. His second shock came again from his mother's words, this time around seven or eight. "My mother, who shrank from dwelling on the hideous doctrine of hell," Myers recalled, "suggested to me that perhaps men who led bad lives on earth were annihilated at death."[19] This was simply more than the boy could take. His father's death about this same time, in 1851, gave little Fred no anguish compared to the idea of such an unthinkable existential horror.

These are significant, even iconic memories, of course. As we shall soon see, Myers would spend much of his adult life essentially rewriting the afterlife as he received it from his father's faith and his mother's shocking thoughts. He would write for decades against all of this, "from the vague emptiness of the conventional heaven to the endless tortures which make the Cosmos the fabrication of a fiend."[20] Hideous indeed.

His father had been teaching Myers Latin since his sixth birthday. At sixteen, he was sent to a classical tutor, then to a mathematical tutor, and then, at seventeen now, on to Trinity College at Cambridge University. At the age of twenty-two, in 1865, Myers was elected fellow and classical lecturer at Trinity. He resigned four years later, to start, as he put it, "the new movement for the Higher Education of Women."[21] In 1871, he accepted a temporary post as an inspector of schools and, in 1872, took a similar but now permanent position. He was appointed to the Cambridge district in 1875, a job that he held until his health collapsed shortly before his death in 1901.

Then there was the family life. In 1880, at thirty-seven, Myers stepped into Westminster Abbey in order to marry a twenty-two-year-old woman named Eveleen Tennant. Evie, as she was called, came from a wealthy family. Alan Gauld cites another woman describing her, not too nicely (but perhaps not inaccurately), as a "barmaid beauty." For his part, Gauld describes her as "without doubt one of the most beautiful girls of her time."[22] Appearances aside, Evie had her own social circles and intellectual interests, which never quite melded with those of her husband. The new couple took up residence in 1881 in Leckhampton House, on the western edge of Cambridge. There they had three children over the next few years. Most of the historians agree that theirs was a stable marriage, but not an entirely happy one. We shall see why later: basically, Evie had married a man married to a ghost.

Myers insists that these events (except for the ghost part) were only the external events of his story. The real events were the inner ones. These, it turns out, involved the loss of not one, not two, but *three* consecutive worldviews. Frederic Myers knew how to let go. Looking back on his life, he traced four major periods of conviction: Hellenism, Christianity, Agnosticism, and what he calls "the Final Faith."

His early life was dominated by the Greek and Latin classics, particularly Virgil and Plato. From sixteen to twenty-three, the classics "were but intensifications of my own being."[23] He *was* the texts he read. This period ended, however, in 1864 when Myers visited Greece and realized that this was a vanished world. He now felt "cold and lonely." He traveled to America in 1865, where on the night of August 28 he swam the dangerous currents of the Niagara River from the Canadian shore to the American one. This death-defying feat felt like a metaphor to him: "I emerged on the American side, and looked back on the tossing gulf. May death, I dimly thought, be such a transit, terrifying but easy, and leading to nothing new?"[24]

After his return to England, he converted to a particularly emotional form of Christianity through the ministrations of a young and beautiful woman named Josephine Butler, in whose particular form of sanctity (and Myers's excessive response to it) many of Myers's friends suspected more than piety. Gauld, for example, describes Butler's erotically charged methods in some delicious detail, summarizing her ministry as "the spiritual seduction of promising young men." "Myers' worship of Christ," he concludes, "was not perhaps quite distinct in his own heart from a worship of Mrs. Butler; and his enthusiasm for her brought some sharp comments from his friends."[25] But such a faith, which did contain doctrinal elements as well, eventually faded too, like his earlier Hellenic ideals. Much later, he would look back: "That faith looks to me now like a mistaken shortcut in the course of a toilsome way."[26]

It was a simple lack of evidence and the rigorous methods of science that did in his worldview this time. Agnosticism and materialism set in, and with them a dull pain and a certain horror before a completely indifferent universe. Not that he did not appreciate the birth of modern science, or even the demanding virtues of an intellectual agnosticism. He most certainly did, as is apparent in his essay "Charles Darwin and Agnosticism." Here he writes warmly of Thomas Huxley and his famous new word. As for Darwin himself, no other man in history, Myers believed, had so completely altered the common worldview by thought alone.[27] He took obvious delight in the fact that the great man was buried in Westminster Abbey, that "Darwin should be laid in the shrine of Peter," as he put it.[28]

Indeed, Myers went so far as to call Darwin "a *liberator* of mankind."[29] Those were his italics too. He meant it.

As an example of what Darwin liberated humanity from, Myers cites the contentious issue of sin. After Darwin, Myers points out, we can no longer see sin as a defect in our relationship to some higher power. We must understand it now in the context of earlier evolutionary development. It deserves no punishment. It is simply an example of our ancient instincts reasserting themselves. Sin is a moment of "arrested development" and nothing more.[30] It was in this way that Myers finally took his revenge on his boyhood's hated hell—by making it look silly and unnecessary in Darwin's bright light. The same move, of course, more or less vaporized traditional Christianity, for without sin, there is no Fall, and without the Fall, there is no need for Redemption, and . . . The house of cards was wobbling, and Myers knew exactly which card to pull out.

What he calls the Final Faith developed slowly and gradually. It took decades, really, and it will take us the rest of this chapter to explain its most basic outlines. Myers tried his hand at the same and managed to summarize his worldview in just eight pages in "Fragments of Inner Life." This was not an easy process for him, since, as he explains, "although my character is ill fitted to illustrate the merits of any form of religion, it is well fitted to bring out that religion's defects."[31] It was not all criticism and deconstruction, though. There was both a positive foundation and a constructive purpose to his final worldview, namely, the "principles of continuity and evolution."[32]

It was finally evolutionary theory, put into deep dialogue with mystical theorists like Plato and Plotinus, that gave him the grid on which he could then locate and make sense of the psychical data.[33] As Myers himself explained it, there were three creedal points: (1) "the fact of man's survival of death"; (2) "the registration in the Universe of every past scene and thought"; and (3) a "progressive immortality" or "progressive moral evolution" moving always "towards an infinitely distant goal."[34] We will treat each of these in turn. For now it is enough to note what it cost Myers to arrive at such a final faith. "I have been mocked with many a mirage, caught in many a Sargasso Sea," he admits in a reference to the large expanse of water in the middle of the Atlantic and its multiple currents that contemporary folklore had held responsible for lost ships, a kind of early Bermuda Triangle.[35]

Myers is best known for the massive, two-volume tome that focuses the present chapter, his posthumously published *Human Personality and Its Survival of Bodily Death* (1903), which is in turn based on a series of papers on the subliminal Self that he published between 1880 and his death in 1901. (In his literary defense, the title was bestowed posthumously by his editors.) Myers himself describes the work in a letter from 1900 as "a big book of some 1200 octavo pages, which I don't expect anybody to read." It is clear that he was already putting the text together in 1896, when he arranged for Richard Hodgson and Alice Johnson to complete it upon his death (HP 1:ix). They would have to do just that. In truth, Myers was hardly writing from scratch in these final years, since much of the text was culled from the first sixteen volumes of the *Proceedings*, the first nine volumes of the *Journal of the Society for Psychical Research*, as well as from the society's other "big book," Edmund Gurney's *Phantasms of the Living* (1886). These are the real source-texts of *Human Personality*, which is not so much a book as an entire corpus and archive crystallized into a book.

The damned thing is haunted.

It is important to point out that *Human Personality* was not the only book Myers wrote. Far from it. Significantly, most of his other published writings had little to do with psychical research and everything to do with what we would today call literary criticism. For example, he published two separate collections of literary pieces: *Essays: Classical* and *Essays: Modern*.[36] The former included three long studies of "Greek Oracles," "Virgil," and "Marcus Aurelius Antoninus." The latter included readings of figures like George Sand, Victor Hugo, Ernest Renan, and George Elliot. Myers also published a separate monograph on Wordsworth, which included both a biographical study and a theological analysis of the poet's "natural religion," and a collection of metaphysical essays entitled *Science and a Future Life*, which included treatments of "Tennyson as Prophet" and "Modern Poets and Cosmic Law."[37]

He was especially fond of the Romantic poets, like Wordsworth, since he considered their poetic access to the deeper realms of the human personality to be superior to that of "the saints and *illuminés* of various creeds." Why? Because there is nothing in a poet like Wordsworth that "any other revelation can invalidate or contradict." In other words, the Romantic poets declared no exact creeds or specific doctrines. Precisely because their subliminal uprushes of genius were simple and evocative, Myers thought that they carried "more conviction" (HP 1:111).

The truth is, as William James pointed out in a eulogy for his friend, Frederic Myers was, in the end, a Romantic thinker. This seems exactly right to me. Frederic Myers was first and foremost a man of letters, a published award-winning poet, an interpreter of texts both ancient and modern, a classicist, a scholar of deep humanist learning and leanings. He may have been writing of scientific themes as an adult, but he often associated mathematical knowledge with Plato's doctrine of reminiscences, and he was studying Latin and reading Virgil at six.[38]

I cannot stress this point enough, as it underlines and emboldens my own hermeneutical and literary approach to psychical phenomena. Nowhere is the textual nature of Myers's soul more obvious than in the famous "cross-correspondences" affair that broke out a few years after his death. This involved different women on different continents (including Alice Fleming, the sister of Rudyard Kipling, who was living in India) receiving bits and pieces of classical poetry and personal allusions, allegedly from Myers, that his colleagues then had to piece together and interpret in order to establish their possible postmortem source. Nowhere do we find a more mischievous suggestion that, yes indeed, for Frederic Myers and his colleagues the soul is a hermeneutical reality, that is, a multilayered text that must be interpreted to be seen at all.

In November of 1899, Myers was diagnosed with Bright's disease. His heart would now enlarge and his arteries deteriorate. On the first day of 1901, he arrived in Rome, where a certain Dr. Baldwin injected him with an experimental serum developed from the glands and testicles of goats. Myers the hybrid wrote to Oliver Lodge of his upcoming visit to Lodge and his daughters: "possibly I shall meet my dear young female friends on my return as a cross between an old goat and a guardian angel."[39] Alas, he would soon be more guardian angel than goat. A few weeks later, on January 17, 1901, Frederic Myers died, at 9:30 p.m.

Myers and the Founding of the S.P.R.

Looking back on his life before he fell ill, Myers found the first clear hint of his Final Faith etched in his diaries on November 13, 1871, in a single brief line: "H. S. on ghosts." H. S. did not stand for the Holy Spirit. It stood for Henry Sidgwick, a lecturer of moral philosophy at Cambridge and a close and important mentor of the young and idealistic Frederic Myers.

Sidgwick was a rigorously honest man with an exceptionally fine mind and a big white beard. By the time of Myers's diary entry, Professor Sidgwick had been losing his Christian faith for years. It wasn't exactly Ruskin's geology and those annoying hammers this time, though. It was the historical-critical study of religion. In 1862, Sidgwick read Renan's *Etudes d'Histoire Religieuse*, which convinced him that there was no real way of understanding early Christianity without contextualizing its beliefs in the earlier Hebrew and Semitic frameworks. Put simply, he realized that Christianity was a historical phenomenon. He could certainly not now pretend, as he described the attitude of another contemporary, that "the Bible had dropped from the skies ready translated into English."[40] Instead, he chose to study Arabic and Hebrew, and he worried about the impossible miracles that seemed to be at the base of his religion.

Such pursuits finally taught him that there was no way to rescue his faith through historical studies. Quite the contrary, he learned that history was a very good way to *lose* one's faith. So he returned to his original training in moral philosophy and theology.[41] That didn't help either. Realizing that he could no longer in good conscience fulfill the terms of his appointment—which required him to affirm the doctrines of the Church of England—he resigned his fellowship and assistant tutorship at Trinity. But his standing in the university was very solid, so he was simply reappointed college lecturer in moral science in 1867. He had lost a great deal of income, as this was clearly a demotion of sorts, but he still had a Cambridge career.

It is important to capture something of Sidgwick's humanity. There are four lovely scenes in Gauld's wonderful history of "the Sidgwick group" that merit recalling here. There was the time, for example, when the famous Neopolitan medium Eusapia Palladino was invited to the Myers's home for a series of experiments. Everyone was preparing for her arrival and practicing for the events that would ensue. "A practice sitting was held," Gauld explains, "at which, to Myers' amusement, Sidgwick threw himself under the table, his long white beard trailing on the floor, to practice holding Eusapia's legs."[42] Palladino was famous for her crude ways and "naughty Neopolitan stories," and she often came on to her experimenters sexually, and not at all subtly. Sidgwick once responded to such a scene by reciprocating. Essentially, he flirted with her ("a fact," Gauld explains, "not made available to the impious"). Eusapia, we are told, was even photographed wearing Sidgwick's academic robes.[43] The gown appears again in the third story. As he aged, Sidgwick's health declined and his doctor told him that he needed more exercise, that he should be riding horses. Sidgwick asked if he could just run himself instead. Yes, the doctor replied. So there was Professor Sidgwick, running through the streets of Cambridge, sometimes even in his academic cap and gown. Finally, there was the time when a German intellectual was trying to convince Sidgwick that the English language is impoverished. After all, it has no word for *Gelehrte* or "learned men." "Oh, yes, we have," replied the good professor, "we call them p-p-prigs."[44]

Sidgwick and Myers, like most of their academic contemporaries, were initially repulsed by the phenomenon of Spiritualism, which had spread in the 1850s and '60s to England from the crude hinterlands of America, where it had first erupted in the spring of 1848 in Hydesville, New York. There the two Fox sisters, aged 12 and 14, began hearing raps in their little house, allegedly from a dead peddler buried in the basement. As with the poor peddler (his initials were C. B., and he claimed to have been slain by a butcher's knife by the previous homeowner, a blacksmith named John C. Bell), these Spiritualist movements would operate with a more or less literal reading of the spirits as objectively real entities that interact with living human beings via mediums, knockings, table tippings, dreams, and the cultus of the home séance.

And then things got wilder. It was one thing when men like Mark Twain or Abraham Lincoln engaged Spiritualist beliefs and confessed to precognitive intuitions of their own or their loved one's deaths.[45] It was quite another when spirits began showing up for "spirit photographs" (which usually amounted to little more than primitive double exposures) or when floating trumpets and accordions played on a literal stage in poor light, for paying patrons no less. Such scenes did not exactly instill confidence in Cambridge intellectuals.

Nor did many of the spirit messages. There were real beauties here, like the one Gauld quotes from the spirit sermon of Reverend H. Snow: "We cannot dwell minutely upon the particulars which go to make up the sum total of the vastness of immensity."[46] What made the situation even more appalling to professional writers was the fact that similar lines were being composed from the spirits of the likes of Emanuel Swedenborg, Saint Paul, and John the Baptist. Gauld dryly concludes: "Of their efforts one can only say that if the great minds of this world degenerate so much in the next the prospect for lesser fry is bleak indeed."[47]

Things were not entirely bleak, however. For one thing, as numerous historians, including Gauld himself, have pointed out, these outlandish belief systems often encoded the most progressive and socially liberal visions of the time, visions that would only find realization decades later when the broader culture in effect "caught up" with what the spirits had been saying for quite some time. On some issues, moreover, the culture has *yet* to catch up with the nineteenth-century séances.

The Spiritualist movement, for example, was often especially liberal and ahead of its time when it came to gender and sexual issues. Discussions around both the mysteries of postmortem sexuality and the practice of an earthly ethic of free love were not uncommon in Spiritualist literature, and both the Spiritualist and especially the later occult communities were *filled* with heterodox sexual ideas, mystico-erotic practices, and alternative genders and sexualities. These included, among other things, the abandonment of dysfunctional marriages for "spiritual affinities" or soul-mates, sexual intercourse with Elementals or subtle beings, ectoplasm emerging from between the legs (read: from the vaginas) of female mediums, the theological identification of the Fall with sex (a quite common equation in the history of Western esotericism), ritual intercourse without orgasm or movement (a practice taught by Thomas Lake Harris and latter dubbed "Carezza"), a famous female religious leader known to her intimates as "Jack" (Madame Blavatsky), and an equally famous male leader who received his most potent magical revelation in a traumatic homosexual ritual encounter that he himself designed (Aleister Crowley).[48]

Then there was Eusapia. Blum explains: "She tended to wake from trances hot, sweaty, and, well, aroused. Several times, she'd tried climbing into the laps of the male sitters at the table."[49] Palladino, it turns out, was hardly alone in her paranormally aroused sexuality. The hidden history of psychical research sparks and arcs with such energies. My sense is that only a small fraction of this material has been reported, and almost none of it has been carefully analyzed and really understood. Hence Eric J. Dingwall, a prominent historian of the field, once shared with the American artist and superpsychic Ingo Swann that he possessed an entire archive of materials on what Swann calls "sexualizing energies" (which Swann sees as metaphysically related to "power energies" or psychical abilities and the "creative energies" witnessed at work in artists, writers, and thinkers). "He kept this collection quite close to his chest," Swann explains in *Psychic Sexuality*: "But in correspondence to me, he indicated that a good portion of it included documents regarding sexualizing energies encountered while conducting mesmeric and psychical research. In fact, it was Dingwall who suggested that a book should be written by 'some daring soul.'"[50] Indeed.

These are finally ontological issues involving some of the deepest dialectical structures of consciousness and energy, mind and matter, spirit and sex. Then there are what we might call the ethical and political dimensions involving the very public category of gender. Most historians agree that what Ann Braude has memorably dubbed the "radical spirits" were a significant force behind the early women's rights movement in both America and England.[51] This was no doubt a function of the fact that the majority of mediums and seers were spiritually empowered women. The men may have controlled the conservative public churches, but the women were running the progressive private séances. This was, if you will, a thoroughly domestic occultism, an often wild, but nevertheless quite real and very effective democracy of the Spirit.

One of the most puzzling aspects of Spiritualism, and indeed of psychical and paranormal phenomena in general, is the confusing ways the seemingly genuine phenomena were unmistakably mixed up with the fraudulent shenanigans, and often in the very same individual—we are back to the fantastic and the key moment of hesitation before a marvel encountered as fiction or fact. Nor does it seem to be a simple matter of either-or, as the true believers and professional skeptics both have it. Rather, it is almost is if the real needs the fake to appear at all, *as if the fact relies on the fiction to manifest itself, only to immediately hide itself again in the confusion of the fantastic hesitation that follows*. Put a bit differently, it is not as if the appearance of the sacred can be reduced to a simple trick, as if the shaman is just a sham. It is as if the sacred is *itself* tricky. Even the well-documented medical placebo, after all, is a fake that has real effects. What to do? I am reminded here of something the contemporary physicist and psychical researcher Russell Targ once shared with me, namely, that he first became aware of the reality of telepathy when, as a young stage magician in New York, he realized that he was receiving genuine telepathic information *from within the mentalist trick he was performing on stage*. The trick was a trick, but it was also, somehow, catalyzing the real deal.[52] This I take as emblematic of the whole problem of the fantastic and the impossible.

One of the classic historical cases of this paradoxical phenomenon is the aforementioned Neapolitan superpsychic, Eusapia Palladino.[53] By all accounts, Eusapia was astonishing. And a cheater. At one point, the S.P.R. refused to study her any longer, since they had a policy not to study anyone who was caught cheating. The policy may have been a reasonable one, but it was not a particularly wise one, and for all the reasons already outlined. After all, Eusapia also did completely impossible things that were judged by the best minds of the time to be quite genuine. In one uncanny scene, with her hands and feet all held tightly by the researchers (remember ol' Sidgwick practicing on the floor?), a chair in the room moved about and the researchers were touched or even pushed from behind. And then this eerie sight: "Looking upwards, Mrs. Myers could see against the ceiling, which was illuminated by light from the note-taker's candle, several kinds of protrusion from Eusapia's body."[54] Like a Hindu goddess, Eusapia grew numerous arms, weird plasmic protrusions whose shadows on the ceiling Mrs. Myers described as resembling a dressed arm (complete with sleeve and cuff), the neck of a swan, and a stump.

Geezus.

The eminent French physiologist Charles Richet, who participated in extensive experiments with Palladino, was convinced of her powers, cheating or no cheating. During one such experiment, he claimed to have held one of her phantom hands for a full twenty-five seconds.[55] It was impossible moments like these with what were called "physical mediums" that led Richet to coin a new word: *ectoplasm* (another paranormal term of elite intellectual origins). It was the same moments again that led William James to muse in his 1896 presidential address about the society's absurd situation. He was particularly flabbergasted by the "phenomena of the dark-sitting and rat-hole type (with their tragic-comic suggestion that the whole order of nature might possibly be overturned in one's own head, by the way in which one imagined oneself, on a certain occasion, to be holding a tricky peasant woman's feet)."[56] In other words, Eusapia.

Palladino, however, was hardly the first physical medium. Indeed, the scene around Myers and his colleagues in England of the 1870s, as they began to venture out into local séances and spirits, manifested the exact same fantastic confusion of fact and fiction, of physics and farce. Consider, for example, the English sensation Daniel Dunglas Home. Home could do things like play accordions without the use of his hands, float out of and back through a second-story window (before three witnesses), and stretch his body as if it were rubber. He was certainly convincing enough. The Roman Catholic Church charged him with witchcraft. An anthropologist had a more rational solution: he seriously suggested that Home was a werewolf with absolute powers over the minds of men. The press, on the other hand, adored him. The eminent scientist and Fellow of the Royal Society William Crookes was not exactly scoffing either. In 1871, he created a sensation when he published an essay, partly about his experiments with Home, in the *Quarterly Journal of Science*. This essay, and others like it later published in Crookes's *Researches into the Phenomena of Spiritualism* (1874) would play a major role in attracting other intellectuals to the subject, including Lord Raleigh, William Barrett (who would later lead the charge to found the S.P.R.), Arthur Balfour (a star student of Henry Sidgwick's who was later to become prime minister), and Sidgwick himself.

It was into this heady mix of the factual and the fraudulent that Frederic Myers stepped with more than a little verve. Two events lured him in. The first took place in the fall of 1873, when Myers had a convincing encounter with what he later described as "my first personal experience of forces unknown to science." We are not told what these forces were—indeed, Myers explicitly refuses to tell his readers "the special phenomena which impressed me"—only that he experienced them.[57] Gauld has put the various pieces together and come up with a plausible scenario. He points out that Myers's diary entry for November 20, 1873, reads: "John King shakes hand." He also points out that Eveleen Myers later described her husband attending a séance with a certain "C. Williams" about this same time. Gauld explains how "a big, hairy hand came down from the ceiling. Myers seized it in both of his; it diminished in size until it resembled a baby's hand, and finally melted in his grasp."[58]

The second event happened on May 9, 1874, when the Spiritualist preacher William Stainton Moses showed his notebooks to Myers and his close colleague Edmund Gurney. Myers was extremely impressed with both the medium and the notebooks. Soon he was encouraging his friends to start up an informal study group around such phenomena. A few years later, William Barrett conceived the idea of gathering together a group of scientists, scholars, mediums, and Spiritualists in order to pursue experiments on psychical phenomena together. On January 6, 1882, he called the first meeting, at 38 Great Rusell Street in London. The group met again on February 20, this time officially forming the Society for Psychical Research.

Sidgwick was elected president. Six working committees were formed: on thought-reading, Mesmerism, the magnetic researches of Karl von Reichenbach (who, in 1845, had published an influential book on a blue cosmic vital force he called "od" or the "odic force"[59]), apparitions and haunted houses, physical phenomena, and finally a Literary Committee, whose goal was to collect and organize all the data. As Gauld explains in some detail, the latter committee easily did the most work. In 1883 alone, the six-member committee wrote more than ten thousand letters, traveled to numerous witnesses in order to interview them, and double-checked their stories in libraries and record offices.[60] Gurney and Myers did most of this work. Even before the S.P.R. was founded, Myers alone had attended 367 séances by his own count.[61] Gurney was known to write up to fifty or sixty letters a day. He became honorable secretary in 1883 at the age of thirty-six, a post that he held until his death at the age of forty-one, in June of 1888, by an accidental overdose of chloroform.[62]

The society's *Proceedings*—for which major figures like James, Freud, Jung, Theodore Flournoy, and William McDougall all wrote—began publication in 1882. Its *Journal* began issues from February of 1884. That same year, Barrett traveled to the U.S., where he helped form an American branch of the society in January of 1885. William James, the Harvard psychologist and philosopher, and Richard Hodgson, a student of Sidgwick's who had come over from England to help, would come to play the major roles on this side of the Atlantic. Myers and James would become close friends.

Those are the institutional and personnel facts. The society's research methods are worth commenting on as well. In a fascinating move, the society members decided that it made the most sense not to go to a far away country where such beliefs and experiences were allegedly still common, but to stay at home and anthropologize their own English countryside and cities. They worked with the Enlightenment principle of a shared humanity or psychic substratum and a subsequent conviction that, if these experiences were possible in the past or in other cultures, they must be possible in the present in their own culture as well (HP 1:7). Accordingly, they did not get on a boat and float to Asia or Africa. They put ads in London newspapers requesting that readers send them written accounts of unusual or inexplicable events suggestive of postmortem survival. In popular parlance, they advertised for ghost stories.

And they received *lots* of them. Early in 1884, for example, Gurney guessed that he had written about 1,600 letters in the last two months, fifty-five that day alone.[63] The first fruit of this work was the 1886 appearance of the volume *Phantasms of the Living* by Gurney, Myers, and Frank Podmore. The book contained 702 documented cases, focusing on what they came to call "crisis apparitions," that is, spontaneous hallucinations of a loved one who in fact dies within twelve hours on either side of the apparition. The book advances the thesis that such hallucinations are essentially telepathic messages sent from the dying agent to the visionary recipient. Myers's *Human Personality* would appear seventeen years later. As is amply witnessed in both big books, the society's methods were primarily ethnographic and empirical, not to mention epistolary. They checked their stories, required signed affidavits from witnesses, and threw out or marked as such any cases that could not be sufficiently verified. Most could not be, with the general pattern of reliable cases settling at around 5 percent of the total data collected.

In this same empirical spirit, the society also functioned as a court of professional skeptics for famous public cases. The society studied the famous founder of Theosophy, Madame Blavatsky, for example. It even sent one of its own, Richard Hodgson, all the way to India to examine the details of her shrine from which "miraculous" letters were said to materialize. Hodgson discovered double-sided drawers opening up into the Madame's bedroom and obtained damning confessions from her servants. In her recent history of the S.P.R., Deborah Blum explains how "Hodgson had scarcely left the building before it mysteriously burned to the ground, turning its secrets into ashes. He'd no doubt that she had ordered the destruction of evidence."[64] The society subsequently declared Blavatsky a patent fraud and said so in its own published *Proceedings* of 1885. Hodgson's dramatic debunking extended to 174 pages of text.[65] One wonders, though, if Blavatsky was not more complicated and interesting than that, if she resembled Eusapia more than a simple stage magician. I wonder anyway.

In any case, Hodgson would become famous among his colleagues for such unflinching and exhaustive demolishings. And so Gurney could write to James about their mutual friend with these words: "His qualities are *absolutely invaluable*; & psychical research ought to insure his life for about a million pounds. . . . He combines the powers of a first-rate detective with a perfect readiness to believe in astrology. (*Don't quote this*, as it might be misunderstood. I should pity the astrologer whose horoscopes he took to tackling.)"[66] Not everyone, of course, was happy about such radical suspicions. The society, for example, suffered a very early and very serious split when the Spiritualist camp among them, including Stainton Moses, took great offense at the way the researchers were treating Spiritualism, that is, critically. The Spiritualists left in protest, leaving the society more or less under the control of what Gauld has called "the Sidgwick group," that is, Sidgwick, Myers, Gurney, Hodgson, and Podmore.

It was not all burning Theosophical houses, forewarned astrologers, and pissed-off Spiritualists, though. There were other moments that approached near luminosity. None were more impressive than the case of Leonora E. Piper, the Bostonian medium whom Gauld describes as "an undoubted lady" and whom James once described, for her lack of intellect and conversation skills, as "that insipid prophetess."[67] But insipid or not, prophetess she was. Gauld, Blum, and many others have told her story in great detail. Indeed, Eleanor Mildred Sidgwick published a 657-page study of Piper in the 1915 *Proceedings*. Obviously, we are not going to repeat such a performance here. It is enough simply to point out the barest impossible facts.

Once William James discovered her, the psychical researchers went to great lengths to test Mrs. Piper. Hodgson went so far as to have her and her family followed by professional detectives, sometimes for weeks at a time. In an attempt to remove her from her usual surroundings, the S.P.R. also took her to England for four months, from November of 1898 to February of 1890, in order to test her further there. The society then offered her two hundred pounds per year if she would let Richard Hodgson control her sittings for the next few years. She agreed.

Like many mediums, Piper's "controls," that is, the spirit-personalities who allegedly spoke through her, changed over the years. Not all were terribly promising, and even here one encounters that strange fantastic mix of the factual and the fraudulent. Mrs. Piper's early controls, for example, included a certain Indian girl named "Chlorine" and Sir Walter Scott, who informed his listeners that there are monkeys on the sun.[68] But Chlorine and Walter quickly disappeared as other controls took over, including a certain "Phinuit" and a young man named "George Pellew."

Pellew was known by many (including Hodgson) as a local historical figure who had been killed in an accident a few weeks before he began speaking through Mrs. Piper. In this life, he was an outspoken critic of psychical phenomena who, as Deborah Blum has it, "had made a half-joking promise" a few months before he was killed. "If Hodgson was right, Pellew was willing to prove it. If he died first, he would return and 'make things lively.'"[69] He certainly lived up to his promise. G. P., as he was called in these sittings, recognized every single person whom he knew while alive who now came to Mrs. Piper: "Out of 150 sitters who were introduced to him," Gauld explains, "G. P. recognized the thirty and only the thirty with whom the living Pellew had been acquainted. He appropriately adjusted the topics and the style of his conversation to each of these friends and often showed a close knowledge of their concerns."[70] Even here, of course, there were mistakes, but there were no more solar primates.

Gauld points out that nearly every serious psychical researcher who came into contact with Mrs. Piper eventually became convinced that her powers were real, and many came to the impossible conclusion that spirits were indeed communicating to the living through her trances and automatic writing. James published well over a hundred pages on her phenomena.[71] And even Richard Hodgson and Frank Podmore, widely known as the harshest of critics and the most difficult to convince, were finally convinced. No one had to burn another house down.

Always the poet, classicist, and philologist, that is, always the lover of words, Frederic Myers dwelt on all of these extraordinary events and colorful personalities through long personal meditations on various Latinized and Hellenized coinages, brave new words that he fashioned out of his own experiences and intuitions. Basically, he took the altered states of consciousness that he encountered in the field and transformed them into the altered words that he expressed in his writing practice. He took all those hundreds of séances and transformed them into the Book as Séance.

In the pages that follow, I would like to trace, both reasonably and speculatively, some of the pathways—psychological, biological, traumatic, fantastic, and erotic—through which Myers accomplished this unique linguistic alchemy. I will dwell on just four of the altered word-states he develops in *Human Personality*: (1) the subliminal; (2) the supernormal; (3) the telepathic; and (4) the imaginal. I will then conclude with a rereading of Myers's initiatory encounter with those "forces unknown to science," which involves a fifth and final altered word-state that I have been honing for two decades of my own life but that also works beautifully with the secret of this Book as Séance—the erotic.

The Subliminal Gothic: The Human as Two

A young André Breton, much inspired by both the early psychical researchers and Freud's later psychoanalysis, pursued a kind of double vision he came to call *the surreal*, that is, the super-real. "I believe," he wrote, "in the future resolution of these two states, dream and reality, which are seemingly so contradictory, into a kind of absolute reality, a surreality, if one may so speak." Not surprisingly, Breton loved Myers. Indeed, he affectionately referred to the elaborate architectonics of Myers's psychological system as a "gothic psychiatry."[72] William James would have agreed. As we have already noted, in a kind of eulogy for Myers he published in the *Proceedings*, James aligned his recently deceased friend with the "romantic" imagination against what he called the "classic-academic" mind, which wants only straight logical lines and neat categorical boxes. James also insisted that in our own immediate experience, "nature is everywhere Gothic, not classic. She forms a real jungle, where all things are provisional, half-fitted to each other and untidy."[73] This was putting it mildly with respect to his old friend. The details of Myers's major text, after all, consist largely of the eerie data of death and apparitions.

This Gothic castle of a book was built with a very particular method, which we might capture, in our own terms and for our own purposes now, as a type of trauma or dissociation theory. Virtually all of the book's data, after all, depended in some way on that most universal of all human traumas and that most permanent of all dissociations—death. But death was not the only trauma Myers treated. He also took the data of early psychiatry and psychopathology very seriously as well. In Emily Williams Kelly's framing, "Myers believed that psychologists needed to begin to single out for special attention situations in which the ordinary relationship between mental and physical functioning seems to be altered or thrown out of gear." Only in this way could they see more clearly "that the correlation of mind and brain might not be as straightforward as it appears under normal circumstances."[74]

In other words, for the psychical phenomena to manifest, it is usually necessary for the normal state of awareness, the social ego, to be temporarily suppressed (as in sleep, trance, or ecstasy) or traumatized (as in an accident or near-death experience). The stars, after all, only come out at night, when the sun goes down. In a stunning comment that foreshadows certain strands within contemporary neuroscience, Myers even suggested that subliminal material and various unusual automatisms might manifest in an especially clear way when the left, language-processing hemisphere of the brain is damaged or suppressed. This is also how Myers thought automatic writing worked: essentially, the right brain and its specific energies become dominant over the left brain and its waking self.[75] I will return to this idea in my conclusion, as, neuroanatomically speaking, I think this is precisely how a writer becomes an "author of the impossible."

Aldous Huxley, who had read his Myers and positioned him in his own psychological galaxy well above both Freud and Jung, put the same traumatic insight this way:

> Nothing in our everyday experience gives us any reason for supposing that water is made up of hydrogen and oxygen; and yet when we subject water to certain rather drastic treatments, the nature of its constituent elements becomes manifest. Similarly, nothing in our everyday experience gives us much reason for supposing that the mind of the average sensual man has, as one of its constituents, something resembling, or identical with, the Reality substantial to the manifold world; and yet, when that mind is subjected to drastic treatments, the divine element, of which it is in part at least composed, becomes manifest.[76]

The situation, however, was more radical than Huxley's chemical metaphor suggests, for in the light of the new physics and his own psychical research, Myers had already realized that fundamental terms like "material" and "immaterial" were beginning to waver. He observed that "it is no longer safe to assume any sharply-defined distinction of mind and matter," and he predicted that "our notions of mind and matter must pass through many a phrase as yet unimagined."[77]

Indeed. We can now make the point even more contemporary. Nothing in our everyday experience, for example, gives us any reason to suppose that matter is not material, that it is made up of bizarre forms of energy that violate, very much like spirit, all of our normal notions of space, time, and causality. Yet when we subject matter to certain drastic treatments, like CERN's Hadron Collider near Geneva, Switzerland, then we can see quite clearly that matter is not material at all, that there is no such thing as materialism, and that the world is way, way weirder than we thought.

Myers, of course, was writing well before quantum theory, which, had he known of it, I am certain he would have mined for new ways of thinking about his psychical data. But he was writing well after men like Sir William Crookes, the pioneering British chemist who was president of both the British Association for the Advancement of Science *and* the Society for Psychical Research and who had performed experiments with mediums and psychics toward the discovery of what he called "a New Force." Most of all, though, Myers was writing after the discovery of the electromagnetic spectrum, hence the language of the latter science became one of the central organizing principles of his theorizing and poetics. Enter the metaphor of *the spectrum* (which, in turn, we might surmise, alludes to the earlier register of *the specter*).

The discovery of electromagnetic radiation taught Myers that our senses pick up only a tiny fraction of what surrounds us at all times. The vast majority of reality is quite literally "occult" or hidden to us. He thus wrote of "the Interpenetration of Worlds," which Kelly glosses as "the interaction between the physical world that our senses have evolved to perceive and what he called the 'metetherial' world, the larger universe that is beyond our direct sensory perception."[78] He even intuited, before Einstein, that space may not be absolute: we must, he reasoned from his psychical data, "be ready to conceive other invisible environments or co-existences, and in a sense to sit loose to the conception of Space, regarded as an obstacle to communication or cognition" (HP 2:262). To employ a less abstract analogy, Myers thought our condition might be like that of a tadpole, "who had learned theoretically that what he was breathing in his pond was not the water but the oxygen dissolved therein,—and who then should . . . raise his head above water . . . [and] perceive frogs and other animals respiring the translucid air" (HP 2:526). We'll see this one again, when we get to Charles Fort and his fishes.

Along similar spectral lines, Myers was convinced that there are no true "breaks" or "miracles" in the universe, that even the most extraordinary events are located along a spectrum that stretches back to the most ordinary ones. Accordingly, he did not argue from the special or completely anomalous case. He argued from the common cases through the less common cases to the relatively rare cases and, finally, toward the horizon of the seemingly impossible ones, which now, precisely because of this gradation or spectrum method, began to look more than a little possible. This is how Frederic Myers became an author of the impossible—through the data of trauma and dissociation, a poetics of the electromagnetic spectrum, a tadpole here and there, and a method of gradation.

So, for example, in the first volume of *Human Personality*, Myers did not just plop down an extreme example of automatic writing and expect his readers to accept it. He carefully introduced his methods (chapter 1) and began with the subject of the disintegration of personality in mental illness in order to show just how malleable and multiple the self really is (chapter 2). If we could track how the self devolves or falls apart, he reasoned, we might also be able to figure out how it evolves into something higher up the spectrum of consciousness. From there he moved slowly to the extraordinary but still accepted "subliminal uprushes" of genius and inspiration in artists, thinkers, and writers (chapter 3), and then to sleep and dreams, those common nocturnal visions in which many strange voices speak through us at night (chapter 4). Who could deny such things? From there it was on to hypnotism, which in its earlier, more robust form as "magnetic sleep" had been widely rejected as preposterous but now as "hypnotism" was being widely studied in the major research hospitals of the time (chapter 5). Immediately after that, Myers took on the related subject of sensory automatisms, such as spontaneous visions or auditions (chapter 6).

This in turn laid the foundation for the second volume, where Myers now ventured into the most extraordinary material on the far end of the spectrum of consciousness. Here we catch sight of phantasms of the dead (chapter 7) and then enter a chapter on motor automatisms (chapter 8). By motor automatisms, Myers referred to phenomena like automatic writing, that is, the paranormal *as writing*. Myers completes his mapping of the spectrum of consciousness with the truly extraordinary subjects of trance, possession, and ecstasy, that is, those phenomena in which the human personality is radically transformed by an altered state, another presence, or even an invading personality (chapter 9). He then concludes with a final philosophical epilogue (chapter 10) and a long series of appendices, which really form the "meat" or base data of the book for the careful and patient reader. The form or structure of *Human Personality* thus reproduces its theory and content: the book begins with an analysis of the normal and evolves gradually into a discussion of the supernormal, ending finally with a discussion of the empirical evidence for postmortem survival.

The psychological castle built in this manner possesses a mindboggling number of rooms, hallways, dungeons, and secret stairwells, but it is also all basically a duplex. It is all, that is, built after the blueprint of Myers's central category of the *subliminal Self.* Myers argued that the human personality can be thought of as operating on two major functional levels, each of which is normally separated from the other by a "threshold" (*limen*). For Myers, in other words, the human personality is a *homo duplex*, or what I have called the Human as Two. There is what he called the *supraliminal* or "above" (*supra*) "the threshold" (*limen*) sense of self that one carries around most of the time as one's social and personal identity and mistakes as one's complete and total self. And there is the *subliminal* or "below" (*sub*) "the threshold" (*limen*) Self that normally manifests only in altered forms of consciousness, such as dreams or creative acts of genius, or under excessive or traumatic conditions that break down or temporarily suppress the operations of the supraliminal personality, as in trance, possession, ecstasy and, finally, death.

Here is how he defined his central term in the opening pages of *Human Personality*:

> *Subliminal.*—Of thoughts, feelings, etc., lying beneath the ordinary *threshold* (*limen*) of consciousness, as opposed to *supraliminal*, lying *above* the threshold. Excitations are termed subliminal when they are too weak to rise into direct notice; and I have extended the application of the term to feeling, thought, or faculty, which is kept thus submerged, not by its own weakness, but by the constitution of man's personality. The threshold (*Schwelle*) must be regarded as a level above which waves may rise,—like a slab washed by the sea,—rather than as an entrance into a chamber. (HP 1:xxi)

Myers did not invent the term *subliminal*, but he did redefine it. As the above quotation makes clear, this redefinition revolved around the idea that the subliminal named a certain dual structure of the human personality.

It would be difficult to overestimate the importance of this distinction between the supraliminal and the subliminal aspects of the human personality for early attempts to analyze and interpret religious phenomena. It was precisely psychological models like this one, after all, that allowed nineteenth- and early twentieth-century writers to think anew about religious experience in a way that was both sympathetic to *and* suspicious of religious claims. They now had a powerful way to explain religious experiences without explaining them away.

But it would also be difficult *not* to misunderstand Myers's particular distinction between the subliminal and supraliminal levels of the human personality. There are at least two problems here. The first is his unfortunate use of the prefixes *sub-* and *supra-* in this context. Together, these two prefixes imply that what goes on "under" the threshold of egoic awareness is less conscious or developed than what goes on "above" it, that the social ego and its sensory capacities are somehow superior to other forms of consciousness and their own respective capacities. Myers recognized the problem and rejected this assumption:

> There seems no reason to assume that our active consciousness is necessarily altogether superior to the consciousnesses which are at present secondary, or potential only. We may rather hold that *super-conscious* may be quite as legitimate a term as *sub-conscious*, and instead of regarding our consciousness (as is commonly done) as a *threshold* in our being, above which ideas and sensations must rise if we wish to cognize them, we may prefer to regard it as a *segment* of our being, into which ideas and sensations may enter either from below or from above.[79]

The second problem, very much related to the first, is the fact that Myers's consistent duplex language seems to suggest a basic dualism in the human personality. Again, Myers recognized the problem and explicitly rejected such a notion.

We must be very careful, then, about how we use a category like the Human as Two, which is my way of relating comparative mystical literature to modern psychological theory. Following Myers, I am using the expression not as a metaphysical statement implying an absolute dualism (which I also reject), but as a helpful heuristic device that captures quite accurately the kinds of functional dualisms that do in fact seem to give structure to human experience throughout the history of religions.

In certain senses, the supraliminal and the subliminal dimensions of the human personality line up closely with what later mainstream Freudian psychology would call the ego and the unconscious. In other senses, they do not line up at all, mostly because Myers's metaphysical conception of the subliminal region of the psyche was far more robust and expansive than Freud's instinctual personal unconscious.[80] The subliminal may at times look like a "chamber" or basement (and Myers was very clear that the subliminal is by no means always positive or inspirational), but it was a basement that Myers insisted could suddenly open out into a vast psychical sea. Myers's subliminal Self was thus much closer to what his most famous interpreter, William James, described as that "continuum of cosmic consciousness, against which our individuality builds but accidental fences, and into which our minds plunge as into a mother-sea or reservoir."[81] This was Jamesian language, with a little Richard M. Bucke thrown in, but it was also pure Fred Myers.[82] Myers's Gothic castle, then, floated on top of the sea, as a haunted island of sorts, with God only knows what swimming in its surrounding waters. But it was much more than that floating castle. It was also the entire sea.

According to Alan Gauld, Myers was mostly influenced in his psychological thought by James's *Principles of Psychology* and so would have rejected what would eventually become the Freudian or Jungian models of the unconscious, whereby one can have a stream of thought or a set of impressions that exists and acts entirely outside conscious awareness.[83] For Myers, in this reading at least, all streams of thought are conscious on their own level. They may be temporarily submerged or subliminal vis-à-vis the ego, but they remain forms of consciousness. They can never really be described as "unconscious." They simply exist along a different band of the spectrum.

Myers's thought on the unity of the Self is also quite complex. On the one hand, he clearly insisted on the "composite structure of the Ego" (HP 1:xxv). That is, he considered any stream of thought that might be recalled and remembered as a "personality." A personality for Myers, then, was essentially a "chain of memory" strung together in a meaningful way. I would rephrase this insight: *on one level, the human personality is a narrative or story that can be remembered.* If the chain of memories is too weak, that is, if these specific memories are forgotten, or if there is no binding meaning or stable story to hold them together, we may have a partial or dual or multiple personality operating, but not a coherent self. Moreover, in something like possession, *another* personality, chain of memories, or story can temporarily take over a body. Obviously, then, the human personality is radically multiple for Myers. It is not just Two.

On the other hand, Myers also insisted on the personality's "abiding *unity*" (HP 1:xxv), on a deep "Individuality," by which he referred to "the underlying psychical unity which I postulate as existing beneath all our phenomenal manifestations," that is, beneath all our other selves.[84] We are thus One *and* Many. He even used, alas inconsistently, the capitalized Self, Personality, or Individuality to refer to the total Self, much in the way Jung later did to express the psychological state of the actualized individual, that is, the human person whose conscious ego is in tune with both the individual and collective unconscious. For Myers, at least, there could be multiple personalities or selves all coordinated within this large super Self:

> I find it permissible and convenient to speak of subliminal Selves, or more briefly of a subliminal Self . . . and I conceive that there may be,—not only *co-operations* between these quasi-independent trains of thought,—but also upheavals and alternations of personality of many kinds, so that what was once below the surface may for a time, or permanently, rise above it. And I conceive also that no

> Self of which we can here have cognisance is in reality more than a fragment of a larger Self,—revealed in a fashion at once shifting and limited through an organism not so framed as to afford its full manifestation. (HP 1:14–15)

Perhaps all of this is clarified somewhat when Myers takes up his methodological metaphor of the spectrum and transforms it into an ontological suggestion. Enter the classic mystical understanding of consciousness as light. This is an ancient and well-worn metaphor, but it takes on a new life in the second half of the nineteenth century as physicists began to discover that visible light is in fact only a small part of a much larger spectrum of energy. Hence Myers's aforementioned "spectrum of consciousness" through which he sought to draw "a comparison of man's range of consciousness or faculty to the solar spectrum, as seen by us after passing through a prism or examined in a spectrascope" (HP 1:xxi). Myers uses such a prismatic effect to suggest that the light of consciousness is not singular at all, that consciousness can be broken up into various bands, much like white light can be separated into a rainbow of colors. Most of the light spectrum, moreover, particularly that beyond the infrared (on the lower end) and ultraviolet (on the higher end), appears well outside the bands of everyday awareness. Similarly, Myers suggested, most of the spectrum of consciousness is entirely invisible to our normal senses and present egoic form of awareness.

But this hardly means that such bands of consciousness are unreal. What we need, then, is a way to see beyond the tiny visible spectrum. We need a new psychical technology, or what Myers called "artifices." "Just as the solar spectrum has been prolonged by artifice beyond both red and violet ends, so may the spectrum of conscious human faculty be artificially prolonged beyond both the lower end (where consciousness merges into mere organic operation) and the higher end (where consciousness merges into reverie or ecstasy)" (HP 1:xxv).

Myers, then, was not so naive as to confuse our present egoic methods of seeing with the real. Science had taught him that much:

> The limits of our spectrum do not inhere in the sun that shines, but in the eye that marks his shining. . . . The artifices of the modern physicist have extended far in each direction the visible spectrum known to Newton. It is for the modern psychologist to discover artifices which may extend in each direction the conscious spectrum as known to Plato or to Kant. (HP 1:17–18)

The issues, in other words, are largely about what we would now call epistemology. Particularly when it comes to the subject of the Subject, that is, to the nature of human consciousness itself, *what* we see is largely determined by *how* we see, and how we see is in turn largely determined by the restricting structures of society and the brain. So the question becomes: By what methods, by what artifices, can we get around these limiting structures to see more, to reflect and refract a broader band of consciousness? More radically still, since the study of consciousness is inevitably performed by consciousness itself, how can we get around the mind-blowing paradoxes of a kind of infinite reflection, of a subject studying an object that is really the same subject? How can we step behind the mirror?

The Supernormal and Evolution: The World as Two

Myers may not have originated the term *subliminal*, but he did coin the term *supernormal*, in 1885, on the analogy of the abnormal to mark "phenomena which are *beyond what usually happens—beyond*, that is, in the sense of suggesting unknown psychic laws." This particular altered word-state was another expression of his spectrum or graduation method. It was also deeply rooted in Myers's specific understandings of evolution. Myers explains:

> When we speak of abnormal phenomenon we do not mean one which *contravenes* natural laws, but one which exhibits them in an unusual or inexplicable form. Similarly by a supernormal phenomenon I mean, not one which *overrides* natural laws, for I believe no such phenomenon to exist, but one which exhibits the action of laws higher, in a psychical aspect, than are discerned in action in everyday life. By *higher* (either in a psychical or a physiological sense) I mean "apparently belonging to a more advanced stage of evolution."[85]

As we have already seen, *Human Personality* in fact begins with the insight that psychopathology and the disintegration of the everyday self can tell us something important about the higher states of psychic functioning, that is, there are intimate psychological connections between the breakdown of the supraliminal self in psychological suffering (what Myers calls the *devolutive*) and the transcendence of the same supraliminal self in the evolved states of genius, telepathic communication, possession, and ecstasy (what Myers calls the *evolutive*). There is a rhyming connection, then, for Myers between what we might call abnormal psychology and supernormal psychology. Psychologically speaking, that connection boils down to a single process expressed in multiple modes, that is, the temporary suppression of the supraliminal self or ego.

This again is why so much of his data involves what we would now call dissociative or traumatic phenomena, that is, states of consciousness in which a traumatic event—usually death as actual or as threatened—separates or dissociates consciousness into at least two fields of operation. In some cases, this leads to abnormal, pathological, or devolutive states. In other cases, this leads to evolutive states of genius and various special powers that Myers called supernormal. In many cases, moreover, both processes can be seen in the same individual. Contrary to what many want to assume, pathological and mystical states are *not* mutually exclusive, and both are related to the suppression of the social ego. Myers saw this very clearly. Hence his rhyming model of the abnormal and the supernormal.

For Myers, the supernormal carried multiple connotations. As its related category of the evolutive suggests, the supernormal was a term that signaled both a particular evolutionary purpose and an entirely natural or "normal" process. We might well say that the supernormal was super natural, but not supernatural. This is how Myers put it in the opening definitions of *Human Personality* (the asterisk signals a word of his own creation):

> **Supernormal.*—Of a faculty or phenomenon which goes beyond the level of ordinary experience, in the direction of evolution, or as pertaining to a transcendental world. The word *supernatural* is open to grave objections; it assumes that there is something outside nature, and it has become associated with arbitrary interference with law. Now there is no reason to suppose that the psychical phenomena with which we deal are less a part of nature, or less subject to fixed and definite law, than any other phenomena. Some of them appear to indicate a higher evolutionary level than the mass of men have yet attained, and some of them appear to be governed by laws of such a kind that they may hold good in a transcendental world as fully as in the world of sense. In either case they are above the norm of man rather than outside his nature. (HP 1:xxii)

As such a quote suggests, Myers was operating with a worldview that mirrored his bimodal psychology. The human being is certainly a material being almost seamlessly embedded in the physical world, but, in the words of Edward Kelly now, the human personality is also "rooted in a hidden, wider environment that underlies and interpenetrates the world of ordinary experience, at bottom a spiritual or 'metetherial' realm lying beyond the material as classically conceived."[86] Just as the Human is Two, so too is the World.

Sort of. It is more accurate to say that, for Myers, the World is One, but that it is experienced by us in two different ways—in a naturalistic and social way via our supraliminal self, and in a spiritual or "transcendental" way via our subliminal Self. What finally renders this Two One for Myers is a firm conviction that *both* forms of consciousness and their corresponding worlds of experience are shaped by "fixed and definite law," and that such a law is at root an evolutionary one. Again, beyond A and B, there is X.

There is another way of putting this. In Myers's spectrum model, the supraliminal self or sense-based ego, that is, a specific personality that has been created by the narrowing of the field of consciousness, is conceived as operating on a specific band along the spectrum of consciousness within a particular social and historical period. This point on the spectrum, however, is neither stable nor absolute. It is transitory and constantly shifting. It is a compromise, a temporary adaptation determined, Myers speculated, by something like Darwin's natural selection.[87] The ego or social self is, if you will, an adaptive response to the cultural and physical environments in which the subliminal self finds itself manifesting at a particular moment in space and time. In another place, Myers seems to intuit the role of culture and language in these evolutionary processes, if only as a metaphor this time: "The letters of our inward alphabet," he writes, "will shape themselves into many other dialects;—many other personalities, as distinct as those which we assume to be *ourselves*, can be made out of our mental material."[88]

In other words, human nature is being written in vastly different ways, and these different languages of consciousness and culture will continue to morph and manifest as history proceeds into the future. Myers is an optimist here. As the human personality continues to evolve, he speculates that it will move further and further away from the primitive, ultrared, instinctual, physiological, or "terrene" end of the spectrum of consciousness and toward the ultraviolet, spiritual, psychical, or "extraterrene" end.

Toward that further end of the spectrum lie what Myers called "*superconscious* operations," that is, capacities that are "not *below the threshold*—but rather *above the upper horizon* of consciousness."[89] He could be quite radical on this point. Consciousness and its sensory capacities, he claimed, are "doubtless still modifiable in directions as unthinkable to me as my eyesight would have been unthinkable to the oyster,"[90] and the human being has "evoked in greatest multiplicity the unnumbered faculties latent in the irritability of a speck of slime" (HP 1:76). In short, just as it has in the history of life on this planet, consciousness will continue to evolve from the normal to the supernormal, and this to the extent that it can gain "a completer control over innate but latent faculty."[91]

As we have already noted, Myers often writes of this double evolution as "terrene" and "extraterrene." He accepted the Darwinian model of natural selection with respect to the terrene or earthly processes, but he was very much a Platonist or, perhaps better, a Neoplatonist when it came to the extraterrene or spiritual processes, that is, he believed that extraterrene evolution flowed from an earlier involution, that that which evolves into our spiritual consciousness was always already there from the beginning. Indeed, he even refers to his understanding of the latter involution/evolution processes as "some sort of a renewal of the old Platonic 'reminiscence,' in the light of that fuller knowledge which is common property to-day." So, for example, he felt it necessary to posit the primordial existence of a "primal germ," which possessed what he called *panaesthesia* or an "undifferentiated sensory capacity" that later evolved into the various sensory organs known to biology and psychology (HP 1:xiv). In another fascinating passage, he calls this "an X of some sort." Whether a carbon atom or an immortal soul, he muses, this X "must have dated in any case from some age anterior to its existence upon our recent planet . . . on which earth's forces began their play."[92] For the modern reader at least, "the heavens" of the spiritual world and "the outer space" of astrophysics here mingle in provocative and suggestive ways.

With respect to the extraterrene evolution of the subliminal Self and its supernormal capacities, Myers explicitly rejected the Darwinian notion that something like a telepathic faculty could be initiated "by some chance combination of hereditary elements." He held rather that "it is not initiated, but only revealed; that the 'sport' [of evolutionary processes] has not called a new faculty into being, but has merely raised an existing faculty above the threshold of supraliminal consciousness" (HP 1.117–18). He recognized, of course, that this view is inconsistent with natural selection in the strict biological sense. Hence his double-language of the terrene and the extraterrene, or what I have called the Darwinian and the Neoplatonic:

> Our human life . . . exists and energises, at the present moment, both in the material and in the spiritual world. Human personality, as it has developed from lowly ancestors, has become differentiated into two phases; one of them mainly adapted to material or planetary, the other to spiritual or cosmic operation. The subliminal self, mainly directing the sleeping phase, is able either to rejuvenate the organism by energy drawn in from the spiritual world;—or, on the other hand, temporarily and partially to relax its connection with that organism, in order to expatiate in the exercise of supernormal powers;—telepathy, teleasthesia, ecstasy. (HP 1:155)

Myers's language here had a rather remarkable pedigree. On the extraterrene side, it went back to Plotinus and Plato, both of whom he read, knew, and loved in the original Greek. On the terrene side, it went back to the very origins of evolutionary biology. Alfred Russel Wallace, the co-creator of the evolutionary thesis with Darwin, attended the first official meeting of the Society for Psychical Research on February 20, 1882. He also attended multiple séances, witnessed the full-blown materializations of various physical mediums, and accepted for publication William Barrett's 1876 paper on thought-transference as chairman for the anthropological section of the British Association (the paper was later suppressed and then finally published in the journal of the S.P.R.).[93] He thus wrote of how an "overruling intelligence" may have something to do with the evolution of mind and morality. He explained to T. H. Huxley his dream of a "new branch of Anthropology" that might be crafted out of a study of Spiritualist phenomena. And he asked his scientific colleagues to pursue "those grand mysterious phenomena of the mind, the investigation of which can alone conduct us to a knowledge of what we really are."[94] In other words, Wallace realized that science leads, inexorably, to ontological questions. Much like Myers, Wallace saw the phenomena of Spiritualism as evidence for a separate, nonphysical line of moral or spiritual evolution.[95] In Myers's own words, Wallace entertained the idea "that some influence, resembling that of man on the domestic animals, may have been brought to bear upon primitive man . . . and that some power of spiritual communion, differentiating man from the lower races, may have been thus originated."[96] We'll return to that idea too: the earth as a farm.

Despite all of this, Wallace was never entirely comfortable with the S.P.R., not because he thought its members were being too credulous, but because he thought that they were being too suspicious. In his mind at least, the researchers were being far too critical of psychical phenomena. Here he was closer to Stainton Moses than Frederic Myers. Accordingly, Wallace completely rejected Myers's notion of the subliminal Self, or any other theory of the unconscious for that matter, as fundamentally unscientific. In his own mind, he was simply trusting his own senses, that is, what he heard and saw at the séances. He was being a good naturalist. Only the jungle had changed.

Wallace's Spiritualist beliefs aside, Myers was clearly working with a similar double-evolutionary model. As we have already seen, there were two lines of evolution for Myers—one that applied to the natural world and one that applied to the transcendental or spiritual world. But, again, they both answered to the same evolutionary law: the A and the B were both rooted in a deeper X. One of the implications of such a conclusion is the notion that human evolution continues after death. In the end, Myers arrived at a kind of mind-body dualism, fully convinced that a mind uses a brain, and that the "human brain is in its last analysis an arrangement of matter expressly adapted to being acted upon by a spirit" (HP 2:254). Thought and Consciousness are not, then, random products of biological processes. They "are, and always have been, the central subject of the evolutionary process itself."[97] Put simply, mind, not matter, is primary, and human evolution is guided by spiritual forces that have, over the course of millions of years, evolved their own bodily receptors and are working still toward the actualization of potential powers that have in fact always been enfolded into the universe. Evolution is exactly what its etymology suggests, then: an "unfolding" of something already present, already there.

Little wonder, then, that Darwin shied away from the word *evolution*, citing its common mystical connotations as inappropriate to his own purely naturalistic understandings. Indeed, the word possessed (and still possesses) an especially rich background in German Idealism and English and German Romanticism. Such authors, drawing on ancient Neoplatonic notions of involution and evolution, the ancient image of the *ouroboros* (the snake biting its own tail), and the symbolism of the spiral, used the language of evolution to express the natural tendency or "way" (*Weg*) of the cosmos to "unfold" its own implicit consciousness or divine Mind. Schelling could thus write that "[h]istory is an epic composed in the mind of God," and Coleridge could declare that "the nurture and evolution of humanity is the final aim."[98] Thus, to paraphrase the famous terms of Schelling, the God who is involved into the universe (*Deus implicitus*) manifests as the God who evolves out of the universe (*Deus explicitus*).[99]

As a striking example of this pre-Darwinian understanding of evolution as a kind of cosmic Mind awakening through history and culture, consider M. H. Abrams's reading of Hegel's masterwork *The Phenomenology of the Spirit*. Abrams approaches this text as a "literary narrative," that is, as a Romantic novel or myth of the mind coming into its own self-revelation. The hermeneutical results are certainly astonishing (and fantastically familiar) enough: in a world in which Spirit or Mind (*Geist*) constitutes both subject and object, as well as the plot of the story, the reader is as much a part of the text as the text is a part of the reader. We are all being written, even as we are also doing the writing. Hegel now reads remarkably like Philip K. Dick's autobiographical descriptions of Valis:

> The spirit, the protagonist of the story, maintains no one phenomenal identity, but passes through the bewildering metamorphoses in the form of outer objects and phenomenal events, or "shapes of consciousness" [*Gestalten des Bewusstseins*], as well as multiple human personae, or particular "spirits." . . . This

> protagonist, the spirit, is also his own antagonist . . . so that the one actor plays all the roles in the drama . . . It constitutes not only all the agents, but also the shifting setting in the phenomenal world of nature and society which it sets up as object against itself as conscious subject or subjects. . . . It constitutes the totality of the plot as well. In a sustained dramatic irony, however, the spirit carries on this astonishing performance all unknowingly. . . . until, that is, the process discovers itself to consciousness in its own latent manifestation, the thinking of the philosopher Hegel, in an on-going revelation with which our own consciousness is privileged to participate as we read. For the reader, no less than the author and the subject matter of the *Phenomenology*, is one of the *Geister* [or spirits] in which the spirit continues to manifest itself.[100]

Put quite simply, Abrams reads the *Phenomenology* as an autobiography of metaphysical Mind evolving into consciousness, but an autobiography told explicitly "in the mode of a double consciousness," that is, in the mode of the Human as Two as both author and reader. In this same context, it should hardly surprise us to learn that Hegel both wrote appreciatively of Jacob Boehme, one of the premiere (if also most baffling) representatives of Western esoteric thought, and drew on the literature of Mesmerism and animal magnetism to forge his own, basically mystical, understandings of "absolute Spirit" and its "magical" relationship to Nature.[101] What I am suggesting here is that it was precisely this same Romantic and essentially mystical stream of thought, now fused with Darwinian biology, that Myers and Wallace picked up on and developed further in the second half of the nineteenth century in the mirror of their own Spiritualist and psychical data.

And all of this in turn led to the grand idea that would have an astonishing run in the twentieth century and is, under many popular cultural guises, still very much with us today, namely, the idea that the supernormal powers evident in the psychical data are early signs of the species' evolutionary advance. Myers at least is quite clear that the history of spirit communication gives witness to "the evolution of human personality" and that his work speaks "of faculties newly dawning, and of a destiny greater than we know" (HP 1:19). He even suggests that humanity may be able to hasten its own evolution and openly encourages his readers to see that their greatest duty is to increase the intensity of their mystical life and so come to recognize "that their own spirits are co-operative elements in the cosmic evolution, are part and parcel of the ultimate vitalizing Power" common to all religions (HP 1:23, 219).

What are these evolving "faculties newly dawning"? There are numerous supernormal capacities posited in *Human Personality*, and all of them are derived from the data, that is, from the stories collected in the field or through the correspondence. Many of these powers, however, are best understood as different manifestations of a form of consciousness that is both nonlocal and nontemporal, that is, a form of Mind not bound by the usual parameters of space and time.

A later writer like Aldous Huxley—the grandson of T. H. Huxley and his agnosticism—would call this form of consciousness Mind at Large and turn to the "artifices" of mescaline and LSD in order to become what he called an aspiring "Gnostic."[102] Such a gnosis for Huxley involved *experiencing*, directly and personally, the brain as a kind of filter (as opposed to the producer) of consciousness. Major thinkers like William James, Henri Bergson, and C. D. Broad had all arrived at a similar conclusion before Huxley. Neuroscientist Edward Kelly has succinctly captured these various "filter" or "transmission" theories of mind by describing them as models "according to which mind is not generated by the brain but instead focused, limited, and constrained by it."[103]

Although Myers would arrive at a more or less identical theory of consciousness, he took no mescaline, nor did he ever use the term "filter." His expressions tended to be much more conservative and classical. Hence the first occurrence of the phrase "supernormal power" appears within yet another of his Greek coinages, *hyperpromethia*, defined as a "supernormal power of foresight; attributed to the subliminal self as a hypothesis by which to explain premonitions" (HP 1:xvii). Similarly, he turns to his Latin in order to coin the word *retrocognition* in order to refer to "Knowledge of the Past, supernormally acquired" (HP 1:xxi).

As the above definitions make clear, the supernormal was intimately related to the subliminal. It was not that Myers's subjects were walking around like Hollywood's superheroes, seeing into the future or the past whenever they wished. Quite the contrary, whatever powers they reported seemed to work almost entirely outside the range of their conscious control, that is, subliminally. If there was an occasional Superman here, and there was, he usually appeared to and within a completely baffled Clark Kent. Hence Myers could write of "a shifting of man's psychical centre of gravity from the conscious to the sub-conscious or subliminal strata of his being—and accompanied by the manifestation of powers at least not obviously derivable from terrestrial evolution."[104] Of course, Superman was not of this earth either.

The clearest evidence of such evolving, subliminal, supernormal powers, Myers thought, could be found in the empirical data of psychical research, but both he and his colleagues recognized that the situation was complicated, to say the least. It is certainly true that the data can suggest the existence of hidden superpowers. But it is also true that such a conclusion finally relies on a particular interpretation of the data. Put more precisely, *the supernormal arose not from the data alone, but from the ways Myers interpreted its patterns and their implied connections*. This is why, I suspect, the very first occurrence of the supernormal appears within his opening definition of the term *coincidental*. "*Coincidental*," Myers writes at the top of his fourth page, "is used when there is some degree of coincidence in time of occurrence between a supernormal incident and an event at a distance, which makes it seem probable that some causal connection exists between the two" (HP 1:xvi). This looks *a lot* like what Jung would later call a synchronicity.

This originary appearance of the supernormal and the coincidental suggests that much, maybe everything, about how we read Frederic Myers comes down to how we manage just three terms: coincidence, cause, and comparison. Let me put it this way. When Mr. A wakes up in the middle of the night and sees his brother, Mr. B., standing at the bottom of his bed dripping wet, and then learns the next day that his brother had drowned the night before, what exactly are our interpretive options here? We can posit a causal X-connection called "telepathy" between the subliminal mind of Mr. B as he died and the subliminal mind of Mr. A as he slept, which is exactly what Myers and his colleagues did. But this, as they would be the first to admit, is a speculative theory, hence Myers's very careful "makes it seem probable" phrase above. We do not *really* have a cause, at least not one we can safely identify and agree upon yet. What we do have are two events that are *meaningfully* connected. What we have, in other words, is *a story, a text, a narrative*, both quite literally in Myers's book—which is filled with hundreds of such stories—but also in the historical world, where these events have indeed come together in deeply meaningful ways for those experiencing them, as if the world is a story telling itself. Jung called this meaningful connection without an obvious cause a synchronicity. In my own terms, we might say that the supernormal arises from the act of reading the paranormal writing us.

If a *coincidence*, then, is a set of two events that appear to be related but for which no obvious *causal* connection can be found, *comparison* is the act of lining up numerous such coincidences until a hidden pattern can be posited and a story intuited. It is crucial to understand here that comparison is not necessarily about identifying causal mechanisms, although it certainly may lead to this, as in Darwin's comparative observations about morphological coincidences between the beaks, wings, and limbs of various species that led to his theory of natural selection. What comparison is *always* about, though, is identifying meaningful connections between apparently separate events or things, that is, between seeming coincidences (which, again, makes the comparative method a very close cousin of Jung's synchronicity, not to mention traditional magic and modern occultism).[105] What sets apart Myers's comparative method is that he will indeed posit a cause between the coincidence of a subjective vision and an external physical event. He will bestow a specific set of meanings on this cause (he will call it supernormal and link it to evolution), and he will give this causal mechanism a new name—telepathy.

Telepathy: The Communications Technology of the Spirit

Visions, of course, can also manifest no coincidence with the physical world. When there is no coincidence of time or fact between a vision and an external event, Myers calls these visions "delusional." When there is such a meaningful coincidence, he calls them "veridical." Which brings us to another coinage, the seeming oxymoron *veridical hallucination*.

Such an expression functioned as one of the central data points of the S.P.R. Indeed, it was one of the earliest data points, as witnessed by the 702 cases of *Phantasms of the Living*. A "phantasm of the living" was defined as the appearance of someone in a dream or vision who was either alive but would be dead within twelve hours or who had not been dead for more than twelve hours.[106] This is perhaps a curious way to describe the "living," but they were trying to be precise and methodical in James's Gothic jungle. Jungle indeed. There were all sorts of weird problems here, from the simple fact that apparitions usually came clothed (hence Deborah Blum's delightful chapter, "Metaphysics and Metatrousers") to the even weirder fact that there were more than a few cases of collective apparitions in which multiple individuals saw the same or a very similar vision (I close this book with a retelling of what is probably the most famous case of this collective phenomenon).

Myers's original reading of collective visions is worth explaining, as it is a good example of how he thought and wrote "off the page." To explain such events, Myers invoked the subject of traveling clairvoyance, that is, the assumed ability of gifted somnambulists to travel in mind to distant places and bring back information that could then be used and verified (as in crime cases). Basically, Myers suggested that a collective apparition may be the sighting of a traveling clairvoyant in some sort of spiritual double or subtle body. He called the "point in space so modified by the presence of a spirit that it becomes perceptible to persons materially present near it" a *phantasmogenetic center* (HP 1:xix). There were even reciprocal cases in the files of the S.P.R. in which the traveling clairvoyant saw an individual at a distant locale *and* the individual saw the clairvoyant, hence the reported "bilocations" of Catholic saints. Gauld takes up such a line of thought and imagines what it would imply about a ghostly apparition. Such a phantasm, he suggests, could be compared to "a traveling clairvoyant who has been permanently cut off from his body."[107] One can catch the glimmers of a general theory of the paranormal taking shape within such thoughts.

Things were not always *this* impossible, though. The classic or modal case of a veridical hallucination involved an often mundane dream or remarkably calm waking vision of a dying or dead loved one that was clearly hallucinatory, that is, a product of the imagination, but also carried accurate and veridical information about the time, nature, or details of the death, all unknown and unknowable to the supraliminal self until the subliminal or telepathic communication occurs. As Myers and company documented, cross-checked, and confirmed hundreds of times, the unsuspecting visionary, sometimes separated by hundreds or even thousands of miles, somehow knows what has happened—an eerie or surreal mix of "subjective" dream and "objective" reality, precisely as Breton intuited.

There is, for example, the simple and brief case of Archdeacon Farler, "who *twice* during one night saw the dripping figure of a friend who, as it turned out, had been drowned during the previous day" (HP 2:17). Or there is the slightly more complex case of Reverend G. M. Tandy, who saw the face of an old friend from Cambridge in his window so clearly that he went out to look for him. Not finding him, he came back into the house, picked up a newspaper another friend had just given him, and read the first piece of news that he saw. It happened to be on the death of the old Cambridge friend whom he had just seen in his window (HP 2:57).

The case sent to "Professor James" about the death of Mrs. Margaret Q. R. is more complex still. Technically, it is more of a veridical audition than a veridical hallucination. Mrs. Q. R. died in her home in Wisconsin on November 5, 1885, at 8:40 p.m. One of her sons, a man named Robert, was working in North Dakota at the time, seven hundred miles away. Shortly after her death, at 9:45 p.m., her two daughters decided to lay down in an upstairs bedroom in order to deal with their grief, when both of them distinctly heard their brother Robert singing "We had better bide a wee." So clearly did they hear the words and tune that they opened the windows of the upstairs bedroom in order to try to determine from what direction the sound was coming. When they got around to the east window, they heard a group now singing the last verse, as the music seemed to float off toward the north. When Robert returned home two days later, his two sisters were astonished to learn that he had in fact been singing that exact song at that exact time at a church function in North Dakota. Not only that, but the telegram announcing his mother's death "was brought to him, and was *held* by the operator so as not to spoil the entertainment by telling him *before* he sang, and we—my sister Mary Q. and I—both *heard* every note and word of that song sung about seven hundred miles away, while our mother's remains were in the parlour under our bedroom" (HP 2:58–59).

Then there are the exceedingly complex cases, which read more like supernatural novellas than simple letters. Myers introduces one such case, which runs to three pages, by describing it as "one of the best-attested, and in itself one of the most remarkable, that we possess." The account was originally published in the *Proceedings* and was sent to the American branch by a certain Mr. F. G. of Boston. The letter writer opens by stating that this event "made a more powerful impression on my mind than the combined incidents of my whole life." It is not difficult to see why.

In 1867, the letter writer's only sister died of cholera in St. Louis, Missouri, at a mere eighteen years. This was a severe blow to him, as he was very close to her and loved her deeply. A year or so later, he was traveling on business and happened to be in St. Joseph, Missouri (which, for non-Midwesterners, is on the opposite side of the state from St. Louis). He had sold a number of orders for his business, so he was particularly happy at the moment. It was noon, and he was smoking a cigar and cheerfully writing out his orders when

> I suddenly became conscious that some one was sitting on my left, with one arm resting on the table. Quick as a flash I turned and distinctly saw the form of my dead sister, and for a brief second or so looked her squarely in the face; and so sure was I that it was she, that I sprang forward in delight, calling her by name, and, as I did so, the apparition instantly vanished.

The cigar in his mouth, the pen in his hand, and the still moist ink on his letter told him that he was not dreaming. Nor did his sister appear ghostly. On the contrary, her flesh "was so life-like that I could see the glow or moisture on its surface, and, on the whole, there was no change in her appearance, otherwise than when alive."

He was so impressed that he ended a business trip he had just begun and immediately took the next train home to tell his parents what he had seen. In particular, he "told them of a bright red line or *scratch* on the right-hand side of my sister's face." His mother rose and nearly fainted when she heard this particular detail. With tears in her eyes, she then "exclaimed that I had indeed seen my sister, as no living mortal but herself was aware of that scratch, which she had accidentally made while doing some little act of kindness after my sister's death." She was embarrassed, and so had covered the little scar with powder and make-up (as she prepared the body for burial, I take it) and never mentioned it to anyone. The writer goes on: "In proof, neither my father nor any of our family had detected it, and positively were unaware of the incident, yet *I saw the scratch as bright as if it [were] just made.*" A few weeks later, his mother died, "happy in her belief she would rejoin her favourite daughter in a better world."

It is interesting to see how the society debated this particular story. Frank Podmore, for example, wanted to argue that the daughter's apparition was a projection of the mother's mind. Obviously, this leaves a good deal unanswered, like how such a projection could extend from St. Louis to St. Joseph, but this is precisely the sort of thing that they came to call *telepathy*. Myers, on the other hand, sees much more. He sees a pastoral or emotional purpose in the telepathic event. More specifically, he wants to read the coincidence as "too marked to be explained away: the son is brought home in time to see his mother once more by perhaps the only means which would have succeeded; and the mother herself is sustained by the knowledge that her daughter loves and awaits her." Myers thus ranks this case as an example of "a perception by the spirit of her mother's approaching death" (HP 2:27–30).

Then there is the related subject of dreams as veridical hallucinations. There are hundreds of cases we could treat here. As a rather arbitrary means of focusing, let us consider just nine pages of the second volume of *Human Personality* (HP 2:209–17). The first thing to remind ourselves here is that Myers understood consciousness not as a discrete or stable phenomenon, but as a broad spectrum of potentialities that are actualized at different points in space and time. Dreams or dreamlike phenomena are spread out *along this entire spectrum*. So there is not one kind of dream for Myers. Quite the contrary, there are different types of dreams for differently evolved states of consciousness. There are normal dreams. And there are supernormal dreams. There are dreams. And there are *dreams*.

Consider, for example, the case of the two elite French intellectuals, Professor J. Thoulet and Professor Charles Richet, both well known to historians of psychology. On April 17, 1892, Thoulet wrote Richet with a most remarkable story. During the summer of 1867, Thoulet was traveling with an older friend by the name of M. F., a former naval officer turned businessman. They were sleeping in adjoining rooms. One night Thoulet awoke suddenly, walked into his friend's room and said, "You have just got a little girl; the telegram says . . ." He began to read the telegram—until, that is, he realized that he had received the telegram in a dream. At that moment, the telegram dissolved in his hands, and he could not read any further. The words he had already read remained, however, fully pronounced and clear in his memory; those he had not been able to read, that he had not allowed himself to consider real, remained as only a "form," as he put it. At M. F.'s insistence, he wrote out what he could, and *drew* the rest as in pictorial form. He had repeated two or three lines of a six-line telegram.

Eight or ten days later, now in Turin on his own, Thoulet received a "real" telegram from M. F.: "Come directly, you were right." He returned to M. F., who showed him a telegram he had received the night before. "I recognized it as the one I had seen in my dream; the beginning was exactly what I had written, and the end, which was exactly like my drawing." Thoulet himself underlines the weirdest part, namely, that he had dreamt of a telegram that had not been sent yet: "I had seen it ten days before it existed or could have existed." Thoulet admits that, were he called into court on this matter, he could not produce a shred of reliable evidence. Nevertheless, "I am obliged to admit that it happened."

Or consider the case of a certain Mr. Edward A. Goodall, a member of the Royal Society of Painters. In the summer of 1869, he was vacationing in Naples when a pack-donkey he was sitting on suddenly fell to its knees, "as if he had been shot or struck by lightning," and threw Goodall to the pavement, injuring his arm. Now bedridden, he awoke suddenly on the third or fourth night to the sound of his own voice saying, "I know I have lost my dearest little May." Another voice, which he did not recognize, answered back immediately and clearly, "*No*, not May, but your *youngest boy*." The next morning he noticed telegraph wires outside and sent a telegram back home. Later, he received two letters from home. The first informed him that his youngest boy was ill, the second that he was dead. The time of death coincided "as nearly as we could judge with the time of my accident." Mr. Goodall speculated that the donkey's collapse may have been caused by "terror at some apparition of the dying child."

It was out of thousands of stories like these that Myers coined the term *telepathy* in 1882, no doubt after the then cutting-edge technology of the telegraph and telegram.[108] Interestingly, two of the three stories that I have just recounted involve precisely this new communications technology. And why not? Early models of Spiritualism had turned to the same kind of language, framing spirit-communications as a kind of "spiritual telegraphy." Gauld also humorously reminds us that the spirits often claimed famous names, with Benjamin Franklin being one of their favorites, "perhaps because his electrical skills made him seem a likely inventor of the 'Spiritual Telegraph.'"[109] In a similar playful spirit, Bertrand Méheust goes so far as to describe Spiritualism as flowing out of a certain "mythology of telecommunications," with the early knocks of the Fox sisters as a kind of celestial Morse code.[110] On the other side of the equation, many of the earliest inventors of the new radio technology—Nikola Tesla, Sir William Crookes, Sir Oliver Lodge, and Lord Raleigh—were all intimately involved in psychical research and sometimes imagined their science along similar occult lines.[111] And it would not be long before the American writer Upton Sinclair would soon frame his own successful experiments with telepathy as a kind of "mental radio," with none other than Albert Einstein writing the preface.[112] The comparisons were simply irresistible.

In the opening definitions of *Human Personality*, Myers defined telepathy as "the communication of impressions of any kind from one mind to another, independently of the recognized channels of sense" (HP 1:xxii). Myers points out that the distance through which telepathic communications take place may be measured in miles or in metaphysical states, that is, between physical distances or between the living and the dead. He also suggests that "[t]he operation of telepathy is probably constant and far-reaching, and intermingled with ordinary modes of acquiring knowledge" (HP 1:xlii). As the researches and writing of the S.P.R. developed, its members eventually came to see telepathy as *the* central category through which the stories they were receiving and back-checking made the most sense. The "telepathic law," as Myers came to call it, thus became the bedrock theoretical construct of *Human Personality*.

The collection of phenomena that this single construct named, however, was by no means singular or simple. To begin with, telepathic events were highly variable, ranging from those focused on some simple projective technology, like the tapping table, crystal ball, or planchette (a kind of automatic writing device invented in 1853 that would later morph into the Ouija Board or "Yes-Yes Board"), to exceedingly complex psychological automatisms, such as automatic writing, trance, and possession states. Words or textual messages were often the literal product, but not always. Myers points out that symbolism, music, and the visual arts are often more natural media for subliminal expressions (HP 1:xxx).

Sometimes, moreover, the message is encoded in an even more basic, and more certain, feeling-tone. Significantly, Myers chose a coinage that literally means "*feeling* at distance" (telepathy), and not "voice at a distance" (telephony) or "writing at a distance" (telegraphy). By doing so, he chose to emphasize the emotional, not the intellectual or verbal, components of these remarkable events. There were at least two very good reasons to do this: (1) as phenomena rooted deeply in the wisdom of the body, telepathic communications appear to escape or subvert the rational censor, which would otherwise deem them impossible and so prevent them from happening at all; and (2) telepathic communications often emerge from highly charged events involving people who care about one another deeply, that is, they often involve the two greatest themes in human emotional experience: love and death. Pathos does indeed seem to be a key for Myers, maybe *the* key, as we shall soon see.

It is also important to note that the category of telepathy emerged from the data of dreams and mediums, and that it was originally a category of *suspicion*, that is to say, it was developed in order to refute the older objectivist model of spirits. In essence, it "reduced" the phenomena of spirit-communication to a human psychical potential theoretically present in everyone. It thus practiced a form of reductionism, but finally found the human nature to which the religious phenomena could be reduced to be ironically spiritlike.[113] Which is not to say that all of the researchers rejected the spirit thesis. They did not. Some of them at least were forced to conclude that telepathic communications could occur either between two living minds, or, more rarely, between a departed spirit and a living one.

It is also important to keep in mind that, in Myers's model, telepathic communications could occur with or without the knowledge of the mind sending them. They could even occur without the knowledge of the mind receiving them, as in Myers's suggestion that sometimes telepathic communications could be received in the day and lay "dormant" until the evening, when the recipient fell asleep and the telepathic communication could surface into dream consciousness. Telepathic communications, moreover, were often couched in symbolic form, as in a dream, and their messages were by no means always clear. In short, as subliminal phenomena, telepathic communications had to cross a psychological threshold in order to appear to the conscious ego at all. Remember the *limen*? We are back to the Human as Two.

And this, of course, is where Frederic Myers becomes a preeminent author of the impossible. He gives us a plausible explanation for why the impossible seems impossible, but is not. He teaches us that the impossible may in fact be a function not of the unreality or fiction of psychical events, but of our own inadequate models of the human personality and our fundamental failure to distinguish between the subliminal Self, which appears to be shared between individuals beyond both space and time, and the social ego, which is clearly limited to the individual personality and quite obviously restricted in both space and time. Because we keep assuming that our full human personalities and our social egos are coterminous and identical, we find telepathic events baffling, fraudulent, that is to say, impossible. What we have to do, Myers suggests, is shift our focus from the supraliminal to the subliminal. What we have to do is cross that threshold. Then the impossible not only becomes the possible. It becomes the real.

The Perfect Insect of the Imaginal

Such a threshold, however, cannot be crossed directly or literally, except perhaps at death. Before that, it can only be crossed through images, myths, and symbols. This, I would suggest, is also why the preeminent data fields of the supernormal lie in comparative mystical literature and the folklore and mythologies of the history of religions, that is, in those human expressions involving symbol and myth. Enter the category of the imaginal.

Those who are familiar with the term inevitably trace it back to the French historian of Iranian Islamic mysticism Henri Corbin, who famously used it to discuss the profound effects mystical experience is said to have on the powers of imagination within his Iranian sources. Following his textual sources (and his own initiatory transmission from a medieval Sufi saint), Corbin understood the imaginal to be a noetic organ that accessed a real dimension of the cosmos whose appearances to us were nevertheless shaped by what he called the "creative imagination" (*l'imagination créatrice*). The creative imagination is an empowered form of what most people experience in its simpler and unenlightened state as the imagination or the imaginary. The imaginal is not the imaginary, though. The imaginal is in touch with and translating a higher dimension of reality, what Myers would have called the extraterrene. The imaginary is the same organ working on a strictly naturalistic or mundane level, what Myers would have called the terrene.

Now it is true that Corbin brought the imaginal into contemporary scholarly prominence. But it is not true that he invented the term. Nor is it true that he was the first major scholar of religion to employ it. The seventeenth-century Cambridge Platonist Henry More appears to have coined the category, in 1642, as "the imaginall" in his *Psychodia Platonica; or, a Platonick song of the Soul*. The first major theorist of the imaginal in the study of religion to use the term in a consistent way, however, was none other than Frederic Myers.

Drawing on over a century of Romantic poetry and literature that recognized the imaginative powers as capable of both floating fantasy and revelatory cognition, Myers understood that the human imagination works in many modes and on many levels. More specifically, he became convinced that in certain contexts, the imagination can take on genuinely transcendental capacities, that is, that it can make contact with what appears to be a real spiritual world or, at the very least, an entirely different order of mind and consciousness. The imaginal is the imagination on steroids. The imaginary is Clark Kent, the normal. The imaginal is Superman, the supernormal. Same guy, different suits. The Human as Two.

As with his categories of the subliminal, the supernormal, and the telepathic, Myers linked the imaginal directly to his evolutionary worldview. Thus in the opening, still Roman-numeral pages of *Human Personality*, Myers defined *imaginal* this way: "A word used of characteristics belonging to the perfect insect or *imago*;—and thus opposed to *larval*;—metaphorically applied to transcendental faculties shown in rudiment in ordinary life" (HP 1:xviii). That's a bit elliptical. What Myers intended to communicate here was the idea that the human imagination under certain very specific conditions can take on extraordinary or supernormal capacities that represent hints of a more highly evolved human nature. In his own more technical terms, such altered states of consciousness were "preversions" that represented "[a] tendency to characteristics assumed to lie at a further point of the evolutionary progress of a species than has yet been reached" (HP 1:xx).

Hence just as the larval stage of an insect looks nothing like the imago or mature image of its adult form (which indeed appears "bizarre" or alienlike in comparison to the larval slug), so too the images of the human imagination can mature into extremely strange but nevertheless accurate evolutionary forms as imaginal visions or veridical hallucinations—Breton's surreal mix of "subjective" dream and "objective" reality again. The imaginal is to the imagination, then, as the adult insect or perfect imago is to its larval slug.[114]

There is a delightful parable of sorts in *Science and a Future Life* where Myers in effect glosses his elliptical definition of the imaginal in *Human Personality*. It goes like this:

> Let us suppose that some humble larvae are dissecting each other, and speculating as to their destinies. At first they find themselves precisely suited to life

> and death on a cabbage-leaf. Then they begin to observe certain points in their construction which are useless to larval life. These are, in fact, what are called "imaginal characters"—points of structure which indicate that the larva has descended from an imago, or perfect insect, and is destined in his turn to become one himself. These characters are much overlaid by the secondary or larval characters, which subserve larval, and not imaginal life, and they consequently may easily be overlooked or ignored. But our supposed caterpillar sticks to his point; he maintains that these characteristics indicate an aerial origin. And now a butterfly settles for a moment on the cabbage-leaf. The caterpillar points triumphantly to the morphological identity of some of the butterfly's conspicuous characters with some of his own latent characters; and while he is trying to persuade his fellow-caterpillars of this, the butterfly flies away.

"This," Myers explains, "is exactly what I hold to have happened in the history of human evolution." And it was Plato who "was the first larva to insist upon the imaginal characters."[115]

Here he is thinking again of Plato's doctrine of reminiscences whereby "sudden increments of faculty" of a mathematical or musical type (as with a genius) are explained by positing a preexisting state in which these forms of knowledge came naturally to the soul. "Somewhat similarly," Myers writes, "I would suggest that telepathy and cognate faculties . . . may be the results of an evolution other than that terrene or physical evolution." Basically, in a telepathic event, we are (re)discovering an innate human potential that evolution is now actualizing in a fuller and fuller fashion. We are realizing that we may not be slugs after all. Still on that cabbage-leaf band of the spectrum, but seeing past it now, Myers concludes that "here is a similarity of structure between our own intelligence and some unseen intelligence, and that what that unseen intelligence is we too may once have been, and may be destined again to be."[116]

Such a line of thinking, of course, did not begin or end with Frederic Myers. We have encountered it already in Alfred Russel Wallace. The truth is that literally hundreds of philosophers, poets, psychical researchers, psychologists, physicists, and philosophers were exploring the idea in the second half of the nineteenth century. Different forms of it, for example, were expressed by the British writer Edward Carpenter and, in a much less disciplined way, by the Canadian physician and Whitmanian mystic, Richard Maurice Bucke, who gave the twentieth century the phrase "cosmic consciousness."[117] It was this same line of thought again that led eventually to a world-class intellectual like Henri Bergson, who philosophically refigured the nature of consciousness in the light of psychical research and what he called the "evolutionary impulse" (*élan vital*), kept a portrait of William James in his office, became president of the London Society for Psychical Research in 1913, and ended his very last book with this very last line:

> Men do not sufficiently realize that their future is in their own hands. . . . Theirs [is] the responsibility, then, for deciding if they want merely to live, or intend to make just the extra effort required for fulfilling, even on their refractory planet, the essential function of the universe, which is a machine for the making of gods.[118]

Who today writes like *that*?

The Telepathic and the Erotic: Myers's Platonic Speech

The subliminal, the supernormal, and the imaginal, then—all on their way to "the making of gods." For Myers, all of this was subsumed within the centerpiece of his system—the telepathic. The "telepathic law," as he called it, is what held everything else together. It was the "gravity" of the psychical world, the binding idea that explained almost everything for Frederic Myers, from spirit communication and poetic or philosophical genius, to crisis apparitions and possession, to the efficacy of prayer, the communion of saints, and the ancient doctrine of the World-Soul, even the actions of a possible Divine Spirit.[119] This is all well known and often discussed in the literature on Myers and the S.P.R.

What is not so well known and, as far as I can tell, seldom discussed is Myers's own clearly stated conviction that the telepathic is related to the erotic, that telepathy is, if you will, ultimately an expression of love or, conversely, that "Love is a kind of exalted, but unspecialized telepathy" (HP 2:282). Some of this may have already been intuited in the curious linguistic fact that the British psychical research tradition emerged out of an earlier discourse on Mesmerism and animal magnetism located largely in France and the delightful coincidence that the French word for "magnet" is, quite literally, "lover" (*aimant*). To my knowledge, however, Myers never engages in such playful speculations.

We need no such speculations, however, in order to establish that the telepathic and the erotic are intimately linked phenomena for Frederic Myers, that, somehow, these two dimensions of the human condition are expressing the same deep metaphysical unity of things. Myers, after all, explicitly tells us exactly this in one of the most dramatic sections of *Human Personality*. In the third chapter on "Genius," we come across an extensive discussion of "the primary passion" (HP 1:111–16). Myers has just completed a long discussion of genius as subliminal uprush in philosophers, mathematical prodigies, poets (Wordsworth, Browning, and Shelley), and contemporary novelists (George Sand, Charles Dickens, and Robert Louis Stevenson), all of whom, he argues, were uniquely skilled at remaining open to subliminal suggestions of great scientific, literary, and philosophical worth. Stevenson, for example, dreamed of possessing a double personality (the Human as Two again). He wrote entire stories after what he called "the Little People" or "Brownies." These were his dream sprites who, with an eye to the bankbook, happily and dutifully appeared in his dreams in order to act out precise plots that he could later write down and sell (HP 1:91). Exactly like Freud, moreover, Myers saw a poet of Wordsworth's status as an "introspective psychologist," that is, as a genius who was accessing on an experiential level what the psychologists were mapping on an abstract theoretical level (HP 1:109). In our own contemporary terms, we might say that, for Myers, great writers are practical mystics.

After such literary studies, Myers suggests that, as far as such subliminal uprushes or impossible authorizations are intellectual, they also tend to be *telaesthetic*, that is, they bring "direct knowledge of facts of the universe outside the range of any specialized organ or of any planetary view" (HP 1:111). *Telaesthesia* was yet another Greek coinage of Myers. The term referred to the mind's ability to access information at a distance without any receiving or sending mind on the other end. He preferred it to the more common French term, clairvoyance, because the latter implies the organ of sight, and perceptions at a distance are by no means always visual. It is also important to note that, although telaesthesia is clearly related to telepathy, they are not the same thing. Telepathy requires another human being, whereas telaesthesia does not.[120] Unlike telaesthesia, moreover, telepathy implies, as its Greek root suggests, a powerful emotional connection. Tele*pathy* implies love, passion, pathos. For Myers, telepathy, precisely because of this strong emotional component, is higher than telaesthesia. In my own terms now, Myers's central category of telepathy is not simply about Consciousness. It is also about Energy.

The reader can almost feel this energy in the text. When Myers gets to the subject of eros, the voice and tone shift dramatically. We are no longer reading a scientific treatise or a piece of literary criticism. Myers becomes a poet again, and he is giving a speech now. But not just any speech. It is as if, with just a few months left to live, he decided to set aside all reservations and say what he *really* thought.

And so he imaginatively enters, he *becomes* one of his most beloved Greek classics, that most famous of all collections of speeches on eros and its sublimation into philosophical ideation, Plato's *Symposium* or "Drinking Party." Fred Myers enters the text, stands up in his turn, and begins:

> Telaesthesia is not the only spiritual law, nor are subliminal uprushes affairs of the intellect alone. Beyond and above man's innate power of world-wide perception, there exists also that universal link of spirit with spirit which in its minor earthly manifestations we call telepathy. Our submerged faculty—the subliminal uprushes of genius—can expand in that direction as well as in the direction of telaesthesia. The emotional content, indeed, of those uprushes is even profounder and more important than the intellectual;—in proportion as Love and Religion are profounder and more important than Science or Art. (HP 1:111)

And he goes on:

> That primary passion, I repeat, which binds life to life, which links us both to life near and visible and to life imagined but unseen;—*that* is no mere organic, no mere planetary impulse, but the inward aspect of the telepathic law. Love and religion are thus *continuous*;—they represent different phases of one all-pervading mutual gravitation of souls. The flesh does not conjoin, but dissever; although through its very severance it suggests a shadow of the union which it cannot bestow. We have to do here neither with a corporeal nor with a purely human emotion. Love is the energy of integration which makes a Cosmos of the Sum of Things. (HP 1:112)

Myers immediately explains that there is no "emotion subliminal" that ranges so widely and shows itself in so many guises as love.[121] Employing his spectrum method again, he explains that at one end of the scale, love is "as primitive as the need of nutrition," that is, it manifests as sex. At the other end, eros morphs into hermeneutics. Literally. Here is Myers: "at the other end it becomes, as Plato has it, the *hermeneueon kai diaporthmeuon*, 'the Interpreter and Mediator between God and Man'" (HP 1:112). We are back to the threshold and the art of interpretation across the gap of two states of consciousness or being.

Myers immediately glosses this rather mysterious line with another: "The controversy as to the planetary or cosmical scope of the passion of Love is in fact central to our whole subject" (HP 1:112). In other words, it all comes down to whether we understand the erotic as something simply sexual and biological, or as something also potentially mystical and hermeneutical, that is, as the "the Interpreter and Mediator between God and Man." It is worth repeating, in my own terms now: by his own stark confession late in life and in his own final statement, a metaphysical understanding of the erotic lay at the very heart and center of Myers's lifework. And by the erotic, I do mean the erotic. I mean *eros*.

So did Myers. The classicist invokes two iconic figures to represent the two poles of this perennial debate about the metaphysical status of "that primary passion": the famous French psychiatrist Pierre Janet, who is made to represent "the physiological or materialistic conception of the passion of love," and Plato himself, whose record of the prophetess Diotima's speech on eros in the *Symposium* Myers unequivocally describes as "unsurpassed among the utterances of antiquity" (HP 1:112, 113). Thus, whereas Janet's "planetary view" sees "sexual instinct as the nucleus of reality around which baseless fancies gather," the "Platonic view" regards such "earthly passion as the initiation and introduction into cosmic sanctity and joy" (HP 1:xxxi). Basically, what we have here is a very clear polarization of the erotic as the sexual and/or the mystical.

Although he plays at a certain balance between Janet and Plato, it is very clear where Myers himself stands on the debate. He stands with Plato and his conviction that it is eros that generates genital desire *and* the creative energies of philosophy, law, poetry, art, culture, and society itself. As if to drive this point home, Myers quotes directly from the *Symposium* for almost two full pages.

There is something about this section on Plato's *Symposium* in *Human Personality* that sets it apart, that *marks it* for me. It is my own intuitive sense, which I cannot prove or establish beyond a reasonable doubt, that it is here that Myers gives himself away; that it is here that we learn about what drove him to research, classify, and write for those two remarkable decades. It is not simply Myers's stated conviction that the primary passion of Love is central to his entire subject. It is not simply the textual fact that his quotes from the *Symposium* in this section are among the longest of the entire two volumes. It is the biographical facts that in the summer of 1873 Myers fell madly in love with his cousin's wife, Annie Hill Marshall, and—more importantly still—that it was her tragic death, on September 1, 1876, that helped catalyze and drive his own anxious questions about the postmortem survival of the human personality. Annie committed suicide, probably in despair over her mentally ill husband, by ineffectively cutting her throat with a pair of scissors and then walking into a cold lake. Myers was devastated.

But he never really let Annie go. As historians Alan Gauld and Deborah Blum have explained in some detail, Myers would love this ghost for the rest of his life. There were early alleged signals from Annie in Myers's extensive sittings with mediums, but it was not until 1899 that Myers received his first clear communication from his beloved, this time through a medium named Rosina Thompson. Myers was convinced now. As a sign of just how convinced, it is worth pointing out that he sat with Mrs. Thompson *150 times* between September of 1898 and December of 1900. And this, of course, was at the very same time he was completing *Human Personality* and, presumably, polishing those passages on Plato's *Symposium*. In any case, it was these late sittings with Rosina Thompson that Myers considered his very best evidence for the soul's survival of bodily death. Annie's continued existence was the final proof that he would soon publish for the world.

Until, of course, his wife found out. The best evidence and final proof was systematically suppressed by Myers's widow, Eveleen Myers, who actively censored her late husband's *Human Personality* by excising all the key passages about Annie Hill Marshall. Blum explains:

> What he could not have foreseen when he composed *Human Personality* was that the evidence that Myers considered strongest—the séances in which Annie Marshall appeared, his many sittings with Rosina Thompson—would not give support to his published argument. His wife had many pertinent records destroyed; more than that, she had refused to allow [Richard] Hodgson to mention them in his edited version of the book.[122]

And that was not all. "Evie Myers wanted every trace destroyed, every scrap of evidence, that her husband had been infatuated with a spirit," Blum explains. She particularly hated her husband's autobiography, "Fragments of Inner Life," in which he "had actually counted the days with and without his beloved Annie."

"I find," Myers writes in these same pages, "that love in its highest—in its most spiritual—form is a passion so grossly out of proportion to the dimensions of life that it can only be defined, as Plato says, as 'a desire for the eternal possession' of the beloved object."[123] He was almost certainly writing about Annie. He had hinted at the same in what I have called the "Platonic speech" of *Human Personality*: "And through the mouth of Diotima," he wrote there, "Plato insists that it is an unfailing sign of true love that its desires are *for ever*; nay, that love may be even defined as the desire of the *everlasting* possession of the good" (HP 1:113). Evie was not the everlasting possession whom Myers desired. And this, quite understandably, infuriated her.

Blum goes on to explain how Myers had given privately printed copies of "Fragments" to his closest colleagues in 1893. Evie demanded that they all turn their copies over to her. She even asked William James to oversee the censorship campaign. Sir Oliver Lodge, head of the physics department at the University of Birmingham, flatly refused, although he agreed not to publish the whole thing.[124] Evie would end up editing the final published version of "Fragments of Inner Life" in 1904. They were indeed now "Fragments" in more ways than one. In her preface, she makes no mention of Annie, only that she has collected other letters of her husband, and that "some day they may be possibly printed, but they are of too personal a nature for present publication."[125] That is all.

As both Blum and Gauld have stressed, then, on some deep level it was Myers's "primary passion" for Annie that provided the spiritual fuel for those two decades of incredible focus, dedication, travel, and writing. Recall that before the S.P.R. was even founded in 1882, Myers had participated in 367 séances. He would sit at many hundreds more, including those 150 times with Rosina Thompson as he approached and entered the writing of *Human Personality*. There are more than a few reasons to approach *Human Personality* as a kind of textualized séance, then. There are all those séances.

On a deeper level, however, we might also speculate that the ritual of the séance structured the text itself, that, through these pages at the end of his life, Frederic Myers was striving to establish contact with his departed beloved, Annie Hill Marshall, as he himself moved toward the threshold to meet her again. We might speculate, that is, that his philosophical quest was driven, exactly as in Diotima's speech, by the altered states of eros, by the love of a deceased Beloved and the forces unknown to science that he appears to have known in her presence, both while she was still living and after she had died. The "passion of love" was indeed "central to our whole subject," as he put it so well, so clearly, so honestly. It was in this way that the erotic subsumed the traumatic in Myers's *Human Personality*. This was how Love finally conquered Death.

Given all of this—some of it easily established, some of it admittedly speculative—I cannot help asking a final question. Was Frederic Myers's conversion to psychical research in the fall of 1873 really connected to shaking John King's hairy hand from the ceiling? Could it have rather been connected to Annie, with whom he had just fallen deeply in love that previous summer? I find it significant that Myers is forever relating his central concept of telepathy to eros, not to hairy hands. It must be admitted that this connection between the telepathic and the erotic is not immediately obvious, unless of course one has experienced exactly such a connection in one's own life. Then it is not only patently obvious; it is crucially important. This, I suspect, is what happened to Frederic Myers.

Recall here that our only source for what Myers describes as his "personal experience of forces unknown to science," which he tells us he will not tell us about, is the very text that his widow later censored and controlled, that is, his "Fragments of Inner Life." Obviously, when Frederic Myers refuses to tell us a secret in a text that was not made public until after his death and that we know his widow subsequently censored, we must be more than a little wary.

Alan Gauld makes a similar point, although he does not ask quite the same question about Myers's initial conversion experience to psychical research. He points out that Myers fell madly in love with Annie Marshall at the exact time he began investigating Spiritualism. He is also very clear that Annie became a veritable mystical presence for him. She was Beatrice to Myers's Dante. "She became at once a symbol and a manifestation of a hidden world of timeless realities, a world once apprehended by Plato, and now obscurely revealed by the strange phenomena of Spiritualism." This, Gauld speculates, is partly explained by the fact that Annie herself showed mediumistic talents and attended séances with Myers.

Certainly Myers was clear enough about his own "endless passion" and its relationship to his psychical researches:

> so soon as I began to have hope of a future life I began to conceive earth's culminant passion *sub specie aeternitatis* [under the perspective of eternity]. I felt that if anything still recognizable in me had preceded earth-life, it was this one profound affinity; if anything was destined to survive, it must be into the maintenance of this one affinity that my central effort must be thrown. . . . For me was there a sense that this was but the first moment of an endless passion.[126]

I am not sure what else needs to be said here, other than the textual fact that some of the most passionate and powerful passages in *Human Personality* have been erased. Many others, though, have survived. What we finally have left are thousands upon thousands of fragments, chains of memory and personality inscribed within twelve hundred pages of words and sentences. Happily, eerily, we can now reactivate and bring to life this human personality in our own intimate readings of what he wrote for us. Frederic Myers's book has become his own séance.

two

SCATTERING THE SEEDS OF A SUPER-STORY

Charles Fort and the Fantastic Narrative of Western Occulture

> If we could stop to sing, instead of everlastingly noting vol. this and p. that, we could have the material of sagas—of the bathers in the sun . . . and of the hermit who floats across the moon; of heroes and the hairy monsters of the sky.
>
> Char me the trunk of a redwood tree. Give me pages of white chalk cliffs to write upon. Magnify me thousands of times, and replace my trifling immodesties with a titanic megalomania—then might I write largely enough for our subjects.
>
> —CHARLES FORT, *New Lands*

Once upon a time, a man named Charles Fort (1874–1932) sat at a table in the New York Public Library or the British Museum in London, spending much of every working day for a quarter century reading the entire runs of every scientific journal and newspaper in English or French he could find. "A search for the unexplained," he explained, "became an obsession" (WT 918).[1] That is something of an understatement. Here is how he joked about a typical day at the office: "I was doing one of my relatively minor jobs, which was going through the London *Daily Mail*, for a period of about twenty-five years, when I came upon this" (LO 630). As he read from the present back into the past, he chose an arbitrary but admittedly even date of 1800 as the place to end his reading odyssey. He had to stop somewhere.

Besides, he reasoned, if the events that fascinated him so were not happening in the modern world, well then, they were of only historical interest and could not speak to his own present questions. The S.P.R., recall, had made the exact same decision before him. Even in the modern world, however, he was only marginally interested in those rare visions glimpsed in fleeting dreams or darkened séance rooms. Oh, he read and thought about such things, a great deal really, mostly through all the issues of the *Journal of the Society for Psychical Research* that he faithfully read in the library. By his own confession, he clearly accepted the reality of psychical phenomena. He affirmed the occult powers of the British superpsychic D. D. Home, and he often used the word "occult" to describe his own materials. But he was deeply suspicious of all talk of (or with) departed spirits, and he wanted no part of Spiritualism, which he associated with cranks and Fundamentalism.[2] In the end, his were mostly "sunlight mysteries" (WT 916), as he called them—strange things that come, usually unbidden, to ordinary people in ordinary circumstances in small towns and on city streets, and then show up in the papers, almost always in confused and baffled ways.

It is precisely this ordinariness that makes Fort's thought so extraordinary. As we shall see soon enough, Fort's radical monism expresses a world in which it is not so much that nothing is supernatural, but rather that *everything* is (LO 655). Fort, that is, locates the paranormal not simply in the rare experiences of a telepathic communication (although it appears here too) or in the invisible mathematical worlds of quantum physics (although he looked there as well, before anyone else, as far as I can tell). He finds it rather, in Colin Bennet's words now, in "the full light of noon on a thronged high street, from crowded rooms, from reports of ship's captains, baffled farmers, puzzled housewives, and scared families."[3] Or, as the poet-journalist Benjamin De Casseres described his friend's books: "There is something tremendously real, annoyingly solid about Fort. His is the first attempt in the history of human thought to bring mysticism and trans-material phenomena down to (or maybe lift it up to) something concrete."[4] Which is to say that Charles Fort discovers the paranormal in the normal.

Which is another way of saying that in Fort's materials and methods, the sacred was in transit again out of its earlier religious registers. The Fortean mysteries, after all, do not involve spiritual flights of ecstasy or unions with beloved deities, much less historically distant prophetic revelations or some singular and complete oriental enlightenment. Part of this is because his seemingly arbitrary 1800 rule effectively prevented him from privileging what had always been privileged, that is, the ancient world and the Bible. Fort would have none of that. What he would have are tablecloths and lace curtains bursting into flames around teenage boys and girls (mostly girls, it turns out), or, even better, rains of fish, periwinkles, frogs, crabs, or unidentified biological matter falling from the sky and piling up in the ditches for anyone to see. Or smell.

Fort, by the way, was not the first American writer to notice the fish. Earlier, Henry David Thoreau had wryly observed that "Some circumstantial evidence is very strong, as when you find a trout in the milk."[5] That is pure Charles Fort.

But how to explain the Transcendentalist trout? Technically speaking, Fort never explained anything. What he was best at was showing how previous religious and scientific methods fail to explain the world as it is. He was particularly hard on what he called the "evil of specialization." Fort felt that specialization prevents us from seeing the hidden connections between different domains of knowledge and data. "He knew," Damon Knight explains, "that we can only see what we are looking for, and he was tantalized by the feeling that there are unsuspected patterns all around us, which would be visible if we only knew where and how to look."[6] Within this kind of broad scanning, specialization is a kind of tunnel vision that effectively blinds people from seeing the hidden patterns of the Big Picture, which emerges only from perceiving the relations or meaningful coincidences between things and events (NL 446–47). Specialists see only what they are allowed to see, what their systems have deemed "real" and meaningful. "Ordinary theologians have overlooked crabs and periwinkles," he noted wryly (LO 548). But he would not. He was an intellectually promiscuous adventurer, a journalist of the metaphysical in search of what we might call, with only slight apologies to Freud, the parapsychology of everyday life.[7]

We could also say that Charles Fort was a *collector*, a collector of anomalies reported in his standard sources that were inevitably offered forced or bogus explanations by the official intellectuals of the time, or, more likely, simply ignored and passed over until the next day's distractions called "news." Though he had worked as a newspaper reporter and editor, he would not be so distracted. He would collect tens of thousands of notes on such anomalies. At one point in 1931, he mentions having written sixty thousand of them (LO 576). Earlier in life, he had organized these into hundreds of alphabetically arranged shoeboxes in his Bronx apartment. So he might write something like this: "March 11, 1924—see Charles Fort's *Notes*, Letter E, Box 27" (WT 977). We'll come back to Letter E in Box 27. And this collecting practice went considerably beyond words. On the walls of his Bronx apartment, he framed "specimens of giant spiders, butterflies, weird creatures adept at concealment . . . and—under glass—a specimen of some stuff that looks like dirty, shredded asbestos which had fallen from the sky in quantities covering several acres."[8]

There are at least two ways to describe such anomalies and Fort's eccentric desire to collect them in glass frames and shoeboxes (and where were all those shoes?): an excessive or impossible way, and a humble or respectable way. The excessive way is to suggest that Charles Fort was a collector of superpowers, which were humble enough sometimes (like the framed insect on his wall that looked exactly like a stick), but at other times they were *really* super. It is difficult to read much of Fort without being struck by his vocabulary of the super. The *normal* of Myers's *supernormal* has dropped away. Everything is potentially just *super* now. Fort thus writes of a super-bat, super-biology, super-cellular, super-chemistry, super-constructions, a super-dragon, a super-egotist, Super-embryology, the super-evangelical, super-evil, super-geography, super-Hibernia, a super-imagination, Super-Israelimus, super-magnets, the super-mercantile, a super-mind, Super-Niagaras, a super-ocean, super-personification, the super-piratic, super-ravages, super-religion, Super-Romanimus, the Super-Sargasso Sea, super-scientific attempts, super-sociology, super-sight, super-things, super-vehicles, super-vessels, super-voyagers, super-whiskeys (with ultra-bibles, no less), and super-wolves. Obviously, the concept of the super was a central one in the thought of Charles Fort. In most of these cases, the expression carries a distinct but expansive meaning, one somewhere between and beyond our own present concepts of the *paranormal* and the *extraterrestrial*. We'll get to that too.

The more humble or respectable way to describe both the events Fort collected and his desire to collect them is to say that Charles Fort was a collector of coincidences. These were coincidences, however, that he felt—he could not quite say why—signaled some larger, and perhaps literally cosmic, truth. He was on the intuitive trail of, well, *something*. Here is how he put the matter:

> Sometimes I am a collector of data, and only a collector, and am likely to be gross and miserly, piling up notes, pleased with merely numerically adding to my store. Other times I have joys, when unexpectedly coming upon an outrageous story that may not be altogether a lie, or upon a macabre little thing that may make some reviewer of my more or less good works mad. But always there is present a feeling of unexplained relations of events that I note; and it is this far-away, haunting, or often taunting, awareness, or suspicion, that keeps me piling on. (WT 861–62)

This is why, beginning in 1906, he began his famous reading practice in the New York Public Library. Charles generally spent his mornings working at home and his afternoons in the library. He and his wife, Anna, would then often go to the movies in the evenings. This was a nightly ritual that appeared to have only reinforced Charles's most basic conviction that "the imagined and the physical" were deeply intertwined, if not actually identical on some level: "According to some viewpoints," he wrote, "I might as well try to think of a villain, in a moving picture, suddenly jumping from the screen, and attacking people in the audience. I haven't tried that, yet" (WT 1010). Which implies, of course, that he had tried other things. Or that he might still try this one.

The couple lived in poverty for a good share of their life together (at one point Charles was hawking all their belongings and breaking up the chairs to heat the apartment) until a wealthy uncle of Charles, Frank A. Fort, died on May 28, 1916, and left his nephew an inheritance that allowed Charles and Anna to live in relative comfort and peace (then a wealthy aunt died, leaving a bit more). Happily, Charles's literary talents early on attracted the attention—stunned worship, really—of the novelist Theodore Dreiser, who once described Fort in a letter to the writer as "the most fascinating literary figure since Poe. You, who for all I know may be the progenitor of an entirely new world viewpoint."[9] Dreiser was not exaggerating. And Dreiser's fascination was echoed by other literary figures, including Booth Tarkington, who described Fort's pen as a "brush dipped in earthquake and eclipse," Buckminster Fuller, who wrote the introduction for Knight's biography, and numerous science-fiction writers, who borrowed generously from Fort's data for their own fictional purposes.[10] Indeed, in many cases, later science fiction reads like a series of imaginative riffs, with techno-realistic pictures now, on Charles Fort.

It was Dreiser who bought and printed some of Fort's early humorous short stories and, more importantly, acted as a literary agent of sorts for

Fort's first and most famous "nonfiction" book, *The Book of the Damned*. Of sorts. Dreiser basically threatened his own publisher: if he didn't publish Fort, he wouldn't publish Dreiser.

When he died at the age of fifty-seven on May 3, 1932, at 11:55 p.m., Charles Fort had published one novel, *The Outcast Manufacturers* (1909), and four really weird books: *The Book of the Damned* (1919), *New Lands* (1923), *Lo!* (1931), and *Wild Talents* (1932). Fort's note to Dreiser upon the appearance of the second and most famous book captures something of their relationship: "I send you this afternoon by express, *The Book of the Damned*. It is a religion. Our beer-man comes Tuesdays."[11] Advanced copies of the last book, on anomalous human beings, were delivered to Fort as he faded away on his deathbed. He was too weak to hold them, much less drink beer on Tuesday.

It is not, however, quite true to say that *The Book of the Damned* was Fort's first work of nonfiction. To begin with, in 1901 Fort had already completed a draft of a youthful autobiography entitled *Many Parts*, only a portion of which has survived. The title is from Shakespeare's famous lines in *As You Like It*: "All the world's a stage, and all the men and women merely players. They have their exits and their entrances, and one man in his time plays many parts."[12] As with Shakespeare's collapsing of the stage into life and life into the stage (or my earlier discussion of the personality as a persona, as a "mask"), Fort denied in principle any stable distinction between fiction and reality. He hated, for example, how books were divided up as "fiction" or "nonfiction" in the libraries (WT 863). "I cannot say that truth is stranger than fiction, because I have never had acquaintance with either." There is only "the hyphenated state of truth-fiction" (WT 864).

Nor, as we have already noted, did Fort believe in any stable distinction between the imagined and the physical (WT 1010). As with Myers's notion of the imaginal, the imagination, properly understood in its true scope, is nearly omnipotent in Fort's worldview. Indeed, it is so powerful (and potentially perverse) that Fort suggested in more than one context that we are all living in someone else's novel, which was not a particularly good one. "Some of us," he observed, "seem almost alive—like characters in something a novelist is writing" (BD 79). There thus can be no final conclusions or firm beliefs or even arguments "in the fiction that we're living," only what he calls "pseudo-conclusions" and "expressions" (WT 1009). The world, after all, may be imagined and written anew tomorrow in some other way, on some other page.

Fort was quite serious about the fictional nature of reality. Hence his two earlier book manuscripts, entitled *X* and *Y* (1915–16), about two complimentary metaphysical forces. As Jim Steinmeyer, his most recent biographer, explains, "the missing manuscript for *X* has always been the Holy Grail of readers of Charles Fort." It is not difficult to see why. In Steinmeyer's reconstruction of the lost manuscript, largely through Fort's correspondence with Dreiser in a three-page letter dated May 1, 1915, it appears that *X* was a more confessional crank version of the worldview that later would be more or less agnostically presented in *The Book of the Damned*. Dreiser was stunned by the thesis of *X*, which involved the idea that all of earthly biological and social reality is a kind of movie (we would now say "virtual world") projected from the rays of some unknown alien consciousness. Dreiser, who then had a dream that seemed to confirm the thesis, summed up Fort's X this way: "

> The whole thing may have been originated, somehow, somewhere else, worked out beforehand, as it were, in the brain of something or somebody and is now being orthogenetically or chemically directed from somewhere; being thrown on a screen, as it were, like a moving-picture, and we mere dot pictures, mere cell-built-up pictures, like the movies, only we are telegraphed or teleautographed from somewhere else.[13]

In short, the paranormal is writing, or projecting, us.

Dreiser's reference to orthogenesis is important, really important. Synthesizing Herbert Spencer's social Darwinism and Ernst Haeckel's monism (both of which the mystically inclined Dreiser loved), Fort moved beyond these systems to develop the idea, widely entertained at the time, that evolution is "orthogenetic," that is, predetermined toward some future goal or end. For Fort at least, the same evolutionary force could be active in one's personal life as well. Hence Fort would often write in his correspondence of the "strange orthogenetic gods" who he felt were guiding him, often in a confused and mixed up sort of way, to do this or that. This was playful, mythical language for sure, but it was also sincere, and it witnessed to a real conviction in a kind of occult spiritual evolution at work in the world.[14]

In *X*, however, Fort seems to have suggested that this controlling force is basically evil, and that, accordingly, we have little for which to hope. Our final goal is "the nothingness of a Nirvana-like state of mechanistic unconsciousness, in which there is neither happiness nor unhappiness." Fort would later back down from this absolute mechanism. He would also back down from his thesis that X was emanating from Mars, which, since Percival Lowell's *Mars and Its Canals* (1906), was commonly believed to be lined by canals and inhabited by intelligent beings. This, by the way, was by no means a new idea, and it was shared by many well-known and respected astronomers.[15] Astronomers aside, Steinmeyer notes that Fort's Martian hypothesis "sounds like science fiction." Indeed, it does.

But if the world is finally a Martian fiction for Fort, it is a fiction out of which we can, conceivably at least, awaken and "step off the page," much like his imagined moving-picture villain stepping out of the movie screen. Fort, it turns out, is not finally bound to a mechanistic Nirvana. Hence Fort's fascinating reference to *X* in a reply to the charge that his writings were inconsistent. "In 'X,'" he mused, "I have pointed out that, though there's nothing wrong with me personally, I am a delusion in super-imagination, and inconsistency must therefore be expected from me—but if I'm so rational as to be aware of my irrationality? Why, then, I have glimmers of the awakening and awareness of super-imagination."[16]

Such striking lines strongly suggest that the acts of collection, comparison, and systematization were not simple or banal activities for Charles Fort. They contained awesome power. They constituted a kind of an occult metapractice that could lead, at any moment, to just such a sudden awakening. Hence Fort's obscure claim that "systematization of pseudo-data is approximation to realness or final awakening" (BD 22). He, at least, collected, classified, and compared to wake up, to become more fully conscious of reality-as-fiction. He wanted out of this bad novel.

Final awakening aside for a moment, Fort was unhappy with both *X* and *Y* and destroyed them, or so it is believed, before he finally set out to write his most famous published work, *The Book of the Damned*. He had also burned twenty-five thousand of his notes earlier in the century.[17] Apparently, he liked to burn things he had written—before, he suggested, they burned him. Living in a cramped apartment in a tenement building stuffed with hundreds of shoe boxes filled with tens of thousands of flammable sheets of paper was not exactly the safest thing to do. But one suspects reasons other than those concerning rational safety codes. Charles Fort, after all, was playing with fire in other ways too, and he certainly did not feel himself unduly bound to the self-imposed limits of reason.

In any case, he was about to experience his own awakening beyond reason's bounds. Still obsessing at the end of the alphabet, he wrote Dreiser in 1918 as he researched and wrote his way to what would become *The Book of the Damned*:

> Dreiser!
> I have discovered Z!
> Fort![18]

The Parable of the Peaches: Fort's Mischievous Monistic Life

Charles Hoy Fort was born on August 6, 1874, in Albany, New York, to an upper-middle-class family. They were grocers of Old Dutch descent. His mother died shortly after his youngest brother, Clarence, was born, when Charles was just four. Their father, Charles Nelson Fort, quickly remarried. Charles and his two brothers, Raymond and Clarence, appear to have hated their father. The boys referred to him in the plural, as "They" or "Them." Charles Nelson Fort was a Victorian authoritarian figure who did things like beat his boys with a dog whip or smack them in the face when they could not pronounce King James English during their Bible lessons. One day, for example, little Charles kept referring to how Moses had "smut" the rock instead of having "smote" it. After adjusting his hat and necktie in the mirror, the father smote his child on the face to fix, once and for all, the boy's poor King James pronunciation.[19]

And this was just the beginning. When the boys got too big to smote, "They" would lock the two brothers "in a little, dark room, giving us bread and water, sentencing us to several days or several weeks of solitude." Already here, though, Fort's redeeming humor shines through. The boys would often sing to make the time go faster. "Then singing patriotic songs, half defiantly because of the noise we were making. About 'Let freedom ring.' Adding, 'Freedom don't ring here.' Hearing our new mother, under the air shaft, laugh at this. Then we, too, would laugh: for we could never be mean when others were not."[20] It is not difficult to see why Charles Fort grew up to question all authority. It is also not difficult to see why Steinmeyer suggests that X was not emanating from Mars but from Albany, New York, that is, from the memories of Fort's hated father and all those terrible, basically "evil," controlling punishments.[21] In this view at least, Fort's paranoid extraterrestrial fantasy finds its psychological origins in overwhelming childhood trauma.

Or was it the physical abuse and emotional trauma that opened him up to the extraterrestrial gnosis?

Interestingly, Fort's intellectual penchant for finding anomalies or contradictions in systems of thought began precisely as the modern study of religion began, that is, with an honest recognition of the contradictions in that same King James Bible—smote, smut, and all. "When a small boy," Fort explained, "we puzzled over inconsistencies in the Bible, and asked questions that could not be answered satisfactorily." He was also quickly growing tired of the dull round of his upper-middle-class life. "We should not have expressed the heresy," he writes in his typical understated humor, "but felt there was some kind of life higher than that of a dealer in groceries."[22] Between the Bible, the groceries, and the solitary confinement, he was also dreaming of becoming a naturalist, and he became fascinated with the problems and promises of classification as these were being practiced in natural history and the museums. Darwin again.

Not that he thought that things could ever be definitively classified into stable essences. Later in life, he would describe himself as a monist. He would think of the world as a vast Oneness where anything could become anything else, where things were not things at all but relations. Early in life, of course, he was not quite so abstract. But he found a way to express a similar intuition, this time in the terms of a prank involving the fruits, vegetables, and labels of Their grocery store. Enter the parable of the peaches. Fort himself tells the story in *Wild Talents* toward the very end of his life. It is repeated in most accounts of his life and work. In other words, it has become something of a legend. It goes like this.

"In days of yore," Fort explains (he wrote like that), he was "an especially bad young one." His punishment was to be sent to the grocery store on Saturdays, where he was forced to labor for his sins. This often involved the task of peeling off the labels from cans of fruits and vegetables of another dealer and pasting on his father's labels instead. In other words, it involved a commercial version of classification as deception. One day he found himself with pyramids of cans, but only peach labels left in his sticky armory. Here is what happened next:

> I pasted the peach labels on the peach cans, and then came to apricots. Well, aren't apricots peaches? I went on, mischievously, or scientifically, pasting the peach labels on cans of plums, cherries, string beans, and succotash. I can't quite define my motive, because to this day it has not been decided whether I am a humorist or a scientist. (WT 850)

The moral of the parable is two-edged and remarkably nuanced. On one level, it appears to suggest that our classification schemes are more or less useful, and more or less deceitful, and more or less profitable. But they certainly do not accurately reflect the true nature of things. We sell someone else's goods and pretend they are ours. On another level, the parable appears to suggest something a bit deeper, namely, that even the real nature of things does not reflect the real nature of things. What appears to be plums, or cherries, or succotash is really all peaches. The deceitful label is true. The fraud is fact. Everything *is* one thing.

I am reminded here of something once quipped about the bizarre facts of astrophysics and cosmic evolution: "Hydrogen is a light, odorless gas which, given enough time, changes into people."[23] Fort would have laughed at that one, and then added: "or peaches."

Fort would continue to live out such mixing and matchings, and eat them. Steinmeyer tells the delightful story of Thanksgiving dinner at the Forts in 1917: Charles served up a new preserve he called "Topeacho," a blend of tomatoes and peaches. He would also invent a dish called "To-pruno," this time with tomatoes and, yep, prunes.[24] Fort delights in such comedic transformations, which he also sees everywhere in the evolutionary process:

> I think that *Thou Shalt Not* was written on high, addressed to fishes. Whereupon a fish climbed a tree. Or that it is a law that hybrids shall be sterile—and that, not two, but three, animals went into a conspiracy, out of which came the okapi. There is a "law" of specialization. Evolutionists make much of it. Stores specialize, so that dealers in pants do not sell prunes. But then appear drugstores, which sell drugs, books, soups, and mouse traps. (WT 976)

We are back to the peach labels.

The peach labels, the tree-climbing fish, and the poor okapi are all in turn reminiscent of another famous Fortean anecdote, that of a board game he invented called "Super-checkers." This invention of Fort, which he apparently constructed some time in the late 1920s, involved the usual checkerboard design, except that Fort's board boasted 1,600 squares. "It was in a moment of creative frenzy," he wrote. "I took a fat lady's gingham apron, some yards of cardboard, and several pounds of carpet tacks, and solved all the problems in the world."[25] By "solving all the problems in the world," what Fort likely meant was that his Super-checkers game was like every other system human beings have invented: it was a *game*, with artificial rules that are more or less useful, but that can also always be bent or ignored and are in the end more or less arbitrary. The Fortean universe operates remarkably like this Super-checkers game. It is much too vast to keep track of, and if it appears to follow the rules we cast for it most of the time, it also "cheats" occasionally, particularly every time a frog or school of fish falls out the sky. Such a universe can hardly be trusted.

Looked at as a whole, what should we make of such a life, at once so ordinary and so extraordinary? And how exactly should we enter the utterly bizarre world of his books? Earlier, I referred to Fort as a journalist of the metaphysical. This is true enough, especially with reference to his early career as a journalist and later newspaper source-texts. But the label finally obscures as much as it reveals. When he has not been read as an inspired prophet, Fort has usually been read as a wit or entertainer, as a major inspiration of pulp fiction and sci-fi literature, or as a countercultural icon.[26] Such understandings all carry their own truths, but such reception histories also tend to obscure the fact that Fort was also a systematic thinker who practiced a very definite comparative method, developed a philosophy of history that was oddly, presciently postmodern, and operated out of a sophisticated dialectical metaphysics that provided all of this with a very distinct grounding or base. I want to treat this Fortean comparativism, postmodern philosophy of history, and dialectical metaphysics, each in turn, before I then approach his dark mythology, and, finally, his magical anthropology.

Recall that the literary theorist Tzvetan Todorov defines the fantastic as "a break in the acknowledged order, an irruption of the inadmissible within the changeless everyday legality."[27] This could just as easily describe a Fortean text. Recall also that Todorov defines the fantastic in terms of a certain irreducible indeterminacy, that is, in terms of the reader's hesitation and indecision about whether what is encountered in the text is illusory or real. "The fantastic," Todorov reminds us, "occupies the duration of this uncertainty."[28] Fort again saw the same irreducible indeterminacy in his subject matter. Hence his reflections on his own wavering opinions about what he calls "the very ordinary witchcraft" of telepathy: "When I incline to think that there is telepathy, the experiments are convincing that there is. When I think over the same experiments, and incline against them, they indicate that there isn't" (WT 962). This indeterminacy is not tangential to the subject. It is no fluke or anecdote. Like a quantum event that can be measured as a particle or a wave—and Fort knew all about this—this indeterminacy *is* the subject.

Todorov cites the Russian theologian and mystic Vladimir Solovyov in order to add an important tagline to his definition of the fantastic: "In the genuine fantastic," Solovyov suggested, "there is always the external and formal possibility of a simple explanation of phenomena, but at the same time this explanation is completely stripped of internal probability."[29] Fort again engages in precisely this rhetorical move: he will often cite scientific explanations for his anomalous events, but only to show how far they fall short, how silly they really are in the face of the offending data. Like a good fantastic writer, he will strip such naturalistic explanations of internal probability.

Like good fantastic literature yet again, Fort's texts fulfill another requirement of Todorov's genre, that is, they integrate the reader into the fantastic world that they are portraying. It is *the reader's hesitation* between a natural, reductive, or fictive reading and a supernatural, occult, or realist reading that constitutes the first and most important condition of the fantastic. Fort accomplishes this through the very nature of his sources, which, after all, are often newspapers with real place-names and real dates describing real events in the same world the reader inhabits. Fort thus brings the fantastic into the real world, or better, he shows that the real world is *already* fantastic, and always has been. By doing so, he dissolves the boundaries between the imaginary and the real and scatters endless seeds of metaphysical confusion.

In the end, however, it may be even more accurate to suggest that Charles Fort is finally a comedian of the fantastic, that it is his humor, above all else, that rhetorically creates the metaphysical hesitations and open-ended nature of his texts. Charles Fort is a very funny writer. As a few typical examples of Fort's delightful style, consider the following scenes. On March 12, 1890, residents of Ashland, Ohio, swore that a ghostly city had appeared over their little town. The pious read it as—what else?—an apparition of "The New Jerusalem." A physicist was a bit more reasonable. He interpreted it as a mirage of Sandusky, Ohio, which happens to be over sixty miles down the road from Ashland. Fort, in his usual style, lampooned both the faithful and the rational explanations. The apparition, Fort wrote, "may have been a revelation of heaven, and for all I know heaven may resemble Sandusky, and those of us who have no desire to go to Sandusky may ponder that point" (NL 459). In other places, he waxes eloquently on the dubious correspondence his dubious books tend to produce: "I have had an extensive, though one-sided, correspondence," he observes, "with people who may not be, about things that probably aren't" (LO 609). Here's another: "Now and then admirers of my good works write to me, and try to convert me into believing things that I say" (LO 641).

It is hard not to like this guy.

There are many things that could be said about the function and import of such textual moments: their rhetorical uses as a protective or qualifying strategy (things that are presented as funny can be true or false, or both at the same time); their entertainment value (it is easy to keep reading this man's big books for more Sanduskys or "things that probably aren't"); or, finally, their philosophical uses as a rhetorical form of transcendence (for to laugh at something is to step outside of it and no longer be bound by its rules). I will get to all of these dimensions of Fortean humor in due time, but for now it seems sufficient to suggest only that any essay or book about Charles Fort that is not funny is not sufficiently reflective of the man or his work. Which is all to say that if the reader does anything with my words below, I hope that he or she at least laughs. If not, this chapter will be about many things, even the fantastic narrative of Western occulture, but it will certainly not be about Charles Fort.

Collecting and Classifying the Data of the Damned: Fort's Comparative Method

Methodologically speaking, Fort was first and foremost a comparativist who understood perfectly well that knowledge arises from how one collects and classifies data. "By *explanation*," he pointed out succinctly, "I mean *organization*" (LO 551). But he also knew that the data themselves are never innocent, that much depends upon *which* data the comparativist selects from the weltering mass of stuff that is the world of information. Fort's most basic comparative principle worked from the conviction that one should privilege "the data of the damned," that is, all that stuff that had been rejected, facilely explained away, or literally demonized by the two most recent reigning orders of knowledge of Western culture, religion and science. Only then, he thought, can we begin to sketch the outlines of a bigger, more expansive and inclusive reality. Only then can we approximate a Truth we may never reach but that is nevertheless worth reaching for.

What this implied and required, of course, was that Fort's thought become inherently and structurally transgressive. If Truth lies outside every system, if every system is only an approximation or partial actualization of this Truth, then a better approach to the Truth can only be had by going outside the present system, that is, by transgressing the proper order of things. "I do not know how to find out anything new," he pointed out with faultless logic, "without being offensive" (LO 547). Still within this same offensive logic, Fort is deeply suspicious of any socially sanctioned truth, particularly any such truth that smells of piety or humility. "I am suspicious of all this wisdom," he writes, "because it makes for humility and contentment. These thoughts are community-thoughts, and tend to suppress the individual." Such "wisdom" or "humility" are nothing but more attempts to reduce the human being to a machine, to a cog in a social wheel. Such community-thoughts are thus seen as "corollaries of mechanistic philosophy, and I represent a revolt against mechanistic philosophy." It is not that he did not see the truth of mechanistic models. Quite the contrary, mechanistic philosophy applies "to a great deal." Fort's point was rather that it does not, and cannot, explain everything, that mechanism can never be "absolute" (WT 975).

Perhaps this rage against herd-thinking or machine-speak is also why the reader can occasionally detect something at once monstrous and beautiful in Fort's raging prose. "I suspect that it may be regrettable," he admitted, "but, though I am much of a builder, I can't be somewhat happy, as a writer, unless also I'm mauling something. Most likely this is the werewolf in my composition" (WT 905). Or, now perhaps hinting at the union of opposites that informed all of his thinking, "that there is nothing that is beautiful and white, aglow against tangle and dark, that is not symbolized by froth on a vampire's mouth" (WT 877).

One of the clearest and most dramatic expressions of this transgressive or offensive aspect of Fort's thought occurs in the very first lines of *The Book of the Damned*. These are worth quoting at length, as they introduce Fort's prophetic voice to the world and set down some of the basic terms of his own system. Here is how he begins in 1919, in what is essentially an oracular voice:

> A procession of the damned.
> By the damned, I mean the excluded.
> We shall have a procession of data that Science has excluded.
> Battalions of the accursed, captained by pallid data that I have exhumed, will march. You'll read them—or they'll march.

He then goes on to define what he means by "the damned" and comments on the radical relativism of human history, where worlds replace worlds that have replaced other worlds:

> So, by the damned, I mean the excluded.
> But by the excluded I mean that which will some day be the excluding.
> Or everything that is, won't be.
> And everything isn't, will be—
> But, of course, will be that which won't be—

He then becomes still more abstract as he introduces his dialectical monism through the classical philosophical terms of existence and being:

> It is our expression that the flux between that which isn't and that which won't be, or the state that is commonly and absurdly called "existence," is a rhythm

> of heavens and hells: that the damned won't stay damned; that salvation only precedes perdition. . . .
>
> It is our expression that nothing can attempt to be, except by attempting to exclude something else: that that which is commonly called "being" is a state that is wrought more or less definitely proportionately to the appearance of positive difference between that which is included and that which is excluded.

At this point, he sounds remarkably like Derrida on *différance*, or Foucault on the *episteme* as a temporary and relative order of knowledge and power. There are clear resonances here. But then one realizes that these resonances are essentially photographic negatives of one another, that Fort is more like the *opposite* of Derrida and Foucault, acknowledging both Difference and Sameness but finally privileging Sameness:

> But it is our expression that there are no positive differences: that all things are like a mouse and a bug in the heart of a cheese. Mouse and a bug: no two things could seem more unlike. They're there a week, or they stay there a month: both are then only transmutations of cheese. I think we're all bugs and mice, and are only different expressions of an all-inclusive cheese. (BD 3–4)

Fort will go on to define "existence" as a shifting, unstable intermediate zone between what he will later call the Negative Absolute and the Positive Absolute, but which he calls here, in a more mythical vein, "hell" and "heaven." "Being" is also defined as that ideal state that includes more and more and excludes less and less until one sees that one is like "a mouse and a bug in the heart of a cheese." Fort's humor is already an expression not of a cynical skepticism or a futile relativism, but of a mystical monism, and laughter unites everything.

Everything spins out of this irreverent monism. Every opinion, which is also every mistake, is a result of privileging some aspect of this Oneness over every other aspect. Error results when parts attempt to be wholes, when the bug imagines itself as fundamentally different from the mouse in the same orange cheese. "To have any opinion, one must overlook something" (LO 559). So too with every standard and opinion. They are all forms of orangeness on a spectrum of reds and yellows (BD 5).

What Fort is most interested in is how much of the world a system must exclude to form an opinion. He was deeply bothered by how easy it is to disregard or damn a datum. Early in his first book, he introduces a metaphor that will help him explain this strange feature of human beings. It will come to play a more and more central role in his other books. Enter, or swim in, the metaphor of the deep-sea fishes:

> I'd suggest, to start with, that we'd put ourselves in the place of deep-sea fishes:
> How would they account for the fall of animal-matter from above?
> They wouldn't try—
> Or it's easy enough to think of most of us as deep-sea fishes of a kind. (BD 26)

And what, he asks, would such a deep-sea fish learn if it bumped into a steel plate that had fallen from some wrecked ship above? Probably nothing at all. "Sometimes I'm a deep-sea fish with a sore nose" (BD 162). Fort calls the metaphysical ocean "above" us—whatever that means—the Super-Sargasso Sea. The Sargasso Sea, we might recall, was that legendary no-place in the Atlantic Ocean where mysterious crosscurrents were said to make whole ships disappear. Fort adds his "super" and makes of the Super-Sargasso Sea a kind of metaphorical space in which he will gather all of his damned data until the waters around the swimming reader are filled with floating and falling debris, "material for the deep-sea fishes to disregard" (BD 119).

It is not simply a matter of stuff randomly falling through the texts, however. Fort is not so simple or so naive. He has a specific means for locating the steel plates of the ship in the deep-sea waters of his data. He knows exactly what it feels like to bump his fishy nose up against something strange and steely. That feeling, that bump, is called a "coincidence." Here is a typical bump on the nose, this one involving the slow falling of stones from the sky or from a specific point in the ceiling of a house:

> Somebody in France, in the year 1842, told of slow-moving stones, and somebody in Sumatra, in the year 1903, told of slow-moving stones. It would be strange, if two liars should invent this circumstance—
> And that is where I get, when I reason. (LO 566)

It is easy to disregard one such report. Merely an "anecdote," as the scientists like to say in their pseudo-explanation. But two now? Then three? Then, with enough time in the library, three dozen from different parts of the world and in different decades? Just how long can we go on like this until we admit that this is real data, and that we haven't the slightest idea where to put it? How long until we see the ship's steel plate bumping up against our now sore noses?

This reasoned comparativism that worked through researched coincidences was very striking to Fort. His data, he felt, spoke far "too much of coincidences of coincidences" (BD 120; cf. BD 183). What, he finally realized, he was really interested in was not the events or the things themselves, which were meaningless in themselves, but *the relation of things* that appears within the comparative method. He knew that this relation was partly a function of his own interpretive inclinations, but he also suspected that it was really "out there," that it was not simply a subjective fantasy on his part. "I have spent much time thinking about the alleged pseudo-relations that are called coincidences," he concluded. "What if some of them should not be coincidences?" (WT 846). In the end, he concluded that at least some of these coincidences were an expression, like everything else, of "an underlying oneness" (WT 850). Coincidences, in other words, are grounded in a deeper Oneness of which they are distant echoes, reflections, or signs. Jung would come to the exact same conclusion later with his notion of synchronicity as an expression of the *unus mundus*, the World as One.

But the world is not all Sameness. There is also real Difference. Like all good comparativists, Fort works through both sameness and difference. His comparativism unites, and it separates, and by so doing it rearranges the world anew. The sameness side is carried by the connections of coincidence as these are glimpsed within the hard work of data collection and classification. The difference side is carried by the competing and contradictory claims of the cultural, religious, philosophical, and scientific systems vis-à-vis one another. Fort does not have to argue against this or that system. He is smarter than that. He simply allows them to be themselves, sets them on the same comparative table, and then watches them deconstruct each other: "We have only faith to guide us, say the theologians. Which faith?" (LO 712). It is really that devastatingly simple.

In the end, however, no Difference can survive the ultimate Sameness. The truth of things for Fort is that we exist in "an underlying nexus in which all things, in our existence are different manifestations" (NL 333). Fort meant this quite literally. Or quite imaginatively. Fort wonders what it all would look like if we hadn't been trained to see horses, houses, and trees. He concludes that to "super-sight" they would look like "local stresses merging indistinguishably into one another, in an all-inclusive nexus" (BD 192). Appearances, then, are just that: appearances. They are not the real. Security and certainty, moreover, are little more than species of a "bright and shining delusion," for "we are centers of tremors in a quaking black jelly" (NL 335).

But this quaking black jelly takes its own forms, becomes its own stories, and we can detect the outlines of these forms and the plots of these stories by carefully and bravely looking at the stuff that is normally disregarded. To interpret the world, then, for Fort is first to accept the data as real data, to not disregard that which has been damned by science or religion as "irrational" or "anecdotal" or "impossible," but to allow all the pieces and parts, and especially the anomalous ones, to fall into place through the bumps in the nexus called "coincidences" until a picture begins to emerge within the black jelly, until a Whole organically emerges from the parts.

The Three Eras or Dominants: Fort's Philosophy of History

In his *Politics of the Imagination*, Colin Bennett has recently read Fort through the prism of postmodern theory. The analogies between Fortean philosophy and contemporary postmodernism are indeed significant and extensive, if not actually astonishing. I have already hinted at them, and I will trace them in my own way shortly. But it also must be said immediately and up front that Fort is finally far too much for most postmodern writers. Whereas the latter almost always lack a metaphysical base, indeed consciously and vociferously eschew one as the Great Sin, Fort clearly possessed a developed and consistent monist metaphysics through which he read, and into which he subsumed, the "differences" and "gaps" of his anomalous material. Moreover, he fully acknowledged these metaphysical commitments. He sinned boldly.

He may, then, have agreed with, indeed presciently foresaw, the postmodern condition and its deconstructionist penchant for seeing reality as a language game in which every term or concept refers only to other terms and concepts within one huge self-referential web of local meaning. He may have also recognized that every such linguistic system of thought is without a final base or stable standard, that it is more or less arbitrary, that it must exclude or "damn" data to exist at all, but that the damned always return to haunt it and, finally, to collapse it. "All organizations of thought," he wrote, "must be baseless in themselves, and of course be not final, or they could not change, and must bear within themselves those elements that will, in time, destroy them" (NL 388). He may have also recognized, acutely, that every form of knowing is an "era knowing" bound to the concepts and assumptions of the culture and clime. "There is no intelligence except era-intelligence" (LO 428). Expressed within another metaphor, intellectual systems are little more than fashions: "I conceive of nothing, in religion, science, or philosophy, that is more than the proper thing to wear, for a while" (WT 993). "My own acceptance," he explained further, "is that ours is an organic existence, and that our thoughts are the phenomena of its eras, quite as its rocks and trees and forms of life are; and that I think as I think, mostly, though not absolutely, because of the era I am living in" (LO 604–5).

But it is precisely that "though not absolutely" that haunts us here. For Fort also suggested that all of these quasi systems with their quasi standards and false senses of completeness are struggling within a "oneness of allness" or "Continuity" (BD 239). There is thus—and he italicizes this—"*an underlying oneness in all confusions*" (LO 542). By means of the inclusion of ever greater swaths of data, human thought *is* developing for Fort, and this toward what he called "the gossip of angels," that "final utterance" that "would include all things." This final utterance, however, must paradoxically be "unutterable" in our "quasi-existence, where to think is to include but also to exclude, or be not final" (BD 249). Thus to think at all is "to localize" for Fort, to mistake the part for the Whole. But, like the self-described metaphysician that he was, he sought to think into infinity, to universalize, even if he knew he must eventually "pull back" in order "to make our own outline" by excluding and including (BD 178). He even hinted that this infinite Truth (which, yes, he capitalized) could be experienced—or, more accurately, *identified with*: "A seeker of Truth. He will never find it. But the dimmest of possibilities—he may himself become Truth" (BD 14).

Obviously, then, if Charles Fort practiced a kind of postmodernism, and I agree with Bennett that he did, it was a paranormal postmodernism akin to what David Ray Griffin has called a "constructive" or "revisionary postmodernism," which Griffin, much like Fort before him, links to both a naturalistic panentheism—that is, to a real metaphysics—and to the anomalous data or "white crows" of parapsychology.[30]

Here is how Charles Fort thought in threes.

Fort liked the number three, perhaps because it had "mystic significance" in earlier religious systems (NL 474), perhaps because Nikola Tesla, the American inventor and "mad scientist," believed that the vibrations he received from Martians on his wireless apparatus seemed to come in triplets (NL 494). Mystics and Martians aside, Fort certainly thought in threes. Indeed, his entire system works through the neat dialectical progression of three Dominants or Eras: (1) the Old Dominant of Religion, which he associates with the epistemology of *belief* and the professionalism of priests; (2) the present Dominant of materialistic Science, which he associates with the epistemology of *explanation* and the professionalism of scientists; and (3) the New Dominant of what he calls Intermediatism, which he associates with the epistemology of *expression* or *acceptance* and the professionalism of a new brand of individuating wizards and witches. Whereas the first two Dominants work from the systemic principle of Exclusionism, that is, they must exclude data to survive as stable systems, the New Dominant works from the systemic principle of Inclusionism, that is, it builds an open-ended system and preserves it through the confusing inclusion of data, theoretically *all* data, however bizarre and offending, toward some future awakening.

The gossip of angels.

Fort gives a date when the Old Dominant or former era finally gave way to the present one: "around 1860." This is when he noticed that the learned journals he was reading begin to lose their "glimmers of quasi-individuality," that is, this is when the data of the damned start to fade away before the higher organizations of aggressively and defensively intolerant scientific explanations (NL 239). This is also, of course, the precise period of Darwin's ascendance. *The Origin of Species* had just appeared the previous year, in 1859. We'll get to that.

Fort is brutal on both religion and science, although he makes, as we shall see, some crucial concessions to each that end up defining the dialectical contours of his own third system. Here are two typical passages on his two great enemies:

> Or my own acceptance that we do not really think at all; that we correlate around super-magnets that I call Dominants—a Spiritual Dominant in one age, and responsibly to it up spring monasteries, and the stake and the cross are its symbols; a Materialist Dominant, and up spring laboratories, and microscopes and telescopes and crucibles are its ikons—that we're nothing but iron filings relatively to a succession of magnets that displace preceding magnets. (BD 241)

Or with more bite now:

> It is my expression that the two outstanding blessings, benefits, or "gifts of God" to humanity, are Science and Religion. I deduce this—or that the annals of both are such trails of slaughter, deception, exploitation, and hypocrisy that they must be of enormous good to balance with their appalling evils. (LO 762)

As the latter passage makes clear, what the two Dominants of religion and science share is their Exclusionism, a basic intolerance that inevitably leads, particularly in the case of religion, to real-world violence. Obviously, Charles Fort was much more than a wit.

The Old Dominant of religion holds a special place in Fort's rhetoric. It is *the* model of intolerance, delusion, and Exclusionism. Deeply immersed in psychical research and its metaphors, Fort often preferred to see the power of religion as a psychological one akin to hypnosis (BD 12).[31] Religion, then, is a kind of consensual trance that settles over an entire civilization and era. Accordingly, one can no more argue with a true believer than one can "demonstrate to a hypnotic that a table is not a hippopotamus" (BD 17). Like the hippopotamus-table, religion is also a lie and a laugh:

> Suppose a church had ever been established upon foundations not composed of the stuff of lies and frauds and latent laughter. Let the churchman stand upon other than gibberish and mummery, and there'd be nothing by which to laugh away his despotisms. . . .
>
> Then we accept that the solemnest of our existence's phenomena are of a wobbling tissue—rocks of ages that are only hardened muds—or that a lie is the heart of everything sacred—

But a lie and a laugh *on the way to something else*:

> Because otherwise there could not be Growth, or Development, or Evolution. (LO 730)

"It is probable that all religions are founded upon ancient jokes and hoaxes," Fort adds a few pages down (LO 793). Then he dissolves the entire category of "religion" back into the human complex from which it arose so darkly, so violently:

> Just as much as it has been light, religion has been darkness. Today it is twilight. In the past it was mercy and charity and persecution and bloody, maniacal, sadistic hatred—hymns from chapels and screams from holy slaughterhouses—aspirations going up from this earth, with smoke from burning bodies. I can say that from religion we have never had opposition, because there never has been religion—that is that religion never has existed, as apart from all other virtues and vices and blessings and scourges—that, like all other alleged things, beings, or institutions, religion never has, in a final sense, had identity. (WT 999)

And we could go on, for a very long time, citing other similar passages. Perhaps we should. Then at least we could recognize the unrecognized "damned" fact that Charles Fort was as radical a theorist of religion as any. But we won't.

The present Dominant of science has taken over and copied the Old Dominant of religion. The priests have changed their vestments for lab coats and exchanged religious dogmas for scientific ones. Thus Fort can write of a "scientific priestcraft" who shout "Thou shalt not!" in their "frozen textbooks" (NL 315). The spirit and structure of their arguments retain the same, essentially religious dimension. As does everyone else's for that matter: "Every conversation is a conflict of missionaries," he writes, "each trying to convert the other, to assimilate, or to make the other similar to himself" (BD 171). But this does not mean that science has made no advances on religion. It most definitely has. Nor does it mean that we should stop proselytizing one another. How else could we make any progress? Thus after comparing a particular chemist to an imbecile, Fort has second thoughts: "I take some of that back: I accept that the approximation is higher" (BD 32). Well, that's a relief.

As his language of "old" and "new" Dominants makes crystal clear, the present Dominant of science is an unmistakable advance over the Old Dominant of religion for Fort. This hardly makes science omniscient or absolute, however. Where science errs for Fort is in its pride, in its arrogance, in its failure to recognize its own limitations. Its absolute materialism and mechanism are particularly odious as well: they are powerful half-truths that imagine themselves to be the whole Truth. Fort hears a storm approaching: "We are in a hole in time. Cavern of Conventional Science—walls that are dogmas, from which drips ancient wisdom in a patter of slimy opinions—but we have heard a storm of data outside" (NL 396). Such thunder outside signals for Fort the approach of a New Dominant, a new era, of which he is the prophet: "affairs upon this earth" are "fluttering upon the edge of a new era," he asserts, "and I give expression to coming thoughts of that era" (LO 712).

He does not imagine, of course, that his particular expressions of this new era are absolute, only that they include more and exclude less and so better approximate the Truth of things. This is why he also calls his New Dominant a species of Intermediatism. This is hardly a grand or arrogant term. It is a humble term. It implies, after all, its own demise. It is an open-ended system "intermediate," in between, on its way to the Truth. But it is *not* the Truth, and it too "must some day be displaced by a more advanced quasi-delusion." It is this sense of being intermediate, of thinking in between, that constitutes Fort's central insight. For him, at least, such a sense opens up to a potential gnosis or awakening in one of his most striking passages:

> our differences is in underlying Intermediatism, or consciousness that though we're more nearly real, we and our standards are only quasi—
>
> Or that all things—in our intermediate state—are phantoms in a supermind in a dreaming state—but striving to awaken to realness.
>
> Though in some respects our own Intermediatism is unsatisfactory, our underlying feeling is—
>
> That in a dreaming mind awakening is accelerated—if phantoms in that mind know that they're only phantoms in a dream. (BD 257–58)

Such an awakening is not restricted to some personal enlightenment or private illumination. Rather, it involves all of human intellectual activity: "In our acceptance, logic, science, art, religion are, in our 'existence,' premonitions of a coming awakening, like dawning awarenesses of surroundings in the mind of a dreamer" (BD 126). Evolution or Progression, in other words, is not restricted to the astrophysical or the biological dimensions. It involves all of human culture.

In order to hasten this eventual awakening, Fort shifts his epistemology within the New Dominant. Both *belief* and *explanation*, or faith and reason, are now replaced by a more humble *acceptance* and a more daring *expression*. The latter two ways of knowing are derived from a historical consciousness that recognizes how bound people's beliefs and explanations are to their time period and, as we say now, its social construction of reality. "All phenomena are 'explained' in the terms of the Dominant of their era," Fort points out in his own terms. "This is why we give up trying really to explain, and content ourselves with expressing" (NL 306). The epistemology of expression, in other words, is a self-conscious knowing that recognizes its own construction and its own relativity and so opens itself up to further evolution. Hence Fort's hostility to naive religious beliefs, which lock us into a previous era's revelations, which prevent us from progressing into the future: "That firmly to believe is to impede development. That only temporarily to accept is to facilitate" (BD 13).

Fort's philosophy of the three eras is important for my own thinking, as it helps clarify my two basic categories of the psychical and the paranormal. In the mirror of Charles Fort's thinking, I would now say this. In Frederic Myers, in what we might precisely now call *the psychical*, the sacred made its transit out of the religious register and into a scientific one. In Charles Fort, however, in what we might now precisely call *the paranormal*, the sacred leaves *both* the religious *and* the scientific registers and enters a still undefined, still irresolvable parascientific register. I have adopted a literary or hermeneutical name for this new indeterminate order of things—the fantastic, the impossible.

Fort, as we have noted, had a simpler name for it. He called it the New Dominant. At least three corollaries materialize out of Fort's New Dominant—what I would call, or better, what I would *express* as a New Science, a New Religion, and a New Self or Soul. In truth, however, what I am calling Fort's New Science and New Religion are really two sides of the same unnamed coin—a New Gnosis. Fort did not speak or write in such a way. But I do in order to rename that New Dominant of his, that new epistemology that draws deeply on both the data of faith and the methods of reason without being bound to either; that works, critically and reflexively, from the empirical data of firsthand psychological experience, however extraordinary or impossible.

There were three scientific traditions that Fort rather liked, with his usual jabs: evolutionary biology, quantum physics, and psychical research. We have already mentioned the evolutionary biology. In both physics and psychical research, Fort detected a breakdown of Exclusionism or a "merging away into metaphysics" (BD 249–50). Both, after all, called into serious question the ultimate separation of things. Both, that is, thought toward the Continuity of Inclusionism. Both also rehabilitated the ancient notion of magic. Fort was especially struck by the magical implications of quantum physics. He was reading authors like Einstein and Heisenberg as they published their theories and experiments in the learned journals of the time. He saw immediately what it would take the broader culture another forty years to realize, namely, that the line between quantum physics and mysticism is a very thin one.

Fort was worried about this in his usual humorous fashion. Alas, he could hardly find a physicist to argue with any longer, so close were their ideas now to his own pet theories, that is, to "an attempted systematization of the principles of magic" (WT 905). Why, this stuff could "make reasonable almost any miracle," he concluded, like "entering a closed room without penetrating a wall, or jumping from one place to another without traversing the space between" (WT 905). Isn't that exactly what electrons do in the new science? He also recognized that these quantum effects could not be restricted to the atomic level. He had, after all, read his Einstein, Tolmon, and Podolsky in the 1931 issues of *Physical Review*, and he knew that they were arguing the same. "The science of physics," Fort concluded, "is occultism" (WT 974). Or again, the "quantum theory is a doctrine of magic" with all those electrons "playing leapfrog, without having to leap over the other frog" (WT 1003). Fort's final conclusion follows logically: it is no longer possible to be a materialist. He thus makes fun of those who think of electrons according to the latest quantum magic, but then refuse to extend this type of quantum magic to things like people, despite the fact that people are made of the very same electrons. Such out-of-date dogmatists remain superstitious materialists, despite the embarrassing fact that matter as such has quite literally disappeared in the very best of their own science (WT 1004).

Just as Fort offers the outlines of a New Science based on quantum physics and psychical research (and, as we shall see, evolutionary biology), he also offers the outlines of a New Religion through the same disciplines. Fort's New Religion was, of course, really a New Heresy: "In my own still hereticalness—and by heresy, or progress, I mean, very largely, a return, though with many modifications, to the superstitions of the past" (BD 38). Heresy progresses by returning to the religious past, not to faithfully repeat or piously mimic it, much less to believe it, but to recover and reinterpret it. "To me," Fort observes in this recovering spirit, "the Bible is folklore, and therefore is not pure fantasy, but comprises much that will be rehabilitated." In any case, he won't write about the Bible. It was written, after all, before 1800 (WT 965).

Much better, because much more recent, are the data of spiritualism and psychical research. Again, much like Myers before him, Fort charts a gnostic path between and beyond science and religion here. He calls the spiritualists and the scientists the "two tyrannies" that bully the data. "On one side, the spiritualists have arbitrarily taken over strange occurrences, as manifestations of 'the departed.' On the other side, conventional science has pronounced against everything that does not harmonize with its systematizations. . . . One is too dainty, and the other is gross" (LO 576).

The data in actual fact are as diverse as they are difficult. He wants to damn stone-throwing poltergeists, for example, until he finds numerous other cases of slow-falling stones in his newspaper and journal researches from all around the world. That gets him thinking. He also is suspicious of prenatal markings or maternal impressions on the developing fetus until he realizes that these are in perfect continuity with all sorts of other phenomena he has read about, like the kitten born with "1921" perfectly imprinted on its white belly (WT 963–64). He begins to suspect that the mind is more powerful than it thinks.

Then there is prayer. This too he ends up rehabilitating. Sort of. Fort certainly does not believe in any personal God. But he recognizes how psychically useful such a God is. What is crucial, he concludes, is not the existence of God, but the *focus* such a belief provides: "The function of God is the focus. An intense mental state is impossible, unless there be something, or the illusion of something, to center upon. . . . I conceive of the magic of prayers." Not that piety is necessary here. Only focus. "I conceive of the magic of blasphemies. There is witchcraft in religion: there may be witchcraft in atheism." So great was the devotion of the faithful that the blood of St. Januarius boiled in its phial in Naples, Italy, reported the *New York Evening World* on September 19, 1930. If the desire would have been stronger to frustrate such a miracle, Fort mischievously suggests, the blood of St. Jaunuarius may well have frozen (WT 1001). Again, the content of the belief matters not. Not a whit. Only the intensity of the mental focus. It's all about consciousness, not custom.

Finally, before we leave the New Dominant, there is what we might call the Fortean Self or Soul, which will become the individuating witch or wizard in his last two books. This is where it gets really interesting, for Fort appears to suggest that the self or soul is not given, but consciously and intentionally created, that we somehow have the power to make ourselves, to bring ourselves into fuller and fuller being out of our quasi existence. The soul or self, in other words, is the result of *practice*. Fort turns to the historical data of witchcraft trials in order to suggest how such a practice may result in the attainment of a subtle body: "it is my expression that out of his illusion that he has a self, he may develop one." After all, in the records of witchcraft trials, we often find "the statement that the accused person was seen, at the time of doings, in a partly visible, or semi-substantial state" (WT 995). Myers's phantasmogenetic center lit up by the presence of a traveling clairvoyant again.

Much of this soul-making, it turns out, has to do with the refusal to surrender to the social surround. Fortean individualism is extraordinary to the extreme. To quasi exist is to aggregate "around a nucleus, or dominant, systematized members of a religion, a science, a society." But true individuals "who do not surrender and submerge may of themselves highly approximate to positiveness—the fixed, the real, the absolute" (BD 232). Quite simply put, the goal of evolution is the soul-actualizing individual, the self who does not submit to the community or consensual trance of society, who wakes up and so ceases to be a phantom in someone else's dream, or, worse, in everyone's dream.

But there is another side to Fort's psychology that is radically reductive, that dissolves the self into an apparent materialism or mechanism. He can be quite funny about this, particularly when he is pillaging Descartes' famous "I think, therefore I am." Here is Fort's version: "I do not think. I have never had a thought. Therefore something or another" (WT 941). Such humor hides a quite sophisticated notion of mental processes. We do not think. We are thought. Fort can write long passages on this that could come straight out of a contemporary textbook on neuroscience (or a Buddhist meditation manual, or a book by Myers on personality as a "chain of memory"):

> I do not think, but thoughts occur in what is said to be "my" mind—though, instead of being "in" it, they are it—just as inhabitants do not occur in a city, but are the city. There is a governing tendency among these thoughts, just as there is among people in any community. . . . So far as goes any awareness of "mine," "I" have no soul, no self, no entity, though at times of something like harmonization of "my" elements, "I" approximate to a state of unified being. . . . There is no I that is other than a very imperfectly co-ordinated aggregation of experience-states, sometimes ferociously antagonizing one another, but most maintaining a kind of civilization. (WT 941–42)

But then he backs up and pulls away from such an absolute reductionism. Fort was no materialist, although his thought possessed profound materialist dimensions. He was, in his own words, a materialist-immaterialist. "We'd be materialists were it not quite as rational to express the material in terms of the immaterial as to express the immaterial in terms of the material. Oneness of all allness in quasi-ness" (BD 265). This was no simple abstract game for Fort. He recognized that modern science could only maintain its strict materialism by disregarding psychical phenomena. Once it recognizes the psychical, it would immediately become "no more legitimate to explain the immaterial in terms of the material than to explain the material in terms of the immaterial." Why? Because the material and the immaterial appear together within every psychical act, "merging, for instance, in a thought that is continuous with a physical action" (BD 53).

In the end, though, this individuality is always unstable in Fort's texts. There is a One and a Many, but the Many appears in the One, not the other way around. "No statement that I shall make, as a monist, will be set aside by my pluralism," he writes. "There is a Oneness that both submerges and individualizes" (LO 552). Hence any identity can only come to be by "drawing a line about itself," that is, by excluding everything else that there is. Such an act appears to be finally futile for Fort, "just as would one who draws a circle in the sea" (BD 6–7).

The only thing, Fort points out with faultless reasoning, "that would not merge away into something else would be that besides which there is nothing else," that is, the Truth or the Universal (BD 9). The individual, then, for Fort is finally not a subject, but a "sub-subject," that is, a form of consciousness within an Ultimate Subject: "Of course we do not draw a positive line between the objective and the subjective—or that all phenomena called things or persons are subjective within one all-inclusive nexus, and that thoughts within those that are commonly called 'persons' are sub-subjective" (BD 51).

The Philosophy of the Hyphen: Fort's Dialectical Monism

Fort's paradoxical notion of the self as at once material-immaterial, as a sub-subject or a wavy circle drawn in the sea of the Universal Subject, is an expression of his wider "philosophy of the hypen," or what we have already encountered as his Intermediatism. This Intermediatism is in turn grounded in a deeper monism, but a monism striving to express itself within a real, if somewhat tenuous, plurality:

> Our general expression has two aspects:
>
> Conventional monism, or that all "things" that seem to have identity of their own are only islands that are projections from something underlying, and have no real outlines of their own.
>
> But that all "things," though only projections, are projections that are striving to break away from the underlying that denies them identity of their own. (BD 6)

This two-tiered system can also be expressed in the terms of a pure relationality in which there are no stable or independent things, but only relations. Fort's local urban environment is called on to express this notion. He compares our existence to the Brooklyn Bridge upon which bugs are seeking some final base or foundation. They never find one, for, alas, even the girders, which they presume to be foundational, are in turn built upon other deeper structures. And so on. In truth, "nothing final can be found in all the bridge, because the bridge itself is not a final thing in itself, but is a relationship between Manhattan and Brooklyn." Having recognized, like a puzzled quantum physicist, that the further one goes down into reality the more and more particles one finds and the less and less stable "stuff" there appears to be, Fort then zooms out and draws his conclusion: "If our 'existence' is a relationship between the Positive Absolute and the Negative Absolute, the quest for finality in it is hopeless: Everything in it must be relative, if the 'whole' is not a whole, but is, itself, a relation" (BD 101–2).

This fundamental relationality of our quasi existence produces a Fortean logic that we might accurately describe as paradoxical and that he consciously and fully recognized as such (BD 190). For the intermediatist, Fort explained, there is one answer to all questions, one solution to all problems: "Sometimes and sometimes not," or "Yes and no." For "everything that is, also isn't" (BD 281). Yes, things seek individuality, but they also depend deeply on other individuals to exist at all. They thus are, and they are not. Or more poetically put, in one of those memorable one-liners: "All things cut an umbilical cord only to clutch a breast" (BD 78).

Galactic Colonialism: Fort's Science Mysticism and Dark Mythology

Almost none of this, it must be said, is what made Fort so beloved among his later metaphysical, countercultural, and occult readers. Again, Fort has not generally been read as a systematic thinker, much less as a paranormal postmodern, which is precisely how I have read him above. He has been read rather, in Damon Knight's popular expression, as a "prophet of the unexplained."

It is often asserted, no doubt to protect Fort from the implications of his own impossible ideas, that he did not finally claim to explain the unexplained, that he did not *really* believe this stuff. Technically, this is true, as we have seen with his constant qualifications, his distancing humor, and his explicit rejection of the entire epistemology of belief. But it is also true that there is a consistent narrative or Super-Story woven into the heart of his four books, a story without which these texts would have little power over their astonished readers.

And this is where things cease to be abstract and philosophical and become eerie and numinous. This is the same fantastic narrative that would later take on visionary, even physical, forms within the UFO phenomenon, a stranger story still that Fort saw in almost every detail over thirty years before it finally appeared on the public stage in the late 1940s. Prophet indeed. What we have here, in the end, then, is much more than a philosophy. It is the beginnings of a new living mythology, a Super-Story, to employ my own Fortean expression.

I have already described Fort's mythology as a species of the fantastic. It can also be thought of as a type of science fiction. But if this is science fiction, it is of a very special kind. After all, although Fort is clearly engaging in a genre of storytelling that looks a great deal like earlier and later science fiction, he is in fact not presenting his writing as entirely fictitious.

Fort recognized, and reveled in, his own radicalism here. Any author, he noted, "may theorize upon other worlds" as long as "his notions be presented undisguisedly as fiction" or, at the very least, as hypothetical. As long as an author follows such a safe lead, he noted quite correctly, "he'll stir up no prude rages" (BD 80).

But Fort was interested in doing precisely this, that is, in stirring up the rationalist and religious prudes. He was also clearly convinced of the general outlines of his own fantastic tale. He had multiple letters published in newspapers like the *New York Times* and the British *T.P.'s Weekly*. They suggested, more or less exactly like his four books, that the earth was being visited by ships from outer space.[32] This did not sound like a man who did not believe his own words, even though he claimed exactly this unbelief in his own texts.

Having said that, it is also true that he works hard to occupy a twilight zone between the imaginary and the real, which means that he must always keep one of those proverbial feet on this side of everyday reality. Hence when he notes the report of a certain Captain Oliver, who "had found, upon the beach of Suarro Island, the carcass of a two-headed monster," he quickly comments: "That is just a little too interesting" (LO 620). Similarly, when "upon good newspaper authority," a dog appears in a story to say "Good morning!" only to disappear "in a think, greenish vapor," Fort draws the line. Even that is impossible for him (WT 862).

Fort, then, is not presenting his data as obvious fiction. But neither is he presenting it as established fact. His unique genres lie somewhere in between fact and fiction. As both real-unreal, a kind of "non-fictional fiction" as he once put it, his Super-Story is yet another expression of his philosophy of the hyphen.[33] It is a unique genre of modern metaphysical literature for which we really do not have a word yet, but for which I would like to propose one now: *science mysticism*.[34]

As I am using the expression, science mysticism is roughly as scientific as science fiction, and just about as disreputable. Appearances aside, neither genre is doing science. Both genres, however, draw heavily on scientific ideas and metaphors in order to construct their fantastic narratives and magical ideas. What sets apart a work of science mysticism like Fort's *Wild Talents* (1932) or Fritjof Capra's *The Tao of Physics* (1975), then, is that such texts claim significantly more purchase on reality than *either* science fiction *or* professional science does. They accomplish this, moreover, through a creative fusion of traditional mystical and modern scientific languages. To hone our terms yet further, we might adopt Fort's own spectral language and say that, while neither science mysticism nor science fiction obtains a complete existence, science mysticism is real-unreal whereas science fiction is unreal-real. But the two genres are clearly dependent on one another and merge in the middle.

What I am suggesting is that Charles Fort took a still nascent science-fiction trajectory and fused it with his own data of the damned in order to create a new genre of writing that I am calling science mysticism. This was science fiction come alive. This was fantasy as fact, or at least quasi fact. Dreiser picked up on something similar when he became enthralled with Fort's *X* and *Y* and described his correspondent in a letter as "out-Verning Verne."[35] This was indeed Jules Verne, and much more.

But there was a crucial third element in the mix that I have not yet mentioned: Western colonialism—"colonial" understood here in both its passive American sense (America as a British colony or, in Fort's title phrase, "New Lands") and in its active European sense (Europe, and especially England, as global colonizer). The base story of much science fiction—that of the alien invasion—was first imagined, it turns out, as a critical response to British colonialism, and by a British writer no less. Enter H. G. Wells's *War of the Worlds* (1898), one of the most important and influential sci-fi texts of all time.

According to the literary critic Brian Stableford, the novel had its creative origins in Wells's private reflections on Western colonialism and in his study of Darwinian biology. Wells had studied biology with T. H. Huxley, the famous bulldog of Charles Darwin whom we met in our previous chapter. Such a training would have likely given Wells the idea of alternate species and alternate evolutionary pathways on other planets. But it was European colonialism that affected him most directly. Indeed, his most famous story came to him when he was walking with his brother and discussing the fate of the Tasmanians, who had recently been decimated by the British colonialists, whose technology far surpassed that of the defenseless islanders. Wells proposed to his brother a scenario in which the tables were turned and the British colonizers became the colonized.

And so Wells's colonizers became Martians, who arrive in southern England, treating the locals as mere bugs to sweep aside, or squash. The result was as electrifying as it was terrifying. As Stableford points out, this story of an alien invasion, of an imperialistic force far superior to anything any human civilization has ever known, "became one of the central myths of twentieth-century Anglo-American science fiction."[36] It would also become, as we shall see in our next two chapters, the central myth of the UFO phenomenon and, as I will explore in my next book, one of the staples of the American superhero comic.

Charles Fort played a central, indeed maybe *the* central role in the creation of this developing Super-Story.[37] Indeed, as is often quipped, if the history of Western philosophy is a series of footnotes to Plato, the history of the paranormal in the twentieth century is a series of footnotes to Charles Fort. Here is how he announced the dark mythology of his Super-Story in *The Book of the Damned*:

> I begin to suspect something else.
>
> A whopper is coming. . . .
>
> The notion that other worlds are attempting to communicate with this world is widespread: my own notion is that it is not attempt at all—that it was achievement centuries ago. (BD 124)

If, then, we are like deep-sea fishes bumping our noses up against things we do not, and probably cannot, understand, Fort suggests now that we are also watched, even manipulated, by "super-constructions" passing above us in the atmosphere, in a kind of psychical space or spatial dimension he likes to call the Super-Sargasso Sea. These super-constructions come in all sorts of shapes and sizes: "one of them about the size of Brooklyn, I should say, offhand. And one or more of them wheel-shaped things a goodly number of square miles in area" (BD 136). Another, according to the report, is "cigar-shaped, with wings, and a canopy on top" (NL 470). And the alleged pilots are as numerous and varied as the shapes and sizes of their spacecraft. They cannot all be trusted: "I think of as many different kinds of visitors to this earth as there are visitors to New York, to a jail, to a church—some persons go to church to pick pockets, for instance" (BD 259).

Later generations would, of course, dub these aerial ships "UFOs." But Fort saw all of this in the teens and twenties of the last century, down to the disc-shaped details and the "falling leaf" motion of their descent (more on this in our next chapter), which he describes, true to his Super-Sargasso Sea, as "falling like a plate through water" (NL 498, 401). He thus studied and wrote about the great airship wave of 1897, when these super-constructions were clearly seen floating over Kansas City, Chicago, Omaha, and Denton (NL 468–47). He also wrote about another passing over El Paso, Texas (NL 487). Not that they were restricted to the U.S. Fort writes about "ships from other worlds that have been seen by millions of the inhabitants of this earth, exploring, night after night, in the sky of France, England, New England, and Canada" (NL 315). His data reached into India as well, mostly through the English newspapers and the British journals.

Fort reads all of this through his historical three-stage model. The data of theology (the First Dominant), he explains, was misinterpreted by the believing theologians, and then later by the scientifically inclined students of psychical research (the Second Dominant). What the theologians, demonologists, and psychical researchers were really studying without realizing it were "beings and objects that visited this earth, not from a spiritual existence, but from outer space" (NL 419–20). Hence, for example, the commonly noted sulphurous smell of meteorites. Fort's Third Dominant, an alien hermeneutic if you will, thus comes with a very heavy existential price, if not an actual moral panic announced with bombs: "Our data are glimpses of an epoch that is approaching with far-away explosions. It is vibrating on its edges with the tread of distant space-armies" (NL 389).

These visitors may intend communication with us through our garbled religious traditions and our confused psychical experiences, both of which we have too easily trusted, but they may well intend something more sinister. In one his most haunting phrases, Fort will admit that, "I think that we're fished for" (BD 264). He doesn't mean this literally, of course, although there are a few cases in his data that look a great deal like people being "hooked" by some unknown force and carried, literally, off the ground.

Such damned scenes aside, the truth is that Fort remains unclear or undecided about almost all of the specifics of his alien hermeneutic, although the general storyline remains quite consistent. Fort, for example, goes back and forth about whether the spaceships are of a material, a spiritual, or some other subtle or "highly attenuated" matter (NL 420). In places, he appears to imagine these ships in quite physical and literal terms. In other places, he suggests that they appear as psychical phenomena, "that some kinds of beings from outer space can adapt to our conditions, which may be like the bottom of a sea, and have been seen, but have been supposed to be psychic phenomena" (NL 507). Or, in another expression still, that "things coming to this earth would be like things rising to an attenuated medium—and exploding—sometimes incandescently" (BD 282). In such passages, Fort appears to be suggesting that different worlds, many different worlds, exist in a sort of parallel fashion. There are "vast, amorphous aerial regions, to which such definite words as 'worlds' and 'planets' seem inapplicable" (BD 136).

Numerous occult and Theosophical authors before him and many science fiction and New Age writers after him invoked the scientific language of "dimensions" to explain what Fort was expressing here. But Fort expressly rejected such language, mostly because he did not understand it and thought it to be an intellectual cop-out: "Oh, yes, I have heard of 'the fourth dimension,' but I am going to do myself some credit by not lugging in that particular way of showing that I don't know what I'm writing about" (NL 567). In other places, he lugs it in anyway, inevitably as a fourth or even fifth psychical dimension (NL 461).

The metaphors also shift dramatically when it comes to the nature of the upper world from which such super-constructions emerge, as if they were floating in our sky. Most basically, these metaphors shift back and forth between images of *water* and images of *land*. The Super-Sargasso Sea image, for example, pounds its waves throughout *The Book of the Damned*. But *New Lands*, Fort's second book, opens with a very different and in some way opposite metaphor, that of "lands in the sky." The opening lines of this second book echo those of the first:

> Lands in the sky—
> That they are nearby—
> That they do not move.
> I take for a principle that all being is the infinitely serial, and that whatever has been will, with differences of particulars, be again—
> The last quarter of the fifteenth century—land to the west!
> This first quarter of the twentieth century—we shall have revelations.
> There will be data. There will be many. (NL 313)

As these opening lines make clear, this new image of land is in fact connected to the earlier image of water through a specific colonial narrative. By "New Lands," Fort is invoking the European experience of "discovering" the new land of America across the waters of the Atlantic Ocean. Much like Myers, he is employing the European discovery of America, which was always there, of course, as a symbol for the acceptance and exploration of all that is occult and unknown to us now, which has always been there, of course.

America, then, is the New Land par excellence, the Land of the Occult that we would do well not to deny simply because we have not dedicated sufficient resources to its discovery and exploration. We have not even admitted its existence yet. "I am simply pointing out," Fort explained in an especially funny passage,

> everybody's inability seriously to spend time upon something, which, according to his preconceptions, is nonsense. Scientists, in matter of our data, have been like somebody in Europe, before the year 1492, hearing stories of lands to the west,

> going out on the ocean for an hour or so, in a row-boat, and then saying, whether exactly in these words, or not: "Oh, hell! There ain't no America." (LO 625)

But there is such an America. And we are called not only to admit this Secret America, but to explore it and expand into it. Interestingly, here the colonized begins to become the colonizer. Fort goes back and forth on this. In places, we are clearly the colonized, hence he compares our sighting of super-constructions in the sky to "savages upon an island-beach" gazing out at three ships in the bay on October 12, 1492 (NL 471). In other places, it appears that Fort has taken this basic Wellsian narrative of the colonizer colonized, accepted its basic claim, and then reversed it. Yes, in truth, we are the colonized, and always have been. But if we can only take seriously the data of our long colonization now, we can cease to be so and can become our own explorers. We can cease being written by the paranormal and become our own authors of the paranormal. We can cease to live in someone else's novel and write our own. We can *expand.*

And we must, whether we will or no. Fort suggests that this is somehow inevitable, that we are born explorers and must have somewhere to go. "The young man is no longer urged, or is no longer much inclined, to go westward. He will, or must, go somewhere. If directions alone no longer invite him, he may hear invitation in dimensions" (NL 313). Fort suggests this expansion is necessary to prevent an "explosion," that we need, as it were, "San Salvadors of the Sky" or "a Plymouth Rock of reversed significance, coasts of sky-continents" (NL 314). He can be quite lyrical about this need to expand, this human drive to explore and colonize, first the planet, then the farthest reaches of inner and outer space: "Stay and let salvation damn you—or straddle an auroral beam and paddle from Rigel to Betelgeuse" (NL 314).

Not that he claims to have gotten very far. He is all too aware of how the adventure has only just begun. Our cognitive maps, including Fort's own, are clearly filled with silly and gross errors: "My own notion is that this whole book is very much like a map of North America in which the Hudson River is set down as a passage leading to Siberia" (BD 213). He was very, very clear about this: "We consider that we are entitled to at least 13 pages of gross and stupid errors. After that we shall have to explain" (NL 389). Given that he thought these "new lands" were just a few miles above us, that the earth was the center of the universe, and that modern astronomy was all wrong about the vastness of space, we must grant Fort significantly more than thirteen pages of gross and stupid errors. One hundred and thirty is more like it. The truth is, as Damon Knight pointed out, that much of *New Lands* is simply embarrassing to read now. We can well understand why Fort needed these new lands to be so close and the earth so stable (he could see no other way to explain how the super-constructions got here so easily), but the fact remains that he was spectacularly wrong about all of this.[38] This is where a concept like dimensions may look far more fantastic, but is in fact far more rational and helpful.

But most of Fort's writing is not about the adventure of our metaphysical expansion into "new lands." It is about *us as someone else's adventure and land*. For now, at least, it is we who are the colonized. Fort could be quite beautiful about these visitors—beautifully terrifying, that is. He had reports, for example, of immense ships that floated before the sun, the moon, and Mars. He gave one a fanciful name, "Melanicus . . . Prince of Dark Bodies." It was a

> Vast dark thing with the wings of a super-bat, or jet-black super-construction; most likely one of the spores of the Evil One. . . . hovers on wings, or wing-like appendages, or planes that are hundreds of miles from tip to tip—a super-evil thing that is exploiting us. By Evil I mean that which makes us useful.
>
> He obscures a star. He shoves a comet. I think he's a vast, black, brooding vampire. (BD 209–10)

A bit further down, he sings again of "the vast dark thing that looked like a poised crow of unholy dimensions" (BD 225).

But why does Melanicus come? What, pray ye, is the poised crow of unholy dimensions after? And why—the "greatest of mysteries"—do these invaders not make themselves better known? Fort finds this "notion that we must be interesting" a very curious one (BD 143). Basically, we're not, so there is hardly a mystery here. "It's probably for moral reason that they stay way—but even so, there must be some degraded ones among them" (BD 162).

There are also what he calls "dangers of near approach." Nevertheless, "our own ships that dare not venture close to a rocky shore can send rowboats ashore," he points out. So "why not diplomatic relations established between the United States and Cyclorea—which, in our advanced astronomy, is the name of a remarkable wheel-shaped world or super-construction? Why not missionaries sent here openly to convert us from our barbarous prohibitions and other taboos, and to prepare the way for a good trade in ultra-bibles and super-whiskeys . . . ?" (BD 162).

But in other places Fort develops the notion that these super-constructions have been communicating with us all along, but only through a sect or secret society.[39] It is these "certain esoteric ones of this earth's inhabitants" who aid these other races in their colonization of us (BD 136). It only takes a few: "We think of India—the millions of natives who are ruled by a small band of esoterics—only because they receive support and direction from—somewhere else—or from England" (BD 152). He will also, however, entertain the more democratic idea that there are some worlds that are trying to communicate with all of us. It depends on the different data and what they suggest (BD 143).

But there are darker possibilities still. Earth may not be a colony at all. It may be a farm:

> Would we, if we could, educate and sophisticate pigs, geese, cattle?
>
> Would it be wise to establish diplomatic relation with the hen that now functions, satisfied with mere sense of achievement by way of compensation?
>
> I think we're property. (BD 163)

Shit.

Which brings us to one of the most striking, and most gnostic, aspects of Fort's system, that is, his notion that the principle mechanism by which we are kept in our pens is religion. What Fort shouts in these most remarkable of passages is what some Jewish and Christian gnostics shouted in the first few centuries of the common era, namely, that orthodox religion, to the extent that it privileges violent deities demanding sacrifice, is demonic not metaphorically, but *really*. Those who do not know believe that they worship God. They in fact worship demons.

I am not exaggerating. Here is a rather typical passage from Fort: "That a new prophet had appeared upon the moon, and had excited new hope of evoking response from the bland and shining Stupidity that has so often been mistaken for God, or from the Appalling that is so identified with Divinity—from the clutched and menacing fist that has so often been worshipped" (NL 428). Here's another, this time on poltergeist disturbances: "Sometimes I am going to try to find out why so many of these disturbances have occurred in the homes of clergymen. . . . Perhaps going to heaven makes people atheists" (LO 693). In a similar gnostic rage against the shining Stupidity we mistake for God, Fort reads the *Chicago Tribune* of June 10, 1889. Fifteen thousand innocent souls were drowned in the Johnstown flood when the dam broke. The survivors threw away, even burned, their Bibles, so obvious was the futility of their faith (LO 764).

This is religion for Fort. A patent lie. A gross fraud. A Bible to burn after the floodwaters have swept away your children.

And a deadly demon. In the winter of 1904–5, a religious mania, a revival, swept through Northumberland, England (LO 650–65).[40] So too did a series of bizarre occult events, as if they were somehow linked to the devotional fervor or "psycho-electricity" of the people, as if the people, Fort suggests, were "human batteries" that the occult events were feeding upon, thus growing more brilliant "with nourishing ecstasies" (LO 655). Terrifying objects appeared in the sky. One "shining thing" followed Mrs. Jones's car, even when it turned from road to road in a vain effort to shake its pursuer. The same damned things were seen hovering over chapels. Things flew about, or seemed to appear out of nowhere, in a local butcher shop. Something was slaughtering sheep in the fields (one is reminded here of the cattle mutilations of contemporary UFO lore). Three different people were nearly buried as dead before they awoke from strangely profound trances. An elderly woman was not so lucky. She was mysteriously burned to a crisp in a case of "spontaneous combustion." Fort does not believe in spontaneous combustions. But he's willing to entertain the existence of "beings, that, with a flaming process, consume men and women, but . . . mostly pick out women." The *Liverpool Echo* of January 18, 1905, put the situation this way in its headline: "Wales in the Grip of Supernatural Forces!" Fort, in his typical suspicions, is not so sure. "Supernatural" is not a word he used lightly. As for the events of Northumberland in the winter of 1904–5, perhaps these were not occult beings at all, but rather "projected mentalities of living human beings" (LO 694).

Maybe. But Fort seems most convinced of the alien-invasion thesis and in a subsequent demonic theory of religion. The two are connected in his mind. We have submitted to our own colonization, and through the very mechanisms of our deepest belief and most heartfelt piety no less. We are thus colonized *from within*:

> Angels.
>
> Hordes upon hordes of them. . . .
>
> I think that there are, out in inter-planetary space, Super Tamerlanes at the head of hosts of celestial ravagers . . . I should say that we're now under cultivation: that we're conscious of it, but have the impertinence to attribute it all to our own nobler and higher instincts. (BD 216–17)

It is easy to imagine a more rational theory of religion. It is difficult to imagine a more radical one.

Evolution, Wild Talents, and the Poltergeist Girls: Fort's Magical Anthropology

Toward the very end of his life, Fort published his last two books: *Lo!* which appeared in 1931, and *Wild Talents,* which appeared a year later in 1932, as Fort lay dying. In many ways, these two books constitute a single work, a vast two-volume meditation on the subject of anomalous human beings, on supermen and superwomen, but also supergirls and superboys. After collecting "294 records of showers of living things," Fort now turns his gaze to falling—or blazing, or telekinetic, or telepathic—people (LO 544). *Lo!* thus opens with a confused, naked man in a city street, seemingly transported against his will and knowledge, like the falling fish, from somewhere else.

From the naked man in the city street, Fort will continue to dwell, relentlessly, on such anomalous scenes and strange powers for the next five hundred pages, as he effectively reverses his theoretical gaze and begins to ponder the question of what *we* must look like to an alien form of intelligence, whether we may constitute some kind of psychical experience or occult dimension *for them.* "I suspect, in other worlds, or in other parts of one existence," he suggests, that "there is esoteric knowledge of human beings of this earth, kept back from common knowledge." "This is easily thinkable," he now jokes, "because even upon this earth there is little knowledge of human beings" (LO 617). He even suggests that "the spiritualists are reversedly right—that there is a ghost-world—but that it is our existence—that when the spirits die they become human beings" (WT, 898). We, in essence, are their heaven.

Fort was quite serious about the occult dimensions of Human Being, about the humanities as mysteries. And he did not restrict this idea to the usual topic of extraordinary forms or altered states of consciousness. He extended it to our *Bodies,* which was precisely the announced, capitalized, and italicized subject of *Wild Talents* (WT 848). This is where the key subject of evolution comes in. Central to both of these last two books was the notion that evolution, or Development, as he preferred to call it in his un-Darwinian capitalized language, has intentionally endowed certain human beings with anomalous physical and psychical abilities toward some distant end or future goal: "There is a fortune teller in every womb," he asserted in another one of those striking one-liners (LO 732). Fort called these evolving magical powers gifted in the womb "wild talents," by which he meant "something that comes and goes, and is under no control, but that may be caught and trained" (WT 1049).

Fort's notion of wild talents appears to be a double echo of both Frederic Myers's earlier notion of spiritual evolution and William James's earlier notion of wild facts. By the latter expression, James referred to the data of mystical literature and psychical research that lie strewn across the surface of history, still unassimilated, still rejected by the scientism of the academic mind. For James, such wild facts always threaten "to break up the accepted system," particularly the accepted scientific system of the universities.[41] This is pure Charles Fort before Charles Fort. And why not? Fort had certainly read his share of William James, although James probably knew nothing of Charles Fort.

Like James again, Fort was very thoughtful and systematic about these matters. Indeed, he had developed an entire evolutionary mysticism and cultural psychology around the notion of such wild talents. He suggested, for example, that they were all "specializations" of some much larger shape-shifting power. Myers and his colleagues had guessed the same thing through their metanotion of the telepathic law, and later parapsychologists would guess again through their similar metanotion of psi. In one of Fort's rougher neologisms, he himself called this metapower *transmediumization*, a term that appears to be a combination of Catholic sacramental theology's transubstantiation (the sacred power of the Eucharistic rite to transform ordinary bread and wine into the actual body and blood of Christ) with the materialized objects and substances (think: ectoplasm) that seemed to manifest through a few talented mediums.

Regardless of its linguistic origins and intended allusions, the term for Fort signaled the ability of the imaginal to become real and the real imaginal, or, in his own words now, "the imposition of the imaginary-physical upon the physical-imaginary" (WT 1048). It is the old controversy of the relationship of mind and matter, he points out. "But, in the philosophy of the hyphen, an uncrossable gap is disposed of, and the problem is rendered into thinkable terms, by asking whether mind-matter can act upon matter-mind" (WT 1055). Here is Fort's clearest expression of the idea:

> The *real*, as it is called, or the objective, the external, the material, cannot be absolutely set apart from the subjective, or the imaginary: but there are quasi-attributes of the imaginary. There have been occurrences that I think were *transmediumizations*, because I think that they were marked by indications of having carried over, from an imaginative origin, into physical being, or into what is called "real life," the quasi-attributes of their origin. (WT 1049)

This is a key idea for Fort, as he thinks it has something to do with evolution and, particularly, with the ways different species can take on strikingly intentional forms, like the insect that evolves into a veritable stick or leaf—the "wereleaf," as he puts it in his typical humor, and then literally pins to his apartment wall: "I have thought of leaf insects as pictorial representations wrought in the bodies of insects, by their imaginations, or *by the imaginative qualities of the substances of their bodies*—back in plastic times, when insects were probably not so set in their ways as they now are" (WT 1024; italics mine). Basically, what Fort is proposing here is a kind of imaginal evolution, a biological process driven by an unidentified, and probably unknowable, Imagination. We are back to Myers's entomological notion of the imaginal on its way to the perfect imago of the insect, in this case a literal insect!

Such a superpower not only drives biological evolution. It also is at the base and center of psychocultural evolution, an especially elaborate process for Fort that selects out different human potentials and actualizes them when they are needed, that is, when they become "marketable" at a particular time and place (he even made up a "job ad" for poltergeist girls in order to joke about how unmarketable this stuff was at his, and no doubt our, particular cultural moment). Such wild talents are latent in us all—"It is monism that if anybody's a wizard, everybody is, to some degree, a wizard"—but they require much discipline and attention to manifest at all, and this is something our culture and our markets simply will not allow: "My notion is that wild talents exist in the profusion of the weeds of the fields. Also my notion is that, were it not for the conventions of markets, many weeds could be developed into valuable, edible vegetables" (WT 1039).

Still within this same model, he considered the advancing social activities of art, science, and religion—whose cutting-edge developments are always considered useless and preposterous by the established offended system (NL 530)—to be expressions of these same human potentials, all aimed at a distant future awakening that no one yet grasps. Evolution, in other words, is not simply about physical mutations. It is also about cultural mutations. Evolution is that process that expresses and represses the wild talents latent in us all.

Fort was especially interested in one particularly strong comparative pattern he had noticed, namely, that these wild talents often manifested in adolescents, particularly, he hints, in adolescents in emotionally difficult or abusive situations, such as orphans or young house servants. Young girls were especially evident. Or vulnerable. There was, for example, the story of John Shattock's farmhouse reported in the *Glasgow News* of May 20, 1878. A hayrack burst into flames when a twelve-year-old servant girl passed by. That was only the beginning. Things around her in the house would move—things like dishes and loaves of bread. More ominously, small fires kept breaking out around her. A priest was sent for, no doubt to perform an exorcism. The stable burned down. Fort noted that such fire scenes were usually very localized and occured in broad daylight, instead of at night when they would have been far more dangerous. Usually, moreover, they broke out in the presence of a girl between the ages of twelve and twenty (WT 919). He was suggesting, I gather, that these pyropsychic scenes served symbolic purposes, that is, that they were meant to express rage and not cause physical harm.

Twelve-year-old Willie Boughs was a different case. The *San Francisco Bulletin* of October 14, 1886, reported on his sufferings in Turlock, Madison County, California. Willie could set things on fire "by his glance." He was thrown out of school for this wild talent, and then he was thrown out of his home by his parents. A kind farmer took him in and sent him to school again. "On the first day, there were five fires in the school: one in the center of the ceiling, one in the teacher's desk, one in her wardrobe, and two on the wall. The boy discovered all, and cried from fright. The trustees met and expelled him, that night" (WT 920). The *New York Herald* of October 16, 1886, reported on the same events. One can only imagine what poor Willie thought.

On a related note, there was that odd recorded ability of human beings who were allegedly capable of setting things on fire by breathing on them. Human dragons. From there Fort paints a veritable X-Men scenario, with potential mutants roaming the streets of New York:

> The phenomena look to me like a survival of a power that may have been common in the times of primitive men. Breathing dry leaves afire would, once upon a time, be a miracle of the highest value. . . . If we can think of our existence as a whole—perhaps only one of countless existences in the cosmos—as a developing organism, we can think of a fire-inducing power appearing automatically in some human beings, at a time of its need in the development of human phenomena. . . . most likely beginning humbly, regarded as freaks; most likely persecuted at first, but becoming established . . . [Then] their fall from importance, and the dwindling of them into their present, rare occurrence—but the preservation of them, as occasionals, by Nature, as an insurance, because there's no knowing when we'll all go back to savagery again . . . Conceive of a powerful backward slide, and one conceives of the appearance, by only an accentuation of the existing, of hosts of werewolves and wereskunks and werehyenas in the streets of New York City. (WT 926–27)

Whereas an author of the impossible like Frederic Myers conceived of telepathic abilities as hints of a *future* evolutionary development, an author like Charles Fort conceived of psychical abilities as fossils of the *past*, as evolutionary leftovers, as it were, that might yet be reactualized again.

As such ideas make more than obvious, Fort's relationship to the Darwinian model of evolution is, to put it mildly, not exactly a traditional one. In places, he clearly rejects Darwinism as "positively baseless," but he immediately notes that it is far superior to anything that preceded it in terms of its organization and consistency (BD 24). In short, it is a better system, a better theory, a closer approximation to the truth of things. What Fort clearly rejects about Darwinism is its purposelessness, that is, its insistence on random selection and mutation toward no particular end. Fort is an evolutionary thinker of sorts, but one who insists on a kind of intelligent design,—an intelligent design, however, without a Designer. He is thus careful to point out that he wishes to give no aid or comfort to anti-Darwinians and fundamentalists. There is no Christian God in his system. We would say now that "God" is an emergent property of a system for Fort: "I am God to the cells that compose me," he would write in *Wild Talents* (WT 877).

The other major difference between Darwin's biology and Fort's metaphysics is that for Darwin only the past can influence the present, whereas for Fort the future also influences the present via orthogenesis, or what he also calls Development. He thus prefers to think of the "Geo-system" as a kind of huge egg, an "incubating organism of which this earth is the nucleus." In more contemporary terms, the earth is a self-regulating ecosystem evolving toward its own innate plan or design:

> In a technical sense we give up the doctrine of Evolution. Ours is an expression upon Super-embryonic Development, in one enclosed system. Ours is an expression upon Design underlying and manifesting in all things within this one system, with a Final Designer left out, because we know of no designing force that is not itself the product of remoter design. . . . it is not altogether anti-Darwinian: the concept of Development replaces the concept of Evolution, but we accept the process of Selection, not to anything loosely known as Environment, but relatively to underlying Schedule and Design, predetermined and supervised, as it were, but by nothing that we conceive in anthropomorphic terms. (NL 528–29)

What it all comes down to is a question of time and whether one privileges the past, the present, or the future. Darwinism concerns itself with present adaptations as the biological results of past challenges and selections, but "there is no place for the influence of the future upon the present," Fort correctly notes (NL 529). There is in Fort's system. Indeed, it is the future that acts as a kind of occult attractor or magnet, pulling everything in the past and the present toward its own superstate, which Fort himself considers predetermined but which he leaves entirely open ended, except for some tantalizing hints about an "awakening." Fort's preferred expression for this cosmic process is "Super-embryonic Development." Human beings are "cellular units" in this Embryo called Earth. It is all "one integrating organism, and we," Fort now sings, "have heard its pulse" (NL 531–32).

It is within this same Super-embryonic Development that Fort began in *Lo!* to conceive of strange human abilities, particularly something he called there, for the first time, "teleportation" (LO 553). Hence the confused naked man in the city street with which the book opens. This is a technical term, first announced in 1931, that would have an incredible run in twentieth-century science fiction, superhero comics, and metaphysical film, from the "Beam me up" of *Star Trek*, through the X-Men's teleporting Nightcrawler, to the recent movie *Jumper*. Teleportation is also a crucial concept for Fort, partly because it helps explain all the falling matter of his earlier two books, partly because it serves a certain balancing or distributive role in the Super-Embryo. Teleportation is the natural mechanism through which the Super-Embryo of Earth distributes things where they are needed at the moment. Although the agency behind teleportation is certainly "not exclusively human" (LO 572)—so Fort can conceive, for example, of the "occult powers of trees" that need rain—it can be harnessed by human beings, if usually unconsciously (LO 571).

Humorously, absurdly, much of this falling stuff makes little sense now. As nineteenth-century documented reports of "manna" in Asia Minor suggested to Fort, the stuff, once needed desperately thousands of years ago, just keeps on falling into the present, despite the fact that no one needs it any longer. "This looks like stupidity," even "idiocy," Fort observes (LO 554, 601). Perhaps this is why his publisher wanted to title *Lo!* his third book, *God Is an Idiot*.[42] Fort rejected this idea—*why* is not clear, as he clearly did think that the common images of God amounted to idiocy, or at least shining Stupidity—but he pressed the point further anyway. "To keep on sending little frogs, where, so far as can be seen, there is no need for little frogs, is like persistently, if not brutally, keeping right on teaching Latin and Greek, for instance. What's that for?" (LO 668) Poor ol' Fred Myers, the Cambridge classicist, would have rolled in his grave at that one. Had, of course, Fred been in his grave, which is doubtful, given what *he* had written.

Some of the most delightful scenes in *Wild Talents* involve Fort's experiments with his own wild talents. Consider, for example, the story of the falling picture. We began this book with an epigraph from *Wild Talents*.

"Read a book, or look at a picture," we began. There is a story behind this. We return now to Letter E in Box 27.

Letter E, it turns out, is a note about how Fort, inspired by his reading in the British Museum Library about poltergeists, had decided to "experiment" while he was living in London, at 39 Marchmont Street, W.C. 1, he tells us with some uncalled for precision. It was March 11, 1924. Fort was—what else?—reading. He heard a thump. He found a picture had fallen near a curtain, which shook vigorously for "several seconds" after the fall. The next morning he examined the brass ring on the back of the picture. It appeared to be sheered in two places by some force. He now recalled two other pictures falling in the apartment. Six days later, he was startled by a loud "crackling sound," as if glass was breaking. But no glass broke. He found a fourth fallen picture on the 28th. He suspected that, "in some unknown way, I was the one doing this." He seemed to hope so anyway. Another fell on July 26. And another on October 22, as he stared at a picture and thought about all the others falling. Then another, this time in the landlady's apartment, on the night of September 28. A year later, on October 15, 1929, now back in New York, "or anyway in the Bronx," Charles is discussing this with Anna. A pan fell in the closet. Fort explains two more experiments in two more consecutive years:

> Oct. 18, 1930—I made an experiment. I read these notes aloud to *A* [Anna], to see whether there be a repetition of the experience of Oct. 15, 1929 [the pan in the closet]. Nothing fell.
>
> Nov. 19, 1931—tried that again. Nothing moved. Well, then, if I'm not a wizard, I'm not going to let anybody else tell me that he's a wizard. (WT 976–80)

But Fort remains troubled by what happened over those months. He can't shake the conviction that there was some relationship between his state of mind and all those pictures falling. He continues to pursue his wizadry, this time with a little more luck. This wild experiment involves him walking down 42nd Street and believing that he could somehow "see" what was ahead of him. An odd phrase pops into his head: "Turkey tracks in red snow." He was working in the library on cases of red snow, so this phrase signaled a connection between what he was reading and what he believed was about to appear in the physical world. He soon comes upon a store window selling fountain pens. They are lined up in the window display, "grouped in fours, one behind, and the three others trifurcating from it, on a back-ground of pink cardboard," that is, like turkey tracks in red snow.

"At last I was a wizard!" (WT 1036).

But then the next experiment fails. And the next. And the next. It is difficult to accuse this man of hubris:

> Say that I experimented about a thousand times. Out of a thousand attempts, I can record only three seemingly striking successes, though I recall some minor ones. Throughout this book, I have taken the stand that nobody can be always wrong, but it does seem to me that I approximated so highly that I am nothing short of a negative genius. (WT 1037)

Still, he cannot shake the hits, so extraordinary did they *feel*. He is equally impressed by "the triviality and casualness of them." Turkey tracks made out of fountain pens in a store window are not exactly about changing the world. Nor are tipping tables in séance rooms. But still, what do these things signal, what do they *mean*? Quite a lot, Fort suggests, for "the knack that tips a table may tilt an epoch" (WT 1045).

But he also recognizes that he only experimented for a month, and that it takes five years to learn the basics of a skill like writing a book. What he seems to be suggesting here is that we get what we want, or more accurately, what our cultures want us to get and so reward. But what if things were different? What if these "coincidences" could be put to some use? If he can take down a picture by just looking at it, why not a whole house? Indeed, why not *build* a house this way too?

> All around are wild talents, and it occurs to nobody to try to cultivate them, except as expressions of personal feelings, or as freaks for which to charge admission. I conceive of powers and the uses of human powers that will some day transcend the stunts of music halls and séances and sideshows, as public utilities have passed beyond the toy-stages of their origins. (WT 1041)

Thus appears the magical outlines of Fort's Third Dominant, the era of witchcraft. Whereas this age of materialism, the industrial era, trains young men "to the glory of the job" and convinces them that "all magics, except their own industrial magics, are fakes, superstitions, or newspaper yarns," Fort dreams of a coming era in which human beings can openly acknowledge, harness, and hone their wild talents (WT 1028–29). Humorously, again as if to protect himself from the implications of his own thought, he imagines "batteries of witches teleported to Nicaragua where speedily they cut a canal by dissolving trees and rocks," but then sees admittedly that there is nothing more reasonable than the taboo against this stuff, since with the advantages of witchcraft also comes the possibility of "criminal enormities" (WT 1041).

And just how would such practical witchcraft be used in warfare? Fort lets loose:

> Later: A squad of poltergeist girls—and they pick a fleet out of the sea, or out of the sky. . . . Girls at the front—and they are discussing their usual not very profound subjects. The alarm—the enemy is advancing. Command to the poltergeist girls to concentrate—and under their chairs they stick their wads of chewing gum.
>
> A regiment bursts into flames, and the soldiers are torches. Horses snort smoke from the combustion of their entrails. Reinforcements are smashed under cliffs that are teleported from the Rocky Mountains. The snatch of Niagara Falls—it pours upon the battlefield. The little poltergeist girls reach for their wads of chewing gum. (WT 1042)

We can smile at such scenes, and laugh at Fort's outrageousness, not to mention his keen psychological descriptions of the gossip of girls. But there would be many others who would seriously posit something called super-psi. And still others who would dream of similar psychotronic displays, namely, cold war psychic spies and something called "remote viewing." And they were perfectly serious.

It was in this way that Charles Fort sang his saga with volume and page numbers. It was in this way that he laid the seeds of a Super-Story through those monistic peaches, that marching data of the damned, the philosophy of the hyphen, the New Era of witchcraft, quantum teleportations, super-constructions in the sky, New Lands, falling fishes, galactic colonialism, evolutionary superpowers, and gum-chewing poltergeist girls. By so doing, he set the table for later writers of the anomalous, of the pulp magazines and early science fiction, the UFO, and those most popular of all possessors of wild talents, the American superheroes.

And us? What should we make of all of this?

For now, it is enough to acknowledge that if Charles Fort had any reliable and truly indisputable wild talent, it was his talent as a writer. Steinmeyer concludes his recent biography with this fair and balanced assessment. American writers like Dreiser, Hecht, and Tarkington, of course, had early on seen something similar, if in a more astonished vein.

I in turn have added my own impossible readings here. More specifically, I have tried to foreground Fort's comparative, philosophical, and hermeneutical practices and show how, through them, Fort came to understand that writing can morph into something that is truly mythical in scope and power, that writing can become a veritable occult practice, an act of the super-imagination through which one can wake up and, some day, step out of the Cave of Consensus. This was his technique anyway for realizing how we are being written by the paranormal, and how we might finally step out of this bad novel and begin to write ourselves.

In the end, then, the real wizardry of Charles Fort resides not in the turkey-track shop window (although those *were* pens), or in all those falling apartment pictures, but in those four wonderful books and the weird ways they might reveal hidden patterns and new meanings and so order the world anew for their stunned readers. If that's not magic, I don't know what is.

BEFORE MOVING
PRIOR TO STAND
VERIFY NO
AND/OR REMOVAL
FOLLOWING ITEMS.
HANDRAILS
LIGHTS
VACUUM HOSES
TOOLING / OPTIC STANDS
14 DEC 2006

three

THE FUTURE TECHNOLOGY OF FOLKLORE

Jacques Vallee and the UFO Phenomenon

> If it were possible to make three-dimensional holograms with mass, and to project them through time I would say this is what the farmer saw. . . . Are we dealing . . . with a parallel universe, where there are human races living, and where we may go at our expense, never to return to the present? . . . From that mysterious universe, have objects that can materialize and "dematerialize" at will been projected? Are the UFO's "windows" rather than "objects"?
>
> —JACQUES VALLEE, *Passport to Magonia*

> Any sufficiently advanced technology is indistinguishable from magic.
>
> —ARTHUR C. CLARKE

When I first read Jacques Vallee, I knew immediately that I had found a writer who had something important to teach us about the history of Western esotericism, about the truths of traditional folklore, about the mysterious attractions of modern science fiction, and about the reality of paranormal phenomena—all those imaginal realities and damned facts that point toward what Vallee has called "the apparent magical qualities of human consciousness."[1] I knew, in other words, that I was reading another author of the impossible.

It was not just what Vallee writes, although that is impossible enough. It was *how* he writes it, how he makes the impossible possible through the sophistication of his suspicions and the complex ways that his comparative imagination puts together the pieces and parts of his historical data in order to form a radically different picture-puzzle of things. I was also fascinated by the way he relates material from the ancient and medieval worlds to our own ultramodern one. He obviously does not consider time absolute, nor does he idolize local culture as the measure of all things. The study of history for him is not about an "us" and a "them," all solipsistically locked into our little decades and languages and cultural practices. It is about a global "we" spanning multiple millennia and countless local expressions of a vast psychical system. Just as significantly, Vallee's comparative imagination adamantly refuses to be located in any single order of knowledge. Here, after all, is a pioneering computer scientist and venture capitalist who purchases rare editions of Paracelsus and writes like a mystically inclined humanist. Even as a young man, he scoffed at the dysfunctional ways his education had separated the literary and the technical modes of thought, and he felt little but disgust for scientists who were contemptuous of science fiction. Fantasy, for him at least, was a mode of serious speculative thought.[2]

He certainly lived up to these youthful ideals. Vallee has speculated about multidimensional universes and mythological control systems worthy of any science-fiction novel (of which he himself has now written five), but he has also helped map Mars, published on pulsar fundamental frequencies, and written books about business strategies and information technology. His business career and cultural presence similarly reflect this double persona. Vallee was an early entrepreneur in the computer industry of Silicon Valley and the development of the Internet. He was also the inspiration for the character of the French scientist Claude Lacombe, played by Francois Truffaut in Steven Spielberg's sci-fi classic *Close Encounters of the Third Kind*.

In terms of my present reflections, Jacques Vallee dwells exactly where I have suggested the contemporary gnostic intellectual dwells, that is, in a modern form of gnosis or forbidden knowledge well beyond reason and completely beyond belief. These are my terms, not his. But his are remarkably, astonishingly close. He too, after all, uses the phrase "beyond reason" to describe his subject matter, and he presents his life as a passionate pursuit of "forbidden science," the title phrase of his published journals that speaks of a radical rejection of reason's claim to exhaust the possible.[3] He is thus dismissive of "the constipated rationalists who are the new arbiters of French thought" (FS 1:192). He similarly scoffs at the Enlightenment rationalist philosophers, who trapped us all in a boring "bureaucratic cage for two centuries" (FS 1:97). And he is positively disgusted with "the old scientists," who deny the very reality of the problem of UFOs. Vallee had already had enough of their reasonable, respectable nonsense in 1961, when he wrote this in his journals: "Our research would be emasculated by their lack of creativity and their need to reduce everything to that dull state of uniformity they mistakenly label as rationalism" (FS 1:52).

Not that doctrinal religion fares any better than dogmatic rationalism within Vallee's deeply personal gnosis. He is profoundly suspicious of institutional religion, which he sees primarily as a kind of social control system, certainly not as a deposit of eternal truths. He thus confesses a "lack of faith in the common images of God." Which is not to say that he does not possess his own spiritual sensibilities. These in fact are profound, as we shall see, but he prefers to label them as expressions of mysticism, not religion. Mysticism, for Vallee, has nothing to do with religion and its doctrinal formulations. Rather, it is "an orientation of consciousness, a direction of thought away from ordinary space-time."[4] We will see that he means this quite literally, even scientifically, in a forbidden sort of way.

Beyond reason and beyond belief, then, Vallee writes as a man who possesses or, better, is possessed by, a form of secret knowledge or gnosis. Such a third way of knowing is closely linked to what he calls "the higher dimensions of mind," which are traditionally expressed through the imagination, the realm of the fantastic, and, most recently, through science fiction. His intellectual heroes are men like Nikola Tesla, that modern American wizard who combined future electrical, radar, and radio technologies with occult ideas in ways so weird that they were genius; Isaac Newton, who practiced his alchemy and astrology behind all that orthodox science; and the hermetic philosopher and physician Paracelsus, whose texts Vallee has studied with care (FS 1:96). Indeed, with respect to figures like the last and their hermetic science, Vallee feels strongly that "whatever else these old hermeticists were doing, they should be credited as the real founders of modern thought" (FS 1:76). For Vallee, Western thought, truly serious thought beyond the surfaces of rationalism and religion, is fundamentally an esoteric project, the outlines and implications of which we have only begun to glimpse. It is still too much for us. So we hide it from ourselves.

It should be stressed that Jacques Vallee's secret knowledge is not simply a function of his mysticism. It is also a function of the U.S. government. Of the air force, to be more precise. Vallee, after all, is a man who worked, in an unofficial capacity, for four years on an independent study of the files of a government project (Project Blue Book) with military professionals and scientists who knew things others did not, should not, and could not know. But Vallee came to realize that such people, with one very important exception, did not really know. How could they? They were naively chasing something "out there," whose absurd, impossible behavior was also clearly "in here." They behaved "like a well-organized insect colony whose life is suddenly impacted by an unforeseen event" (FS 1:55). Their idea of research was to form commissions composed of rocket scientists and chase UFOs with jet fighters with the intent of shooting one down. These were not profound puzzles capable of transforming our understanding of the world and ourselves. They were simply "targets." In *Fastwalker*, one of his later English novels, Vallee puts his own thoughts in the mind of a puzzled fighter pilot. "What is wrong with us," the pilot muses to himself, "that we automatically call any object in the sky a *target*, as if we had to shoot down anything we don't understand?"[5] This kind of military thinking struck Vallee as primitive and silly, if not actually stupid. It was certainly futile.

What Jacques Vallee came to know, in other words, could not be explained as something strictly objective *or* subjective. It was both. And it was neither. When Vallee writes of the paranormal—and this is what *really* drew me to his impossible writings—he is not thinking of purely internal states or subjective conditions, however interesting and profound. He is thinking of fundamentally anomalous events that routinely appear on radar screens. He is thinking of a potentially hostile force that deeply concerned nation-states and their militaries for decades, of an advanced future technology that has easily escaped our best fighter jets, and of a puzzling presence of truly mythological proportions that has secretly shaped our folklore, our religious beliefs, and our cultures for millennia. He is thinking of something that is mythical and physical, spiritual and material *at the same time*.

If the reader is now confused, then so much the better. Rational certainty and religious belief are the enemies here; confusion, our delivering angel; absurdity and suspicion, our flapping wings. Hence the fundamental weirdness of the situation at hand deserves restating.

And then underlining.

And then highlighting.

What, after all, we are approaching here is a particular moment in Western cultural history when the mystical and magical qualities of human consciousness became the object of tax-funded secret research programs, where the paranormal became a matter of national security, and where governments tracked occult forces on radar systems and chased them with supersonic planes.[6] We are also approaching the idea of a future technology of folklore through which we might imagine parallel universes and holographic visions projected back through time in order to reprogram our own cultural software, with or without our present permission. In such a fantastic world, a UFO may remain a physical "object," while at the same time functioning more like a symbol or metaphysical "window" into another plane or dimension, a portal in space-time through which we imaginally encounter not an alien race from another planet but our own evolved species from another time.

Forbidden Science (1957–69)

I visited Jacques Vallee in his San Francisco condominium. The flat looks out high above the local buildings toward the city skyline and the iconic pyramid of the Trans-America tower. I had asked to meet him and to see his library. The latter request was very much related to the former, as I had spent time in other writers' libraries and found this an especially direct pathway into their authorial souls. These are symbolic spaces whose details are all significant: which books are there (or not there); how they are organized; what sort of art sits alongside which books; and so on. The Vallee Collection, which spills out into rooms and hallways, did not disappoint. The present chapter is a very partial record of what and whom I encountered on two separate visits in those rooms and hallways high above the city.

Jacques Vallee was a war baby. He was born among exploding bombs, on September 24, 1939, in Pontoise, France. The doctor was unable to come over the bridge during the attack, so a local nurse delivered him amidst the sound of the first German air strike. The Nazi Panzers would soon arrive, and the Vallee family would flee for Normandy (FS 1:35). Vallee's free associations with the cultural timing of his birth are interesting. He notes that this was the year that the film *The Wizard of Oz* and the superhero Batman appeared. These are hardly random associations, as Oz-like magical balls of light would float through his own later texts, Kansas and all, and a paranormal Batman would even make an anachronistic appearance, eerily, in the London of 1837, almost exactly a century before Bob Kane dreamed him up again, this time as a quasi-criminal superhero.[7] Vallee also notes that this was the year President Roosevelt received a letter from Albert Einstein and Leo Szilard suggesting that atomic energy could be used to make a bomb, and that, at the time of his birth, Sigmund Freud lay dying in London, in exile—from the same Nazis that were bombing Pontoise, I would add (FS 1:446). As a young boy, little Jacques witnessed the war's atrocities: the Germans "would fire pitilessly at the bodies of helpless Allied pilots swinging down from the bright blue sky at the end of their white parachutes." But he also remembers affectionately how the war ended: "Soon came the mighty rumble of Patton's tanks, behind which marched tall, laughing Americans with chewing gum in their mouths and nets over their helmets" (FS 1:37).

Vallee thus grew up in postwar France in the 1940s and '50s, fully aware that there were forces beyond his little neighborhood and country that could have a tremendous impact on his life and world. As a teenager, he followed with fascination the amazing wave of UFO sightings in France, indeed all across Europe, in 1954. Three years later, he watched the first *Sputnik* satellite fly overhead, on Sunday, 24 November 1957, at 5:54 p.m., he is careful to note in his journals. The French Astronomical Society published his account of it (FS 1:11). As a young man, he studied physics and astronomy, completing an M.A. in astrophysics. In June of 1961, he began working as a government employee on the artificial-satellite service of the Paris Observatory, where he saw tape recordings of visual readings of UFOs intentionally and systematically destroyed (FS 1:48). "There were films, too" (IC 46).

It was at this time that his boss, a man named Paul Muller, received a letter from Aimé Michel, a well-known interpreter of the UFO phenomenon whom Vallee had read and much admired. Michel wrote Muller, offering to donate his rich files on UFO sightings to the observatory (Michel, Vallee explained to me, believed that he was dying of a brain tumor at this point in time and wanted these materials preserved in an appropriate institution). "You see," scoffed Muller, not knowing that Vallee had corresponded with Michel, "that's another letter for the crackpot file. Although properly speaking, Aimé Michel is not really a crackpot, he is a crook." The cruel comment stung Vallee so badly that he insists on including it in the original French: *Ce n'est pas un fou, c'est un escroc* (FS 1:49). He would never forget those words. He wrote Aimé Michel that same night and asked to meet him. The next January he resigned from the observatory. Later, Muller would deny in a French television interview that astronomers ever see anything but satellites, shooting stars, and planes. "A bundle of lies," Vallee comments in his journals, "but the French public swallows it" (FS 2:349).

And this was only the beginning of the cruelty and the censorship. Years later, Vallee would learn of how the Condon Committee papers—a study commissioned by the air force in the fall of 1966 at the insistence of Michigan Representative Gerald R. Ford to study the UFO problem at the University of Colorado[8]—were locked up by the university and then transferred to a private home, where, it was rumored, they were subsequently burned (FS 1:51). He would also learn about what happened in the radar room in July of 1952, when seven UFOs, on two consecutive weekends, no less, were buzzing around Washington, D.C., and F-94 fighter jets were scrambling in the sky. This is how Michael D. Swords, the biographer of Major Donald E. Keyhoe, one of the early founding fathers of ufology, described the scene: "The case was huge. It made banner front-page headlines. Radar at Washington's National Airport had tracked a cluster of objects over restricted airspace near the Capitol building. Visual confirmation came from commercial flights and jets scrambled by the Air Force. The government was agog from the Pentagon to the President."[9] According to Vallee, an officer in the radar room ordered two men to go outside and take pictures. They did. The photos were developed on the spot. They clearly showed what everyone else was seeing outside, that is, luminous objects darting about in the sky. The photographs were immediately confiscated and the men in the room ordered to say nothing (FS 1:151). Later, some of Allen Hynek's files at Northwestern were stolen by a group of individuals. No one ever found out who they were (FS 2:402). There is no end to such stories of cover-ups, confiscations, even suspicious deaths.[10]

It was because of stories and scenes like these that Vallee finally decided to publish his private journals. A crucial historical event had occurred, he believed: whole "new classes of phenomena that highlighted the reality of the paranormal" had appeared in the historical record. The government and the military, moreover, had deliberately denied and consciously distorted the data with the result that scientists, much less the public, never had "fair and complete access to the most important files." In short, "the public record was shamelessly manipulated" (FS 1:4). Vallee points out that this had been widely assumed and often alleged, but never effectively proven. His published journals, he feels, prove it (FS 1:3).

Vallee's interest in UFOs began during the European wave of 1954. From France to England to Italy, the headlines and airwaves were filled with stunning and confusing reports. Falling "angel hair" was particularly common in Italy, as it had been at Fátima forty years earlier with the perfectly timed, monthly apparitions of a being from the sky (FS 1:128). During the three-month wave of sightings, Vallee gathered newspaper clippings and glued them into a book. It was the next year, though, in May of 1955, that he finally observed a UFO for himself. His mother saw it first. She screamed for her husband and son to come out into the yard. Her husband, who scoffed at such things, would not budge. Her son, though, rushed down into the yard: "What I observed was a gray metallic disk with a clear bubble on top. It was about the apparent size of the moon and it hovered silently in the sky above the church of Saint-Maclou." The next day his best friend Philippe told him that he saw the same thing from his house half a mile away and even had time to watch it with binoculars.[11]

After reading Aimé Michel's *Mystérieux Objets Célestes* in the summer of 1958, Vallee struck up a correspondence with the author. Michel had argued that such beings, if real, must be so superior to us that anything we think about them carries the intellectual weight of an eight-year-old boy staring at the equations of Einstein's blackboard. Yes, a young Vallee answered back, but even the eight-year-old may grow up and outsmart Einstein. Moreover, perhaps their superior evolution carries superior methods of education; perhaps, he implied, they can teach us. Besides, from the reports that were circulating in the newspapers, they appear to be "morphologically human," and this "implies a similarity of level between us and them" (FS 1:22–23). Whereas Michel had already begun to despair of any effective communication with such alien forms of intelligence, Vallee was hoping for an evolutionary education, for a cultural mutation.

In November of 1962, Vallee and his wife, Janine, traveled to the United States on the *Queen Mary*. Once they had landed and adjusted, they moved first to the University of Texas at Austin, where Jacques worked as an astronomer on a project to develop the first computer-based map of Mars. Here the Vallees also expanded their use of IBM cards to organize their UFO data with a sense of relief. After all, they did not "have to hide anymore" (FS 1:71). They would soon move on to Chicago, where Jacques worked as a computer programmer and, eventually, completed a Ph.D. in computer science at Northwestern University. There he worked as a research assistant for an astronomer named J. Allen Hynek, the director of the Dearborn Observatory at the university. Within two years of meeting him, Vallee would describe Hynek as a "mystical man," and this despite Hynek's public persona as an arch-skeptic. He would also muse, with some marvel, how Evanston was the home of *Fate* magazine, "that popular standard of occult lore" (FS 1:132).

Indeed, the lead cover story of the first issue of *Fate* was written by none other than Kenneth Arnold, the American businessman and pilot who, around 3:00 p.m. on June 24, 1947, saw nine silver, crescent-like disks flying in formation near Mount Rainier in Washington State. This is the event that, by all accounts, initiated the public craze around UFOs. Remarkably, Arnold's essay is completely devoid of sensationalism or exaggeration. In it, he simply describes what he saw, and saw very clearly. This was a no-nonsense kind of guy. To prove his credentials, he discloses his pilot's license number (33489), describes his high-performance Callair airplane, and even gives the reader the plane's national certificate number (33355). Not exactly the stuff of high fantasy.

Here are the reported facts. Arnold was helping with a search for a downed marine transport plane. He was cruising at about 9,200 feet on a beautiful, clear day when a "bright flash" or reflection caught his eye. He could not find the source at first but eventually located what he described, in the precise language of a trained pilot, as "a chain of nine peculiar-looking aircraft flying from north to south at approximately 9,500 feet elevation and going, seemingly, in a definite direction of about 170 degrees north to south." Their high speed or precise formation did not immediately bother him, but the fact that they did not have tails did. "The more I observed these objects," he explained, "the more upset I became, as I am accustomed and familiar with most all flying objects whether I am close to the ground or at higher altitudes." He tracked them for two and a half to three minutes and noticed that when they were flying straight and level, "they were just a thin black line."[12]

When he landed to refuel, he reported the sighting to the authorities, as he feared the objects might be of Russian origin (this was, after all, Washington State, and military officials had long suspected that any Russian spy plane incursion would come from the northwest over the Bering Strait). In an interview with journalists (they were waiting for him on the ground in Pendleton, Oregon, when he landed again), Arnold compared the flying objects to speedboats in rough water, to flat shiny pie pans reflecting the sun, and to saucers skipping across water. A journalist by the name of Bill Bequette picked up on the last metaphor and coined the expression "flying saucer" (despite the fact that the crescent craft Arnold reported were not saucer-shaped at all). A new English expression was born. So too was an entire mythology, one thankfully not organized around "flying pie pans."

When Vallee arrived at Northwestern University, Hynek was the government's chief scientific consultant on the air force's Project Blue Book, the successor of two earlier projects, Project Sign and Project Grudge.

Project Sign had been established in the fall of 1947, after one of the most well-known UFO flurries in U.S. history (including Arnold's original sighting and the infamous Roswell incident in New Mexico, which followed just two weeks after Arnold's sensational news), when Lieutenant General Nathan F. Twining concluded that the saucers were indeed "something real and not visionary or fictitious."[13] The real worry here was best expressed by Major Keyhoe. Keyhoe, noting the tendency for the saucers to be sighted over military and nuclear facilities, put the matter in its scariest terms: "It looks as though they're measuring us for a knockout."[14]

Project Sign was replaced by Project Grudge the next year, which was then revised again as Project Blue Book in 1952. Like its earlier incarnations, Project Blue Book was about studying UFOs and assessing their potential threat to national security. Most ufologists, however, including Vallee, argue that it was mostly about *not* studying the phenomenon too deeply, downplaying or simply ignoring the most difficult cases, and calming the public. In short, it acted primarily as a public-relations campaign, not as a serious research initiative. By this time, the air force seems to have concluded that, whatever the damned things were, they were not a threat to national security, not an immediate one anyway. They were right about this.

Still, there remained a real question, and a real question that the U.S. government took very seriously for decades. Hynek worked for the government on the UFO problem for twenty-two years, from 1947 to 1969. Because of his carefulness, Hynek was often cast as a complete skeptic by the sensationalizing and frustrated media (the Michigan "swamp gas" case was the most oft-cited incident here[15]), but in fact Hynek, like Lieutenant General Twining, would become convinced of the reality of UFOs—a reality, however, that he was careful not to define in any naively objectivist fashion. Vallee worked closely, if unofficially, with Hynek on Project Blue Book for four years, between 1963 and 1967, and played a key role in changing Hynek's view of the problem. During this time, they became very close friends. The collaboration between the two men helped produce Vallee's first two books, *Anatomy of a Phenomenon* (1965) and *Challenge to Science* (1966), the latter which he co-wrote with his wife, Janine. Hynek published his own book, *The UFO Experience*, in 1972. This was the book that announced to the public his famous tripartite model of close encounters of the first, second, and third kinds. The two friends also co-wrote a later volume together, *The Edge of Reality* (1975).

Anatomy of a Phenomenon begins with a historical correction that is in some sense the key to Vallee's entire corpus on these aerial mysteries. When Vallee wrote his first book, it was commonly assumed that the language of "flying saucers" (and hence their sightings) began in the spring of 1947, with Arnold's famous story. Many people still assume this. Vallee begins his book in 1965 with a section entitled "As Old as Man Himself" in order to correct this false assumption. Here is the first sentence of his first book: "On January 24, 1878, John Martin, a Texas farmer who lived a few miles south of Denison, saw a dark, flying object in the shape of a disk cruising high in the sky 'at a wonderful speed,' and used the word 'saucer' to describe it."[16]

"The legend of the flying disks has existed throughout history," Vallee asserts.[17] A provocative chapter of ancient sightings from around the world follows to underline this point. Ezekiel's bizarre vision of all those fiery "wheels" (or "discs"?) that tradition has mistakenly, and rather bizarrely, called a "chariot," along with the prophet's subsequent "abduction" to the Tel Abib Mountains, make their standard appearances.[18] But so do numerous other, lesser-known, unidentified flying objects, including large flying shields, "cloud cigars," and various sorts of aerial armies and ghost ships. The sightings over Nuremburg (April 14, 1561) and Basel (August 7, 1566) are particularly impressive. They were so obvious and dramatic that popular drawings were made and preserved. Jung reproduced these drawings in his classic study *Flying Saucers: A Modern Myth of Things Seen in the Sky* (1958), a pioneering analysis that clearly influenced later French authors like Paul Misraki, Aimé Michel, and Vallee himself.

The Basel Broadsheet of 1566 clearly shows dozens of black and white round objects in the sky. The white objects seem to be flying directly out of the sun, not unlike what happened at Fátima in 1917. The Nuremberg Broadsheet of 1561 shows a number of classic UFO shapes, including the spear, the cross, the circle, a kind of crescent-wing, and a weird tube form from which circular objects are popping out in great numbers, as if from some toy ping-pong gun. Some of the circular objects appear to be attacking a town in the lower right corner. Smoke arises ominously from this corner scene. Much later in the book, Vallee will treat the classic and most dramatic example of a flying saucer before the flying saucer: the case of Fátima again (FS 1:160–64).

Vallee points out that space travel has only very recently become a technological possibility, hence the earlier accounts were not interpreted, and could *not* have been interpreted, as ships from outer space.[19] What I have called the alien hermeneutic, then, is a very new interpretive possibility, dependent on the imaginative universe of modern science fiction, modern cosmology, and the advanced technology of our space programs. Through the latter, we now have a way of "reading back," which can all too easily become a kind of "believing back" or "projecting back." Vallee, as we shall see, is very astute here, striking a balance that acknowledges the privileged position from which we can now see the past, even as he cautions us against naive backward projections from a literalizing and historically naive sci-fi imagination.

At this point in his career, Vallee was clearly open to the widely held belief that UFOs were evidence of extraterrestrial civilizations attempting contact or, more darkly, reconnaissance. This, of course, was exactly what Charles Fort had argued in his own language of galactic super-constructions. This was also the U.S. government's initial concern (after they had ruled out Soviet technology) when they initiated their own secret studies in the late 1940s. Vallee treats the major available theories of contact, including Paul Misraki's theory of extraterrestrial intervention in the history of religions, in chapter 7.

It is, however, the modern scientific version of potential alien-human contact that captures his real attention here.[20] Vallee attributes the first truly scientific expression of the theory to Dr. J. E. Lipp, who had written a classified report in 1949 on the subject for the air force's Project Sign.[21] Chapter 2 reflects Dr. Lipp's government-classified theory, bearing a title that could have come straight out of a *Fantastic Four* comic book or *Star Trek* episode: "Probability of Contact with Superior Galactic Communities." Basically, Lipp had concluded that visits from Mars, the usual science-fiction scenario, was unlikely at best, since civilization there would probably be no more significantly advanced than it is here. We, after all, share the same star. Visits from other solar systems within our galaxy were more likely, he thought. The vast interstellar distances traveled in such a scenario would remain a constant problem, however, as would the second-rate nature of our galactic neighborhood: "A super-race (unless they occur frequently) would not be likely to stumble over Planet III of Sol, a fifth-magnitude star in the rarefied outskirts of the Galaxy," Lipp cleverly wrote.[22] Vallee picks up on that parenthetical "unless" and does the math. He comes up with eight billion inhabitable planetary systems in our galaxy alone.

Vallee also develops a classification scheme for organizing UFO sightings in this first of his books. We learn from his journals that Vallee began developing this typology back in France as a kind of secret telephone code, so that he and his colleagues could speak openly with each other on the phone about UFO landings, free from worry that their rationalist colleagues would overhear and report them (FS 1:64). There were five types of UFOs in the published system of 1965: (1) those perceived on the ground or near the ground; (2) those that appear as large cylinders surrounded by cloud formations, often oriented vertically (the classic "cloud cigar"[23]); (3) aerial forms hovering in the sky or flying in an interrupted path, usually associated with some ground target or site; (4) aerial forms flying straight through the sky with no such flight patterns; and (5) those that appear as distant lights.[24]

Vallee would continue to develop and change his typologies, but his efforts would eventually be superseded by the classification model Hynek developed for the Center for UFO Studies (CUFO), which he then published in his *The UFO Experience* (1972). This system would be made world famous through Spielberg's adoption of it in his movie title *Close Encounters of the Third Kind* (Hynek was a consultant for Spielberg and makes a close-up cameo appearance in the final landing scene). There were three kinds of close encounter (CE) for Hynek: close encounters between human and alien of the first kind (CE1), in which there is visual contact but no interaction is experienced; close encounters of the second kind (CE2), in which there is interaction but of an abstract kind (for example, car ignition failure or radiation burns, as portrayed early in the Spielberg movie); and close encounters of the third kind (CE3), in which aliens or humanoids are clearly seen. Hynek was never comfortable with what would become the category of close encounters of the fourth kind (CE4), as in an abduction or onboard experience, which is how Spielberg's movie really ends, at the base of Devil's Tower in Wyoming—the new mountain of revelation. As for his part, Vallee would not only accept the necessity of this fourth category as a phenomenological descriptor; he would also add a fifth, that is, close encounters of the fifth kind (CE5), in which humans are physically harmed (or, ironically, healed) in some lasting way by the encounter.[25]

Space prevents me (forgive the pun) from treating the rest of *Anatomy of a Phenomenon* or its quick sequel, *Challenge to Science*, which picks up on the cultural histories, statistical analyses, and scientific reflections of the first book to advance the thesis of extraterrestrial contact further still and to develop a new typology. It is worth noting here, though, that this second book features a symbolically significant foreword by J. Allen Hynek. In it, Hynek writes of looking for the "signal" in all the "noise" of the UFO accounts and compares this detection work to Madame Curie searching through tons of pitchblende in order to isolate a tiny amount of radium, even a bit of which, of course, changed the world's conception of matter forever. Hynek remains open to whether their own signal in the noise is of a physical or psychological nature, "or even a heretofore unknown phenomenon" (as we have already seen, this *tertium quid* or "thought of the third" occurs throughout the literature of the impossible). But he had concluded that there is indeed radium in the pitchblende and that "it is in every respect a challenge to science."[26] *Challenge to Science* picks up on such opening thoughts to, well . . . challenge science. Vallee's general methodology and intellectual orientation, however, remained largely scientific. It was essentially science challenging science, though. This would soon change.

The Vallees moved backed to France in the fall of 1967 and settled in Saint-Germain. There Jacques quickly became disillusioned with his own little bourgeois dreams. He began to feel as if he were running away from his vision and vocation: "In which time, on which scale do I want to live? Back in the United States, Saturn rockets are climbing straight up in the sky. And here I am, wondering if I will ever own a little cottage of my own someday" (FS 1:331). He also realized that there was a real mental and cultural gap between the French and the Americans, and that the future with which he identified was being lived in America, not in France (FS 1:336).

The Vallees would soon move back to the States, first to New Jersey in November of 1968, and then, in December of 1969, to that "secret California where everything is crashing through the old barriers" (FS 1:283). But not before Vallee had had something of a revelation within the occult bookstores of Paris and the old French and Latin documents of the Bibliothéque Nationale. He bought boxes of rare esoteric books and added them to his UFO library. He encountered the books of Charles Fort for the first time. In the summer of 1968, he visited Scotland, the country of the Little People and the Good Neighbors, as he liked to call the land after its local legends. He had begun applying for a passport, not yet back to the States, but to a truly impossible place called Magonia.

Passport to Magonia: From Folklore to Flying Saucers (1969)

It was neither *Anatomy of a Phenomenon* nor *Challenge to Science* that came to represent the deeper worldview of Jacques Vallee. It was *Passport to Magonia*. This third book represented a major shift in Vallee's thinking about UFOs, and it is in many ways the most important in his corpus. It is certainly the most iconic. As the book's subtitle—*From Folklore to Flying Saucers*—suggests, Vallee effectively argues in these pages that the modern flying saucer cannot be understood without taking into account the striking parallels that exist between the bizarre behavior of contemporary UFOs and the earlier appearances of various occult beings in the history of folklore, magic, witchcraft, and religion: angels, demons, elves, fairies, sylphs, Little People, leprechauns, elementals, succubae and incubi—that sort of thing. This basic parallelism between traditional folklore and the UFO phenomenon, which he would soon enrich and radicalize further in his next book with what he calls "the psychical component," is Vallee's grandest comparison and signal contribution to the subject.

Such a folklore approach was not entirely new. As Thomas E. Bullard points out, the attempt to relate ancient mythology and UFOs goes back to the origins of the ufological literature, which was rife with interpretation of things like the Hindu *vimanas* or mythical sky "vehicles" representing ancient spaceships. There are many forms of this "ancient astronaut" thesis, some of them perfectly outrageous, some of them oddly suggestive, if never quite entirely persuasive.

Even an elite figure like Carl Sagan could speculate very seriously about a "central Galactic information repository," with advanced civilizations employing starships in order to explore the Milky Way and monitor the evolution of life and culture within different solar systems. He calculated how often each technical civilization might be visited by another in such a scenario: about once every thousand years. He imagined "colonies of colonies of colonies," and he deftly used the mythical memories of contact with European colonizers from North America and sub-Sahara Africa in order to suggest that other "contact myths" may encode ancient encounters with galactic astrononauts, who "would probably be portrayed as having god-like characteristics and possessing supernatural powers." After teasing his readers with an utterly bizarre ancient fresco from central Sahara depicting, in the words of a French archaeologist, "the great Martian god" (just a human in ritual mask and costume, we are reassured), Sagan zeroes in on a series of Sumerian myths as particularly suggestive of extraterrestrial contact. "Sumerian civilization is depicted by the descendents of the Sumerians themselves to be of non-human origin," he writes. "A succession of strange creatures appears over the course of several generations. Their only apparent purpose is to instruct mankind. Each knows of the mission and accomplishments of his predecessors. When a great inundation threatens the survival of the newly introduced knowledge among men, steps are taken to insure its preservation." As for the gods themselves, they are associated with individual stars, the cuneiform symbols for *god* and *star* being identical.

"Such a picture is not altogether different from what we might expect if a network of confederated civilizations interlaced the Galaxy," Sagan concludes, noting, of course, the hypothetical nature of his thought experiment. Then he immediately speculates about a possible interstellar base on the far side of the moon and suggests one possible reason for intervening in another planet's evolution: "to head off a nuclear annihilation." These, of course, are all standard tropes in the ufological literature, not to mention science fiction, which Sagan also approvingly cites, this time in the person of Arthur C. Clarke.[27]

But Bullard recognizes that Vallee is doing something different here: in his terms now, Vallee's "message was actually subversive of this standard view and the beginning of a new perspective on UFOs, one that diminished them from the answer for all mysteries to just one offshoot of a large mystery encompassing religion, mythology, folklore, and paranormal experience."[28] This is exactly right. Vallee has shared with me that when he wrote *Passport*, he thought of himself as following in the footsteps of Charles Fort. "Let's face it, he was right." Vallee, though, was especially interested in what Fort missed, how his method could be developed and advanced further.

He was also deeply influenced here by his training in advanced mathematics and his awareness that mathematical theorists commonly think about the impossible. Mathematical theory, Vallee explained to me, often has to confront the fact that two contradictory theories can explain the same data. A solution is inevitably found not by choosing one of the contradictory theories, but by going to the next, third level. Similarly, he remains convinced that the UFO phenomenon will never be solved by the believers or the rationalists. More or less exactly like Fort, he thinks that we have to reject the dogmatisms of both religion and science and confront the phenomenon *on its own terms* (in the study of religion, we would say that the phenomenon is *sui generis*, that is, "of its own genus" or "its own thing"). We cannot begin by assuming what UFOs are. We cannot begin by assuming that they can be reduced to normal physics or normal psychology. Obviously, they cannot be. They are their own thing.

Much like Myers and Fort before him, Vallee's is also a strong comparative method. He works with both hard and soft data—metal and chemical physical traces, photographs, spatial and temporal coordinates, medical reports, police investigations, and richly complex first-person narratives of sightings and abductions. He insists that the enigma of the UFO cannot be understood by restricting the data to, say, American cases, or European cases, or, for that matter—and this constitutes his real originality—to the second half of the twentieth century. Only a wide sweep through space and time can provide the broad comparative perspective necessary to decipher the mystery.

He thus sees his task as one of collection, classification, comparison, and, finally, theorization. The latter, moreover, must always remain open and tentative and, in the end, perhaps even literally impossible, for, as his friend and colleague Aimé Michel used to insist, a full theory may well be completely beyond the reach of the human brain with its present cognitive and sensory capacities. The reader might recall that Vallee had once debated with the older master on this very point in his first youthful letter. He appears to be coming around to his old friend's position now. He thus ended his most recent essay, in 2007, with the following lines from William Irwin Thompson:

> We are like flies crawling across the ceiling of the Sistine Chapel: We cannot see what angels and gods lie underneath the threshold of our perceptions. We do not live in reality; we live in our paradigms, our habituated perceptions, our illusions; the illusions we share through culture we call reality, but the true historical reality of our condition is invisible to us.[29]

There is a double edge to such a line of thinking. One edge suggests that, as flies, we can never really know the meaning of the visions across which we crawl so ignorantly. The other suggests that, if we could fly back a bit and obtain a true historical consciousness, this might constitute a true gnosis, that is, an effective deliverance from culture and consciousness as they presently co-create (and co-constrict) themselves. We could see how consciousness and culture interact to create our experience of reality, which is never complete or entirely trustworthy. A truly radical historicism, that is, a knowledge of "the true historical reality of our condition," would thus become *an awakening*.

Vallee suggests that flying saucers and folklore have something very important to teach us here. The lesson is not an easy one, however. For although UFOs are still quite real for Vallee in *Passport to Magonia*, they are no longer probably extraterrestrial, and they are almost certainly not literally true. They are not what they appear to be. Often, in fact, the stories, which really happened, are really absurd. Deception and absurdity, Vallee insists now with a growing conviction, are part of what the phenomenon is communicating, what it intends to teach us about the nature of our world. They are *designed* or even *staged* to confuse us, to baffle us, to shock us into another level of consciousness and culture, rather like the mystical paradoxes of Zen Buddhism and Jewish Kabbalah, Vallee suggests in an especially insightful aside (IC 27). Hence those humorous, nonsensical, but vaguely profound statements made by the occupants of the American "airship" wave of 1897, widely reported in the newspapers across the country. Here is one: "We are from Kansas." Here is another: "We are from

ANYWHERE, but we'll be in Cuba tomorrow" (IC 29). A technological koan in the sky. A metaphysical joke.

This is a different man writing in 1969, or perhaps it is the same man allowing himself to write now in a very different way. The statistics, databases, and scientific methodology of the two first books now float into the background, and a distinct and quite beautiful lyricism enters the text.[30] This is how Jacques Vallee became an author of the impossible. This is how he opens and so offers to us a *Passport to Magonia*:

> This book is an attempt to build a bridge—a tenuous and fragile one—between a fancy and a myth. It is not a scientific book. It could be called a philosophical book, if there were a philosophy of nonfacts. It is not a documentary, unless the dreams of children at play and the cries of women burned alive can be documented. Yet many lives have changed (secretly, unnoticeably sometimes), and, indeed, many innocents have been burned alive because of that fancy. This book is a tribute to all the people who dared preserve a dream. (PM vii)

Vallee intends to preserve that dream too. He also intends to extend, interpret, and theorize it, to perfect or realize it.

Central to this theorization that is also a realization is one core theme that he finds in his comparative data: "visitation by an aerial people from one or more remote, legendary countries" (PM viii). There are many names for what Fort had called his "New Lands," but Vallee rhetorically and mythically privileges one of them: Magonia. Vallee adopts the name from one of his medieval countrymen in France, Archbishop Agobard of Lyons (779–840).[31] When he died, Agobard left an account of how he saved four people from being stoned by the locals when they, or so the locals believed, fell from such a place in the sky. Since the myth of Magonia is central to Vallee's literary imagination, the original ninth-century text, *De Grandine et Tonitruis*, is worth citing precisely as Vallee cites it. Archbishop Agobard relates the event in a skeptical, somewhat disgusted mood:

> We have, however, seen and heard many men plunged in such great stupidity, sunk in such depths of folly, as to believe that there is a certain region, which they call Magonia, whence ships sail in the clouds, in order to carry back to that region those fruits of the earth which are destroyed by hail and tempests; the sailors paying rewards to the storm wizards and themselves receiving corn and other produce. Out of the number of those whose blind folly was deep enough to allow them to believe these things possible, I saw several exhibiting in a certain concourse of people, four persons in bonds—three men and a woman who

> they said had fallen from these same ships; after keeping them for some days in captivity they had brought them before the assembled multitude, as we have said, in our presence to be stoned. But truth prevailed.[32]

Sort of. Not everyone agreed with the archbishop's assessment of Magonia, including the later alchemists and the hermeticists, men whom Vallee praises as "remarkable for the strength of their independent thinking," who belonged to "a major current of thought distinct from official religion" (PM 10). One such independent thinker appears in the occult novel and Rosicrucian classic named after this same central character, *Le Comte de Gabalis* (probably written by Abbé Montfaucon de Vilars). The count saw the former events of Magonia quite differently than the archbishop.

> In vain the four innocents sought to vindicate themselves by saying that they were their own country-folk, and had been carried away a short time since by miraculous men [*hommes miraculeux*] who had shown them unheard-of marvels, and had desired to give them an account of what they had seen. The frenzied populace paid no heed to their defence, and were on the point of casting them into the fire, when the worthy Agobard, Bishop of Lyons, . . . came running at the noise, and having heard the accusations of the people and the defence of the accused, gravely pronounced that both one and the other were false. That it was not true that these men had fallen from the sky and that what they said they had seen there was impossible. . . . Thus the testimony of these four witnesses was rendered vain.[33]

Basically, what we have here is a ninth-century version of the modern alien abduction account, complete with a subsequent official denial by the major authority of the time, the church, and a later esoteric revisioning that worked to deny the ecclesial denial. Where Agobard saw religious impossibility and folk ignorance, Le Comte de Gabalis saw evidence of a real experience. Putting aside for a moment the historical truth of these events, which will forever elude us, it is easy to see Vallee's comparative point: the basic narrative of an aerial people visiting (or abducting) humanity is a very old and stable one. It is not a twentieth-century invention, although it now speaks our language. We have indeed morphed "from folklore to flying saucers."

Vallee proceeds to demonstrate this basic comparative point through numerous themes. First and foremost among these are the similarities he noticed with the help of some unpublished notes of Evans-Wentz (an American folklorist specializing in the popular mystical traditions of

Tibet and Scotland) between the fairy-faith of Celtic lore and contemporary ufology.[34] "The recognition of a parallel between UFO reports and the main themes of fairy-lore is the first indication I have found that a way might exist out of this dilemma [of the UFO phenomenon]," Vallee explains (PM 111).

Vallee's method here is quite interesting. He begins with the hypothesis that *the absurd is meaningful*, that the dilemma signals new thought, that we should be looking for the cracks or glitches in the stories in order to begin divining their latent messages. Much like dreams, UFO accounts do not mean what they seem to mean. They point to something else, or to somewhere and somewhen else. They often have the quality of dreams, but they are also physical events. They look a lot like physical dreams. In my own terms, they are hermeneutical events, meaning events that share in both the mythical and the physical.

Hence Vallee hones in on some of the most bizarre features of contemporary UFO reports—like Joe Simonton being fed crispy pancakes on board a spaceship, with the pancakes as souvenirs to prove it no less—in order to highlight the inadequacy of a purely technological interpretation. Fairies too, after all, fed their guests (PM 25). They also abducted human beings for reproductive reasons, much as aliens are said to abduct human beings today for genetic ones (PM 105). Similarly, the manner in which UFOs are said to create circular landing patterns or "UFO nests," as they are called, reminds Vallee of the fairy-rings and magic circles of Celtic lore (PM 32–38). Precognitive dreams announcing an alien encounter also function in both mythologies in very similar ways.[35] Vallee concludes: "It would be nice to hold on to the common belief that the UFO's are craft from a superior space-civilization, because this is a hypothesis that science fiction has made widely acceptable" (PM 56). But this cannot be a complete answer. Why? Because the theory looks too much like a belief. It looks too much like the Celtic faith in fairies, or the medieval belief in lutins, or the Christian belief in demons, satyrs, and fauns. Or whatever. Put simply, Vallee locates the UFO phenomenon squarely in the history of religions, where the human witness "is the only tangible vehicle of the story" (PM 44).

Which is not to say that Vallee interprets the modern encounters strictly in traditional religious terms. Such an alien hermeneutic, after all, works *both* ways. That is, the traditional religious accounts can be read in "alien" ways just as easily as the modern alien accounts can be read in traditionally "religious" ways. The point is not to reduce one "false" register to the other "true" one. It is to confuse and destabilize *both* registers. Put more radically, the point is not to adopt this or that symbolic system as somehow literally true. The point is to be simultaneously sympathetic to and suspicious of *all* symbolic systems, and then finally to entertain the impossible possibility that the controlling intelligence communicating with us through all these systems is a human one, that is, a form of human consciousness far beyond our present, hopelessly materialistic and restrictive notions. We are not who we seem to be. We are alien to ourselves (PM 57). We are, quite literally, *fantastic*.

Vallee also wishes to make a historian's point, namely, that we have a very unique opportunity before us, an opportunity to observe and study folklore in the making. Note again Vallee's extraordinary synthesis of material and mythical realities:

> When the phone rings in Wright-Paterson Air Force Base, and a local intelligence officer transmits the observation of a motorist who has just been "buzzed" by what he describes as a flying saucer, we are really witnessing the unique conjunction of the modern world—with its technology—and ancient terrors—with all the power of their sudden, fugitive, irrational nature. We are in a very privileged position. . . . We feel . . . that we can almost reach out into the night and grab those lurking entities. We are hot on their trail; the air is still vibrating with excitement, the smell of sulphur is still there when the story is recorded. (PM 78)

Sulphur indeed. We read, for example, of a "parallel universe" called Elfland where time operates in an Einsteinian fashion *way* before Einstein. And we meet a sylph who teaches a Renaissance scholar named Facius Cardan truths about the material nature of existence (as continuously created in every moment) that would fit nicely into a modern textbook on quantum physics, but "which antedates quantum theory by four centuries" (PM 101–2, 105–6, 163). Some of these are glitches, more damned facts, as Fort would say. Some of them, if true, seem more like huge rips in the fabric of our reality. This is how Vallee writes anyway. Impossibly.

And then there is the subject of the sexual. Thankfully, Vallee is a self-described "passionate man" who does not feel the usual American puritanical squeamishness about the subject (FS 1:101). Quite the contrary. "Thought and sex are the only human activities which are not totally ridiculous," he wrote in the spring of 1959 (FS 1:31). He continued to write openly, gently, humorously about such intellectual-sexual connections. And to collect books. His library includes an entire section dedicated to the history of erotic mysticism and sexual magic, with everything from Aleister Crowley and Tantra to Wonder Woman. When I asked him about this particular collection, he explained to me that he understands the history of sexual magic through the esoteric categories of alchemy, that is, he understands the energies of the body to be mutable and, when alchemically transformed through technique or accident, as capable of granting access to different levels of consciousness.

It is also worth noting in this context that Vallee's beloved wife, Janine, appears in his journals, always beautifully and graciously. "Since September," he writes on 22 February 1961, "I have been working on a new science-fiction novel entitled *Dark Satellite*. I am writing very fast, swept along by passion and Janine's kisses" (FS 1:41). Janine's presence would grow more and more central to his writing. She read all of his manuscripts—every line, every word. She was his constant critic and "guardian angel," the skeptic he could always trust. It was Janine who prevented Jacques from ever getting too involved in ufology, "from ever slipping into a belief system," as he put it to me.

Such personal details are also emblematic to the extent that they demonstrate a real appreciation for the demonstrable erotics of human life in all its multiple dimensions. It comes as no surprise, then, when Vallee insists that the sexual component is central to the alien narratives, and that it points again to the history of folklore and religion, this time to the folklore of witchcraft and sexual magic. Succubae enticing medieval mystics, fairy-women seducing men into a kind of parallel universe, and the witch's magical intercourse with the Devil or demons—these are all encountered again in the dramatic sexual episodes of the modern UFO encounters (PM 116–25). Vallee features what is probably the most famous case of such alien sexual encounters: the Brazilian episode of Antonio Villas-Boas, first reported in English in 1965 in three separate issues of *Flying Saucer Review*.[36]

On October 5, 1957, twenty-three-year-old Antonio Villas-Boas witnessed a powerful searchlight sweep the family corral in São Francisco de Salles, Minas Gerais. Ten nights later at about 1:00 a.m., as Antonio worked his night shift, what looked like a red star descended, floated above his International tractor, and landed. Four short, suited, and helmeted humanoids seized Antonio and took him aboard a ship, where, now joined by a fifth, they stripped him, washed his body with some sort of strange liquid gel (perhaps an antiseptic or an aphrodisiac), drew some blood from his chin, and left him in a room to wait . . . for a short, gorgeous woman, it turns out. She walked in stark naked, with large oblong blue eyes ("like the slit eyes of those girls who make themselves up fancifully to look like Arabian princesses"[37]) and blondish-white hair, thin lips, a pointed chin, and a grunting sexual aggressiveness.

After Antonio became aroused and the woman had had her way with him ("That was what they wanted of me—a good stallion to improve their stock"[38]), another male humanoid came in. The woman gestured to her stomach, then to Antonio, smiled, pointed to the heavens, and left with the man. A series of events then followed, including a failed attempt on Antonio's part to steal a dial of some sort, after which Antonio was ushered out before the machine zipped off, like a bullet, toward the south. It was 5:30 a.m. He had spent four hours and fifteen minutes on board. Antonio later drew the ship in some detail, including an abstract script above the door. He also developed symptoms that suggested radiation poisoning.

The case of Barney and Betty Hill, a mixed-race couple from Portsmouth, New Hampshire, is equally bizarre and equally important, as theirs is the first fully documented abduction account in the literature. John G. Fuller's *The Interrupted Journey*, which recounts the case in careful detail based on the hypnosis treatment of Dr. Benjamin Simon, is an undisputed classic in UFO studies.[39] The event was not as sexualized as the Villas-Boas case, but it did involve classical (and absurdly primitive) surgical procedures that appear to carry reproductive connotations.

Arriving home from a vacation in Canada in the early morning of September 20, 1961, the couple could not account for two hours they seemed to have "lost" on the ride home. When Betty told her sister details about an encounter with a huge flying structure that tracked them and that Barney saw quite clearly through his binoculars, Betty's sister suggested that Betty test her car with a compass for possible (electromagnetic?) radiation. The compass went wild near strange circular marks on the trunk. The couple notified Pease Air Force Base, and Betty wrote NICAP (National Investigations Committee on Aerial Phenomena), one of the primary organizations dedicated to studying such events at this time. They could not sleep over the next few weeks and months, and they were suffering from nightmares.

Put under hypnosis by Dr. Simon in 1964, a story began to emerge. They had encountered a UFO in the White Mountains of New Hampshire on Highway 3. It followed them, buzzed them, and then blocked their way with a landing. Short, gray-skinned men abducted them and took them aboard their spaceship against their will. They communicated with each other in a language completely foreign to the Hills, but when they spoke to the Hills, it was in English, with an accent: "I did not hear an actual voice," Barney explained. "But in my mind, I knew what he was saying. . . . It was more as if the words were there, a part of me, and he was outside the actual creation of the words themselves" (PM 94). Barney recalled them putting some kind of cup over his groin. Betty remembered watching in horror as alien creatures inserted large needles into her abdomen, as part of a pregnancy test, she was led to believe. Barney recalls noticing huge slanted eyes that extended to the side of their heads: "Oh, his eyes were slanted! But not like a Chinese—Oh, Oh." Think: Spider-Man.

It would be quite easy, of course, to read all of this as some kind of simple shared hallucination, the result of too much driving on a mesmerizing dark highway in the middle of the night later called up and constructed by hypnosis. It would be easy, but wrong. Vallee's unique access to the air force records (Report No. 100-1-61, in the files of the 100th Bomb Wing, Strategic Air Command, Pease Air Force Base, New Hampshire, prepared by Major Paul W. Henderson, to be militarily precise) gave him a crucial piece of information of which Fuller, Simon, and the Hills were completely unaware, namely, that the object seen by the Hills and at the core of their hypnotic, dreamlike tale was picked up by military radar (PM 90). Once again, the paranormal turns out to possess physical characteristics, in this case both magnetic (the compass scene) and radar effects. It acts like a material myth, a physical dream. It behaves like a folktale, but it also shows up on a military radar screen and appears in an air force file. Not your typical religious experience.

Vallee's conclusion about the sexual component of such incredible stories is something of an ironic understatement: "For Villas-Boas or Betty and Barney Hill would certainly have had a hard time before the Inquisitors if they had lived in the seventeenth century" (PM 124). We are back to the opening lines of the book, where the cries of women burned alive are promised to be preserved and defended. I would add another observation. Since Gordon Creighton believed that Villas-Boas was a Caboclo (a person of mixed Portuguese-Amerindian blood) and Betty and Barney were a mixed-race couple, what we are confronted with here is the historical fact that the two earliest full-scale abduction reports involved an explicit theme of hybridity—a hybridity, moreover, acted out on both the human *and* the alien-human levels—"an act of procreation between beings of different worlds," as Creighton puts it with respect to the first case.[40]

But what does it all mean for Vallee? *Passport to Magonia* concludes with a flurry of bold speculations and seemingly rejected hypotheses. Vallee is certain of only one thing now, namely, that science is not up to the task of explaining the UFO phenomenon. The latter, he believes, cannot be studied by itself. It is rather "an instance of a deeper problem," which is to say that it is a paranormal problem (PM 157). So how to proceed?

Science-fiction readers, Vallee points out, already have a working hypothesis at hand. It goes like this:

> There exists a natural phenomenon whose manifestations border on both the physical and the mental. There is a medium in which human dreams can be implemented, and this is the mechanism by which UFO events are generated, needing no superior intelligence to trigger them. This would explain the fugitivity of UFO manifestations, the alleged contact with friendly occupants, and the fact that the objects appear to keep pace with human technology and to use current symbols. . . . It also, naturally, explains the totality of religious miracles as well as ghosts and other so-called supernatural phenomena.

Unfortunately, such a theory cannot explain the physical traces, the very real chemical, radioactive, magnetic, and medical effects of the hard data in the files. A more Fortean speculation follows: "We could also imagine that for centuries some superior intelligence has been projecting into our environment . . . various artificial objects whose creation is a pure form of art" (PM 159–60).

Vallee rejects such speculations as scientifically groundless, but one suspects—I do anyway—that he is more drawn to this kind of impossible science-fiction thinking than he will allow himself to admit in print here. Vallee, after all, had already won the prestigious Jules Verne Prize in 1961, at the age of twenty-one, no less, for his first science-fiction novel, *Sub-Space*, and he would go on to publish four more science-fiction novels, the last in English, *Fastwalker*.[41] The Jules Verne medal is now proudly displayed among his books, significantly in the section on parapsychology and paranormal studies. These hidden streams of influence flowing between the occult, the UFO phenomenon, and the literary art of science fiction run very deep indeed throughout the twentieth century. And this is before we even get to the various subcultures of American space technology, which I cannot treat here but which are well worth flagging.[42]

Not yet ready in 1969 for a fully public science-fiction thesis, Vallee offers instead three final propositions, which are hardly any less bold, namely: (1) that the behavior of a superior intelligence, whether from the stars or from some other dimension of this planet, would not necessary appear sensible to our own cognitive and sensory capacities; (2) that the puzzle of time and, I assume, the possibility of time-travel, renders intergalactic or multiple-earth scenarios more, not less, likely; and (3) the subject of UFOs as a whole suggests "a myth that could be utilized to serve political or sociological purposes" (PM 162). Time travel aside for a moment, it is the last proposition that is in many ways the most radical. With the social-control thesis, Vallee suggests that the UFO encounters have every mark of feeling staged. It looks as if we are being duped. Vallee does not claim to know whether such a cosmic hoax is being perpetrated by an alien race from another planet, or by our own race from a distant time in the future or from another dimension right now. But he is willing to ask the question, which is saying quite a bit.

The Invisible College (1975)

The Invisible College (1975) represents a development of the ideas and theories first set out six years earlier in *Passport to Magonia*. There would be other developments and ideas, of course, but it is probably not too much of an exaggeration to suggest that these two books constitute the heart and soul of Vallee's thinking on the subject of UFOs. That the first is named after a legendary land in the clouds whose existence was denied by a major representative of the church and the second after a group of contemporary intellectuals interested in paranormal matters who were meeting secretly in the late 1960s and '70s out of fear that such interests would threaten their academic and professional standing in the universities should alert us to the "impossible" nature of their subject matter from the perspectives of faith *or* reason. Vallee is perfectly aware of this. He states very clearly that his speculations "will contradict both the ideas of the believers and the assumptions of the skeptics" (IC 28). Again, beyond faith and reason there is gnosis.

It was Hynek who suggested that they call themselves "the Invisible College" in order to capture the deeply felt sense that they were pursuing a kind of forbidden knowledge, that they were after a new form of science that was not yet acceptable to the powers that be.[43] The same year Vallee's book appeared Hynek explained the history of the expression in, of all places, the *FBI Bulletin*. The FBI had requested the piece, why, Hynek was never sure (FS 2:251). Vallee provides his readers with the relevant passage in his own introduction. Here is Hynek writing for the FBI now, as quoted by Vallee at the beginning of *The Invisible College*:

> Way back in the "dark ages" of science, when scientists themselves were suspected of being in league with the Devil, they had to work privately. They often met clandestinely to exchange views and the results of their various experiments. For this reason, they called themselves the Invisible College. And it remained invisible until the scientists of that day gained respectability when the Royal Society was chartered by Charles II in the early 1660's.[44]

And so Hynek, Vallee, and their confidential colleagues met too, throughout the late 1960s and early '70s, working quietly in the background and refusing to be intimidated by either the conservative attitudes of their professional colleagues or "those three fierce paper dragons, Bizarre, Magic, and Ridicule" (IC 114–15). They also hoped for their own Charles II, who never appeared, and for their own Royal Society, which never materialized.

It is not difficult to see why. The group's basic theory as publicly explained by Vallee is a difficult truth for most people to swallow. No, I take that back: it's an impossible one. What he was arguing, after all, is that UFO appearances may be part of a huge "control system," a kind of mythological thermostat on the planet designed to adjust and control the belief systems of entire cultures over immense expanses of time.[45] As he described it in his journals, this control system "acts upon human consciousness, preventing it from going beyond certain limits" (FS 2:454). Vallee seems to have in mind a kind of cosmic Puppet Master, a "manufacturer of unavoidable events," as he puts it in one of his short stories, who pulls the strings of history from above and prevents us from developing our own psychic potentials.[46] The religious doctrines and mythologies of the human imagination are the main object of control and adjustment here. Put crudely, we are being manipulated by our own belief systems, which are in turn being implanted, influenced, and guided by "alien" forces well outside our conscious selves.

The precise nature of this "outside" is debatable, and Vallee never stops suggesting that that outside may still be a human one, that is, I gather, that we are all part of some immense form of Mind or Cosmic Consciousness that is playing tricks on itself. This, of course, is basically what Fort suggested with his playful suggestion that he himself was an inconsistency, or a consistency-inconsistency, in the mind of some super-imagination. Either way, the implications would be disturbing for the reasonable or the believable. It is not an easy thing to entertain the possibility that one's deepest-held beliefs are mechanisms of control, that one is bound, defined, and restricted by one's own, largely unconscious, categories, that one is secretly a puppet or, to employ the more modern neuroscientific reductionism, that we are all biological robots programmed to believe that we are not robots.

Vallee, it turns out, had long felt part of an esoteric intellectual community. Originally, he seems to have understood this community as stretched out through time and available to him in books and old manuscripts. Later, he and Hynek decided to turn this historical textual community into a contemporary social one. Vallee then gave their esoteric community an exoteric form. He turned their private discussions into a public book. He never, though, lost his sense of the forbidden nature of what they were up to. He never lost, that is, his gnostic orientation to the world. In the foreword to the 1996 edition of his published diaries from the late 1950s and '60s, he is especially sensitive—and, in my opinion, especially correct—about how the subject of their Invisible College's study lay well outside—that is, *offended*—the acceptable academic categories of knowledge and possibility:

> This diary was written by a young scientist as he wandered into the minefield of the paranormal, a taboo subject among academics and a source of some fascinating questions: What should a small group of researchers do when they find themselves confronted with a phenomenon that does not follow the recognized laws of nature? How far should they go in alerting their colleagues and the public in the absence of definite proof? Can they really hope to influence an academic community that is notoriously enamored of the status quo and intimidated by political intrigue? (FS 1:1)

Toward this end, Vallee had offered five working theses in *The Invisible College*. First, he points out, humorously but accurately, that "unidentified flying objects are neither objects nor flying." They commonly materialize and dematerialize at will and often synchronize with the subjective states of those witnessing them (for example, they are sometimes "announced" precognitively in dreams), which eliminates the simplistic term "object" from any proper description. Moreover, they maneuver in ways that violate the most basic laws of possible flight patterns, which renders a term like "flying" equally suspect. Second, UFOs have been active throughout human history, always appearing and acting in the cultural terms of the place and time. This, of course, is essentially the thesis of *Passport to Magonia*. Third, the structure of space-time as we know it implies that the question "Where do they come from?" may be meaningless, and may be better asked as "*When* do they come from?" That is, UFOs may come from a place *in time*, in the future, no doubt, perhaps even our own future. Fourth, the key to the UFO phenomenon "lies in the psychic effects it produces (or the psychic awareness it makes possible) in its observers." Vallee writes here of lives deeply changed by encounters with UFOs and of "unusual talents" developing with which their possessors may find it very difficult to cope (a clear analogue of Myers's supernormal powers and Fort's wild talents).

Fifth and finally, Vallee sees meaning in the absurdity of the narratives, a meaning he will call the *metalogic* of the encounter stories. Such a metalogic, which appears as absurdity from the outside, more or less guarantees that the encounters will be rejected by the elite members of the target society (that is, by professional academics and scientists), even as the symbols conveyed through the encounters are absorbed at a very deep and much more lasting unconscious level. The absurdity of the extraterrestrial explanation, in other words, is a kind of intentional ruse or cloaking technique that allows the phenomenon to accomplish its real work, which is symbolic and mythological.

> Everything works, in my opinion, as if the phenomenon were the product of a *technology* that followed well-defined rules and patterns, though fantastic by ordinary human standards. The phenomenon has so far posed no apparent threat to national defense and seems to be indifferent to the welfare of individual witnesses. . . . But its impact in shaping man's long-term creativity and unconscious impulses is probably enormous. The fact that we have no methodology to deal with such an impact is only an indication of how little we know about our own psychic world. (IC 30)

"Our own psychic world." This is the central teaching of *The Invisible College*. By *psychic*, Vallee does not mean "psychological." He means "the interactions between consciousness and physical reality."[47] Thus if *Passport to Magonia* was about constructing "a picture of a different level of existence, a reality that seems to cut through our own at right angles . . . what I call the reality of Magonia" (IC 6) (recall Couliano's Flatland thought experiment with which we began these reflections), then *The Invisible College* is about exploring "the psychical component" that appears to be a common core result of human exposure to UFOs. This is the book's most important, and most daring, contribution. Vallee notes that it came only gradually to him, as the frequency and richness of the close-encounter cases became both overwhelming and inescapable. The amount of evidential data was just too great.[48]

It is not simply the psychical component, however. Vallee also intuits profound similarities between UFO abductions and "the initiation rituals of secret societies."[49] Moreover, he suggests a similar phenomenology at work in both UFO encounters and the modern out-of-body experience (OBE), particularly as the latter is mapped by the American businessman turned metaphysical writer Robert Monroe.[50] Monroe's books are especially provocative for their elaborate descriptions of out-of-body states, literally thousands of which Monroe experienced throughout his life. Vallee cites three descriptions from Monroe's notes, from the nights of

September 9, 16, and 30 of 1960, in order to gloss the meaning of the UFO encounters. Note both the fantastic nature and the disillusioning honesty of Monroe's descriptions:

> I suddenly felt bathed in and transfixed by a very powerful beam. . . . I was completely powerless, with no will of my own, and I felt as if I were in the presence of a very strong force, in personal contact with it. It had intelligence of a form beyond my comprehension and it came directly (down the beam?) into my head, and seemed to be searching every memory in my mind. I was truly frightened because I was powerless to do anything about this intrusion.
>
> The same impersonal probing, the same power, from the same angle. However, this time I received the firm impression that I was inextricably bound by loyalty to this intelligent force, always had been, and that I had a job to perform here on earth. . . .
>
> It is an impersonal, cold intelligence, with none of the emotions of love or compassion which we respect so much, yet this may be the omnipotence we call God. . . . I sat down and cried, great deep sobs as I have never cried before, because then I knew without any qualification or future hope of change that the God of my childhood, of the churches, of religion throughout the world was not as we worshipped him to be—that for the rest of my life, I would "suffer" the loss of this illusion.[51]

As a comparative point, Vallee then offers the story of the twenty-eight-year-old French legionnaire on duty in Algeria, who in March of 1958 saw an immense UFO (one thousand feet in diameter) descend within a few hundred feet of him and "zap" him with a beam of gorgeous, ecstatic, emerald light. He became depressed when it departed. He later recalled how in the presence of the object time seemed to run very slowly, as if he were in another world.

Though a real admirer of an author like C. G. Jung, Vallee seriously questions the usual psychologization of these experiences: "Are we faced here with something more than a projection of Jung's archetypal images, a psychic technology whose applications know few if any limitations in space and in time?" He can see no better way to explain the data and the clear "pattern of manifestations, opening the gates to a spiritual level, pointing a way to a different consciousness, and producing irrational, absurd events in their wake." This, he suggests, is a technology "capable of both physical manifestations and psychic effects, a technology that strikes deep at the collective unconscious, confusing us, molding us—as perhaps it confused and molded human civilizations at the end of antiquity" (IC 140).

He is quite serious about that word: *technology*. And he relates it to another: *physics*. A chapter dedicated largely to the Marian apparitions at Fátima, Lourdes, Knock, and Guadalupe follows in order to study what he calls, rather shockingly, "the physics of the B.V.M.," that is, the physics of the Blessed Virgin Mary. He arrives again at the same conclusion:

> We are faced with a *technology* that transcends the physical and is capable of manipulating our reality, generating a variety of altered states of consciousness and of emotional perceptions. . . . The B.V.M. may dress in golden robes and smile radiantly to children, but the technology which "she" uses is indistinguishable from that of gods and goddesses of other tongues and garb; it is also indistinguishable from the technology surrounding the UFO phenomenon. (IC 153–54)

A psychic technology. The physics of the Blessed Virgin Mary. A technology that transcends the physical and is capable of manipulating our own individual and collective realities. These are jarring phrases that strike at the very roots of the way we separate and divide our experience of the world into subjective appearances and objective realities, into "religion" and "science." There are three final points to make with respect to such phrases before we graduate from *The Invisible College*.

The first is to suggest a double whammy. What Vallee, after all, is most interested in here in his fourth book on UFOs is building a bridge between the UFO data and the evidence that has been amassed for psychical phenomena over the last two centuries, beginning, as we have seen, with Myers and the S.P.R. This is a truly incredible proposal, as either subject alone is sufficiently outrageous to merit complete exclusion from the boundaries of intellectual respectability. Vallee happily ignores such exclusions and treats the two damned fields *together*, essentially doubling (if not squaring) the provocations of his thought.

The second point to make is that the psychic technology Vallee imagines depends on the manipulation of *time* as well as space.[52] What I read him reading in the history of folklore is a *future* technology projected, somehow, back into our present. Such a hypothesis—which is a common trope in science fiction, not to mention well within the imagination, if not the present technology, of contemporary physics—implies that these need not be space aliens from another planet. They may well be human beings from another time, from the future. They may be *us*. The future technology of folklore that Vallee is imagining here, in other words, is a technology that we may be using on ourselves to manipulate our own past, to control, as it were, our belief systems and mythologies that lie well below the present political system or cultural fad of the day.

It is precisely these religious systems that control our history for Vallee, hence his privileging of Jung in the concluding third part of *Fastwalker*: "It is not starvation, not microbes, not cancer," Jung writes and Vallee quotes now, "but man himself who is mankind's greatest danger; because he has no adequate protection against psychic epidemics, which are infinitely more devastating in their effect than the greatest natural catastrophes."[53] Hence, to employ an overused metaphor that is nevertheless quite apt here, mythologies and beliefs can be seen as the "operating systems" of that cognitive and behavioral software we call culture. What Vallee is imagining, then, is a kind of "re-writing of the computer code" from the future, before the viruses that determine us now can take over and crash the system for good.[54]

Third and finally, it is worth underlining the basic disillusionment, which is also an awakening, that appears with such poignancy in *The Invisible College*. Monroe had confessed his own disillusionment with respect to religion. Vallee now expresses his own with respect to science. Vallee once thought that science was enough, that it would eventually recognize the reality of paranormal phenomena and so generously and definitively expand our conception of what it means to be human. Essentially, he believed that science could and would rewrite our code. *The Invisible College* closes with the confession that he no longer possesses such a faith. Science cannot supply the key to our psychic crisis. How could it? Its strict commitment to a method that only recognizes objects prevents it from even admitting the presence of psychical phenomena, which are objects and subjects at the same time. How can a method that denies the very reality of the subject study the magical and mystical qualities of that subject? The answer: it cannot.

Nor, though, will we find our answer "in some secret file in Washington."[55] The solution to our psychic crisis, he suggests in the very last lines of the book, "lies where it has always been: *within ourselves*. We can reach it any time we want" (IC 209). Which is to say, once again, that the solution lies well outside the present parameters of the scientific method. It lies rather in the fundamental mystery of human consciousness, in the subject doing the science. It lies in us.

The Present Technology of Folklore: Computer Technology and Remote Viewing in the Psychic Underground

Vallee had very good reasons to end his book on a note suggestive of both government intelligence and the primacy of human consciousness, as the lived context in which he wrote *The Invisible College* was deeply informed by a small group of elite government-sponsored scientists interested in artificial intelligence, information theory, quantum biology, the mind-matter interface, and the physics of consciousness. Vallee interacted with these scientists at SRI, an independent research institute in Menlo Park that contracted with the U.S. military for various secret research programs. Vallee in fact worked for one SRI program, which was not secret at all, and became indirectly involved in another, which definitely was.

The first program was something called the Augmentation of the Human Intellect, for which Vallee worked for a little over one year, from February of 1972 to April of 1973. This project was erratically managed and frustrated him, but in its more interesting moments it also involved him in cutting-edge technology and government conferences that were a part of the early development of a global communication network sponsored by the Pentagon called the Arpanet.[56] The Arpanet would eventually morph into the Internet in the early 1990s, effectively changing the world of communications, and just about everything else, in the process.

The same project also put him in touch with individuals who worked for the intelligence community, including the NSA (National Security Agency), whose initials were jokingly said to stand for "Never Say Anything" or "No Such Agency" (FS 2:160). Vallee quickly grew disillusioned with such people once he realized how little they actually knew about paranormal subjects and how impossible it was to ever really know who was telling the truth. It all struck him as a very silly and childish game. Hence the negative conclusion of *The Invisible College* concerning those "secret files in Washington." He had had quite enough of all that.

The second SRI program, housed one floor down from the first in the Electronics and Bioengineering Laboratory, was a research project that was initially conceived as a series of quantum biology experiments designed to answer the question of whether the human mind can affect very small-scale quantum processes. If such a thing were possible, a kind of mind-matter interface could in turn be imagined that might allow for the mental control of quantum machines and supersmall circuits. Through a series of truly remarkable events, this initial research project quickly morphed into a very different sort of animal, this one dedicated to exploring the intelligence potentials of using gifted psychics to accomplish what came to be known as "remote viewing."

Historically speaking, this program was originally set up by Stanford alumn Harold Puthoff in the spring of 1972. Puthoff is a laser physicist who had written a textbook on quantum physics and had worked as a naval officer for the Defense Department laboratory before he arrived at SRI. After hearing Puthoff lecture at Stanford, Russell Targ, another accomplished laser physicist at that point working for Sylvania, approached Puthoff and asked to join his research group.[57] This was no sudden interest on Targ's part, though. In 1965, he had founded the Palo Alto Parapsychology Research Group (the PRG), a small collective of scientists, intellectuals, and interested individuals (including Vallee in the early '70s) who met regularly—for a time, according to Vallee, in an A-frame house built exactly on the top of the San Andreas fault—to discuss issues surrounding the subject of parapsychology. It was in this way that Puthoff and Targ became the early leaders of the SRI group.

Much had already transpired by the time Targ joined Puthoff, however. It all began when a New York artist by the name of Ingo Swann saw a research proposal that Puthoff had written in the office of a colleague in New York. Swann wrote Puthoff on March 30, 1972, outlining his psychokinetic experiments in the psychology department of City College of New York and suggesting that he may be able to help Puthoff investigate quantum biological effects, that "boundary between the physics of the animate and the inanimate."[58]

Puthoff invited Swann to SRI for a set of initial experiments in June of that same year. Physicists from Stanford's Physics Department and its Linear Accelerator Center joined Puthoff in testing Swann's alleged abilities. They certainly set the bar high enough. Swann arrived only to learn that they wanted to see if he could manipulate the recorded output of a superconducting magnetometer or quark detector, a kind of supersensitive compass used to register subtle magnetic fields that was located in a vault below the building. It was protected by "a mu-metal magnetic shield, an aluminum container, copper shielding, and most important, a superconducting shield."[59] To the great puzzlement of the physicists, Swann successfully and dramatically altered the output of the magnetometer in their presence. He even described a gold alloy plate that was part of the apparatus. "Impressed" was a gross understatement. Puthoff invited Swann back for an eight-month series of experiments.

Upon his return, though, Swann quickly grew bored with the standard parapsychological tests and suggested instead that he be allowed to view distant places and objects, anywhere in the world. "There was an awkward silence."[60] Finally, they decided to give in to Swann's request, as a diversionary game, if nothing else. The results were no game, though. They were stunning. They initiated a three-year double-blind study of what they were now calling "remote viewing," an expression chosen for its relative neutrality over better-known terms, like the earlier psychical research categories of "telepathy at a distance" or "traveling clairvoyance," or the occult expression "astral travel."

Not that Swann was any less fantastic. Vallee, who was working at SRI just one floor up when all of this transpired, notes that Swann's impossible ability to describe and manipulate the magnetometer through several feet of concrete and even stop its output resulted in one government-related group contemplating killing him, for if he could do this, "he could just as easily detonate a nuclear weapon at a distance" (FS 2:192). Vallee describes another scene in which "all hell broke loose" when Pat Price, their other star seer, remotely viewed a supersecret site, even noting the codes and labels on some important files locked inside cabinets.[61] "They didn't know whether to shoot us or congratulate us," Puthoff told Vallee (FS 2:214). Intelligence breaches aside, the results of Targ and Puthoff's experiments with Pat Price at SRI were almost immediately published in the prestigious British science journal *Nature*.[62]

Vallee's journals from this time, which he appropriately entitles "Psychic Underground," are especially fascinating, exploring things like "our psychic computer conference" and "the software of the soul" (FS 2:317, 471). In the privacy of his journals, he could even speculate in a kind of techgnostic code about "a level of reality where information is common to all beings." "Perhaps," he went on, "that level has singularities—points that stick out of the information fabric. Each of these singularities becomes the root of an individual being."[63] (One is reminded here of Myers's notion of the personality as a "chain of memory.") In another entry, he explains how Puthoff once confessed to him that he was called from time to time by some secret group within the government to have his psychics do remote viewing of places where suspected UFO bases were located (FS 2:211). When Vallee, then, published an exoteric public document in 1975 about the existence of an esoteric "invisible college" interested in combining the cutting edges of mysticism, science, and technology, he very much meant it. There was indeed just such an invisible college at SRI, and he was on its faculty.

Vallee, however, did not simply speculate about these matters in his published and private writings. He also contributed concrete research models toward their study, professional dissemination, and practice. He made at least two major contributions to the remote-viewing program at SRI. One was a position paper he addressed to Puthoff and Targ dated January 8, 1973, and entitled *Alternative Scenarios for Long-term Research on Paranormal Phenomena*, which essentially argued for a "mixed strategy that combined open and secret research" (FS 2:504). This is clearly the model the group adopted, hence Vallee's *The Invisible College*, which appeared two years after this position paper. Hence Targ and Puthoff's *Nature* essay and their *Mind-Reach* (1977), a book that sets out in surprising detail the early history and theory of the secret remote-viewing program at SRI. Indeed, they even traveled to Prague, Czechoslovakia, in July of 1973 to share their parapsychological researches with colleagues in Eastern Europe and Russia, who were deeply involved in similar research projects. Puthoff summarized their work at SRI. Swann gave a paper on Scientology as an appropriate paradigm for studying and extending paranormal powers.[64]

The other contribution Vallee made to the SRI remote-viewing project was his suggestion to Ingo Swann that the group consider using "addresses" to locate targets in what they were beginning to suspect was a kind of hyperdimensional field of superconsciousness.[65] Working on the model of a computer programmer, Vallee essentially argued here that the human mind needed some such address to locate what it was seeking, even if it were an artificial or "virtual" one (FS 2:196). The group eventually adopted this idea, at first using longitude and latitude coordinates (which are arbitrary artificial constructs anyway) and later, at least in the Stargate Program at Fort Meade, shifting to arbitrary computer-generated numbers after the unusual discovery that, indeed, the nature of the "address" did not matter.[66]

It was also during this time that the SRI group engaged in detailed experiments with Uri Geller, the Israeli superpsychic who had become famous for his psychical and telekinetic feats, including multiple apparent teleportations that would have delighted Charles Fort. Geller had come to SRI through *Apollo 14* astronaut Edgar Mitchell, himself a dedicated psychical researcher.[67] Significantly, Geller attributed his powers to a childhood encounter that he had at four or five in a Tel Aviv city garden, where a beam of light from a hovering, high-pitched UFO struck him down, "exactly like that scene in the John Travolta film, *Phenomenon*," he explained. Shortly after this, a spoon "melted" in the little boy's hand as he tried to eat his mother's soup.[68] Vallee treats Geller at some length in *The Invisible College*, basically concluding that his powers were a mixture of trick and truth.

What should we do with such impossibilities? I have written my own two chapters on a tiny slice of this story, as it intersected the history of the

Esalen Institute in Big Sur, California, through Targ.[69] The truth is, however, that we now have extensive accounts of these government-funded psychical activities by the scientists, remote viewers, and military officials who were intimately involved, and these from a variety of philosophical perspectives and moral evaluations.[70]

Historians of American religion have not even begun to process and evaluate these histories, which is rather odd given the base fact that the entire program was founded on what is essentially a religious presupposition, namely, that human consciousness is not bound to the body or brain. I wish to emphasize this point. Indeed, I wish to force the issue by pushing it to its completely impossible but perfectly real extreme. Consider the case of Joseph McMoneagle. In a stunning second chapter of his book *Mind Trek*, McMoneagle describes collapsing in an Austrian restaurant in 1970 and finding himself floating above the street in the rain outside. He marveled at how the raindrops passed through his arm and how he had no visible feet. "I understood very clearly by that time that I couldn't really die." The experience was exhilarating. So he decided to follow the car that was rushing his body to the hospital. He might as well have been Superman: "The entire trip was spent cruising just above the car, zipping up, down, and through the overhanging telephone and electric wires." After being pulled up and out of the emergency room, backwards, "as if I were falling upward through a tunnel," he felt a warm sensation at the back of his neck, which then spread to the rest of his subtle body and intensified . . . and intensified . . . and intensified . . . until it approached a state of being he calls "*exceedingly-outrageous-fantastic*." We return to the familiar theme of the mystical and the erotic: "The closest I can come to giving an example that most people would understand is that it was like the peak of a sexual climax times twelve times ten to the thirty-third. That would be twelve with thirty-three zeros after it. (Sexual peak × 12^{33}, or a normal climax times 12,000,000,000,000,000,000,000,000,000,000,000.)" The math carried theological connotations for McMoneagle. "So this is what God is like!" he exclaimed. He knew immediately that he "had been absorbed by a Being of Light, with unimaginable qualities and quantities of power, goodness, strength, and beauty." Then a voice in the Light commanded him to "Go back. You are not going to die."[71]

It would be easy, of course, for the skeptic to declare all of this "purely subjective," except for the historical fact that Joseph McMoneagle, empowered by these unimaginable metaphysical energies, returned to life as commanded and became the premiere remote viewer for the U.S. government's secret paranormal program. Now he could do things like remote view, in 1979, the interior of an immense Soviet Naval structure in northern Russia, including a weird submarine inside that fit no present standard. He also estimated the launch to be about four months in the future. McMoneagle was angered when he learned that the analysts scoffed at his work for a number of reasons, including the fact that the building was well off the water and so could not contain an immense sub. McMoneagle had his "I told you so" moment, though. About four months later, within just a few days of his prediction, American spy satellites showed the never-before-seen *Typhoon* submarine (560 feet long) being floated out to sea through a channel the Soviets had recently dug from the building to the icy waters. Physicist Edwin May, who directed the remote viewing research from 1985 until 1995 and worked very closely with McMoneagle, described his friend and colleague to me as "the most certified psychic in the country."[72] The intelligence community certainly agreed. In 1984, it awarded McMoneagle a *Legion of Merit* for "producing crucial and vital intelligence unavailable from any other source."[73]

So much for the "purely subjective."

Never quite happy with the leadership and direction of his research group, Vallee resigned from SRI on April 9, 1973, in order to manage his own software-development group for two teleconferencing projects on the Arpanet at something called the Institute for the Future. He would now be working even more closely with the science policy makers in Washington, including the National Science Foundation. In 1976, he pursued these business ventures further and became an independent computer entrepreneur in Silicon Valley, much to the disappointment of Hynek, who always thought he should be a professor somewhere, like him. But Vallee had seen firsthand what happened to university professors when they showed too much freedom of thought and theory. He certainly wanted none of that. And he treasured the intellectual freedom that a life in the visionary computer industry would give him (FS 1:424). He would now apply to high technology and the business world the exact same critical-thinking skills, the same interdisciplinary boldness, the same magical structures of consciousness that he had applied to astronomy and folklore. It was a career decision that, by all measures, worked. Vallee would become a successful international businessman, even as he continued to write science-fiction novels, books on finance and computers, and more creative works of ufology.

In the standard terms of the latter field, *Passport to Magonia* and *The Invisible College* were a one-two punch that had exiled Vallee, permanently, from both the rationalist debunkers of the scientific world and the true believers of the UFO community. Reason and faith had abandoned him, and he was left alone now, very alone, in his difficult gnosis. He had become, as one later interview title put it, "a heretic among heretics."[74] There were some major well-established academics who quietly supported him, usually behind the scenes. He lists psychologists Fred Beckman of the University of Chicago and Douglas Price-Williams at UCLA, as well as theoretical physicist Peter Sturrock at Stanford University (FS 1:421). But, for the most part, Vallee and Hynek were alone in their published convictions. And they felt it. "Sometimes I get the awful feeling that I am the only human being who doesn't know what UFOs are," Vallee would later confess after Hynek had died (FS 1:419).

As the decade closed, Vallee published *Messengers of Deception* (1979), a book that argued that some of the UFO flaps were orchestrated by the military to manipulate the public. It was a book that he had a difficult time writing. The material troubled him, and he feared that it was too far ahead of its time to be fully appreciated (FS 2:418). He was right. The book antagonized his closest colleagues in ufology and left other researchers completely puzzled. Even the channeled aliens didn't like it. They asked him, through a friend named Valerie, to change the title, which they apparently found offensive. "Let's see how they will stop me," Vallee answered in his usual combination of humor and intellectual conviction (FS 2:443). Aliens aside, the final result of the book for some of his closest friends was a kind of despairing conclusion that little, if anything, could ever be learned in a field so deeply intertwined with religious cults and secret military intelligence, two fields whose business is often indistinguishable from lying.[75] It was a sobering conclusion.

The Alien Contact Trilogy and the Mature Multiverse Gnosis

Vallee, however, did not despair. In the late 1980s and early '90s, he published three more books on the subject of UFOs. These became his Alien Contact Trilogy: *Dimensions* came out in 1988, *Confrontations* in 1990, and *Revelations* in 1991. In 1992, he then published his early journals up to 1969, *Forbidden Science*, as well as a study of UFO sightings in the quickly collapsing U.S.S.R., *UFO Chronicles of the Soviet Union*, a subject connected to his earlier remote-viewing activities at SRI. Together these five books represent what we might call Vallee's mature position—a mature position, however, that was strikingly compatible with his earlier writings. In truth, he had not changed his mind in any significant way since *Passport to Magonia* and *The Invisible College*. He had, however, become more convinced of the multidimensionality of the cosmos; he had expanded his materials into Latin America and Russia; and he had become much more sanguine about the violent aspects of the phenomenon and the intricate webs of deception that surrounded it, seemingly from almost every side.

Sections of the Alien Contact Trilogy are reworkings of earlier writings. Other parts present new material and new ideas. As a whole, the effect of the trilogy can be summed up by the dedication page to Fred Beckman in the third book: "to Fred Beckman, who urged me to look under the bed." These indeed are scary, boogeyman books. Vallee gave up writing the last book not once but twice, so repelled was he by the cultish material.

Dimensions begins with a foreword by Whitley Strieber, the science-fiction author and self-confessed abductee, who offers a fascinating definition of the alien experience as "what the force of evolution looks like when it acts on conscious creatures."[76] All of the classic Vallean themes are present in the pages that follow: the notion of a high technology that is at once physical and psychical, the control system thesis, the present privilege of observing folklore in the making, the metalogic of alien absurdity, the emblem of Fátima, the complexities of censorship and secrecy and their shaping of the phenomenon, the likely temporal or terrestrial origins of the phenomenon, and so on. Indeed, in many ways, *Dimensions* is a summary of all of Vallee's earlier books.

But there are different accents. For example, the control thesis is linked to human evolution in a quite direct way now, hence the relevance of Strieber's opening definition.[77] There are also developments around the idea of a multidimensional universe, an idea which was already present, of course, in *Passport to Magonia*. Indeed, this is the real point of *Dimensions*. The universe is not a universe. It is not One. It is a multiverse. It is a Many. Hence Magonia, "made visible and tangential only to selected people," is now speculatively defined as "a sort of parallel universe, which coexists with our own."[78] As I pointed out with respect to the impossible possibility of time travel, such a theory is well within the parameters of possibility in contemporary physics. Indeed, it is predicted and expected by a number of theorists.[79]

Vallee continues to interpret the UFO phenomenon within this same expectation. The UFO phenomenon does not thus represent an extraterrestrial visitation. "Instead it appears to be inter-dimensional and to manipulate physical realities outside of our own space-time continuum."[80] He openly acknowledges those before him who came to the same conclusion, particularly Charles Fort, whose famous line he now cites: "We are property." This is no invasion, Vallee observes in agreement. "It is a spiritual system that acts on humans and uses humans."[81] How? Through psychic processes we have not even begun to fathom, working on levels of human consciousness we know next to nothing about—hardly a positive assessment. Still, communication does take place. Contact is made. "I believe," Vallee concludes, "that the UFO phenomenon is one of the ways through which an alien form of intelligence of incredible complexity is communicating with us *symbolically*."[82] Put in my own terms, Vallee has concluded that the paranormal is a hermeneutical reality.

If *Dimensions* is the most metaphysical of the trilogy, *Confrontations* is the most disturbing. Its subject matter is a collection of cases, mostly from Latin America, that involved the chasing, wounding, even apparent murder of human beings in the presence of UFOs. Fort had declared that "We are fished for." *Confrontations* suggests something equally discomforting, namely, that sometimes "We are hunted for." I am not being metaphorical here. Some of the cases Vallee treats in this second book are dramatic examples of hunters being hunted, oddly in ways remarkably similar to their own hunting techniques (more weirdly still, there are other classic encounter cases of fishermen being fished for).

Deer hunters in the Parnarama region of Brazil sit in hammocks in trees at night and use flashlights to hunt for deer in the brush below. In the early 1980s, these deer hunters began reporting incidents of being caught in the bright beams of "chupas" hovering above them. One was chased and "hit" by the beam all night long, after which he developed odd purple marks all over his upper body. Another, named Raimundo Souza, was not so lucky. His hunting partner described how when Raimundo struck a match in their hammock one night, a chupa immediately appeared above them, as if the match had revealed their position. The partner climbed down in terror and hid in the bushes all night long. The next morning he found his partner dead on the ground, with purple marks on his body. Vallee is careful to note that the cause of death in such cases is seldom clear. A fear-filled heart attack and subsequent fall could have easily killed Raimundo. It was the number of these cases, and the absolute sincerity of the witnesses, that impressed Vallee. And why wouldn't they be so open and transparent about what they had experienced? "Nobody has ever ridiculed these people. Their intelligence has never been insulted by the pundits of the *New York Times* or the arbiters of rationalism of *Le Monde*."[83]

And then there was the Brazilian wave of 1977, a wave from July to September during which UFOs appeared every evening around the island of Colares. They arrived from the north or emerged directly out of the immense mouth of the Amazon *every single night for three months*. The horror of the events virtually emptied the island. Everyone who could leave did, including the chief of police. Vallee describes the bizarre scene:

> The objects were never alone. On numerous photographs taken by journalists they are seen accompanied by smaller probes. They exhibit a variety of shapes that would drive an aeronautical engineer to insanity. They range in size from starlike objects to things as big as two 737s end to end. . . . There was a superior technology at work over Colares, and all the observers could do was to film it and watch in awe.[84]

Dr. Wellaide Cecim Carvalho de Oliveira chose to stay. She shared with Vallee the odd symptoms she treated over and over. Her patients all had the same story, which was basically a version of that of the deer hunters. A weird immobilizing beam about one inch in diameter would hit them, always on the upper body. Blackened wounds of red or purple would appear immediately. Hair would fall out the next day. Within a week, they were fine, though. The doctor witnessed a UFO too, but her experience was completely different. It was the most beautiful thing she had ever seen. "She hoped it would land and take her."[85]

As for the photos the journalists took and the reels of film the Brazilian military recorded (in full view of the population), Vallee states that the latter are now buried in some military drawer and that an unnamed American firm purchased the entire set of photographic negatives from the Brazilian newspapers: "Somebody in the United States owns a collection of records that contains the proof of the reality of the phenomenon"[86]

If *Dimensions* is the most metaphysical of the trilogy and *Confrontations* the scariest, *Revelations* is the most depressing. Here Vallee takes a hard look at the orchestrated hoaxes, media manipulations, and "hall of mirrors" that define so much of the discussion—including that around the famous cases of Hangar 18, Majestic 12, and Area 51—and effectively make any open public research well nigh impossible. The signal is not only lost in the noise. It is completely drowned out by the noise. This was a return to and amplification of the earlier thesis of *Messengers of Deception*.

In 1992, immediately after his Alien Contact Trilogy was complete, Vallee published two more volumes: *UFO Chronicles of the Soviet Union: A Cosmic Samizdat* and his early journals, *Forbidden Science*. The former book treats about forty cases that were being discussed in the Soviet Union after the waves of 1966–67, 1977–79, and 1989. Vallee had already played a rather central role in ufological circles in the Soviet Union in the summer of 1967, when he published with Russian science-fiction writer Alexander Kazantsev a pro-UFO article in a Russian magazine more or less equivalent to the American *Popular Mechanics*. The piece was picked up by *Trud*, a major labor union newspaper, and republished in its August 24th issue of that same year, which promptly sold over 22 million copies and went on to become something of a collector's item.

By the time Vallee arrived in the Soviet Union in January of 1990, then, he discovered that he was something of an underground legend, and that *Passport to Magonia* had been circulating for years in samizdat form, that is, in a retyped version secretly distributed among trusted friends and close colleagues. He learned that many Soviet intellectuals were comfortable with his control-system thesis, which they had picked up from *The Invisible College* ("invisible colleges are second-nature to us," one of them noted, no doubt with a smile[87]). He also discovered that they were more than familiar with the polymorphous or shape-shifting nature of UFOs (one case featured a UFO that "divided itself into eight parts that reunited into a single block, turned into a torus, then a cylinder"[88]); that they were quite comfortable with various parapsychological ideas; and, finally, that they were even guessing that these sightings might express "another form of our existence here."[89] *UFO Chronicles of the Soviet Union* is very much about this cross-cultural mirroring, about this "intense feeling of a mystery shared."[90]

Indeed, Vallee discovered here more or less exactly what the visionaries of the American Esalen Institute had discovered in the 1970s and '80s in their own travels through the Soviet Union, namely, that this was a land especially rich in occult and mystical traditions. Vallee quotes a pair of healers who held a particularly provocative thesis about why. "We're ahead of you in the study of the paranormal," they told him in complete confidence, "because the Western churches killed all your witches in the name of their dogma. You only have yourselves to blame if you have fewer gifted psychics. You've eliminated their genes from the gene pool."[91] Historical (and biological) questions aside, such a comment captures beautifully a certain Russian mystical anthropology that came to impress Vallee deeply.

Confirmations continued to mount in this frozen land as Vallee met with various researchers, scientists, and journalists and visited places like the City of the Stars, the Russian space center where cosmonauts were being trained. He was surprised to learn that some of his Russian colleagues were speculating about the multidimensional nature of the universe and some supercivilization's manipulation of space and time through their own psychotechnology. The Russians were doing more than speculating on psychic technology, though. They were also using their own to investigate the encounter scenes. More specifically, they were employing something they called "biolocation," which was essentially a form of dowsing for fields of energy that they believed were left over from a living organism's previous movement through a particular area (what Myers had called a phantasmogenetic center). Vallee, who was never really convinced of the legitimacy of this technique, was puzzled by how completely even otherwise skeptical intellectuals accepted the realities of such biofields and the legitimacy of such biolocation techniques. He was also amused by how badly the Western press muddled this particular issue. When the *New York Times* picked up on one Russian sighting and subsequent site visit that included the biolocation technique, they printed it as "bilocation," thus rendering an already puzzling news event virtually meaningless.[92]

His early journals, as already noted, appeared under the title *Forbidden Science* in 1992. They came out in a second edition in 1996. The epilogue to the latter edition is a concise summary of his mature gnosis, which was still defined by an impossible double conviction: in the metaphysical reality of Magonia, and in the foolishness of accepting the standard ufological readings. The ufonauts, he wrote now, "continue to behave like the absurd denizens of bad Hollywood movies," and their "technology is a simulacrum—and a very bad one at that—of obsolete human biological and engineering notions" (FS 1:419). The encounters and abduction stories still struck him as staged. Alien camp.

Still, he continued to insist that the phenomenon is a real one, that it possesses a physical as well as a psychical component, that it has been with us for a very long time, and that it operates through a multidimensional universe of which our own familiar space-time is a subset (FS 1:420–21). This is an insight Vallee comes back to constantly, even as he walks through his beloved Paris: "A few hours in these narrow streets are enough to convince me that the true meaning of existence lies in parallel worlds for which this city provides a secret metaphor" (FS 2:488). It was French author Jacques Bergier (whom we will meet below, in chapter 4, as the coauthor of the immensely influential 1960s Fortean classic *The Morning of the Magicians*), who pushed Vallee in the 1970s to see that the main lesson to learn from the UFO phenomenon was that the universe we live in is not single, not one (*uni-*). It was Bergier who gave Vallee the word *multiverse*. He also encouraged him to think about how such a multiverse might become a stage for elaborate control systems.

In turn, Vallee suggested to Hal Puthoff in 1978 that both UFOs and Puthoff's continuing remote-viewing work at SRI may be related to the manipulation of other dimensions. He also thought that Western esoteric traditions "flow from the same idea" (FS 2:422). It is certainly true enough that, at least since Giordano Bruno, speculation about multiple worlds has been entertained in this broad tradition.[93] It is probably not until Edwin A. Abbot's delightful *Flatland: A Romance of Many Dimensions* (1894), however, that the model of multidimensionality has been this explicit.

In another fascinating move, Vallee connected this insight to the superior cosmic being American science-fiction writer and literary gnostic Philip K. Dick experienced and wrote about in his novel *Valis*. With Dick's Valis (or Fort's mysterious X), we could hardly be any closer to the impossible vision of Jacques Vallee, with all those shape-shifting aliens and their intentional reprogramming of our religious software: "It is at the level of multiple universes and control systems of consciousness that the UFO phenomenon becomes scientifically interesting, not at the simplistic level of a search for the 'propulsion system' of unidentified flying objects" (FS 1:431). Jacques Vallee was thinking of Philip K. Dick, and of Valis.[94]

Sub Rosa: The Three Secrets

It should be patently obvious by now that the models of reading and writing the history of religions that Jacques Vallee ascribes to are fundamentally esoteric ones. For the sake of summary and some semblance of a conclusion, I would like to isolate—perhaps artificially but I hope also helpfully—three secrets within this thought. Two of them are structural. We have encountered them before, many times in fact, but never quite named them. The third is biographical. I have kept it here, like some precious buried treasure, for the end.

The first Vallean secret constitutes what we might call *the gnosis of the future*. This involves a particular hermeneutic that privileges the imagination, and more especially the imaginaire of modern science fiction, in order to interpret the past and the present from the perspective of the future. In many ways, this is simply an "impossible" extension of standard historiography, which involves a thinking about the past from the perspective of the present. Here that structure of historical consciousness is radicalized further to the extent that it is projected into the future and imaginatively applied back to the present. In essence, it renders the present past. Put a bit differently, Jacques Vallee *thinks backwards*, from the future to the present and then, like the rest of us, to the past.

Thus, even when he entertains a very traditional idea like that of reincarnation, he finds himself asking a very untraditional question, namely:

Why must reincarnation move from the past to the present? Why not from the future to the present? Why, that is, might not reincarnation also work "backwards"? "I've always wondered why people have always reincarnated from the past," he muses in a 1993 interview. "Those few times when I've had feelings of remembering another life, it was from the future."[95] Whether understood as a specific memory of a real future life, as a tapping into some larger cosmic Memory Matrix, or as an active fantasy become hermeneutic, such a feeling from the future expresses perfectly what I want to call Vallee's gnosis of the future.

The second Vallean secret is very much related to the first. We might call it *the gnosis of multidimensionality*. This, of course, is the idea with which we began this book, namely, the idea of multiple dimensions of space-time and its implications for thinking about the history of religions. But such an idea is hardly restricted to the hyperabstract categories of space and time. The idea defines Vallee's understanding of mysticism as "a direction of thought away from ordinary space-time." It also, potentially at least, might inform and expand our most basic models of mind and text, of consciousness and culture. It might morph, that is, into a new paranormal hermeneutics. Within such a new way of reading, we might perhaps better understand how multiple dimensions of consciousness become crystallized into the multiple meanings of a cultural system, or how a vast Mind becomes a vast text with multiple levels of meaning, each, as it were, an altered state of the Mind that projected it. Nothing is simple. Nothing is one. Everything is multiple. Everything is many. This is the mind-blowing secret that both the believer and the skeptic miss, as each tries to collapse the many dimensions of reality into a fundamentalist Flatland of simple faith or pure reason. In the end, neither move can possibly get us to where we want to go for the simple, but fantastically complex, reason that *this is not what is*.

This second secret is crystallized in Vallee's central symbol of Magonia. Within such a multiverse, historical events of a profound religious nature cannot be read as strictly causal or materialistic processes. They cannot be exhausted by reason or context. How could they be? Time is not structured like a one-way arrow, despite what we naively assume in our "behind the times" pre-Einsteinian imaginations. Rather, the structure of time, like that of space, is multidimensional. It can be bent, manipulated, transcended. There are alternative worlds, even whole parallel universes, beyond the ken of our little Flatland and the pathetic little strip of the electromagnetic spectrum that we are able to detect and record with our itty-bitty senses. We are so many "electromagnetic chauvinists," as Michael Murphy likes to put it.[96] That is to say, we assume that what we see and hear is all there is. But it's not. Not even close. Trained in astrophysics and the immensities of space revealed to him through the super-vision of the modern telescope, Vallee never makes this gross epistemological mistake. He is not an electromagnetic chauvinist. He is keenly aware of the smallness of our sensory perceptions and the normal intellectual capacities that they shape, control, and limit.

But he is also personally familiar with other modes of intuitive knowledge, what I have called gnostic modes, that do not rely on these senses. His journals, for example, are peppered with examples of tantalizing precognitive dreams and remarkable synchronicities or what he calls "intersigns," the latter which he takes as evidence that reality itself—very much like a Freudian dream—is "overdetermined."[97] One does not explain or "prove" such thinking to others. One *recognizes* it in another as something of one's own impossible truth. One has either been resynthesized by Valis, or one has not. "Whoever possesses this 'other kind' of thought," Vallee wrote as a young man, "recognizes it at once. It comes with the feeling that we do not really 'exist' any more in this world than a single note in a symphony exists, or a single spark in the fireplace. We are both creators and tributaries of the universe we perceive" (FS 1:20).

It is this same gnostic or reflexive sensibility, this same notion of writing and being written, that inspired Vallee to write in his journals about an "esoteric history," of a mysterious attraction he feels "of an unseen presence that seems to be speaking to us across the centuries of darkness" (FS 1:76). It is this same esoteric attitude again that teaches him that texts, and particularly mystical texts, are not rational objects with simple literal meanings. Each is a multidimensional universe of meaning designed, rather like a UFO, to shatter one's inherited categories and so offer a potential passport into another, richer dimension of existence—a passport to Magonia. "For those who have pierced the barrier," Vallee writes, "words have never represented more than the emerging part of thought. Beyond words are the second meaning, the third meaning, the true ones" (FS 1:41). One, two, and beyond both, a third: this again, at the risk of overemphasizing the point, is a classic mystical or gnostic structure of reading and thinking.

It is important to point out that none of this is an abstract, strictly intellectual project for Vallee. His entire alien corpus is based on intuitive glimpses, flashes of insight, and other planes of consciousness that he has experienced since his youth (FS 1:19). "Perhaps it is true that I have been here, inside this particular body, for nineteen years," he wrote as a young man. "But in reality I feel that I have always existed" (FS 1:18). Indeed, even then he experienced his historical persona and body as something other: "I was created in the form of a man. This is supposed to be obvious: 'I am a man.' Yet there is an infinite distance between 'me' and 'the man I am'" (FS 1:34).

Such an alien-ated gnosis is even more apparent in Vallee's understanding of the God of the Bible, a rather disturbing deity whom some of the early gnostic Christians considered a demiurge, that is, a half-wit creator god who was not worth their worship or respect. This, of course, is Fort's "bland and shining Stupidity." It is also why Fort's editor wanted to call his third book *God Is an Idiot*. The true Godhead of the ancient gnostics, of course, was none of this. The true God, the Father, the One, was something completely beyond the god of the Bible, a God beyond god. With Fort, Vallee shares an almost identical sensibility. He told me quite simply that he does not believe in "the God of the Bible." He had put the same in print, though, and much more, over a decade ago: "The notion of the 'good yet frightful God' of the Bible and the Gospels seems like a swindle to me: It is the biggest, most cruel confidence game in history. . . . Simple human dignity should make us reject all that with indignation" (FS 1:113). Hence the "groveling plea" of the Catholic Requiem, the "religious malady" that gives us endless conflicts "from Ireland to Palestine," and the utterly bizarre phenomenon of "good" Christians, "good" Muslims, and "good" Hindus building atom bombs (FS 2:124, 110).

Which is not to say that he rejects the various scriptural accounts as groundless. He accepts the ambiguous and always fallible historical record that something happened, that is, that a series of profound religious events occurred, which were then recorded in scriptures by way of human memory and community. But he sees no reason to assume that such paranormal events were authored by an ultimate deity. Quite the contrary. "The correct conclusion, in my opinion, would be to acknowledge that an unrecognized form of life and consciousness exists close to our earth" (FS 1:75). What we have, then, is a lower deity, a devilish demiurge, as the early gnostic Christians would have put it. "Other forces manifest," Vallee wrote as late as 1996. "We call them ghosts, spirits, extraterrestrials. When all else fails we abjectly turn them into gods, the better to worship what we fail to grasp, the better to idolize what we are too lazy to analyze. I am in search of a different truth" (FS 1:434–35).

This is radical stuff, but it is radical stuff that many are likely to miss or too quickly dismiss. What, *really*, is going on in an author like Jacques Vallee? It is one thing to sneer at the ufological reading of the Marian apparitions at Fátima, which, as we shall see soon enough, were not originally Marian, or Ezekiel's vision of the chariot, which even by internal textual standards was clearly no chariot. It is quite another to come up with an explanation for all those spinning disks, or to realize the theological implications of what is being suggested, symbolically, through such an alien hermeneutics. Just *who* is being more suspicious here? An author who frames the world religions in categories derived largely from Christian or at least Western philosophical assumptions about the nature of human being? An author who reduces the metaphysical to the present materialism of orthodox science or to the reigning contextualism of this or that social science? Or an author who denies *all* the traditional religions *as well as* the materialisms and contextualisms of modern theory for an imaginative leap into an impossible new world?

We need not believe in the literal existence of aliens—do not misread me here—in order to recognize and admire the boldness of such a move. Nor need we be surprised that such thinking occurs well outside academic respectability. Where else *could* it occur? Authors like Fort, Vallee, and Michel write entirely outside of the typical professional boundaries of the field. This leaves them open to the usual charges of inadequate linguistic preparation, a lack of appreciation for local context and historical detail, and so on. But it also empowers them, enables them to think things that no one within those safe, respectable boundaries would dare think, much less write about. As a consequence, they come up with impossible ideas that, if taken seriously, "could bring Theory to its knees" (FS 1:128).

An exaggeration? The UFO phenomenon as made possible, that is, as interpreted by an author like Jacques Vallee, not only challenges our most basic notions of consciousness and reality. It calls into serious question "the entire history of human belief, the very genesis of religion, the age-old myth of interaction between humans and self-styled superior beings who claimed they came from the sky, and the boundaries we place on research, science and religion" (FS 1:429). One would be hard-pressed to come up with a more radical proposal with respect to the study of religion.

Certainly Vallee experiences this gnosis as profoundly dangerous. He thus references Gershom Scholem's classic study *Major Trends in Jewish Mysticism* and its discussion of Merkabah or "chariot" mysticism, a tradition based on Ezekiel's vision of that mysterious chariot and abduction. Jewish tradition, Vallee notes, forbade the study of the chariot until the scholar was over thirty. Angels and archangels were said to attack the unprepared traveler, and a great fire was said to burst forth from inside the visionary's body in order to devour him: "I think I know what that great internal fire is," Vallee notes elliptically in his journals (FS 1:185).

There is, again, more here than meets the eye. Vallee is not engaging the history of Western esotericism as a scholar of Western esotericism. He is engaging the history of Western esotericism as a Western esotericist. This becomes particularly obvious when we look at his personal relationship to the Rosicrucian tradition, one of the more well-known esoteric traditions of the modern West. Here, in *the gnosis of the rosy cross*, we arrive, finally, at the third secret of Vallee's thought.

Vallee was first introduced to the Rosicrucian tradition in college at the Sorbonne, when a young woman with whom he had many philosophical conversations approached him one day after her grandmother's death. She presented Vallee with a package that contained one of her grandmother's books, Sédir's *Histoire et Doctrines des Rose + Croix* (FS 1:17–18). The book would have a major effect on the young man. He treasured it for years. It taught him the basic structure of esoteric thinking. In 1960, he applied for formal membership in the Rosicrucian Order through a French branch. He received course materials every month in the mail, complete with simple ritual instructions. By the first day of 1964, however, he was expressing disgust with the contradictory mumbo jumbo of occult literature, and by 1966 he had dropped out of any formal relationship with the Rosicrucian tradition. But he never abandoned what he took to be its most basic teachings: its insistence that there are many levels of truth in scripture, history, and science; that private study, solitude, and a fierce independence of thought are all crucial to the search for esoteric truths; that, for the sake of not being noticed, one should adopt the religion of one's place and time, but also realize that the external forms are irrelevant, since the path is the same; that such secrets cannot be institutionalized and are available to a sufficiently prepared intellect at any time and anywhere; and, finally, that an effective initiation into these secrets cannot come from any human being or human institution (FS 1:222).

Nor was he alone in his Rosicrucian inspirations. Astonishingly, Allen Hynek was equally indebted to the exact same tradition. On Saturday, November 12, 1966, Hynek picked up Vallee in a little white sports car at Stapleton Airport outside Denver. They were both on their way to a meeting of the Condon Committee at the University of Colorado in Boulder. On the way, Vallee was surprised to hear Hynek begin waxing eloquently about why he became a scientist: to discern the limits of science and to fathom that which lay beyond it. He was even more surprised to learn that Hynek had been studying the Rosicrucian tradition for years. Hynek explained to him how his own hermetic studies had begun with Max Heindel, after which he moved on to Manly P. Hall (whose *The Secret Teachings of All Ages* he had purchased, at great cost, on May 1, 1931, at the age of twenty-one[98]), and finally to Rudolf Steiner, whom Hynek considered "the deepest of the group."[99] He also joined the American branch located in San Jose, California. Vallee then records the following comments from Hynek, still, I gather, in the little white sports car somewhere between Denver and Boulder:

> I always admired the old traditions which state that there is no such thing as a physical Rosicrucian organization. The only valid Rosicrucian Order, they claim, is not on this level of existence. And they insist that the true initiation, the only illumination of the spirit that counts, cannot come from any human master, but only from nature herself. When I read this I dropped my membership to the San Jose group. I continue to wonder if there may be a genuine Rose + Croix that remains invisible. (FS 1:233)

Invisible. That is a significant and familiar word. It leads one to guess that when Hynek named their secret study group "the Invisible College," he had much more in mind than the sixteenth-century scientists who still lacked royal protection and support. He had in mind the esotericists, the hermeticists, the Rosicrucians. The study of UFOs that Hynek, Vallee, and the Invisible College undertook in the 1960s and '70s, in other words, was no simple scientific pursuit. It was an esoteric practice, a secret school, a scientific mysticism modeled, partly, after the Rosicrucians whom both Vallee and Hynek loved and were reading, unbeknownst to each other until that little white sports car. Aimé Michel was certainly not far off the mark, then, when he wrote to Vallee that "Ufology is not a science but a process of initiation. One starts with field investigations and ends up studying Arab mystics" (FS 2:68). That certainly is an accurate description of Vallee's intellectual-spiritual path.

Or Hynek's. Hynek spoke passionately and often, if usually in private, of a twenty-first-century science that would take the paranormal seriously and so free us from our own present cultural provincialism (FS 1:5). He pursued an active interest in truly anomalous phenomena and became fascinated with parapsychology, especially the alcoholic psychic Ted Serios, whose impossible ability to imprint images on photographic film psychoanalyst Jules Eisenbud has documented and philosopher Stephen Braude has analyzed, both with great care (FS 1:240). Hynek was also interested in ghosts, astral travel, psychic surgery, and LSD research (FS 1:262). And he had a rich library of parapsychology, which he willed to Vallee on his death, on April 27, 1986. Vallee still proudly displays his deceased friend's parapsychological library in his own. He was especially pleased to show me Hynek's immense illustrated copy of Manly Hall's *The Secret Teachings of All Ages*, in which Hynek penciled notes to himself (and now to us) in the margins.

Three forms of secret knowledge thus shape the thought and so the texts of Jacques Vallee: the gnosis of the future, the gnosis of multidimensionality, and the gnosis of the rosy cross.

Toward the very end of *The Invisible College*, after invoking the psychological conditioning models of behaviorism to suggest that we may be a bit like rats in someone or something's giant experiment, Vallee writes this:

> There is a strange urge in my mind: I would like to stop behaving as a rat pressing levers—even if I have to go hungry for a while. I would like to step outside the conditioning maze and see what makes it tick. I wonder what I would find. Perhaps a terrible superhuman monstrosity the very contemplation of which would make a man insane? Perhaps a solemn gathering of wise men? Or the maddening simplicity of unattended clockwork?[100]

This was not a new idea for him in 1975. Indeed, he had expressed the same sense of things bluntly in his journals as early as 1958, on December 22, to be exact: "Everything we see is fake, a stage drowned in movie fog.... Slowly, revolt after revolt, torture after torture, this earth will eventually emerge into its true history. In the meantime I am eager to learn what is outside all these events; I want to see the mechanism beyond time itself" (FS 1:28). He was nineteen when he authored these lines.

Vallee returned to this sentiment again as late as 2007, in "Consciousness, Culture, and UFOs." He was now sixty-eight. Although confessedly frustrated with "this festival of absurdities" to which the public prominence of alien abductions and hypnotic regression had effectively reduced the study of aerial phenomena, Vallee insists that he has not lost his hope that "someday we will be able to sort out the signal from the noise and get to work on the real UFO phenomenon" (FS 1:208–9). This is precisely what he and Hynek had written in *Challenge to Science* all the way back in 1966. Vallee no doubt has his old friend and fellow Rosicrucian traveler in mind when he writes:

> Let me remind you again that the phenomenon is indeed a real manifestation in a physical sense.... We are dealing with physical objects that interact with their environment through the emission of light and other electromagnetic radiation,

> through mechanical and thermal effects, and through psychophysiological changes in the witnesses who are in close proximity to the phenomenon. . . . The believer's mistake is to ascribe meaning and credence to the secondary perception, the mental image created by our brain to account for the stimulus. The skeptic's mistake is to deny the reality of the stimulus altogether, simply because the secondary perception seems absurd to him or her. What we take to be reality may, in fact, be a mere appearance, or projection, onto the "screen" of our four-dimensional space-time world from a much more complex, multidimensional, more fundamental reality. More than two thousand years ago, Plato described this very scenario in his allegory of "the cave," where sensory reality turned out to be mere shadows on the cave wall, projections from the higher reality of Ideal Forms beyond the cave. Real progress lies between the two equally close-minded attitudes of the believer and the skeptic.[101]

Which is to say that real progress lies in the attitude of the gnostic, the man or woman who does not confuse the two-dimensional shadows on the flat cave wall with the "other dimension" outside, who understands that symbols are just that—symbols. They are not literally true. But neither are they completely false. Truth shines through them. They are not the truth.

The Hermeneutics of Light: The Cave Become Window

This same spirit was borne out beautifully in my first meeting with Vallee, with which I began and with which I will now close. As we sat in his living room and got to know one another that December day high above the city, Jacques began speaking of my books that he was reading and their specific use of the word "hermeneutics," a term that was new to him but with which he was quite taken now. It is not difficult to see why. Recall that the term, as I have used it here at least, encodes an approach to the paranormal as meaning and story and insists on the interpreter's creative role in the interpretation. Such a definition could easily be used as a kind of poor paraphrase for Jacques Vallee's corpus of work on the UFO encounter. Since 1968, he has cautioned his literalizing readers away from any naive objectivist interpretation of the UFO phenomena. He has recognized for forty years now that these encounters have every mark of being staged, that they have something to do with the magical and mystical structures of human consciousness, and that they draw on ancient mythology and folklore—in a word, that they are *stories*. He has also shared with me a more personal fact, namely, that, although he has known some successful remote-viewing experiments, most of his own mystical experiences, which have involved intimations of the future, have inevitably come to him *during writing*.

It is not difficult, then, to see why he was so attracted to this particular term among the literally hundreds of thousands that I had sent him in the form of my books. It captured quite well what he had been doing his entire adult life. And then he went further still. He proposed an analogy, the analogy of stained glass for what he called "hermeneutics in action," that is, an interpretation of higher-level symbols from the point of view, and for the benefit, of the common person. He spoke specifically of how stained-glass windows are able to refract an infinite cosmic light that has traveled from untold distances and times before it takes shape in the glass and is able to express itself in the human symbolic language of metaphor, symbol, and word. He also spoke about how the light of the imaged windows is never the same. It is different each day, each hour, even each minute, as the sun moves overhead and beams down on the glass at different angles and with different intensities.

Such an analogy took on an entirely different light, literally, when we entered Jacques's study. One entire wall is dominated by five beautiful stained-glass windows, each of which he has made with his own hands. It took him three years in all to construct them. Here are the central symbols of his literary corpus and his mystical life on display, in full living color, no less. At the top of each stained glass window there is a single glowing rose. Everything that takes place in that room is thus truly and literally sub rosa. There also, in the first window, is a familiar friend, Bishop Agobard. He is holding a book in his hand entitled—what else?—*Magonia*, as he blesses a man coming down from a beam of light to protect him from the crowd below, which no doubt wants to kill him as some kind of demonic magician.

I saw many other symbols in those five windows. As I looked, the light laughed as often as it shone. There was, for example, a grinning, cartoon-like devil modeled, Jacques told me, after a similar imp from the Cathedral of Chartres. He held a prism in his hands so that he could screw up the heavenly light beaming down from above. There was also a knight holding the Holy Grail, the Egyptian goddess Isis signaling secrecy with her finger over her mouth as she held the *Liber Mundi* or Book of the World (again, reality or nature as a secret text to be read). There was an alchemical furnace; the Queen of Heaven emerging, Picasso-like, from different dimensions; the priest Melchizedek; and the medieval nun, mystic, painter, and writer Hildegaard of Bingen. I must admit that I understood little of this. My time was too brief and the symbols too personal, intimate, and playful. But one thing was obvious enough. It was clear to me that, for Jacques Vallee, there is a cosmic light shining through the earthy metaphors and colorful symbols of the history of religion, mysticism, and folklore. The paranormal is very real, although it is always refracted, reflected, and filtered through the magical structures of human consciousness (including that little cartoon devil), which we still do not understand because we have continued in our science to look out instead of in. This is our most fundamental and most important secret, our psychic existence sub rosa.

And so we spend our days in a cramped Cave of Consensus, watching so many fake movies on a foggy screen or dark wall, pretending that it's all real, all "out there." Sometimes, however, just sometimes, our cave wall becomes a stained glass window and we see another kind of light shining through reality. What was once a hard "object" now becomes a translucent "window." Most, of course, even now continue to mistake the colored glass for the light itself. Most replace the cosmic with the earthly, the universal with the local, the symbol with the truth. Unable to distinguish between the two, they do not know. They experience and believe. Or they do not believe. They reason and deny the literal truth of the symbols. Both the believer and the skeptic capture an important part of the situation, but both are wrong about the other part.

Others, however, somehow manage to shake loose from both their religious and rational chains, turn around, and look back at the projector and its brilliant beam of light. Then everything changes, instantly and forever. They have been granted a passport to Magonia. They leave the cave. Now the problem is not the movie. It is the people watching the movie, who do not yet know that they are watching a movie.

four

RETURNING THE HUMAN SCIENCES TO CONSCIOUSNESS

Bertrand Méheust and the Sociology of the Impossible

> No culture is able to achieve the integral fullness of the real, nor can any develop all the potentialities of the human being, for the latter is always in excess of itself. . . . Each culture explores certain sectors of the real, privileges and develops certain dimensions of experience, and, because of this fact, sacrifices other dimensions, other possibilities, which return to haunt it (the return of the repressed!), against which the culture protects itself through a number of mechanisms.
>
> —BERTRAND MÉHEUST, *Le défi du magnetisme*

> *Les mythes se pensent dans l'homme.*
> Myths think themselves in man.
>
> —CLAUDE LÉVI-STRAUSS, *The Raw and the Cooked*

Unlike Jacques Vallee and despite his own intense interest in the subject, our fourth and final author of the impossible, Bertrand Méheust, has never seen a UFO. Nor again, despite his voluminous writings on the history and interpretation of psychical capacities, has he been the recipient of unusual telepathic gifts or precognitive or imaginal visions. He does, however, often experience very strange and striking coincidences.

One such event happened in the spring of 2008, around and indeed apparently mirroring a symposium to which I had invited him at the Esalen Institute in Big Sur, California, on the nature of consciousness and postmortem survival. It began on the plane to San Francisco from France. Méheust was reading my *Esalen*, and more particularly the opening pages where I discuss the hermeneutical nature of synchronicity, that is, the phenomenon of striking coincidences involving texts whose reading and interpretation coincide precisely with the world revealing itself as a text to be similarly read and interpreted. As he read and interpreted my words on the synchronicity of reading and interpretation, the man seated next to him broke in. He was a Buddhist meditation teacher who had taught at Esalen. He had also been involved with the Indian philosopher of consciousness Krishnamurti. They chatted for hours, much of it about Krishnamurti and his ideas about the unconditioned nature of consciousness. When the two got off the plane, the public address system in the airport synchronized with their conversation and called them to return to consciousness: "Calling Mr. Krishnamurti. Mr. Krishnamurti. Will Mr. Krishnamurti please come to . . ."[1]

"I am known for that," Bertrand explained to me with a grin as he finished telling me this story soon after he landed. "My friends know it happens often. Some of them think that this is because I think in connections, making connections between things that no one else has thought to combine. Maybe that's it. Maybe I am a Connector."

I would put it this way. Bertrand Méheust is a super-comparativist who sees connections where others do not and cannot. Until, that is, he writes about them. But he does more than write about such invisible connections. He also attracts them to himself through his existential openness to a universe in which everything is really and truly connected. His, then, are not simply comparative patterns. They are also comparative events.[2]

A Double Premise

I begin with this story related to Méheust's reading of my own written work not to prove anything purely and simply objective, but to acknowledge a certain synergy between our writings and to take it yet further. I take it as a *sign with which to think.* And why not? Bertrand Méheust practices what I have called a hermeneutical mysticism, which is to say that he experiences the world as a series of signs or meaning events to read, interpret, and then write out again in his own written work. And as he reads and writes, he is read and written. This is how he lives, how he comes to be.

It is in this spirit anyway that I would like to suggest that Bertrand Méheust's written corpus can be read as flowing from a double premise, which the reader is free to read as Méheust's or my own. I end my chapter reflections with Bertrand Méheust, then, not simply because most of his books appear after those of our first three authors of the impossible (although he and Jacques Vallee are really contemporaries), but also because his intellectual training and hermeneutical—really Hermetic—sensibilities are extremely close to my own. In essence, then, these are also my conclusions.

The first part of our double premise involves the claim that the humanities have something important to offer the study of psychical and paranormal phenomena. By the humanities, I mean all those fields of study within the modern university that focus on the nature and construction of meaning, value, beauty, and narrative in the history of human experience as the latter has been crystallized in such activities as philosophy, religion, art, literature, and language. By the humanities, I mean all those forms of thought that intuit that reality is not just made up of matter and numbers and causality (which is what the natural sciences assert), but also of meaning and words and stories. By the humanities, I mean *the study of consciousness encoded in culture*.

The second part of our double premise involves the claim that psychical and paranormal phenomena have something important to offer the humanities, that such phenomena can help bring the humanities back to consciousness, if you will. The simple truth is that we have quite a few ideas and some general consensus about what culture is, but no real idea, no real consensus about what consciousness is. When, then, intellectuals try to create comparative systems that can relate consciousness to culture and culture to consciousness, they naturally falter and fall back into cultural systems, that is, into things we know something about, like discursive practices, histories, social systems, power, and politics. Basically, they reduce consciousness to culture.

Accordingly, intellectuals are generally quite resistant to the possibility that consciousness can effectively reveal itself as fundamentally beyond or against culture (although the ideal notion of a "counterculture" certainly hinted at this possibility[3]). And the vast majority of intellectuals would positively deny that consciousness can exist without culture. Psychical and paranormal phenomena, on the other hand, strongly suggest that certain, very special forms of human consciousness are in actual fact not reducible to local cultures, even if they must finally express themselves in the terms and languages of those very cultures. They provide us with some of the most suggestive evidence that *consciousness and culture cannot be collapsed into one another but work together, in incredibly complex ways, to actualize different human potentialities, different forms of reality, different (im)possibilities.*

The encoding of consciousness in culture, then, is no simple material process, as if consciousness and culture are "things" that can be objectified, quantified, and measured separately. There are no such things. Nor is there any Archimedean point for the humanist, no perspective from which everything can be definitively measured and judged once and for all as a stable object. Quite the contrary, the humanist study of consciousness is practiced *by consciousness*. Which is to say that this is an inherently reflexive practice, a meditation in the mirror, with all the mindboggling paradoxes of subjectivity and objectivity that such an image suggests. "The eye with which I see God," Meister Eckhart wrote, "is the same eye with which God sees me." The exact same thing is true of the mystical humanities and the study of consciousness by consciousness.

This encoding of consciousness in culture, moreover, is a radical dialectical process between two forms of human experience (one internalized as consciousness, one externalized as culture) that is as much about repression as expression, as much about the suppression or wilting of potentialities as their education and actualization. And no conscious culture can do it all. To develop one set of human skills is inevitably to ignore, and probably discourage or even demonize, another. What is possible and impossible within a particular temporal and spatial frame, then, is to a very large extent psychoculturally loaded, constructed, or even determined (take your pick).

At first glance, this may sound reductive and relativistic, and to some extent it is (depending on what you pick), but only if one's perspective is restricted to that of a single psyche or culture. This is where the most radical act of all comes in: *comparison*. Radically conceived (as I am conceiving it here), comparison respects no cultural or religious system as representing *the* truth of things. From the perspective of the larger, indeed universal, psychocultural processes captured under the comparative rubrics of "anthropology," "history of religions," or "cultural psychology," however, such a method can point to collective forms of consciousness, levels of metaphysical freedom, and degrees of imaginal power virtually unthinkable in contemporary theory.[4] In culture, any culture, we are bound to that which is deemed possible. In the comparative imagination that can relate consciousness to culture and culture to consciousness, we begin to free ourselves for the impossible. We begin, with Fort, to step out of the movie screen and, with Vallee, to leave the rat maze.

What an author of the impossible like Bertrand Méheust finally teaches us, then, is that we really do shape our worlds, even if we do not fully determine them. We are magicians all. But as whole cultures extended through centuries of time, we are much more than a collection of knowing and unknowing magicians stumbling about with their consensual spells called Language, Belief, and Custom. We are veritable wizards endowed with almost unbelievable powers to shape new worlds of experience and realize different aspects of the real. We are authors of the impossible.

Méheust and the Master

Bertrand Méhuest was born on July 12, 1947. His only complaint to his mother was that he was not born three weeks earlier, on June 24, the day Kenneth Arnold spotted those nine skipping, shining discs over Washington State and so initiated a new era in the mythology of the West. Arnold was a wealthy businessman flying his own private plane. Méheust was born into a poor family with few financial resources and even fewer social connections.

As his birth-wish might suggest, Méheust's early work and first book, in 1978, were on ufology. He would go on to complete an M.A. in 1981, for which he wrote a thesis on William James. Between 1985 and 2003, he worked almost exclusively on the history of animal magnetism and psychical research. He would be awarded a Ph.D. in philosophy from the Sorbonne for this work in 1997. He would also produce two major works of historical scholarship, a two-volume history of this same material (his Ph.D. thesis) and a study of the nineteenth-century superpsychic Alexis Didier (1826–86).[5]

One of the major influences on Méheust's thought was the enigmatic spiritual teacher, ufologist, and mystical writer Aimé Michel, the same man who had such a powerful influence on the young Jacques Vallee. It was Michel, in fact, who helped Méheust find a publisher for his first book on flying saucers and science fiction, which appeared in March of 1978, after which both men engaged in a long and fruitful correspondence.[6] Since Michel was a key figure in the early lives of both Vallee and Méheust and played a central role in a kind of Fortean renaissance in France, it is time now to meet him more fully and introduce the French metaphysical movement that he helped inspire: fantastic realism.

Aimé Michel was a living paradox. A humpbacked dwarf of a man who suffered intensely throughout much of his life and wrote about his body as "the Machine," he thought in cosmic terms and looked upon humanity as a transitional species evolving toward a spiritual identification with the entire universe. His was both a deep and painful pessimism and a nearly limitless cosmic optimism.

There were biographical reasons for this gnosis, for this radical vision of the Human as Two. As a young child on his first day of school, little Aimé was cruelly stricken down by polio. He would lie paralyzed for three years. He was now essentially locked into his own consciousness and unable to communicate with the outside world, and this at a crucial stage of psychosocial development. Aimé gradually learned to observe the intricacies of his own mental processes. These, Méheust points out, now moved outside the habitual or normal channels of social thought and made strange connections. Michel even claimed that he learned to think without words. He also observed his fellow playmates, with whom he could not play, as entranced "somnambulists" acting out a dreamlike social script—the consensual trance.

The result of this three-year meditation was a kind of permanent childhood, a stable altered state of consciousness that left Michel remarkably open to the inexpressible, the improbable, and the nonhuman, an openness that others, including and especially Bertrand Méheust, felt as a kind of "aura" or philosophical charisma, as an alien presence. Aimé Michel was a stranger among men, a being between worlds, in his own words now, "neither man nor woman, neither from here nor from there" (*ni homme ni femme, ni d'ici ni d'ailleurs*). This is how, Méheust explains, Aimé Michel was "born a philosopher," not in the vein of a professional academic, but in the lineage of a Socrates, a Descartes, or a Pascal.[7]

This is also how he lived. In his adult life, Michel sought out nature's solitude, thought and wrote well outside the French academic system, and lived a life of eccentric holiness through which he came to understand the physical phenomena of mysticism (ascetic practices, stigmata, levitation, and psychical powers of various sorts) to be both signs and engines of an evolving superhuman (*surhumain*) that would eventually reveal itself and unite the thought of humanity with the very thought of the Universe—a kind of cosmic consciousness coming to be.[8] Like Bergson before him, Michel saw the strongest evidence for this process in the transformative experiences of the mystics and the data of psychical research. He also understood the baffling appearances of UFOs in a similar light—for him, these phenomena, about which he wrote before almost anyone else in France, were portents of our own superhuman future.

This was no sugarcoated optimism, however, no simple vision of a clear, happy future. There was another side to Michel's view of the human, a darker, more pessimistic, more tortured side. As we have already had occasion to note with respect to his correspondence with Jacques Vallee, Michel constantly stressed the limits of human knowledge and our fundamental inability to understand what might be at stake in something like a UFO or a truly alien form of consciousness. For Michel at least, such an alien-to-human communication really is impossible, at least for now. He was also appalled by what Méheust calls "the mystery of cosmic evil," and especially "the absolute scandal" of the suffering of animals.[9] For Michel, we are caught in a cosmos with hopelessly inadequate sensory, cognitive, and moral capacities. We are thrown into a world and a body that bring us, and so many other sentient creatures, unspeakable suffering and untold pain.

Aimé Michel also had a fascinating take on modern science. He eventually came to the conclusion that physics and science as a whole are the richest and most promising veins of a new mystical worldview. Such disciplines, after all, had revealed a world far more fantastic than any previous religious or mythical register. Charles Fort, of course, had seen the same. I mean, who needs, really, a bilocating saint or a witch turning into a crow when *everything* is teleporting all the time on a subatomic level and birds were once dinosaurs? It was precisely this kind of thinking that so inspired Aimé Michel. He in turn inspired a French metaphysical movement that exploded around the publication of a single blockbuster book.

Louis Pauwels was a French editor and publisher who, with his collaborator, the chemical engineer and former Resistance fighter Jacques Bergier, published *Le Matin des Magiciens* in 1960. The book came out in England as *The Dawn of Magic* in 1963, and a year later in the U.S. as *The Morning of the Magicians*.[10] The same movement spawned its own magazine, *Planète*. It was in the pages of the latter periodical, edited by his friend Louis Pauwels, that Aimé Michel set down the outlines of his vision and its quest.

Although the invocation of magic and a certain cosmic spirituality were the primary rhetorical strategies here, what these authors were really proposing was what they called a *fantastic realism*. The authors explain their approach to the impossible:

> We call our point of view *fantastic realism*. It has nothing to do with the bizarre, the exotic, the merely picturesque. There was no attempt on our part to escape the times in which we live. We were not interested in the "outer suburbs" of reality: on the contrary we have tried to take up a position at its very hub. There alone we believe, is the fantastic to be discovered—and not a fantastic leading

> to escapism but rather to a deeper participation in life. . . . The fantastic is usually thought of as a violation of natural law, as a rising up of the impossible. That is not how we conceive it. It is rather a manifestation of natural law, an effect produced by contact with reality—reality perceived directly and not through a filter of habit, prejudice, conformism.[11]

Such ideas, of course, were distant echoes of Myers and the S.P.R.'s search for "the telepathic law" and a true science of religion. They were also essentially Fortean. What Pauwels and Bergier were ultimately after, then, was precisely what Fort represented for them, that is, "a new mental structure" that was not binary, "a third eye for the intelligence" that could say yes and no at the same time, like the subatomic particle that is also a wave, they pointed out.[12] In short, Fort's philosophy of the hyphen.

I am not speculating here. I am simply taking the authors at their word. They tell us that the phrase itself, fantastic realism, was indebted to both the surrealism of André Breton, whom Pauwels describes as "a very great friend," and the general methods of Charles Fort, whom the authors openly acknowledge as "one of our most cherished idols," who "before the first manifestations of Dadaism and Surrealism . . . introduced into science what Tzara, Breton and their disciples were going to introduce into art and literature."[13] Indeed, it was at Pauwel's instigation that *The Book of the Damned* first appeared in France, in 1955.[14] It hardly made a mark. So Pauwels tried again, this time with Bergier.

They made a mark.

A deep mystical humanism, or what they called "That Infinity Called Man," constitutes one of the deepest messages of the book. And the accent was definitely now on the *mystical*. Whereas Breton, for example, had explored the Freudian regions of sleep and the unconscious, Pauwels and Bergier were now exploring "their very opposites: the regions of ultra-consciousness and the 'awakened state.'" Central to this awakened state—the constant phrase invokes Gurdjieff—was the realization that the line between the imaginary and the real is a very thin one, that reality seen truly is truly fantastic.

Science Fiction and Flying Saucers

Méheust's first book appeared in 1978: *Science-fiction et soucoupes volantes: Une réalité mythico-physique*, or *Science Fiction and Flying Saucers: A Mythical-Physical Reality*.[15] The book was a study of the UFO phenomenon, his first love and in many ways the subject that defined the direction and metaphysical shape of everything that would follow. Méheust explained to me that he did not understand what he was writing when he began this first book. He was following a series of deeply felt, but still vague intuitions. He was practicing what he called a "hermeneutics of the self," which is to say that he was discovering what he thought not as he thought, but *as he read and wrote*. It was almost as if the book was "channeled," he confessed. The phrase is a common one among creative writers who do not experience their writing as entirely subjective events, who sense their words and ideas as coming, somehow, from outside them. This, of course, is often literally true in the simple sense that the act of reading is an "outside influence." But often the influences, even the reading influences, feel far weirder than that, as if external events are reading and writing the author as the author reads and writes. It is as if one is reading the paranormal writing one.

So it was with Méheust and the origins of *Science Fiction and Flying Saucers*. The work began as another comparative event involving the reading of a book, similar to the events with which I began this chapter. It was 1974, and a twenty-seven-year-old Bertrand Méheust was rummaging through the library of his family's loft when he came across an old science-fiction novel, Jean de la Hire's *Roue fulgurante* (*The Lightning Wheel*). The cover featured a flying disc-shaped machine surrounded by a halo of light. He opened the book. The story began with the heroes being lifted into the humming sphere by a beam, losing consciousness, and awakening to find themselves in a brightly lit room. This was by no means a great work of literature. Indeed, the few pages Méheust read in the attic struck him as rather incoherent.

Then he saw the publication date: 1908. This stunned him. The date was so shocking because it was (and still is) widely assumed that the "flying saucer" did not appear on the cultural scene until 1947, when American pilot Kenneth Arnold sighted his nine silver disks. The first widely publicized abduction, we might also recall, did not occur until 1961, when Barney and Betty Hill reported their experience of "losing" two hours on the road and later remembered, under hypnosis, being abducted by aliens on board a spaceship.

But here was a set of strikingly similar images and an abduction story *in 1908*, and in a forgettable science-fiction novel no less. How could this be? Méheust recalled that some years earlier, while reading Jules Verne's *Robur le conquérant* (1885), he had been much intrigued by the similarities between Verne's famous flying Albatross machine and the strange flying vessel or floating ships that were seen across America and widely reported in the newspapers of 1897. It was if Verne's science-fiction image had become an experienced cultural reality across the American landscape, and that within just twelve years (SF 223–29).

These two comparative events of reading Jean de la Hire and Jules Verne in effect "lived out" or intuited the thesis and comparative method of the book before there was a book. The focus of the work is a series of elaborate demonstrations of the historical coincidences that appear to exist between the narrative and visual frames of the UFO experiences of the second half of the twentieth century (1947 to the present) and the science-fiction stories of the first half of the twentieth century (1880–1945). Flying discs accompanied by buzzing noises, harmful or healing beams of light zapping people, abductions via levitation or teleportation, large-headed dwarves or humanoids, physical examinations on board a spaceship in a lighted room—point by point, detail by detail, Méheust demonstrates with texts and glossy pulp-fiction art how the later encounters "realized" or reenacted the earlier sci-fi scenes, and this down to astonishing details. Rhetorically, Méheust is mischievous here. So, for example, he will present three encounter stories without telling the reader which ones are "fictional" and which ones are "real" until a few pages later. Through techniques like this, he shows, over and over, that it is simply impossible to tell the difference between fiction and lived reality within the two sets of stories.

The treatment of pulp-fiction art and comic-book images pushes this point still further. Méheust, for example, reproduces a fairly typical cover of *Astounding Stories* from June of 1935, this one illustrating a version of the classic sci-fi abduction and medical experiment scenario that would become a standard feature of the later UFO accounts. He can also juxtapose a few panels from a French comic book from 1945, this one involving an odd globe-shaped spaceship with little men hopping from its portal, and a strikingly similar drawing based on a real-life UFO encounter from 1967. To employ the language of the British psychical researcher Hilary Evans, what we appear to have here is neither exactly fiction nor pure fact. It is "faction."[16]

The same could be said, of course, about that strange fusion of fact and fiction we call "religion." And indeed, like Vallee before him, Méheust is very clear that the UFO phenomenon manifests all sorts of folkloric, religious, and spiritual themes. For example, he was interested in the parallels with the history of Christian mysticism, which involves things like beams of light bestowing mystical illumination and effecting levitation (SF 17, 120–21, 164). Méheust was especially impressed with the profound physical dimensions of mystical events that the English Jesuit Herbert Thurston and his own French master, Aimé Michel, had written about.[17] Thurston was a well-known expert on the lives of the saints. Through his association with the S.P.R., he had become convinced that the extraordinary transformations of the body (stigmata, luminosities, seeming imperviousness to pain or fire, various magical or psychical powers, even apparent human flight in the cases of Teresa of Avila and Joseph of Copertino) reported in the hagiographical literature were real. He had also become convinced that they were somehow related to the psychical phenomena studied by the S.P.R. This all struck Méheust as terribly pertinent to his UFO literature, of both the fictional and experiential types, since it seemed to suggest a link between mystical states of consciousness and highly unusual physical phenomena. Sometimes, moreover, the parallels were nearly exact, as for example when St. Francis was "zapped" by the beams of light that bestowed on him his stigmata wounds (UFO encounters often zap people with beams of light and leave odd scars or wounds).

Méheust began to suspect that just as Christian mysticism had produced a certain type of fictional literature that clearly exaggerates but also preserves the experiences of the saints, so too the UFO phenomenon produces a certain type of fictional literature, science fiction, that exaggerates but also preserves the experiences of the witnesses and contactees. The comparative model, then, looks like this: mystical event : hagiography :: UFO phenomenon : science fiction. That is to say, Christian mysticism is to the hagiographical literature as the UFO phenomenon is to the science-fiction literature.

There were differences, of course. The hagiography, after all, was written after the lives of the saints and for the edification of the faithful, some of whom would then imitate this literature and become future saints, thus establishing the typical dialectical relationship between consciousness and culture, or in this case between sanctified subjectivity and public textuality. The science-fiction literature, however, was written for cheap adolescent entertainment and was generally not known by the later abductees. This is the central intellectual scandal of Méheust's first book. How exactly *does* one derive the absolutely terrifying and often completely debilitating traumas of the later UFO abductions from an earlier lowbrow literature sold literally for pennies to pimply adolescents? This is a question Méheust asks himself and his readers in the strongest terms (SF 59, 202).

Contrary to first expectations, whereby one would simply reduce the later abductions to the earlier cultural fantasies that had entered the public realm, Méheust's own understanding of this morphing of science fiction into occult experience is much more complicated, as he sees these alien narratives as engaging real metaphysical ground *and* as being dependent on the earlier imaginal frame of science fiction. That is to say, in my own terms now, Méheust refuses to reduce consciousness to culture, while at the same time he demonstrates how consciousness must express itself through culture, and in this case popular culture. He shows how consciousness encoded in culture is finally *fantastic*.

Méheust thus refuses, like a good author of the fantastic, to allow the reader to settle into any comfortable conclusion concerning the final nature of the experiences under discussion. As he repeatedly reminds his reader, the central idea of the book is the mindboggling observation that these experiences clearly possess both physical *and* psychical components (SF 237). UFOs leave traces on radar screens and landing marks on the ground. Entire militaries worry about them, and fighter jets routinely chase them. They occasionally heal people (SF 150). They also occasionally kill people (SF 146–47). They clearly cannot be reduced to subjective fantasies. But they also, just as clearly, behave like dreams, like myths or "super-dreams" seen in the sky (SF 117, 200, 215, 229, 289, 296).

Moreover, and more bizarrely still, they are mischievously omnipotent in their ability to show themselves to us in quite outrageous ways, as in a picture window, while at the very same time *completely* eluding any lasting or conclusive contact. We have more than enough evidence, up to eighty thousand cases reported around the world, Méheust notes. And yet we have nothing, not a single piece of incontrovertible evidence. Working much like a mystical text, they reveal themselves only to conceal themselves. Apparently, they can never be known as they are. The UFO, then, is "the unnameable thing" (*la chose innommable*) that clearly manifests intentional properties but frustrates all psychological and sociological explanations. Whatever it is, it exists "before all determination" (SF 19, 33–35). Accordingly, the UFO phenomenon creates epistemological conditions that are inherently solipsistic, circular, and maddeningly paradoxical for those who attempt to engage it (SF 277–78). In a word, my word anyway, they are hermeneutical realities.

These unnameable things, these damned things, as Fort would say, express themselves in the cultural fantasies of the time and place. They can also be scarily mimetic, as, for example, when they literally hunt hunters or fish for fishermen, as we saw with Vallee's study of the Latin American cases (SF 201, 203). They are thus hardly objective things "out there." They are objective things "out there" *and* subjective things "in here." They are interactive, participatory realities that cannot be understood outside the forms of consciousness that perceive and experience them, that is, *us* (SF 75).

Méheust has many ways of expressing this central paradox of his book (which is also the central paradox of this book). It is certainly not an easy idea, one all too easily collapsible into a simple subjectivism, as if UFOs, poltergeists, or telepathic communications were just our cultural or psychological projections; *or* a naive objectivism, as if UFOs were spaceships piloted by Martians or Venusians and poltergeists were pissed-off dead people named "Joe" and "Kathryn." Méheust avoids both of these rationalist and religious extremes, consistently arguing instead for a richer and more nuanced position.

That position comes down to this. The world is not simply composed of physical causes strung together in strictly materialistic and mechanical fashion requiring, say, a physics for their complete explanation. The world is also a series of meaningful signs requiring a hermeneutics for their decipherment. Whatever they are, UFOs "vibrate in phase" with our forms of consciousness and culture. We thus cannot even conceive of them outside or independent from their observation. This most basic of facts puts into serious doubt the adequacy of any traditional scientific method. Such methods, after all, work from an ideal of complete objectivity, which in turn demands an effort to eliminate all interference with the observer. But what if the observer is the very mode of the apparition? What if the observer is an integral part of the experiment?

For his part, Méheust argues that the naive idea that consciousness is a clean "mirror" separate from the objects that it reflects needs to be abandoned immediately and put into the museum of bad ideas. He cites the physicist Von Neumann here, who wrote that "the conception of an objective reality has thus evaporated" (SF 321). Méheust had arrived at the same conclusion twenty pages up: "We therefore find, but now transposed into the domain of the symbolic representation, the paradoxes of microphysics: as with the electron, the notion of a UFO independent from its human observer is nonsensical" (SF 302). The implications of all of this for the study of the UFO phenomenon as a "mythical-physical reality" are immense: "*one is not able to envisage [the UFO phenomenon] independently from our consciousness; what is more: there can be no question of eliminating that part which the human spirit adds to it; it is, on the contrary, an essential component of the phenomenon*" (SF 321).

Such a hermeneutical shocker carries other shockers. There is the notion, for example, that a meaning or a representation can become an efficient cause in the physical world (SF 302), that there is such a thing as "a concrete action of a meaning" (*l'action concrete d'un sens*) (SF 305). But how? How, Méheust asks, can something entirely without location, mass, or energy, like a meaning or bit of information, interfere with solid objects, with things? After a fascinating footnote on Freud's letter to Karl Abraham in which Freud suggested that biological evolution may be driven by unconscious mental representations, that is, that consciousness may somehow be able to imprint itself on physical forms (remember Fort's "wereleaf"?), Méheust finally plays his cards and suggests that reality appears to possess two sides or faces: a public face involving physical matter and causality, and an esoteric face (*une face ésotérique*) involving the presence of meaning and information (SF 307).[18] This is how, for Méheust, a meaning (*un sens*) can really and truly structure a physical event involving matter, as in an experience of synchronicity (SF 263). Reality *really is* double-faced. It is matter, and it is meaning. It is "it," and it is "bit."[19] Not only is the Human Two. So too is the World.

Méheust also employs mythical language to say the same thing. Hence he can describe the entire UFO phenomenon as a "technologized Hermes," after the Greek trickster god of lucky finds, language and communication, doorways, and dreams (and the etymological base of our own "hermeneutics").[20] Here he points out that in reading the abduction narratives one often has the impression that the victim has "penetrated" into the UFO as if it represented "the other side of the mirror." Like Alice in Wonderland, the victim has somehow entered another universe, this one of an atemporal and nonspatial order. The UFO has in effect acted like a "windowsill," even like a "reality changer." Méheust is particularly struck by all those stories in which a gardener, hunter, fisherman, or driver is engaged in some utterly banal activity when—pop!—another reality opens up in the very midst of the mundane activity. He thus sees these narratives as a return of the repressed Hermes archetype, as a lived embodiment of that most basic of Hermetic principles, "where the high and the low cease to be perceived as contradictory" (SF 215–17).

Very much related to these Hermetic notions of the UFO functioning as a windowsill, reality changer, or portal and of paradoxically joining the spiritually profound and the mundane (or the culturally lowbrow) are the key issues of *the absurd* and *the symbolic function*. We might recall that Vallee had highlighted the utter absurdity of many of the UFO narratives. He felt that this absurdity was not accidental or meaningless, that it was somehow part of the message. Aimé Michel highlights the same in his preface to Méheust's book, "Requiem pour des chiméres trés anciennes" ("Requiem for Some Very Old Chimeras"), a potent little gnostic essay in which the author expresses his disgust with "the ideologues and the theologians," that is, with the representatives of reason and faith, neither of whom, he suggests, have really confronted the facts of the case at hand. Such facts, Michel admits, appear both fantastic and absurd. But does not this nonsense itself make sense? Is not this genre of absurdity entirely appropriate, even expected, before the possible presence of another thought (SF 68)? Hence Michel's fantastic realist mantra, which is also Méheust's mantra, "to envisage everything and to believe nothing" (SF 323). Méheust follows the master here, pointing out, for example, that the UFO phenomenon acts like a "super-dream" (*sur-reve*) that works through a process of radical "absurdization" (SF 289).

Méheust's most profound treatments on the absurd, however, involve his notion of the symbolic function embedded in the UFO narratives and encounters. For Méheust, the symbolic function is about communication between different orders of reality, orders *so* different that they cannot communicate to one another in any straightforward or simple way. As an expression of the symbolic function, then, the religious image, the myth, or, in some cases, the dream does not work like a simple word or a precise number. Its meaning is not, and *cannot*, be a straightforward one. There can be no direct or one-to-one translation, not because the process is being intentionally deceptive or ridiculous, but because a fisherman is trying to talk to a fish. We are back to the Flatland insight.

Méheust thus notes the central role of "bubbles" or crystal-like "encasements" common in both the sci-fi and encounter literatures. Aliens are often imagined or seen floating around in them, revealing themselves through the bubble, and yet also *not* revealing themselves by staying inside the bubble. Such transparent encasements, such revealings that conceal, symbolize for Méheust the symbolic function itself to the extent that they are all about permitting "the otherwise impossible encounter between two heterogenous realities" (SF 195). Such symbols are relays, as it were, from something invisible and structurally unknowable, something truly alien, to our own local forms of culture and consciousness (SF 310). That is to say, in my own terms now, *to the extent that it permits at least some type of communication across radically different metaphysical orders, the symbolic function renders the impossible possible.*

It also, alas, renders the possible impossible to the extent that a culture or a person loses the ability to think symbolically. So deprived, people literalize their cultural myths and symbols and fall into all sorts of genuine absurdities, including the absurdity that UFOs are nuts-and-bolts machines piloted by aliens from outer space. This, Méheust points out, is simply to mistake our own cultural moment—which happens to be imbued by a modern sci-fi register and a cold war space race—as somehow privileged and absolute, that is, as applicable to all place and time in the universe.[21] For Méheust at least, this is definitely not what the UFO encounters are about. They are not literal messages. They are not what they seem to be. They symbolize. They translate across metaphysical orders. They reveal the sacred in the mode and code of the day.

And that code is largely pop cultural. Faithful to his Hermetic principle about joining the high and the low, Méheust dedicated this first book to the religious revelations of popular culture, that is, to the high revealing itself in the low. Not surprisingly, other pop cultural allusions appear alongside all those spinning, darting, shining discs.[22] Sometimes this is a rather subtle process, as, for example, when Méheust refers to the astonishing displays of the UFOs as their "special effects," as if what we are witnessing here is a Hollywood movie (SF 16, 132). At other times, the pop cultural allusions are more direct and obvious. The French comic-book character Tin Tin appears to be one of his favorites. The character makes appearances in both *Science-fiction et soucoupes volantes* (SF 283–84) and, a bit later, in *Somnambulisme et médiumnité*, to which we will return.

Superman also makes an appearance or two. The first occurs in a discussion of the alien as a modern technoangel, a theme that began to appear in the 1930s (SF 121). "Transcendence is always armed," Méheust notes, citing one of his favorite authors, Gilbert Durand (SF 121). This is especially obvious in the history of the biblical and Islamic angel, which often looks remarkably like a heavenly military general. So too with the alien and his high-tech weaponry, which Méheust sees as an example of the "technological avatar of the angel." Such a process culminated in the U.S., Méheust suggests, with the wildly popular appearance of Superman in 1938. The mythical ground had been laid by the earlier science-fiction pulp magazines. And Superman, of course, was essentially a crashed alien. He descends from the sky from another world literally called the Hidden (Krypton) or the Mystical to save us.

Méheust's fullest treatment of Superman, however, occurs in his discussion of the odd behavior and general comportment of the saucer occupants in the sci-fi narratives and UFO encounters. One never sees saucer occupants performing biological functions, such as eating, drinking, or defecating, he reminds us. Such biological functions have been erased, as if they were not necessary for the message.[23] In essence, Méheust suggests, the UFO occupants do not behave like biological creatures. They behave like *signs*. They are like puppets on a string, or representations in a store window display. Or comic-book characters.

They are also astonishingly, impossibly invulnerable. In one famous American incident, the Hopkinsville case, a farmer and his family shot at the things multiple times. They just bounced back and continued on their terrifying way around the farmyard and farmhouse. It is here that Méheust invokes Superman and the comic books again. "One has the impression," he writes, "that, if [the superheroes] visually distinguish themselves from the flying saucers, they are nevertheless taken from the same substance, they share all their privileges, that the same force controls all the details of the manifestation" (SF 283–84).

Exactly.

The Challenge of the Magnetic and the Shock of the Psychical

In 1992, Méheust published a second, much less speculative book on flying saucers, this one on the abduction narratives in the comparative light of ethnography and folklore, *En soucoupes volantes: Vers une ethnologie des récits d'enlèvements*, or *On Flying Saucers: Toward an Ethnography of Abduction Narratives*.[24] If the first book was written by a young and passionate ufologist, this second one was written by a careful and qualifying anthropologist. Méheust frankly worried that the success of his first book—and it was quite successful, both culturally and commercially—was due to its "mistiness." He also knew that in order to get a university position, which is what he really wanted, he would have to mask his real thoughts. So he put aside all of his bold speculations and true convictions and hid them behind the mask of scholarship and objectivity. The result was disappointing. The people who were interested in the fascinating fusion of science fiction and flying saucers lost all interest in his work. The ufologists saw him as a traitor. And the university scholars, well, they were never interested in UFOs in the first place. The second book landed with a dull thud.

In 2007, now looking back with three decades of such sobering experiences and a certain intellectual maturity, Méheust sat down to write a new preface for the second edition of the first book. Here again, he expressed himself in a careful and cautious vein about the whole matter of UFOs. He remained impressed with the phenomenon as a whole, but he had also become convinced that he had underestimated the epistemological difficulties of the inquiry, and especially "the irrepressible tendency of the human spirit to modify the real in the sense of that which the culture of the moment proscribes." He had underestimated, that is, "the work of the successive filters through which the real passes before it appears to us" (SF 21).

This is a *key* distinction, and one central to my own thought as well. Folklorist Thomas E. Bullard captures the same point, beautifully, in the very title of his essay "UFOs: Lost in the Myths." His point here is the same one that Eliade made in "Folklore as an Instrument of Knowledge" with respect to paranormal phenomena and the history of folklore, namely, that there is an experiential core to these myths and legends, and that we ignore this experiential base at considerable cost. Here is how Bullard puts the same idea:

> In a sense the myth has fared all too well. It hides the fact that the UFO mystery is not a single question but two, one about the nature of the UFO experience, the other about the human meanings of UFOs. To overlook this distinction leads to dismissal of the whole phenomenon as a cultural reality and nothing more, without any careful reckoning with the experiential core.[25]

This, of course, is the same idea that authors like Hynek and Vallee had called "the signal in the noise." I will return to this notion of "the work of the successive filters" and the two hermeneutical levels of the paranormal problem in my conclusion.

Happily, the historical scope and metaphysical depth of this cultural filtering process was precisely the subject of Méheust's third book, if, that is, one can call a twelve-hundred-page, two-volume tome a "book." *Somnambulisme et médiumnité* was the doctoral dissertation he wrote for his Ph.D. at the Sorbonne. It is divided into two chronological volumes: volume 1, *Le défi du magnetisme*, or *The Challenge of Magnetism*; and volume 2, *Le choc des sciences psychiques*, or *The Shock of the Psychical Sciences*.[26] The first volume begins on May 4, 1784, the date of the marquis de Puységur's discovery-production of somnambulism in a twenty-three-year-old peasant by the name of Victor Race, and carries the story forward to the early 1840s, the rough date of the beginning of the magnetic tradition's cultural decline after a series of official commissions by the French government and medical profession. The second volume returns to the magnetic origin point of 1784, but then carries the story forward further to 1930, the approximate date of this tradition's absorption and eclipse within Western intellectual culture. Finally, Méheust ends the volumes with some reflections on the state of the French academy with respect to the paranormal at the very end of the twentieth century.

The work is far too large and venturesome to capture even in a second book, much less a brief chapter such as this, so I will restrict myself here to focusing on four major themes that are especially relevant to the themes at hand: (1) Méheust's notion of *l'oubli du magnetisme* or "the forgetting of [animal] magnetism" within Western intellectual culture, a two-century process that coincides with the erasure of the paranormal within intellectual culture and its subsequent migration into "the safety" of popular culture; (2) the related notion of "shock zones" or "stop concepts" through which he explains how later systems of thought—like Freud's psychoanalysis, Breton's surrealism, or Bergson's creative evolution and philosophy of consciousness—both beat back and incorporated the earlier metaphysical defiances and shocks in order to preserve, but also to expand slightly, the epistemological boundaries of Western culture; (3) the central idea of *décrire-construire* or "description-construction," which in turns builds on the aforementioned theory of human consciousness as a reservoir of potentialities that can be actualized within different worlds and persons at different places and times through various intellectual practices, psychological techniques, social interactions, and institution building; and (4) the recurrent theme of psychical capacities or extraordinary human powers within this history, basically what Myers called supernormal powers, what Fort called wild talents, and what Vallee referred to as psychical capacities.

1. The Great Forgetting. It is a commonplace in humanistic circles today to hear that such-and-such truth is a "social construction," or that this or that claim is a product of an "episteme," that is, a particular order of knowledge that is held together by elaborate networks of power established by earlier cultural battles whose winning arguments have been institutionalized in carefully controlled hierarchical structures and minutely monitored social and intellectual practices. We thus might believe that we are indeed "thinking freely," but the patterns and tracks, if not troughs, of our "private" thoughts have in fact been laid down before us by quite public practices and battles. We do not think. We are thought. As William Blake might say, we labor with "mind forg'd manacles," that is, conceptual chains strapped around our flaming brains by the prejudices, bigotries, and idiocies of previous generations. Along similar but more objectively stated deterministic lines, one also often hears that any truth claim is ultimately really only a "discourse," that is, a language game that makes good sense within its own rules and grammatical structure, but little or no sense outside of them. Such claims, deeply indebted to French figures like Michel Foucault and Jacques Derrida, are general features of what we mean by poststructuralism and postmodernism today.

One way of thinking about Méheust's project is to read it as an elaborate delineation of these fundamental postmodern insights with respect to the nineteenth- and twentieth-century cultural wars surrounding animal magnetism and psychical research, but toward a very specific, and deeply subversive, end. Basically, what Méheust demonstrates is how the present regime of power and knowledge—a regime defined by materialism, determinism, objectivism, and scientism—came about through the disciplining, suppression, and finally forgetting of the metaphysical shock of the psychical, which can indeed be read with the tools of postmodernism *but finally overflows and overwhelms these*. Méheust, in other words, employs the tools of poststructuralist thought in order to think beyond poststructuralism. He relativizes the relativizers, as the sociologist of religion Peter Berger might say.[27]

Thus, for example, when he discusses Pierre Bourdieu and the notions that all of our linguistic and geographic borders are the result of conflicts, compromises, and transactions, that the real is not given but constructed, that "society is the seat of a permanent battle around its definition," he is careful to remind his readers of that which is common in all of this, which is precisely that which is often forgotten, namely, humanity itself (SM 2:121). Not that this human base is entirely stable. The limits of our human faculties, he suggests, were not in 1900 what they were in 1800. The very structure and capacities of our sensorium change with our social practices and intellectual categories, over which we ceaselessly fight. And not for nothing, it turns out: worlds of experience and possibility are indeed at stake.

Vigorous psychical phenomena are less common, or at least less reported, today than they were in the first half of the nineteenth century. Is this because we are not as credulous today, because our predecessors were being duped and we no longer can be? Or is it because the older epistemological limits were less stable, more fluid, and had not yet fully enforced the specificities of our present mental universe? It is not so absurd to ask, then, "if the culture in which we live has not finished completing the occultation of a psychism *sui generis*" (SM 2:122–23). It is not so absurd to ask, that is, if we have forgotten our own innate nature, whether we have, as it were, fallen into a certain cultural unconsciousness.

For the story Méheust tells, the nineteenth century was the turning point, the space and time in Western culture where and when consciousness defiantly suggested that it might be fantastically free of the spatial and temporal strictures that were then beginning to be seen as absolute. It all began on May 4, 1784, when a career military man and artillery colonel, an aristocrat by the name of Armand Marie Jacques de Chastenet, marquis de Puységur (1751–1825), attempted to put a young peasant by the name of Victor Race into a Mesmeric "healing crisis." That didn't happen. Instead, Race *woke up asleep*. More specifically, he began to manifest a calm, lucid state of consciousness in which he ceased to speak in his village accent, took on a learned tone, and began to respond not to Puységur's vocal commands, but to his unspoken thoughts. It was as if Race had some immediate access to his magnetizer's innermost processes and desires.

Puységur was understandably stunned. He would write two years later of encountering in Victor "a being I do not know how to name" (*un etre que je ne sais pas nommer*).[28] The two men (or the two men and the Being), ten years apart and from vastly different social backgrounds, became close collaborators in a shared exploration of this extraordinary state of mind. Victor, it turned out, could predict in these states the future course of his own treatment and healing with calenderical precision. More astonishingly still, he could also diagnose the conditions of other patients and prescribe effective treatments for their ills.

Puységur quickly discovered other somnambulistic subjects with similar abilities in the same district of France. The area was now a kind of psychic contagion zone. Puységur named this new technique *somnamublisme provoqué* or *sommeil magnétique*. It was the last expression that would finally stick and enter the English language as "magnetic sleep." By "magnetic," he referred to the strange metaphysical energies, at once physically palpable and mentally directed, that commonly manifested themselves in these altered states of consciousness. The eventual result of such seemingly humble beginnings was an extremely broad and diverse intellectual, therapeutic, and medical movement that spanned much of the Western world, but especially France, Germany, England, and the U.S. The efflorescence in France was the earliest, although it waned under the Napoleonic wars and, when it revived under the Restoration, so too did the rationalist forces poised against it, mostly from the academy (SM 1:384–93). An official commission was organized under a certain Doctor Husson, the chief medical officer at the Hotel-Dieu. It studied the matter for five years only to issue a report in 1831 that concluded that most of the magnetic phenomena were in fact quite real and effective.

A scandal erupted, and, as sometimes happens in the history of psychical research, if a skeptical body does not like the conclusions of one study, it simply organizes another, avoids research altogether, or just lies about the facts.[29] Hence the next commission was directed by Dubois d'Amiens, who, not accidentally, also happened to be the major figure in the anti-magnetist crusade. A certain Doctor Burdin, who was a member of this second skeptical commission, offered three thousand francs to anyone who could perform a traditional magnetic feat, that is, read a text through some opaque obstacle (often a blindfold, but envelopes, buried pages further down in a book, and other strategies were also used). A young girl named Léonide Pigeaire stepped forward. She appeared to be able to do exactly this, that is, read with her eyes laboriously sealed by a veritable shroud (a photo of which appeared in the newspapers and is reproduced on the cover of the first volume of *Somnambulisme*). The intellectual and cultural environments would not be swayed, however. The two camps went to war over experimental protocol, the experiments were not able to take place, and, as Méheust puts it, "magnetism was vanquished by forfeit."[30]

After the negative Dubois Commission report and the retraction of the Burdin prize in 1842, the magnetist movement essentially lost whatever status it had in the professional medical community. It hardly disappeared, however. Indeed, numerous major literary figures, philosophers, intellectuals, and anthropologists saw very clearly what was at stake, that is, what the magnetic phenomena suggested about human nature and its latent capacities, and pursued these with passion and dedication. This latter humanist defiance held for another century as the movement hopped the pond to the U.S. and the channel to England, where it merged with the later movements of Spiritualism and the psychical research tradition of the S.P.R.

Méheust's *Somnambulisme et médiumnité* is the story of that initial efflorescence and subsequent disciplined suppression and forgetting. I have listed a few representative moments in the introduction, so I will not repeat them here. It is worth citing Méheust's final thoughts on this long forgetting, however. Toward the very end of the two volumes, Méheust puts the matter as starkly as he can. If we were to reproduce in France in the second half of the twentieth century what was happening intellectually in the nineteenth century, or even in the first three decades of the twentieth, he points out, we would see names like Barthes, Bourdieu, Deleuze, Derrida, Foucault, Lacan, Levi-Strauss, Morin, Ricoeur, and Sartre debating the existence of psychical abilities in places like *L'Homme*, *La Revue de métaphysique et de morale*, *Diogéne*, and so on (SM 2:501). Such a thing, of course, can hardly be imagined. We have forgotten that much. We have rendered what was once possible completely impossible.

2. Guardians of the Threshold. Historians of psychology generally acknowledge Puységur's role in "the discovery of the unconscious," but they usually relegate this role to a subordinate one, to that of a catalyst, as Henri Ellenberger put it in his famous study.[31] For Méheust, this is an inappropriate reading-backwards, an illegitimate adoption of a later ideology that is then anachronistically imposed on an earlier system that did not subscribe to the rules and limitations of the later ideology. And indeed, Puységur's magnetic sleep, much like Myers's subliminal Self, was no Freudian unconscious. This was a form of mind of immense metaphysical proportions and astonishing psychical abilities. Accordingly, authors like Méheust and Adam Crabtree reject the notion that Puységur's magnetic sleep was somehow an ill-formed or incomplete version of a later Freudian psychoanalysis.[32] Rather, Méheust argues, Freud's psychoanalysis acted in effect as a "Guardian of the threshold" (SM 2:441), a compromise-formation that, by incorporating, refashioning, and domesticating select aspects of these new models of the psyche, rendered them relatively harmless to the reigning materialism and scientism of the day. In one of Méheust's most striking images, psychoanalysis was a kind of "back fire" (*contre-feu*) set in the hills to stop the spread of an approaching metaphysical blaze (SM 2:213). The image is nearly perfect, as it suggests, correctly in my opinion, that psychoanalytic theory participated in the same fiery nature of that which it battled and finally stopped.

Méheust also points out, again correctly in my opinion, that an epistemological system like that of psychoanalysis grants very particular insights that the earlier mesmeric and magnetic models simply could not (e.g., oedipal and libidinal dynamics), even as the earlier models granted very particular insights that psychoanalysis could not (e.g., telepathy and the subliminal Self). Freud thus opened the Western world up to a "new continent" of the psyche with features ignored by the earlier models and now intricately described with what Méheust calls a kind of hallucinatory precision: enter the domains of the primary processes, the archaic, and the infantile. One of the results of Freud's stunning success, however, was that the earlier discoveries of the magnetists and psychical researchers were effectively overshadowed. Eventually, they more or less disappeared (SM 2:415). There is no "free lunch" for Méheust, then, no perfect system. Every system, *any* system, conceals as it reveals and reveals as it conceals. As Fort once put it so precisely, to "save" one class of data is inevitably to "damn" another: "To have any opinion, one must overlook something."

This, then, is a story of more than a forgetting, more than a simple suppression. For, as we see here with psychoanalysis, Méheust argues that major twentieth-century intellectual movements incorporated aspects of psychical research, but primarily as a strategy to resist them, to stop them in their tracks, as it were. In this way, these movements functioned like those immense padded stops at the end of a train line that are designed to stop the momentum of a moving locomotive in an emergency. Méheust defines these "stop concepts" (*concepts butoirs*) as "notions which, no doubt possessing an incontestable heuristic power, have at the same time a strategic function, that of limiting, by tacit convention, an obscure domain of experience, thus stopping the flight of thought into the unknown" (SM

2:208). In effect, such concepts function on a cultural level as means to stop a moving "train of thought." They are defense mechanisms invoked by the internal logic of a social system in a cognitive or metaphysical emergency.

By far, Méheust's most extensive and analyzed example here is again psychoanalysis, particularly in its notion of the unconscious and its methods of dream interpretation. Personally speaking now, I find this view of psychoanalysis as a kind of *cultural shock zone before a psychical challenge* especially convincing, as it helps me to relate what are essentially two opposite and seemingly exclusive views of psychoanalysis: one, about which I have written a great deal, as a kind of secular mysticism that is uniquely suited to the interpretation of mystical literature (especially erotic mystical literature); the other, by far the more orthodox reading, as a purely materialist and reductionistic method that has no place in its worldview for the mystical or the paranormal. What Méheust does, for me anyway, is show how *both* of these positions are true, how psychoanalysis, in effect, comes to be *between* the two competing worldviews, acting as a buffer or stop zone between them. This seems exactly right to me.

But it is not just psychoanalysis that protects Western culture from the moving train of the psychical. Méheust also treats, among many other figures: Arthur Schopenhauer, who, Méheust suggests, understood the superconscious state of magnetic lucidity to correspond to a direct experience of the life-force in which the World is perceived, in his famous titled phrase, as Will and as Representation (SM 1:314); André Breton's surrealism and its "occult background" (SM 2:322–32); Emile Durkheim's sociology and its valorization of highly individualized forms of ecstatic consciousness made possible, paradoxically, by the fusion of collective enthusiasms (SM 2:260–61); psychofolkorist Andrew Lang's anthropology of the soul and its constant evocation of "region X" (SM 2:276, 293); Mircea Eliade's history of religions, with its constant references to mysticism, occultism, and the fantastic (SM 2:277–78, 294–95); and any number of literary oeuvres, including and especially those of Arthur Conan Doyle and Victor Hugo.

3. To Describe Is to Construct. Méheust's grand historical thesis about "the forgetting of magnetism" carries with it a second major thesis about the inner workings of consciousness and culture, which is also a kind of insight into the metaphysical consequences of history. This is the striking notion that human intellectual and social practices, particularly in their naming and institution-creating functions, somehow circumscribe reality, somehow create the real for a particular place and time. In a single phrase, *to describe is to construct*. Méheust captures this idea in his French hyphenated expression, *décrire-construire*, which appears consistently throughout both volumes. We might gloss this Méheustian gnomon this way: "to acknowledge openly and to describe authoritatively some aspect of the real is to make possible a psychological experience of the same." Méheust himself comes very close to this gloss when he broaches what he calls "an historical and epistemological enigma," namely, the manner in which *décrire-construire* functions as "the actualization and/or the inhibition of potentialities." To describe-construct, in other words, is also to describe-select (*décrire-selectionner*) and to describe-point (*décrire-aiguiller*) (SM 2:116). It is as if our intellectual and social practices "switch on" and "switch off" a set of latent universal human potentials.

In order to get a proper handle on what Méheust is arguing here, it is perhaps helpful to get a handle first on what he is not arguing. As a personalized, psychological truth, after all, Méheust's sound bite seems to reflect rather closely one of the central ideas of the American metaphysical tradition, from the nineteenth-century Mind Cure and New Thought movements, through Norman Vincent Peale's *The Power of Positive Thinking*, to the human potential movement and the contemporary New Age. In its most exaggerated and radical forms, this idea boils down to the notion that a single individual can create his or her own reality through acts of intention and affirmation. This, essentially magical, idea is evident in a whole variety of modern mystical texts, from the channeled classic *A Course in Miracles* to the most recent breezy bestseller *The Secret*.

There are certainly links between the modern metaphysical literature and nineteenth- and early twentieth-century magnetic and psychical literature. But this is not exactly what Méheust is arguing in these two volumes. His thought is much more sociological, although it never ceases to be psychological as well. That is to say, he is much more interested in the broad social processes and institutional structures, not to mention the outright cultural wars, that produce a sense of the real in any given place and time. He is interested in things like government commissions, published essays and books, and medical and scholarly careers won and lost over ideas. More technically, he is interested in how our methods of inquiry end up constituting both the subject that seeks to know and the object that is finally known. Which is all to say that Bertrand Méheust is much closer to Michel Foucault than to *A Course in Miracles*.

Which is not to say that Méheust is arguing exactly what Foucault argued, or that he would disagree completely with the fundamental premises of a text like *A Course in Miracles*. Framed in my own terms now, Méheust's thought appears rather as an elaborate attempt to relate consciousness to culture and culture to consciousness, and to demonstrate, in the process, how these two dimensions of human experience effectively constitute each other in a never-ending cycle of dialectic and debate. Méheust, then, would likely not accept that a single psyche can somehow create a new reality from whole cloth. But neither would he deny the possibility that an individual psyche, temporarily freed from its cultural constraints (which include the personal ego), might demonstrate "impossible" powers and capacities. That which is possible, after all, is relative. He would thus insist that a culture's sense of reality—what is possible, what is impossible—is largely circumscribed or "set up" by social practices, historical institutions, and previous cultural battles by which the lines were drawn and the real circumscribed. Essentially, we write ourselves, but as social groups now, not generally as single lone individuals.[33] Which implies, of course, that we can, singly or together, unwrite and author ourselves anew.

What I personally find so remarkable about all of this is what it implies about what we might call the metaphysics of history. What we seem to have here, after all, is a basic sense that, although there is a fundamental base to what human beings experience as reality, this reality behaves differently in different historical periods and linguistic registers. Things that are possible in one place and time are impossible in another, and vice versa. Put a bit differently, we think, feel, and experience today according to the battles of yesterday, but had these battles come out differently, we would be thinking, feeling, and experiencing quite differently now. The world can be otherwise. The impossible is possible. Fort had it exactly right again then: "Or that the knack that tips a table may tilt an epoch."

4. Magical Powers as Actualizations of the Self. All three of these major themes—the cultural forgetting of animal magnetism and psychical research, the concept of intellectual systems as shock zones or "stop concepts," and the sociology of the impossible embedded in the French sound bite *décrire-construire*—play in turn into Méheust's elaborate discussions and analyses of the various secret powers that manifested themselves, that began to reveal their secret identities, as it were, at the center of this two-century story. Enter our fourth and last theme: the magnetic ability, what will become the supernormal capacity in Myers and company, the wild talent in Fort, and, eventually, the pop-cultural superpower. In historical fact, it was precisely the alleged existence of these magnetic powers—which seemed patently, shockingly obvious to those who witnessed them—that constituted the basic metaphysical challenge of the magnetic and psychical currents. It was the powers and what they implied about human consciousness that so scandalized French intellectual society. It just couldn't be. But it was.

True to form, Méheust refuses to buffer the shock for us, or just barely does so. He thus writes of "these faculties that seemed to belong to the mythical" (*ces facultés qui paraissaient relever du mythe*) (SM 1:150). These indeed were faculties of mythological proportions. He writes of such capacities at this juncture of European history as if they were quantum events, not yet fully real, but certainly not unreal either. They were "quasi facts" of sorts, possessing a structural instability that is also a rich potentiality, capable of manifesting in any number of directions.[34] Before such states of consciousness, the very foundations of rationality and the real came into question and were negotiated. It was before them that what will become modernity and modern rationalism took shape: "*it is precisely*," Méheust insists in his own italics, "*on the foundation of the question of [magnetic] lucidity, posed as a sort of horizon, that this world is able to manifest itself*" (SM 1:151).

Put simply, in the fantastic states of magnetic lucidity that were so prominent in the early decades of the nineteenth century, Western intellectual culture was issued a profound metaphysical challenge. It encountered a fork in the road. It chose to take what would become a rationalist and materialist path. But it could have chosen otherwise. Which implies, of course, that it might still. Again, the real is fluid for Méheust. What we know as modernity, and now as postmodernity, is by no means the last word. Both are moments, Fortean fashions to put on and take off, temporary choices in the ongoing dialectic of consciousness and culture.

Various, wildly various, occult powers make their appearances throughout the two volumes. Méheust, for example, discusses how the senses become empowered within a kind of hyperaesthesia (SM 1:156). He also treats the "spiritualized life" (*la vie spiritualiseé*) as a life in which the entire physical organism has become strangely empowered, mystically zapped, spiritually electrified, or, to employ the simpler scientistic language of the day, *magnetized* (SM 1:314–15). Within such a magnetic state, a kind of superhearing might manifest (SM 1:167). Or a supersight, including a kind of X-ray vision that forced the coinage of two new technical terms: *endoscopy* and *exoscopy*. Endoscopy, literally an "inside-sight," was the alleged ability of the somnambulist to see and diagnose the condition of his or her own internal organs. Exoscopy, literally an "outside-sight," was the alleged ability of the somnambulist to see into someone else's body and deliver a diagnosis. Such powers, it turns out, went all the way back to 1784 and the original scenes with Victor Race.

Méheust points out that these particular visual abilities, lacking any clear historical precedent with which to make some comparative sense of them, were among the most puzzling and the most capricious of all the magnetic phenomena. The learned consensus was that endoscopy was generally more reliable than exoscopy (SM 1:179–80). Later, moreover, endoscopy, now renamed *autoscopy* (in 1904), literally a "self-sight," would take on yet another form and approach a kind of microscopic vision that could describe internal bodily tissues and structures normally visible only under a microscope (SM 1:184). Things, in other words, hardly cleared up with the coinage of new words. On the contrary, they became more fantastic still.

There were other powers too, many of which Méheust treats in a section entitled "The Magnetic Phenomenology" (SM 1:146–216). These include: spontaneous and provoked sympathetic reactions to another's pain or suffering; the transposition of the senses; seeing through or by means of an opaque body (e.g., reading a book above the head or with the tips of the fingers); *voyage mental et voyance*, what we would today call clairvoyance or remote viewing (SM 2:136); mental suggestion (in the strong sense now, that is, mentally suggested without the use of the voice); and precognition (*faculté de prevision*). And then, of course, there was also "the sixth sense" coined by and subsequently omnipresent in the early magnetic literature itself (SM 1:317).

There were, of course, numerous theorizations of these powers, theorizations grounded in both practice and experience. These theorists were men whom Méheust describes as "theoreticians-practitioners of magnetism, men of the world engaged in the groping quest for a new epistemology" (SM 1: 254). The Comte de Szapary, for example, described the state of magnetic lucidity as a "third state" in which the life of the body and the superior functions of the mind clarify or enlighten one another until they provoke the emergence of new faculties (SM 1:315). J. P. F. Deleuze suggested that such powers are always present but well hidden, effectively and necessarily suppressed by the pressures of daily life and practical action. They thus only manifest in exceptional states of consciousness, like somnambulism, or in sudden interruptions and sufferings, within traumatic and dissociative conditions, as we would say now. Such inner hidden faculties are like the stars in the day sky—they are always there, shining, but they are completely invisible until the sun sets, that is, until the sun of the waking consciousness is temporarily suppressed (SM 1:287–88). Julian Ochorowicz would articulate a similar sensibility, which had been more or less common with the magnetic theorists since Puységur, namely, that the powers of mental suggestion and the forms of magnetic lucidity evident in rare and gifted subjects almost certainly exist "in germ" in every human being (SM 1:582; cf. 1:157). We are all secretly, nocturnally gifted. We just live in the day, oblivious to our own secret stars.

Another theorist compared the figure of the somnambulist to that of the mythical figure of Proteus, who had similarly received a gift, but a gift that takes a thousand different forms that are virtually impossible to pin down. The sheer diversity of the magnetic phenomena across the human body and senses is indeed overwhelming (hence Fort's adjective of *wild*). It appears that the magnetic state renders the obvious diversity normally seen in human beings much more extreme, and even more individualized (SM 1:255–56). The celebrated somnambulist Alexis Didier, to whom we will soon return, consistently insisted on the same point. For him, the central character of the states of magnetic lucidity is their variability. For others, this "fugitive" or "anarchic" character of the magnetic phenomena, this boundless reservoir of potentialities, should profoundly transform our image of the human being and, consequently, render any final model of human nature, and so any general or universal method of therapy, impossible (SM 1:257).

In the light of such impossible potentialities and possible actualizations, human nature begins to be seen as fundamentally contextual *and* unconditioned, that is, as dialectical. Hence the data of anthropology with respect to shamanism and the realization, already intuited by the magnetic theorists with their studies of mediums and somnambulists, that the ecstatic and his or her environment constitute a single system. So, for example, many shamans have claimed that they cannot access their magical powers without the presence of a group. And similarly, the social group is continually influenced by the presence and dramatic rituals of the shaman (SM 1:274–75). Together, the psyche of the shaman (or medium, or somnambulist) and the cultural group "make each other up."

Such insights, Méheust reminds us, put into stark contrast the naive objectivism of the scientific method with respect to paranormal phenomena, a method whose philosophical assumptions about determinism, objectivity, nature-as-given, and stable "facts" can only operate by effectively denying, suppressing, or even destroying this psychocultural Gestalt. Méheust articulates the counterproposition as "the idea that the phenomena of somnambulism are not invariable manifestations of the human soul, but that they should be thought of as the actualization of hidden virtualities—an actualization rendered possible only in certain contexts, and therefore variable" (SM 1:275).

There is a moral contribution to make here as well, for there was also a "dark side" to the nineteenth- and early twentieth-century theorizations of the magnetic powers, particularly surrounding the potential for evil that numerous thinkers saw in such occult capacities—essentially, a modern version of the traditional lore around black magic. Or, alternatively, we might detect what will later be theorized as a "fear of psi" and watch how the natural paranormal capacities of the human being are almost always demonized, from the early modern Inquisition trials, where such abilities were literally linked to the devil, to the most recent Hollywood movie or television hit, where the gifted one is forever getting hunted down and dying. God forbid such an anomalous person be happy, healthy, and content. Who would want to watch that?[35]

Thus Puységur was convinced that something like thought transference was quite real. He had, after all, observed it. But he refused to propagate this discovery too openly for fear that it would be used for nefarious purposes (SM 1:521). Later, there would be quite serious discussions among medical doctors and intellectuals about how psychic criminals might employ mental suggestion in order to manipulate other people, like puppets, for various criminal ends. There was even talk of performing "experimental crimes," that is, of seeing whether a person could be mentally forced to commit an "experimental suicide" (with a revolver loaded with blanks) or perform "fictitious poisonings." Philosophically speaking, things were even more serious, as these same theoreticians began to realize what such thought experiments implied, namely, "a funeral hymn for free will" (SM 1:541–45). Was everyone, in the end, a puppet whose strings are being pulled by someone else? By something else? How *do* I know where my thoughts, desires, and motivations come from? How do I know that they are really mine? Shades of Fort's X and Vallee's cosmic Puppeteer. Hence the common link between psychical phenomena and paranoia. It was for both moral and materialist reasons, then, that the medical community waged an effective war against the notion that one human being could have occult influence over another (SM 1:593).

Not that materialism could not sometimes use the same ideas toward immoral ends. Méheust goes to some length to show how different the moral sensibilities of the psychiatrists and the later theorists of hypnotism—all more or less committed to materialism—were to the sensibilities of the early magnetists. Whereas the magnetists considered themselves to be "listening to the voice of Nature" and submitted themselves carefully and humbly to forces they did not claim to control or predict, the psychiatrists and hypnotists considered themselves to be superior to their (mostly female) subjects, whom they often grossly manipulated for scientific ends (SM 1:430–31). Their experiments at Nancy in France and elsewhere were thus often cruel and famously voyeuristic. For Méheust, then, "*the central operation of the science of hypnotism is to eliminate completely the magnetic hypothesis of an occult interaction between two human beings*" (SM 1:595). Once the interpersonal spiritual dimensions were removed from the transactional space, a kind of materialistic manipulation could follow, with some quite disturbing medical and symbolic consequences.

Consider the case of Charles Binet-Sanglé, a medical doctor whose authoritarian fantasies regarding occult influence recorded in his *La fin du secret* or *The End of the Secret* (1922) literally end volume 1 of Méheust's *Somnamublisme et médiumnité*. Binet-Sanglé had adopted one of the theories of telepathy common in his time: the mental-radio thesis (today cognitive processes are all about computers and mental software—we never learn). Telepathic influences were not occult, spiritual, or even necessarily human forces in this model. They were rather completely material processes, mental radio waves, as it were, sent and received over large distances by brains.

In this materialist model of "brain waves," the doctor recognized the potential benefits for the State's effective control and manipulation of individuals. He dreamed of recruiting telepaths to be put in the service of the State, mostly from the "backwards" races, like the Negroes or the Tibetans, or from those races predisposed to regression, like the Jews (of course). The best candidates, he thought, would be prepubescent Jewish girls. They would receive special training. They would be gathered in *camps* (Méheust italicizes this word). They would be forced to take drugs, like hashish. They would be trained in a strict vegetarian diet. And they would be required to remain virgins, a discipline that would be imposed on them by hypnotic suggestion. Through such an elaborate discipline, they would no doubt develop extraordinary metagnomic powers: "Nothing," Méheust explains, "would escape their vigilance: the secrets of intimacy, the secrets of correspondence, intentions, past actions, hiding places, [or] diplomatic and military espionage activities" (SM 1:596). There is no need, Méheust points out in the very last line of volume 1, "to underline the posterity of these phantasms" (SM 1:597).

It would be a serious mistake, though, to claim—as many ideologically driven skeptics have claimed—that the paranormal somehow automatically leads to fascism or right-wing politics. Méheust is very clear on this point: the full history presents us with no necessary relationship or link between the psychical data and any particular political system. Moreover, there is a fairly strong, if by no means definitive, trajectory through the history that links the magnetic and the psychical with degrees of autonomy, liberty, and freedom still unknown to any political system. This was already apparent in the ways that the Being whom Puységur could not name related to the marquis in ways that would have been entirely inappropriate for a young peasant like Victor Race. The Being manifesting in Victor's magnetic states, in other words, possessed its own autonomy and liberty and would have nothing of the usual deference and submission required before someone of Puységur's social rank.

Similar levels of autonomy and freedom were intuited in the magnetic discourses on belief and the whole phenomenon of "suggestion." The theorists realized that the content of the belief or the suggestion (much less the literal magnets themselves that were sometimes used) mattered little, if at all. What was important was the power or conviction in the belief (recall that Fort would later express the exact same insight into the irrelevance of belief and the centrality of mental focus). For these authors, in other words, "the fundamental suggestion is the belief in the power of suggestion." *Ideas are forces*, they realized, and the most powerful idea of all is the idea of the force of ideas. In this way, the theorists encountered the dominant psychic determinism of their era, refracted it through their own practices with mental suggestion and magnetic healing, and inverted it into a kind of radical freedom for which we still have no real models, much less a stable practical institution (SM 1:574).

Méheust, it should be noted, is hardly alone in linking nineteenth-century psychical phenomena to liberal political practices and democratic values. We have already noted the remarkable case of Spiritualism and social reform around gender issues. To take another particularly striking case that bears directly on my repeated insistence that there is a profound link between psychical phenomena and literary phenomena (that is, that the paranormal is a hermeneutical reality), consider the recent work of Bruce Mills, whom I briefly alluded to in my introduction. Mills has persuasively argued that Edgar Allan Poe, Margaret Fuller, Lydia Maria Child, and Walt Whitman all turned to the critical literature on Mesmerism, where they learned that the true power of mesmeric practices lay not in any literal "fluid," but in the power of the imagination and the nature of signs, gestures, and beliefs that such practices artfully employed. Puységur, we might recall, was the first to realize this. He quickly concluded that the materialism of Mesmerism was mistaken and that what was in fact at work in these extraordinary states was not "fluids," tiny "atoms," or the "workings of the spheres," but the nearly omniscient and seemingly omnipotent power of a vast magnetic Mind. Although they differed, of course, on the nature of this mind, even the most official critics recognized the truth of this basic psychological insight.

Hence Mills quotes from Chauncy Hare Townshend's *Facts in Mesmerism*, in which he approvingly cites the following lines from the Commission of the French Academy of Science and its report on animal magnetism:

> That which we have learned . . . is, that *man can act upon man*, at all times and almost at will, by striking the imagination; that signs and gestures the most simple may produce the most powerful effects; that the action of man upon the imagination may be reduced to an art, and conducted after a certain method, when exercised upon patients who have faith in the proceedings.[36]

Mills's own point is simple but profound here, namely, that the psychological insight of the above quote is "as applicable to literary creation as to medical practice or social reform."[37] In other words, what the Mesmerists could do with their patients via magnets, touch, and the passing of hands in a healing practice, the authors could do with their reader via words, plot, and mood in a writing practice. Both, after all, were drawing on the same imagination, the same power of signs and symbols, and the same psychology of belief. This was particularly obvious after Puységur and his colleagues realized that the magnets and related rituals of mesmeric practice were not necessary, that they were artful and useful props, but certainly not literal physical causes.

This is how, Mills suggests, American writers of the nineteenth century intuited "a link between the mesmeric and literary arts" and came to understand the incredible power of signs.[38] This is how the call for a national literature and the subsequent American Renaissance it produced "evolved into attention to the state of one's own mind, to those manifestations of the highest states of mind, and to the effects of literary choices on readers' psychological states."[39] Such authors were writing their way to a distinctly American aesthetic that could accommodate and nurture what Mills calls "transition states" in a democratic culture. In my own terms, they were writing their way to a democratic mysticism rooted in literature and individuals as opposed to doctrinal systems and institutions. They were laying the foundation for America's religion of no religion and its various and diverse "altered states of consciousness."

Finally, there is Méheust's treatment of the common evolutionary reading of the emergent superpowers, evident, as we have already seen, in figures from Alfred Russel Wallace and Fredric Myers to Richard Maurice Bucke and Henri Bergson. These thinkers were hardly alone in their conclusions. In 1902, for example, Jean Jaurés asked whether "the man of extraordinary and unknown powers" may not signal some "new progress of consciousness and life on our planet." Why, after all, should we consider the present form of man, the "normal" form, the last term or expression of the species? Jaurés then posited a classic *homo duplex* doctrine by which the human being is seen as possessing two distinct but related forms of consciousness: one familiar and normal, the other manifesting in the altered states of hypnotism and still considered abnormal. Fusing these two forms, Jaurés speculated, might well lead to "the creation of a new humanity." This, however, would by no means be easy, he thought. It would likely be no easier and no less filled with suffering than that unimaginably long evolution that has already carried life from the amoeba to man (SM 2:157).

Joseph Maxwell, writing in 1922 on the history of traditional magic in the present light of psychical research, thought more or less the same: "magic," he wrote, "leads us to consider the human being as an entity whose evolution has not ended, whose powers are not yet fully developed" (SM 2:283). This too was a sensibility very much in line with the intuitions of the magnetic theorists, "for whom," Méheust writes, "the somnambulist trance permits a return to a very ancient form of experience, but also to a recovery of some latent potentialities in order to re-actualize them and use them to make a contribution to the evolution of humanity" (SM 2:298).

Hence that whole field of psychofolklore by which earlier forms of magical experience and folklore are revisited and reread through the categories and findings of contemporary psychical research. The past is recovered, but in a new form now. The anthropologist, folkorist, and historian of religions Andrew Lang is usually credited with bringing this method into prominence, but Lang knew well that he did not invent the idea. He knew, that is, that the early magnetic theorists had arrived at the same realization a full century before him (SM 2:273).

Such evolutionary thinking would find a uniquely gifted voice in the philosopher Henri Bergson and his earlier cited description of the universe as *une machine à faire des dieux*, that is, "a machine for making gods." Here also we should place Bergson's central notion of the *élan vital* animating the universe. Although Bergson followed Christian mystical theology in his position that mysticism represented a more evolved stage of the spiritual life than psychical abilities, he also thought that it was what Méheust describes as "the potentialities evolving through the psychic phenomena" in which this *élan* manifests in human nature in a way that can be scientifically, collectively, and cumulatively studied. In this way, Bergson thought, a new vision of human nature and its psychical evolution can eventually be made available to the public, and this in a manner that mystical accomplishments, however profound, could never supply (SM 2:253).

"If Only One of These Facts . . .": The Impossible Case of Alexis Didier

One of the features of Méheust's work that makes it so remarkable, and so refreshing, is the fact that he does not avoid the question of whether the magnetic and psychical phenomena are real or not.[40] When I spoke to him about his work, he shared with me his observation that this is a question that must not be asked in French intellectual circles. Such phenomena can be discussed as "representations" to be sure, but never empirical facts, never genuinely veridical cognitions of something out there. If Méheust had been a traditional French intellectual (or a traditional American one, for that matter), he would have gone in precisely this direction. He would have "bracketed" the truth claims of the phenomena and treated them as pure forms, as "representations" or "discourses," to use the safe, postmodern catchphrases in fashion today.

He does not do this. And this constitutes his most important intellectual intervention. In essence, he forces his readers into a kind of philosophical corner: "If these facts are real," he asks, "what does this mean?" And more specifically, "If these facts are real, how must we now reread intellectual history and its defensively dismissive treatment of magnetic, psychical, and paranormal phenomena?" These are rhetorical questions. Méheust thinks that the phenomena are very likely genuine. They are not only representations or simply discourses (although they are certainly those things too). But once we postulate such an (im)possibility, the history of animal magnetism and psychical research looks *very* different indeed, as does the intellectual antireception of these practices and inquiries. It all looks like a vast forgetting, a massive cultural repression, a tragic denial of our own potential nature. All of this is implied but never really stated as such in *Somnambulisme et médiumnité*. Méheust was still being careful. He still hoped for a university position.

He didn't get one.

And so, after publishing his immense temporal and intellectual map of the Great Forgetting, Méheust decided to make his implicit philosophical challenge more explicit. In order to do this, he zoomed in on a single historical figure and in 2003 published *Un voyant prodigieux* or *A Seer Extraordinaire*, an in-depth case study of a mid-nineteenth-century figure whom many consider to be the most gifted magnetic seer of the century, Alexis Didier (1826–86). As with all books, there are many ways to read this one, but it is difficult to miss the ways Méheust employs the biographical details and historical documents (part 1); the elaborate reception of Alexis by journalists, literary figures, intellectuals, and skeptics (part 2); and the various critical approaches to the phenomena that he heralded (part 3) as one long argument about the empirical reality of the magnetic phenomena under study and, most of all, about what these impossible phenomena imply about the still possible nature of human consciousness and culture. As with his first flying-saucer book, he is setting down a metaphysical challenge. As with his two-volume dissertation, he is asking us to remember that which we have forgotten.

Méheust begins the book with a quote from Kant's response to Emanuel Swedenborg, his *Dreams of a Spirit-Seer*, which includes the following line on the data of clairvoyance: "Such a capital witness, such a perspective of astonishing consequences, if one is able to presuppose that *only one* of these facts is guaranteed" (VP 7). The line captures well what William James would later make famous as the white crow argument. It only takes one white crow to prove that all crows are not black, James pointed out. So, too, it only takes one proven case of telepathy to establish that the mind is not bound by the brain and the body. The Jamesian white crow became a kind of battle cry or philosophical symbol for early (and later) psychical researchers, but the faultless logic it represents is already present in Kant's honest philosophical frustrations with the dreams of the Swedish spirit-seer. It only takes one.

Or a thousand. From about the age of fifteen to the age of twenty-five, when he more or less retired from exhaustion and a variety of health problems (perhaps brought on by his various healings and feats), Alexis Didier demonstrated an entire spectrum of psychical powers that baffle the modern reader even more than they baffled the princes, intellectuals, aristocrats, journalists, and medical professionals who sought him out in the 1840s and '50s in such great numbers. The latter, at least, lived in a cultural climate that could still remember a time when such powers were widely accepted as real and so were often experienced as such. But even they had to remember. Alexis came on the French scene just after the magnetic movement had been thoroughly defeated in the public arena and had gone underground. The receptive actualizing climate was no more. Because of both this repressive cultural climate and the incredibly short span of the seer's public career, Méheust sees Alexis as a kind of Icarus figure, a tragic being who attempted to fly too high, who tried to expand the human condition past where his culture, and his own body, was willing to go. His wings melted. His career was cut short. A mere decade or so is all. It was over almost as soon as it began.

I cannot possibly summarize all the stories Méheust recounts in his exhaustive study. One iconic example will have to do, the one that Méheust himself treats as iconic, that is, the one with which he begins his book. Rev. Chauncey Hare Townshend was an Episcopalian priest, an author of an early book on Mesmerism (briefly cited above in our discussion of Mills), an intimate friend of Charles Dickens, and the latter's literary executor.[41] Townshend also wrote poetry, painted, and practiced animal magnetism himself. In October of 1851, he sought out Didier and spent a few hours with him in Paris. He subsequently published an account of his experiences in the form of a letter dated November 25, 1851, in *The Zoist*.[42]

The reported facts are these. Townshend visited the home of a certain Mr. Marcillet, who was the magnetizer of Didier, in order to arrange a meeting with the famous clairvoyant. Marcillet brought Didier to Townshend's hotel room at 9:00 p.m. that same evening. At Marcillet's suggestion, Townshend magnetized Didier himself. After a few minutes of magnetic passes and some strange, quite ugly convulsions of his face, Didier passed into a calm state and gave his usual signal that he was there: "*Merci*!" Once Marcillet saw that Didier was successfully magnetized, he left the two men alone in the hotel room and departed.

Townshend immediately began to test Alexis "in the matter of seeing distant places," a particular power the French called *clairvoyance à distance* but which is very similar to what we have already encountered in its American cold war form as remote viewing. With no Russians to spy on, Townshend asked Alexis if he wished to visit his house in thought. "Which?" Alexis responded. "For you have two! You have a house in London and one in the country. Which shall I go to first?" Townshend asked him to visit the country home. After a pause, Alexis responded, "I am there!" Alexis's eyes were now wide open but "blank" and staring, like a sleepwalker's, with his pupils fixed, dull, and dilated. In this odd stare, he described a chateau with a garden around it and a very small house to the left. All exact. He was looking at water now too. Townshend's windows looked out onto a lake.

Alexis now entered the salon and commented on the numerous paintings hanging on the wall. He found it curious that they were all modern paintings, except for two, one of the sea and one of a religious subject. Townshend shuddered. Alexis went on. "There are three figures in the picture—an old man, a woman, and a child." He described the painting in significant, and correct, detail—of Saint Ann in the process of teaching the Virgin Mary to read, it turned out. Townshend asked him what the painting was done on. Alexis described a blackish-gray stone substance that was bumpy. It was, in fact, a black marble base that was rough and bumpy.

Alexis then proceeded to describe his other home in London, on Norfolk Street. He gave descriptions of the two female servants, especially the young one who struck him as pretty. He described the salon, the library, the elaborate carved frame of a mirror over the chimney, and then, suddenly, a portrait that appeared reflected in the mirror. He described in detail the painting, of the Holy Family this time. Townshend asked him the name of the painter. He replied that he had been dead for some time and, after some effort, he murmured "in a very cavernous voice," that it was Raphael. "The fact is," Townshend explains, "the name of Raphael is written dimly in gold letters on the hem of the Virgin's garment."

After a few more uncannily accurate descriptions of paintings, Townshend asked Alexis to read through some kind of opaque obstacle. Alexis successfully read in turn lines or words from Lamartine's *Jocelyn*, a popular French magazine, and an English novel, all a number of pages down (determined by Townshend) from where the book or magazine was opened. At Alexis's request, Townshend now produced a letter in an envelope that he had recently received from a particular lady. Alexis described its contents in impossible detail and then proceeded to describe "the whole history of my fair correspondent—how long I had known her, and many minute circumstances respecting herself and our acquaintance—something too about the character of her sister, and (to crown all) he wrote . . . both the Christian and family name of her father!" One gets the sense that Townshend had some sort of romantic relationship with the woman in question. In any case, he confesses that he cannot make her or her family's name known in print and that the case would be much stronger if he could indeed be more specific. As with the psychical data emerging from Myers's relationship to Annie Hill Marshall, the erotic appears to be intimately related to the paranormal, first as a generative force, then as a reason to censor and weaken the report.

Mr. Marcillet now returned. Townshend continued with his test. He quizzed Alexis about himself and his health. He was astonished by the answers. The conversation finally turned to religious subjects, particularly the question of life after death. "*Dieu seul le sait*," Alexis made clear. "Only God knows that." "It is true," he went on, "many somnambulists pretend to make revelations about a future state. But the proof they are all wrong is, that no two of them agree: all give different accounts."

As the magnetic session ended, Alexis awoke with the same convulsions and grimaces with which he had entered the altered state an hour before. He came back. He was now no longer the gifted seer. He was a young man, timid and respectful to his social senior. It was 10:00 p.m. Marcillet and Didier left. Townshend was left alone with his thoughts.

Toward the end of the letter, Townshend reflects with his readers about the events he has just recounted. Alexis did make a few mistakes "once or twice," and he did ask Townshend to concentrate on what he wanted him to see (a significant detail that naturally invokes an alternate but equally paranormal process, that of telepathy). Townshend believed that much of Alexis's success was a function of his own trust in the seer's powers. He had no doubt that, had he been impatient or distrustful, "Alexis would have lost his clairvoyance, and perhaps attempted to supply it by guessing. This is the history of most of the mistakes and apparent want of truth of somnambulists. We have no patience with them, and will not *observe the conditions* requisite for the development of their clairvoyance." "But a thousand negations," he goes on, "are nothing before *one* affirmative proof." One white crow is all it takes. And Townshend now had a whole flock of them fluttering about in his brain.

I have spent so much space on the Townshend-Didier scene for a simple reason. Any attempted summary of the history of psychical research and modern paranormal phenomena—including the halting one I have sketched here and there throughout the present set of chapters—is all too prone to impressions of secondhand rumor and suspicions of sloppy thinking, as if the authors of the last two centuries were somehow not as smart and careful as those of this one. Nothing could be further from the truth. The truth is that Méheust's study of Alexis Didier reaches to nearly five hundred pages and explores virtually every imaginable criticism and reading, and that in this it resembles and extends the work of such earlier researchers as Frederic Myers, William James, Richard Hodgson, and Hereward Carrington, all of whom we have met above. Such invocations, however brief, are worth making here, since there is much nonsense written about the history of psychical research, with the greatest nonsense of all being the ignorant claim that it was never carefully done.

This in fact is one of the major points of Méheust's study of Didier—how elaborate and careful many of the experiments in fact were. The real point of the book, however, is not to defend the nineteenth-century intellect before the dogmatic skepticism of contemporary intellectual culture. It is to establish the genuineness of Didier's powers, and then to tease out their philosophical and anthropological implications. Basically, it is one immense "If, then . . ." exercise. And once the "if" is established, the "then" that follows is, as Fort would say, a real whopper. In brief, Méheust shows that Alexis Didier—as a kind of mutant prodigy who magnifies, like a human microscope, powers that lie still tiny and invisible in all of us—presents us with truths that strike at the very heart of our cultural assumptions about humanity and its place in the natural world. These invisible powers now rendered visible through such an excessive being, Méheust argues, possess an "immense polemical and heuristic impact" (VP 18).

Méheust reflects here on the dueling perspectives of the sociologist and the parapsychologist: whereas the former brackets the epistemological truth of the visions and reads the visionary through the contexts of his or her social and cultural environment, the latter more or less ignores the cultural context in order to focus exclusively on the objective truth of the visionary cognitions. Such a sectarian division of labor, he points out, essentially paralyzes the inquiry and prevents any real progress toward an adequate resolution of the question at hand. Such different approaches—which align more or less with the methods of the human and natural sciences—need not be seen as opposed, however. They can also be understood as complementary. Consciousness and culture.

The sociologist's approach to the seer as a privileged revealer of a social reality ought to be revived, then, but only if we can acknowledge that the argument can be reversed, that is, only if we can acknowledge that the social reality to which the seer gives witness witnesses in turn to the reality of the seer's experiences. This is a perfect example of the kinds of reflexivity or reversal in modern theory that I have identified as "gnostic": If all the gods are projections of human nature, as modern projection theory argues so convincingly, then might not human nature itself be considered a veritable supergod?[43] Peter Berger put the same "flip" this way in his *A Rumor of Angels*: "If the religious projections of man correspond to a reality that is superhuman and supernatural, then it seems logical to look for traces of this reality in the projector himself."[44]

In order to demonstrate his own point, Méheust invokes Alison Winter's historical study of the effective use of magnetic anesthesia during surgical operations in India in the Calcutta practice of the Scottish surgeon James Eisdale.[45] The impossible phenomenon, which dated from about 1845 to 1851, is well attested: working for up to two (sometimes even eight) hours a day on each patient, local medical workers under Eisdale's instruction were able to magnetize whole rows of suffering subjects. Eisdale would then come into the hospital, test the magnetized trance of a particular patient, and then perform the requisite surgical procedure.

Some of these operations were especially dramatic (huge scrotum tumors were his specialty, and amputations were not unknown), and, although we have no data from the patients themselves, most of the surgeries were reported as being both successful and as accompanied by little or no apparent pain.

Winter approaches these historical events through a classic cultural-context argument, that is, by suggesting that the profound social inequalities between the elite Western surgeons and their patients, who were often impoverished charity patients as well as colonial subjects, set up a certain "physiology of colonial power" that made the practice work. She also points out that, unlike in Britain, where the mesmerized often displayed power over the mesmerists, in Eisdale's Calcutta hospital the whole point was to render the mesmerized subject completely unconscious and entirely passive beneath the surgeon's knife. These events were sometimes veritable spectacles, moreover, with Eisdale essentially performing minor tortures (burning coals were sometimes used, for example) on the patient to test the depth of a particular trance.

Yes, of course, Méheust answers, such scenes do in fact reenact the social conditions of Victorian society and British colonial power, and they are inexplicable without such historical contexts. But they also *did* happen, and this also needs to be explained. Precisely because many of the surgeries were successful, they "constitute at the same time an enigma for the psychologist and the physiologist" (VP 20). The perspectives of the sociologist and the parapsychologist, in other words, can be joined, can be made complementary, but only if we are willing to step out of *both* our antihistoricism *and* our resistance to the metaphysical implications of the actual historical data. But how to go about this? Méheust proposes an elegant model of human potentiality and cultural actualization: "If the alleged facts reveal themselves as sufficiently attested, then it is also necessary to consider them as a potentiality of the human spirit, rendered possible by a certain context" (VP 21). Again, this seems exactly right to me.

Finally, before we leave Alexis, it is worth commenting on a particular section of the book where Méheust manages to synthesize, implicitly anyway, all three of his major works: on flying saucers, on the history of animal magnetism, and on Alexis Didier. The section involves the relationship between the Didier phenomena and major French and English literary figures, particularly Honoré de Balzac, Alexander Dumas, Charles Baudelaire, and Sir Arthur Conan Doyle.

Here Méheust points out that the same year that Alexis appeared on the French scene as a young magnetic prodigy, 1842, Balzac published his

Ursule Mirouet, a major novel that features scenes in it that eerily replicate the performances of Didier. In fact, Balzac based the novel on his reading of the mesmeric and magnetic literature, so this is not entirely surprising, but the degree of the correspondences is striking. The comparative case is stronger still with a later novel, *Louis Lambert*, the novel that Balzac considered his major work, where he speaks in the first person, and where he revealed his own metaphysical system. Méheust is blunt: "*Alexis, in effect, is Louis Lambert*—but a Louis Lambert who has left the universe of the novel in order to develop his presumed gifts in reality" (VP 237).

The details are certainly analogous enough. Both figures are cast as prototypes of the Romantic hero, that is, as a precocious genius who is prematurely spent by the excessive use of his extraordinary gifts. Both men are described as short, fragile, given to illness, pale, and effeminate. Both men are empowered by a strange, "almost superhuman" force that first appears just short of puberty, that is, at twelve years of age. Both men's superpowers, moreover, involve the mysteries of textuality and the act of reading. Whereas Lambert possesses a strange ability to enter the labyrinthine world of a text and reconstruct the intentions and intimate meanings of the author, Didier takes this gift even further with his psychometric power by which he takes an object and "reads" the previous owner's personality and history via its energies and memories. Lambert can gulp down nine to ten lines with a single look. Alexis can read lines ten to twenty pages down from where the book is open. Finally, both men fail in their vocations. Lambert's secret diaries, which are found by a priest of his boarding school, become the means by which his reputation is ruined. Similarly, when Alexis is attacked by the clergy and accused of being in league with Satan, his niece decides to burn his journal. He also loses his reputation among the academy, which ignores him completely (neglect, as Fort pointed out, being the easiest and most effective form of damning a datum). Both men's health breaks down as a result of their respective misfortune. Lambert suffers from catalepsy and dies at the age of twenty-eight. Didier suffers from epilepsy and ends his career at roughly the same age.

How to explain this correspondence between fiction and reality? We have been here before, of course, with the flying saucers and the science fiction. Méheust offers the most obvious and reasonable answer, namely, that Didier had read Balzac. Perhaps, but that hardly explains everything—we are, after all, dealing with technically impossible matters here, not common skills that one can learn from simply reading a novel. True to his earlier writings, Méheust argues that the impact of literature on society is much deeper and much more mysterious than we realize. More specifically, he invokes his *Somnambulisme et médiumnité* and its central notion of *décrire-construire*. Something else is going on here, he suggests. A reality is constructed through elaborate social processes, including the processes of literature, and then it is experienced by gifted visionaries as physically real. The impossible is thus rendered possible, here by literary means.

The case is similar with Alexander Dumas, who assisted in séances with Didier and wrote about magnetic scenes, particularly in his *Joseph Balsamo*. The scenes look a lot like those involving Alexis.

The case is somewhat different with Charles Baudelaire, however, as this particular fiction-fact parallel involved Baudelaire's mystical theory of poetry, which, or so Méheust suggests, was essentially a reworking of psychometric convictions involving the "auratic perception" of physical objects. Psychometry is the practice of handling an object—a shirt, a lock of hair, a bracelet—that a person owned (or was) and "reading out" the identity or chain of memories allegedly inhering in that object. Didier's theorization of his own psychometric practices is a perfect example of psychofolklore, that is, the reinterpretation of a traditional religious practice or doctrine in the light of present paranormal experience and psychical research:

> The past, for me, is not dead, but living. There is a pious belief that leads one to preserve religiously, encased in gold or precious stones, the relics of saints, and that encourages one to believe that something of their souls, of their spirits, of their hearts, in a word, of their personalities, remains in these fragments of their dead bodies. For me, I see them re-existing entirely in body, in soul, in spirit, in holiness, within the least particle that they have touched during their lives, and I feel their real presence, as if they were again on this earth.[46]

Through a kind of occult historiography involving the act of touch, when Alexis "reads" an object, the past comes alive. He physically "feels" and "remembers" it. So too with an inspired poem for Baudelaire—the correspondences and connotations of the words invoke a certain palpable nimbus of nostalgia and remembrance. They carry, as it were, a certain "physical meaning" that can be reinvoked and re-experienced by the sensitive reader. The state of consciousness of the poet is thus reactivated and reactualized in the act of deep reading. Reading has become a genuine mystical act, and poetry has become a kind of divination, even communion with the soul of the "dead" author. Put more precisely, *in Baudelaire the psychometric has become the hermeneutic*.

Finally, there is Didier's role as a kind of "transcendental detective." The use of psychics to solve crimes is something one often hears about in the modern world, mostly on The History Channel and in other popular, and sometimes dubious, venues. Regardless, the phenomenon is embarrassingly well attested in the historical literature and appears to be genuine in that most lowly of senses, namely, in the sense that it sometimes works. Skeptics may dismiss such things, but detectives and police departments use what works.[47]

The newspapers of the time were certainly convinced. They reported on Didier's activity here as well, including the time he remotely tracked a man named Dubois who had stolen twenty thousand francs and was visiting gambling houses in Brussels and Spa, where he was finally arrested at Didier's direction.[48] According to Méheust, such scenes appear to have influenced Sir Arthur Conan Doyle and his most famous character, Sherlock Holmes. Méheust believes that Doyle read about Didier in English sources that were widely available, took a psychical practice with which he was very familiar, that is, psychometry, and transposed it "into a mythical capacity for hyperdeduction" (VP 248). An ancient practice, that of divination, was thus given a very modern garb, and an entirely secular genre was born as a result—the detective novel (VP 247–48).

The Collective Mind: Bateson, De Martino, Vallee, and Jung

One way to get a handle on a thinker's thoughts is to compare his or her system to those of other thinkers who have addressed similar subjects. Since we are at the end now of our readings of our four authors of the impossible, a brief comparison of these four might also serve us well as the beginning of a conclusion.

As we have seen, Bertrand Méheust has written at great length about the history of the mesmeric, magnetic, and psychical research traditions in France. But he also knows the British and American psychical research traditions, and he wrote his M.A. thesis on William James. In many ways, then, his concerns are so close to those of Frederic Myers that it seems almost pointless to point this out. My first chapter on Myers and this fourth chapter on Méheust, then, can be thought of as the beginning and the end of a circle, or, more true to my own gnostic imagination, as a written snake biting its own textual tail. In the end, then, it is probably more fruitful to focus on the middle movements of this hissing book and reflect for a moment on Méheust's thought in relation to that of Charles Fort and Jacques Vallee. I will address the Vallee-Méheust correspondence in this present, penultimate section and the Fort-Méheust correspondence in the last.

Bertrand Meheust's relationship to Jacques Vallee is a very obvious one. The two men know each other. They have read each other's work. They were both partly inspired in their youth by the same older teacher: Aimé Michel. Both, moreover, approach the data looking for "the signal in the noise" (SF 243), and they hear very similar things, particularly concerning the profound connections between folklore and flying saucers. Méheust clearly acknowledges the similarities in approach, as does Vallee.[49]

Méheust observes that Vallee's work, especially in its earlier incarnation, is more interested in the occult dimensions of the phenomenon, and that Vallee moved closer to his own present methodology as his work progressed (it is important to keep in mind here that virtually all of Vallee's corpus predates Méheust's, with the important exception of the latter's science-fiction and flying-saucer book of 1978). This is not an unreasonable reading. In Vallee's early writings, one can indeed get the sense that the mythological control system that he was writing about was controlled by some kind of alien mind. In his later work, Vallee appears to have come to see this control system more as a kind of spontaneous collective mind. That is to say, he has effectively intuited the ways that the ideas and structures of a society interact and regulate themselves, much as Méheust would intuit later on in his *Somnambulisme et médiumnite*. It is this approach to a kind of collective mind and its spontaneous self-regulation that really unites our two authors of the impossible and links in turn their books to those of previous authors, especially Gregory Bateson, Ernesto de Martino, and C. G. Jung.

As for Vallee on Méheust, Vallee embraces the incorporation of science fiction into the discussion (indeed, he has written five science-fiction novels, and he pioneered the folklore approach), but he also points out that unexplained aerial phenomena hardly began in 1947. Indeed, Vallee's very latest work, with an independent scholar named Chris Aubeck, who co-founded a collaborative network of librarians, students, and researchers on the Internet called the Magonia Project, works very much against this "modernist fallacy" by focusing on five hundred cases of unexplained aerial phenomena *before 1875*. And it is not just the modernist fallacy Aubeck and Vallee write against. It is also what we might call the "Western fallacy," for these phenomena are by no means restricted to Europe or North America. Not even close. Chinese, Thai, Japanese, Indian, Russian, Egyptian, and Arab accounts, for example, are all listed and discussed in their latest work.[50] Vallee, then, reads Western science fiction not as simply productive of a later living folklore involving flying saucers (although it is that too), but also as a kind of literary intuition or imaginal realization of something that has been with us, with all of us, for a very long time. Vallee, in other words, points toward a realist conclusion that is in no way dependent on modern science fiction.

Where is Méheust with all of this now? "My own concern," Méheust explained to me, "is the ecology of mind." He was very enthusiastic about such a notion when he first encountered it in the American anthropologist and cybernetics theorist Gregory Bateson. His thought goes well beyond Bateson's in terms of its metaphysical reach, but the sensibility is much the same. For Bateson, "mind" is not something restricted to the human skull. Nature has mind. So too do ecological systems. Mind is the intelligence of a collective system or network, of "the patterns that connect," as Bateson put it so famously in a line that could well function as a motto for the comparativist. This poetic expression captured Bateson's understanding of mind as any complex system that can process information and self-correct. Cells, societies, and ecosystems are all forms of such mind, which may or may not possess consciousness. All minds, though, rely on multiple material parts. Hence there can be no final separation of the mental and the physical. This is why Bateson detested dualism, supernaturalism, or any other theory or theology that separated what he called the "necessary unity" of mind and nature.[51]

The implications for the study of the paranormal seem obvious enough, although to my knowledge Bateson did not seriously study or write about the subject. Méheust did, however, and he was especially keen on demonstrating, through a work like *Somnambulisme et médiumnité*, how the mentality or form of mind of a particular culture shifts, changes, and morphs over time, that is, how it regulates itself. Hence, again, what is possible in one historical period becomes impossible in another, and vice versa. It is on this crucial point—which is also the central point of these four chapters—that Méheust also invokes the work of the Italian anthropologist Ernesto De Martino, and especially the latter's *The Magical World*.

As we have already noted in the introduction, De Martino suggested that the data of ethnography, folklore, and psychical research point to "the paradox of a *culturally-conditioned* nature, and all its embarrassing implications."[52] More specifically, he argued under section titles like "The Problem of Magical Powers" and under rubrics like "paranormal studies" and "paranormal phenomenology" that reality behaves differently within different linguistic codes and historical periods. Magical practices presume a form of human consciousness or collective mind that is much more embedded in the natural world than our own present form of mind in the West. We have moved out of this state of mind in order to gain certain things (foremost of these being the individual), but we have also lost certain things (like our communion with the natural world).

This is an especially powerful idea with strong parallels and resonances in thinkers ranging from Henri Bergson's notion of an *élan vital* guiding the evolution of human consciousness, through John Gebser's notion of an evolving human sensorium that cognitively and sensually constructs reality in different ways in different historical periods, to Charles Taylor's *Sources of the Self* and his notion that the boundaries around the experience of the Western self are more stable now. In De Martino, the thesis is expressed in an especially strong way, and he does not hesitate to draw on parapsychological material to make his point. Accordingly, assessments of De Martino's *The Magical World* range from readings of it as a youthful mistake out of which the anthropologist, thankfully, matured, to celebrations of the little anomalous book as the key to his entire lifework. Clearly, however we read De Martino's corpus, the base notion that reality appears to human consciousness differently in different cultural frames, that the real is malleable, that the impossible becomes possible and the possible impossible, is fundamental to Méheust's corpus.

Finally, it is worth pointing out that there is an unmistakable lineage of thought from C. G. Jung to both Jacques Vallee and Bertrand Méheust. Both Vallee's and Méheust's writings on UFOs often come very close indeed to Jung's famous notion of an archetype, that is, a permanently unconscious ("unidentified") universal psychical pattern that can break into our physical world and express itself through local myths and symbols, even, in the case of synchronicities, through physical events. For Jung, flying saucers were what I would call "physical meanings." Essentially, they were planetary poltergeists that appeared in the heart of the twentieth century in order to correct and balance Western culture's gross materialism and statistical leveling of the real.

A bit of historical background is necessary here. Jung finally published his little book on flying saucers in 1958, not to publish yet another book, but to clear up the misunderstandings sparked by an interview that he had given to *Weltwoche* in Zurich (published on July 9, 1954). News of what Jung had said (and often of what he had not said) spread like wildfire around the world. Whereas he had been very careful to qualify his conclusion and remained agnostic about the ultimate ontological status of the flying saucers, what was reported often boiled down to the simplistic idea that "flying saucers are real." Over the next few years, different versions of this interview appeared in all the major UFO research publications, including *Flying Saucer Review* (May–June 1955), the *APRO Bulletin*

(July 1958), and NICAP's *UFO Investigator* (August–September 1958). In August of 1958, Jung felt it necessary to issue a statement to the United Press International in order to clarify his position, which was really quite subtle. That same month he also wrote a personal letter to Major Donald E. Keyhoe, a retired military official who was heading up the National Investigation Committee on Aerial Phenomena (NICAP) and who is widely considered to be one of the founders of modern ufology. All of this was no doubt designed to appear in conjunction with the book.

In his 1954 *Weltwoche* interview, Jung expresses his central thesis that the UFO phenomenon may be an attempt by the collective psyche to balance itself, to dream itself aright after a long night of materialism, that the real lesson here is not little green men but our own hopelessly inadequate understanding of our own psychic worlds. His language is much more abstract, but he is essentially arguing what Charles Fort had argued, namely, that by damning the anomalous, modern science "flattens" reality into a bleak and shallow surface "average," whereas, deep down, it is much more wild and ambiguous.[53] This Jungian hermeneutic, which would come to have an immense influence on the later ufological literature, is captured succinctly by Bullard:

> Picking up Jung's implications that UFOs are too important to be just spaceships, these interpreters recast all paranormal phenomena as a glimpse of some larger reality. It may be the juncture where psychic and physical worlds join, a parallel universe, or an imaginal realm, but it is now slipping through the cracks in our everyday continuum, breaking into awareness through altered states of consciousness or gradual weakening of a rational, materialistic worldview. In these speculations UFOs fast-change from physical to mental or spiritual roles and back again. They are deceivers and shape-shifters, tricksters on a mission to violate boundaries and sow confusion. They are agents to rearrange human consciousness.[54]

When Jung finally published his book on flying saucers in 1958, he was still attempting to clarify himself, still struggling with the glowing trickster in the sky. He certainly began humbly enough: "The conclusion is: *something is seen, but one doesn't know what*."[55] What followed was a series of speculations and dream interpretations, much of it engaged with parapsychology, all of which Jung presented as highly tentative. One can almost feel his bewilderment—and his desire not to be misunderstood again.

Although Méheust is critical of Jung's desire to overread the circle-shaped objects as mandalas, that is, as balancing archetypes of psycho-spiritual wholeness, the Jungian influences and even conclusions of Méheust's first book are both obvious and conscious ones. These include the framing of the phenomenon within a certain dream-logic (SF 117, 200, 215, 229, 289, 296), or even *as* a "super-dream" (*sur-reve*) projected into the sky (SF 289), and a serious and sympathetic discussion of Jung's own model for relating consciousness and culture, his archetypal and collective unconscious theories (SF 184). Finally, Méheust even documents how literal "*mandala*-machines" appeared in the early pulp science-fiction stories, often controlled by Hindu, Buddhist, or vaguely Oriental wizards and sages (SF 99–100, 215–20). Such moments, complete with pictures, hardly work to undermine Jung's speculations.

Agent X: Projection Theory Turned Back on Itself

Méheust points out that Jung's *Flying Saucers* book was not the only thing, and perhaps not even the most significant thing, that the depth psychologist published about the subject. He also published an account of a dream involving a UFO he had in October of 1958 (SF 269). It is certainly not surprising that Jung would have such a dream at that point in time. This was the same year, after all, that he published his *Flying Saucers* book. The interpreted meaning of the dream is another matter, however, another matter that takes us straight into Charles Fort land and, through that strange land, back to Bertrand Méheust.

Jung's dream came fourteen years after he had a heart attack (in 1944) and an attendant series of visions and dramatic out-of-body experiences, some of which he recounted in chapters 10 and 11 of his oral autobiography under the titles "Visions" and "On Life after Death." It is in the latter chapter and in this general context of relating personal visions as he ended his career and approached death that Jung finally relates his UFO dream. The dream involved a number of lens-shaped metallic disks flying around his house and above the lake that spread out nearby. One such flying lens, he explains, possessed "a metallic extension which led to a box—a magic lantern." At sixty or seventy yards out, the flying disc pointed the thing straight at him. Jung awoke astonished and, still half-asleep, thought to himself: "We always think that the UFOs are projections of ours. Now it turns out that we are their projections. I am projected by the magic lantern as C. G. Jung. But who manipulates the apparatus?"[56]

This is the most basic question behind the books of Bertrand Méheust.

It was also the most basic question behind the books of Charles Fort.

Fort used the letter X to express this dramatic reversal of projection, this sudden sense that we are the projections of someone else's dream, movie, or novel. Fort used it to express the extraterrestrial force that he believed was projecting the fiction of our world. He also toyed, tongue in cheek, with different possibilities here, never really settling on an answer. Humor or no, however, it is difficult to read him and not come away with the sense that Charles Fort was fairly certain that X is out there, that it is real, and that we are not.

Perhaps not surprisingly, there are many Fortean scenes in Méheust. Méheust, for example, like Fort, seriously treats the colonial-invasion reading of UFOs by comparing science fiction's apparent pop-prediction of the 1947 Arnold sighting and its aftermath to the divinatory practices of the Aztec prophets under Montezuma's reign. As the story goes, the Aztec prophets had predicted the coming of some new gods, who then showed up on cue, as well-armored Spaniards, it turned out, to sack the Aztec kingdom. The moral of the story is clear enough, and rather disconcerting, to say the least. Méheust softens the blow, however, when he suggests that the Aztec "predictions" were likely based on more or less accurate information, a kind of visionary rumor that was traveling through the New World at the same time as the Spaniards made a number of early landings and forays into the continent (SF 54–56).

Then there is Méheust's recounting of a stunning case of seeming teleportation involving an Argentinian couple. The couple got in a car in Buenos Aires, drove into a cloud, lost consciousness, and awoke to find themselves, car and all (now with scorched paint), in an unknown alley in Mexico. Since they were on their way to a party back in Argentina, their friends reported them missing when they did not show up. The Mexican authorities were not amused. Since there was no record of them crossing the border, they accused the couple of entering the country illegally. So, if we are going to believe such an account, we have a whole bevy of "witnesses" (really anti-witnesses), some scorched paint, and the Mexican government to account for here—a typically Fortean scene, for sure (SF 161–62).

Alien invasions and teleportations aside, however, in the end Bertrand Méheust is not Charles Fort. (But who is?) To begin with, he is not nearly as paranoid. Yes, he takes Stanislas Lem's disturbing novel *Solaris*, about a planet whose life-forms are totally controlled by a surrounding unknowable plasma field, as a framing device to get at the epistemological dilemmas the student of UFOs encounters, as if the entire field is a mythology unconscious of itself (SF 295–96, 323). And, yes, he plays with the idea of "source X" possessing a kind of complete mental control over us (SF 135). This is not a new question. We saw the nineteenth-century psychical theorists asking the same question: If telepathy and mental control (*l'induction mentale*) are real possibilities, how *do* I know these are my thoughts and not someone else's? But, in the end, Méheust never really goes there. As for being embedded in a myth, this is not necessarily a bad thing for the author. Indeed, myth may be precisely the means through which we can best approach the unknowable (SF 295). It need not be a form of unconsciousness. Quite the contrary. It may be seen as "a divine incarnation as literature" (*un avatar littéraire*) (SF 185). The mystical as the hermeneutical again.

When Méheust, then, writes of "Agent X," he is not writing about an alien being from Mars controlling us like puppets or projected movie-screen characters. He is much closer to Andrew Lang's psychofolklore and its anthropology of "region X" (SM 2:276, 293). He is speculatively postulating an irreducible form of mind or consciousness that may (or may not) lie behind the rich historical dossier of magnetic, psychical, and paranormal phenomena. He is being honest about the data and about what it suggests to him. He is certainly no true believer. He too is "reducing," but to a form of collective Mind that is finally irreducible.[57]

With respect to the UFO phenomenon, he can write in 2007 that "that which interests me today is less the flying saucer (that is to say, the collective mythological dimension constructed and attested by the coincidence of science fiction and the flying saucers) than the UFO, that is to say, the X that it perhaps reveals" (SF 28). Put simply, Bertrand Méheust does not believe in flying saucers per se, but he accepts our own almost total ignorance of what lies behind the mythology of the flying saucer, and he labels this ignorance, like a buried treasure (or a dangerous ray that makes the invisible visible), with the sign of "X."

The same ambiguous sign could be placed over the entire history of animal magnetism and psychical research, indeed over the entire history of religions. There is every reason to believe that something is indeed appearing there, but, much like Jung's flying saucers in the American sky, "*something is seen, but one doesn't know what*." That, it must be said, is not a terribly satisfying conclusion. But it is an honest one. Obviously, we have not yet come into full consciousness. We are still evolving, to what or whom remains unidentified.

Conclusion

BACK ON THE PAGE

> For the mountain, the body of things, needs no key; it is only the nebulous wall of history, which hangs around it, that must be traversed. . . . True, history may at bottom be an illusion, but an illusion without which no perception of the essence is possible in time. The wondrous concave mirror of philological criticism makes it possible for the people of today first and most purely to receive a glimpse, in the legitimate orders of commentary, of that mystical totality of the system, whose existence, however, vanishes in the very act of being projected onto historical time.
>
> —GERSHOM SCHOLEM, letter to Zalman Schocken, October 29, 1937

> Miracle is essentially "sign."
>
> —FRANZ ROSENZWEIG

We have climbed up Scholem's mountain of revelation (or was it Spielberg's Devil's Tower?) through the mists and myths of history and ventured off the two-dimensional page of our Flatland materialisms into multidimensional realms and bizarre ideas that are impossible. Taking up Aimé Michel's advice to the aspiring savant or gnostic, we have "considered everything and believed nothing." It is time now to come back and profess what we have seen in our four fantastic readings.

Or what we think we have seen.

In truth, I have already come back and professed what I think in the last chapter, where I sketched in the mirror of Bertrand Méheust's scholarship my own working position on the real around a metaphysical dialectic of consciousness and culture. That is indeed what I think, and that chapter should be read accordingly. Those are my conclusions. But I also recognize that all of this raises other important issues that are not directly addressed by such a model. Here at the end, I would like to address some of these, however briefly, toward a future form of thought whose precise contours I do not pretend to understand yet. What follows, then, should be approached not as a final conclusion or a statement of certainty, but as an open-ended thought experiment that approaches a kind of sci-fi "What if"? There are at least three dimensions of this future thought that I would like to explore here.

First, there is what is perhaps the most basic issue of all for the student of religion: the sacred. Such a word, which encodes both the positive and negative aspects of religious experience (the divine and the demonic), has a long history in the field, as I explained in the introduction. But it has fallen out of favor recently. Something needs to be said about this eclipse and how it might be linked to the eclipse of the psychical and the paranormal in the same field.

Second, I would like to pick up my thesis about the paranormal as the fantastic one last time and suggest a future theorization of this model via the history of religions, psychical research, and contemporary neuroscience. More specifically, I would like to return to an old Western stream of thought that we have already encountered—the filter or transmission thesis—and put it into dialogue with the much older mystical doctrine of the *homo duplex* or the Human as Two, my own dialectical model of consciousness and culture, and contemporary neuroscience.

Third, I would like to suggest how we might finally become our own authors of the impossible, how we might wake up from our own cultural and religious projections and realize, with a start, that the real is not any of these fictions, but that it is indeed really and truly this fantastic.

The Eclipse of the Sacred and the Psyche in Modern Oblivion

Fact or fraud, trick or truth, whatever paranormal phenomena are, they clearly vibrate at the origin point of many popular religious beliefs, practices, and images—from beliefs in the existence, immortality, and transmigration of the soul; through the felt presence of deities, demons, spirits, and ghosts; to the fearful fascinations of mythology and the efficacy of magical thinking and practice. But if the paranormal lies at the origin point of so much religious experience and expression, it should also lie at the center of any adequate theory of religion. Once, after all, we recognize that these experiences are often genuine and real in the simplest sense that they are experienced as such by those undergoing them, that they are not faked (and that even the intentionally faked tricks are mimicking the spontaneously generated experiences), then we immediately find ourselves at a very interesting and fruitful fork in the road—a fork that, as far as I can tell, is a win-win situation for the open-minded student of religion.

If something, for example, like modern neuroscience can reduce all of this impossible material to neurological processes, frontal lobe microseizures, cognitive grids, and evolutionary needs, then so much the better. We will have a genuine and genuinely powerful theory of religion that we should pursue with all of our resources and courage, absolute cultural relativisms and historical contextualisms be damned (in a Fortean sense, of course). If, however, such a new approach, like every other promising method of the past, cannot finally deliver the goods, if, for example, cognitive science can provide us with all sorts of evolutionary reasons and neurological correlations for the normal workings of the brain and the usual forms of religious ideation but few, if any, genuine causal mechanisms for the really wild stuff, then we are just as clearly onto something big and important here. After and beyond our A and B, we have found our X (not that we know what to *do* with the damn thing, but at least we have found it).

Either way, it seems to me, the study of religion wins, and wins big. So why look away? Why continue to tolerate a kind of armchair skepticism that has everything to do with scientistic propaganda and nothing at all to do with honest, rigorously open-minded collection, classification, and theory building, that is, with real science and real humanistic inquiry? True enough, anomalies may be just anomalies—meaningless glitches in the statistical field of possibility. But anomalies may also be the signals of the impossible, that is, signs of the end of one paradigm and the beginning of another.

In my own mind at least, I have written these four chapters as serious engagements with the anomalous if not toward the next big thing, then certainly toward a more adequate theory of religion. The bald truth is that it is still very difficult to advance a truly adequate theory of religion. As I explained in chapter 4, we have theories *about* religion that attempt, and more or less succeed, to explain the encounter with the sacred, which lies almost entirely outside our rational grasp, in terms of something else, which is relatively within our rational grasp: society, psyche, body, politics, brain, and so on. The last forty years of theory have in many ways been very much about a quick retreat from any real encounter with the sacred *as sacred*.

Indeed, the sacred as sacred—or what we have encountered here as the psychical and the paranormal as the experiential core of comparative folklore, mysticism, and mythology—is *precisely* what has been eclipsed in the contemporary study of religion. The field has denied, in principle, what Jacques Vallee so clearly saw with respect to the impossible within mathematical theory and the ufological material, namely, that the phenomenon can only be understood on its own level and on its own terms, and that, moreover, it can only be misunderstood if reduced, without remainder, to our physics, our psychology, our cultures, our ethnicities, our materialism, our politics, our ethics, or whatever.

One of many features I find confusing about this categorical rejection of the sacred as a "thing to itself" (other than the assumed omniscience of Immanuel Kant and the almost total erasure of Buddhist and Hindu epistemologies, many of which hold that one really can know reality-in-itself directly and immediately) is the odd conflation of the *sui generis* nature of the sacred and the believer's perspective, as if they were somehow the same thing, as if taking the sacred seriously is equivalent to surrendering one's intellect and critical faculties to the faith-claims of the religious traditions. This is simply not true. The sacred *is* a critical category that can seldom be fit into the categories of faith and piety. It offends the epistemology of faith as commonly as it offends the epistemology of reason. Very much like the paranormal, it is a *third thing*. Hence my historical and theoretical reflections on the sacred as the paranormal in the present book. But it is just this kind of reductive materialism, usually joined to some retooled form of Marxism (it's all economics and oppression) or Foucauldianism (it's all discourse and power), that now defines so much of the study of religion. By so doing, the field has, in effect, denied its own subject matter, much as the fields of psychology and neuroscience have done with respect to the psyche and the mind, which they now more or less (mostly more) deny even exist.

We can trace the latter eclipses back to two different points in the twentieth century. The first, 1913, was the year J. B. Watson proclaimed a new behaviorism, a completely natural science that focused only on observable objective behaviors and from which subjective words like "consciousness" and "mind" were quite literally banned. The second historical point, the decade of the 1950s, was when functionalism, the logical theories of Turing machines, and early digital computer modeling began to take over experimental psychology, leading the field to the useful but dubious conclusion that computation is the same thing as consciousness. Edward Kelly has described the latter developments as "the continuing failure of scientific psychology to come fully to grips with the inescapably dual nature of its subject matter—in short, with the mind-brain problem that lies at the heart of our discipline."[1]

I would suggest that these two eclipses within contemporary intellectual life, of the sacred and of the psyche, are fundamentally related, for whatever the sacred is or is not, it is intimately tied to the deepest structures of the human psyche. To erase one is to erase the other. Mircea Eliade, then, had it exactly right when he wrote that, "the 'sacred' is an element in the structure of consciousness and not a stage in the history of consciousness."[2] Put more bluntly in the form of my own paraphrase: "We cannot, as a species, 'outgrow' the sense of the sacred and become purely secular, and this for one simple reason; we *are* that sense of the sacred." This is why the comparative study of religion really does belong in the research university and at the very heart of any truly serious humanistic, philosophical, or scientific inquiry into the nature of human being. The sacred and the human are two sides of the same coin.

Obviously, there are real problems with such a position. For one thing, the religious nature of the human being and its universe are inherently ambiguous. It is indeed true that our world can be lived and understood, extremely well, it turns out, without any reference to the sacred at all. The coin, then, need not be flipped. It also works lying on one or the other side.

Until, of course, it "flips" again.

Consciousness, Culture, and Cognition: The Fantastic Structure of the Mind-Brain

It turns out that there is a good neuroanatomical reason why we have no theory of religion, but only theories about religion. It is the same reason, moreover, why the universe can be experienced in purely materialist terms or in deeply religious terms. It goes something like this . . .

If the nature of the sacred is intimately tied to the nature of human consciousness, it follows that the sacred is in turn intimately involved with the human brain. Accordingly, in order to begin to understand all of this, we need to propose methodologies that can integrate the humanities and the sciences, that is, that can integrate what I have earlier called the dialectic of consciousness and culture with what the neuroscientists now call cognition. What would such a method look like?

As a thought experiment, I would propose a dual approach through contemporary neuroscience and psychical research, that is, a double-method that can embrace both brain *and* Mind without naively conflating the two. I would also propose putting both neuroscience and psychical research in turn in deep dialogue with the history of religions and literary theory, that is, with the textual or hermeneutical components of paranormal experience—in short, with the fantastic, or what I have called the impossible.[3]

We have already had many occasions to consider what has come down to us as the filter or transmission thesis. Although it appears in different forms, this bimodal psychology or rationalized form of the old mystical doctrine of the Human as Two was first proposed, as we saw in chapter 1, in the nineteenth century by individuals like Frederic Myers and William James in order to explain the supernormal data of psychical research. It was then taken up in the twentieth century and developed further by thinkers like Henri Bergson, C. D. Broad, Aldous Huxley, and Albert Hofmann, the discoverer of LSD, who felt it was the only adequate explanation for the astonishing phenomenology of altered states of consciousness triggered by his new chemical catalyst. We encountered it again in chapter 3 with Jacques Vallee's stained-glass windows filtering an ever-shifting cosmic light. And again in chapter 4 with Bertrand Méheust, who underestimated, in his own words, "the work of the successive filters through which the real passes before it appears to us."

For anyone who attempts to take seriously the data of *both* the natural sciences *and* the history of religions, such a conclusion, it seems to me, is nearly inescapable. Mind is not the brain, but Mind is indeed filtered through the brain with all its mindboggling evolutionary, neurological, cultural, linguistic, emotional, and historical complexities.[4] We are *both*. The Human is Two.

Obviously, we need a new metaphor here. Unfortunately, there are problems in every direction we turn. The analogies of the filter or a transmission, for example, are clearly crude ones, and they almost certainly mislead with all of their dualistic assumptions. My own intuitive sense is that paranormal phenomena are expressions of a deeper nondual reality that possesses both "mental" and "material" qualities that manifest according to the subjective or objective structure of an experience or experiment. In the mystical terms of Méheust, the real possesses two faces: a public face involving cause and matter, and an esoteric face involving meaning and mind. I also suspect, with thinkers like Vallee, that the common absurdities of paranormal phenomena are functions of this same nonduality and, as such, are designed to pop us out of our dualistic, either-or ways of thinking about the world (or just really, really confuse us). This is yet another reason why the paranormal and the mystical should not be separated, why we cannot study the one without the other: both forms of experience are pointing to or expressing this nondual or both-and level of the real.[5]

Edward Kelly has highlighted another problem inherent in the transmission metaphor: it can imply a more or less perfect one-to-one communication, as in a television reception. This is certainly not what Myers had in mind, or James, or Huxley. Here the metaphors of the filter or reducing valve are much more appropriate, as they imply a selection, a narrowing, and a loss of an original More. For these reasons, Kelly prefers the metaphor of "permission" over that of "transmission."[6] I could not agree more. And I would take Kelly's metaphorical re-visioning one step further and suggest a complimentary metaphor that is already implied in the literature but not, in my opinion, emphasized nearly enough: the metaphor of "translation." What is permitted to cross the threshold, after all, is not only filtered, selected, and narrowed. It also comes through *in a different form*, whether this is a dream, a vision, a symbol, a text, or a drawing. In a word, it is *translated*. But this implies that, if we wish to understand something about the communication's source, we must translate it back, that is, we must interpret it. This, of course, has been my basic point throughout these chapters, and it remains my final point here at the end. Psychical and paranormal phenomena are hermeneutical realities. They work like texts and stories. They are about meaning as much as they are about matter. There is always a gap. The fisherman cannot talk to the fish without using symbols and signs (or just a hook).

Many other metaphors have been proposed over the centuries. In the ancient world, we encounter images like Plato's Cave with its primitive, projective "movie technology" (a background fire casting shadows of objects on a cave wall, distracting chained prisoners from the transcendent Sun completely outside the cave), the Upanishadic passage on the *atman* or transcendent Self and the ego as two birds sitting on the same tree, or the gnostic teaching of the *syzygos* or angelic Twin. In the modern world, we have models like Abbot's nineteenth-century Flatland, Fort's projecting Martian X, and Philip K. Dick's Valis.

Personally speaking now, I find Plato's Cave, Abbot's Flatland, Fort's X, and Dick's Valis far more "accurate" descriptions of what consciousness and the human brain are up to in a real-world mystical event than some of the present talk of task-oriented modules, cognitive templates, attribution theory, folk theories, and domain specificity, *not* because the former are literally true (they are not) *or* because the latter are false (they no doubt capture something important), but because the theological, mystical, and literary metaphors deliver far more imaginative impact. They are closer to the lived experience of things. They capture something of the wonder, awe, and sheer terror of a real-world psychical or paranormal event, when Mind beams through the brain with a force and power that can only be approximated by ecstatic, mystical, or sci-fi language.

The cognitive scientific computer metaphors appear much too abstract and "dry" in comparison. They also happen to be unbelievably boring, a fact that, all humor aside, carries real philosophical weight for me. In other words, I find the cognitive scientific models incredibly useful and even convincing as explanatory models for the commonplace (boring) functioning of the brain and the social construction and stabilization of the ego, that is, of the normal sense of self and identity, including and especially religious identity.[7] But I find these models virtually useless when it comes to admitting, much less understanding and explaining, the wilder data of comparative mystical literature with which I am the most familiar. They just don't work.

Philosophers of mind and cognitive scientists do not *have* to be this boring. Douglas Hofstadter and Daniel Dennett, for example, anthologized portions of a beautiful little book entitled *On Having No Head* by D. E. Harding in their classic volume *The Mind's I*. The essay treats the day, Harding explains, "when I found I had no head." "This," he insists with complete clarity, "is not a literary gambit, a witticism designed to arouse interest at any cost. I mean it in all seriousness: *I have no head*."[8] How did he come to this impossible conclusion? Harding was trekking in the Himalayas when he suddenly discovered that he was not at all who he thought he was. He explains:

> Somehow or other I had vaguely thought of myself as inhabiting this house which is my body, and looking out through its two round windows at the world. Now I find it isn't like that at all.... Victim of a prolonged fit of madness, of a lifelong hallucination.... I had invariably seen myself as pretty much like other men, and certainly never as a decapitated but still living biped. I had

> been blind to the one thing that is always present, and without which I am blind indeed—to this marvelous substitute-for-a-head, this unbounded clarity, this luminous and absolutely pure void, which nevertheless is—rather than contains—all things.[9]

Now staring into a mirror, he puzzles again at the sheer lunacy of confusing consciousness with the brain, the ego, or the body:

> In my saner moments I see the man over there [in the mirror] . . . as the opposite in every way of my real Self here. I have never been anything but this ageless, adamantine, measureless, lucid, and altogether immaculate Void: it is unthinkable that I could ever have confused that staring wraith over there with what I plainly perceive myself to be here and now and forever![10]

Similar insights into the nature of the Human as Two have recently come from a Harvard-trained brain anatomist by the name of Jill Bolte Taylor. On the morning of December 10, 1996, Taylor experienced a massive stroke that shut down the left hemisphere of her brain. As a neuroanatomist, she knew exactly what was happening as it happened. She watched her linguistic, memory, and identity processing disappear like cotton candy on a tongue. Deprived of its neurological base, it just all melted away. But as these cognitive capacities blipped out, something else blipped in, something stunning. In my own terms now, she knew consciousness as consciousness instead of as culture. In her own neuroanatomical (and religious) language, as her left side gradually came back online over the next eight months, Taylor found herself alternating "between two distinct and opposite realities: the euphoric nirvana of the intuitive and kinesthetic right brain, in which she felt a sense of complete well-being and peace, and the logical, sequential left brain."[11] Consciousness and culture were gradually coming back together, and with them, her sense of social reality and personal identity.

This still sounds more than a bit like the reduction of Mind to brain, even if it is to two brains now. But there was more, and Taylor seems to find religious language the only really adequate means to express it. "By the end of that morning, my consciousness shifted into a perception that I was at *one* with the universe. Since that time, I have come to understand how it is that we are capable of having a 'mystical' or 'metaphysical' experience—relative to our brain anatomy."[12] Obviously, her language is very careful here: "a perception," "relative to our brain anatomy," and those scare quotes around "mystical" and "metaphysical" are guarded and ambiguous.

But then there is that italicized word: "I was at *one* with the universe." Like her double-sided brain, Jill Bolte Taylor is alternating between two different worlds of meaning, two different possibilities, and *exactly* like a good fantastic author, an author of the impossible, she cannot decide which is the real.

Or can she? The human being now appeared to her as "an electrical being; an apparition of energy smoldering around an organic lump."[13] She entered the space of the fantastic, that is, she felt "bizarre, as if my conscious mind was suspended somewhere between my normal reality and some esoteric space."[14] She was "comforted by an expanding sense of grace." She was in "a void of higher cognition." She "soared into an all-knowingness."[15] More stunning still, she now knew the brain-body as a kind of UFO window, "a portal through which the energy of who I am can be beamed into a three-dimensional external space." The body now revealed itself for what it is, "a marvelous temporary home." She marveled at how she could have spent so many years unaware of this, never really understanding "that I was just visiting there."[16] Like an alien.

We are not who we think we are, she concluded:

> I shuddered at the awareness that I was no longer a normal human being. How on earth would I exist as a member of the human race with this heightened perception that we are each a part of it all, and that the life force energy within each of us contains the power of the universe? How could I fit in with our society when I walk the earth with no fear?[17]

Evolutionary biology now took on a whole new light too: "At the level of our DNA, we are related to the birds, reptiles, amphibians, other mammals, and even the plant life. From a purely biological perspective, we human beings are our own species-specific mutation of earth's genetic possibility."[18] In short, Taylor realized that we are all transhuman: "*What a bizarre living being I am. Life! I am life! I am a sea of water bound inside this membranous pouch . . . I am cellular life, no—I am molecular life with manual dexterity and a cognitive mind*!"[19]

Being in one's "right mind" also took on new meaning. To our right mind, Taylor explains, "the moment of *now* is timeless and abundant." Time, history, and the clock are no more. Our right mind, moreover, is "free to think intuitively outside the box." It is "spontaneous, carefree, and imaginative." It is also the source of some of our deepest ethical sensibilities and political dreams. One might even say that it is the ultimate source of democracy itself: "The present moment is a time when everything and everyone are connected together as one. As a result, our right mind perceives each of us as equal members of the human family."[20]

Not so the left mind. It is analytic and thinks in units of linear time. It divides, dissects, analyzes, and insists on "details, details, and more details about those details."[21] It also goes on and on (and on) about "the insignificant affairs of society."[22] It chatters to us constantly in order to shore up the social ego with all its ethnic, racial, national, cultural, and religious convictions. None of this, however, is really real. Thus, in one of Taylor's most striking passages, she marvels at how she finally realized that, "I really had been a figment of my own imagination!"[23] In short, the ego was revealed for what it is—a social construction. And consciousness was revealed for what it is—a presence of mythological proportions that is filtered through the brain and body, but is in fact neither.[24] In Taylor's own words, "I was simply a being of light radiating life into the world."[25]

Finally, consider the recent work of Mario Beauregard, the neurobiologist of religious, spiritual, and mystical experiences (RSME) at the University of Montreal who recently published *The Spiritual Brain* with journalist Denyse O'Leary. Summarizing his own research with contemplative Carmelite nuns in the context of the vast literatures on the philosophy of mind, neuroplasticity and OCD, the placebo effect, near-death experiences, and psi research, Beauregard exposes and criticizes what Karl Popper called the "promissory materialism" of contemporary science as fundamentally incapable of explaining the most basic facts of consciousness. Promissory materialism is the notion that, even though there are gaps in our knowledge now, eventually materialistic science promises to explain everything, including human intention, imagination, and that mystery of all mysteries—consciousness itself.

Not so, no way, Beauregard argues. Science may indeed eventually throw some light on the nature of consciousness, but only if it is willing to abandon its unquestioned, uncritical commitment to the metaphysics of monistic materialism. The limits of scientific materialism here are captured in the joke about the man searching for his car keys. Another man comes up and asks where he thinks he lost them.

"In the basement," he answers.

"So why are you looking out here in the driveway?" he asks in confusion.

"Oh, because the light is much better here."

This, Beauregard suggests, is more or less how materialism functions as an unquestioned dogma in contemporary science. Its dogmatic methods preclude even looking at data that suggest that its monistic materialism is deeply flawed, that there might really be something worth looking for in the dark. Thus anything that cannot be explained within its Flatland philosophy—like paranormal phenomena, or the notion that evolution might display intelligent dimensions—is relegated to the tired tropes of "irrationalism," "anecdote," or "pseudoscience." Often, moreover, individual scientists who are brave enough to question the metaphysics of materialism or, worse yet, offer real scientific data that seem to violate its absolute principles, are ruthlessly denied, shamed, or otherwise humiliated in the profession. They are "damned," Fort would say.

But scientific rationalism is not at all the same thing as scientific materialism, and there are very good, perfectly rational reasons to advance a nonmaterialist science that posits the Mind as distinct from the brain, that understands brain as a kind of supersensitive receptor or reducing valve that the Mind uses to interact with the material world. In other words, the filter thesis.

What Beauregard finally proposes is really quite stunning, or better, really quite impossible (since it is all in perfect sync with the paranormal phenomena that we have been examining all along here). He begins by quoting Nobel Prize–winning neuroscientist Charles Sherrington on the futility of looking for Mind in the brain: "If it is for mind that we are searching the brain, then we are supposing the brain to be much more than a telephone-exchange. We are supposing it to be a telephone-exchange along with subscribers as well." Beauregard then offers his own "psychoneural translation hypothesis," or PTH for short. The PTH "posits that the mind (the psychological world, the first-person perspective) and the brain (which is part of the so-called 'material' world, the third-person perspective) represent two epistemologically different domains that can interact because they are complementary aspects of the same transcendent reality."[26]

The ways in which the neuroscientist turns to hermeneutical and semiotic terms is quite remarkable here. Not only is this a "*translation* hypothesis," but Beauregard argues that trying to look at neurons to understand consciousness is like trying "to determine the meaning of messages in an unknown language (thoughts) merely by examining its writing system (neurons)," and this, I would add, while denying, in principle, that there is an unknown speaker to detect and decode at all. Basically, materialist neuroscience operates exactly like religious fundamentalism here: it denies the gap between meaning and text, between right-brain consciousness and left-brain culture, between intention or conscious cause and neural correlation. Now there is *only* the text, *only* the rational methods of the left-brain, *only* the neurons. Such a materialist view of the human being also, as Beauregard reminds us, completely denies the very possibility of human freedom, human responsibility, and moral agency. There is, after all, nobody in there, at all. The political implications of all of this border on the appalling.

Beauregard's nonmaterialist neuroscience works very differently. It does not deny, of course, all the material processes of the body and the brain or of the physical world in general (although he constantly reminds us that quantum physics has definitively demonstrated that there is no such thing as "matter," and that quantum probability collapses before an observer, hence the hopelessly outdated notion of an objective "materialism"). But it does not make the mistake of reducing mind to these material processes without remainder. Rather, it begins with mind, intention, and human freedom, and then shows how this consciousness communicates its messages through our shared neurobiology, that is, through the body and brain.

This "informational transduction mechanism," as he puts it, is described as "a paramount achievement of evolution that allows mental processes to causally influence the functioning and plasticity of the brain. It is somewhat like writing our spoken words down in a symbol system that can be read by others at a distance." In essence, a kind of microtelekinesis within the brain itself.

Beauregard's invocation of biological evolution here is not tangential. It is in fact part of a much larger evolutionary mysticism in which he understands his neuroscience and the history of human culture in general:

> A teleologically oriented (i.e., purposeful rather than random) biological evolution has enabled humans to consciously and voluntarily shape the functioning of our brains. As a result of this powerful capacity, we are not biological robots totally governed by "selfish" genes and neurons. One outcome is that we can intentionally create new social and cultural environments. Through us, evolution becomes conscious, that is, it is driven not simply by drives for survival and reproduction but more by complex sets of insights, goals, desires, and beliefs.[27]

This, of course, comes very close to what I have identified above as the dialectic of consciousness and culture. Here, though, the influence of consciousness is extended back into the biological realm as well. In this model, at least, consciousness was implicated in biological evolution before it came into its own, became conscious of itself, and took up the task of cultural evolution.

Finally, after almost three hundred pages of robust criticism of monistic materialism and a discussion of the scientific evidence for his own thesis about how the brain mediates but does not produce religious, spiritual, and mystical experiences, Beauregard insists again that *psyche* and *physis*, or mind and matter, "represent complementary aspects of the same underlying principle," that neither can be reduced to the other. Here finally we seem to have an answer to the rather sensationalistic question touted on the back cover: "Did God create the brain, or does the brain create God?" The answer? Both.

Beauregard is perfectly aware that his thesis about the brain mediating transcendent religious experiences has been advanced before by William James, Henri Bergson, and Aldous Huxley. Indeed, he cites these very authors on the idea that "the brain can be compared with a television receiver that translates electromagnetic waves (which exist apart from the TV receiver) into picture and sound." But he goes much further than a simple acknowledgment of intellectual debt. He reveals his own direct knowledge, even gnosis, of the psychoneural translation hypothesis, that is, he describes his own mystical experiences, which he classifies under what Richard Maurice Bucke called "Cosmic Consciousness." These, he explains, occurred in 1987 within a serious bout of chronic fatigue syndrome (the theme of trauma-as-trigger again):

> The experience began with a sensation of heat and tingling in the spine and the chest areas. Suddenly, I merged with the infinitely loving Cosmic Intelligence (or Ultimate Reality) and became united with everything in the cosmos. This unitary state of being, which transcends the subject/object duality, was timeless and accompanied by intense bliss and ecstasy. In this state, I experienced the basic interconnectedness of all things in the cosmos, the infinite ocean of life. I also realized that everything arises from and is part of this Cosmic Intelligence.[28]

The nonmaterialist neuroscience that flows from *both* the third-person perspective of professional science *and* the first-person perspective of mystical experiences suggests for Beauregard that "the death of the brain does not mean the annihilation of the person." If the brain, after all, is a receiver or a reducing valve and not the producer of consciousness, then the destruction of the filter or reducing valve hardly implies the end of consciousness. The TV can go on the blitz, even be demolished, but the television program, like the Truth in *The X-Files*, continues to be "out there." It is completely unaffected by what happens to this or that television set.

But the situation is even more radical than this, for Beauregard, if I read him correctly, seems to be proposing, to stick to our metaphors, that the television program "out there" actually helped create the circuitry of the TV-brain. In his own terms, mind or consciousness represents "a fundamental and irreducible property of the Ground of Being," and "mind, consciousness, and self profoundly affect the physical world," including the evolutionary processes themselves. "It is this fundamental unity and interconnectedness that allows the human mind to causally affect physical reality and permits psi interaction between humans and with physical or biological systems."[29] The universe is finally mental as well as physical. Or, in the words of the physicist James Jeans, "the universe begins to look more like a great thought than a great machine."

Beauregard concludes his book by writing of "a trend in human evolution toward the spiritualization of consciousness." He suggests that a nonmaterialist science may even "accelerate our understanding of this process of spiritualization and significantly contribute to the emergence of a planetary type of consciousness."[30] This acceleration of the evolution of consciousness through the cultivation and promulgation of a truly adequate science of the human spirit may sound utopian to some, but it is exactly what Frederic Myers had argued over one hundred years ago now in *Human Personality and Its Survival of Bodily Death.*

We have come full circle.

I do not offer any of these three thinkers as the last word on psychical and paranormal phenomena. Nor do I mean to argue that, in neuroscience, we now, at last, have all of our answers. I do not believe that, not for a second. Nor do I mean to suggest that what emerges from the brain as producer or filter is always somehow good or wise, or, for that matter, left or right. I understand that consciousness is as unitary as it is modular, that most significant brain processes display a "horizontal" or "global" patterning across both hemispheres and cannot be located simply on the "left" or "right." Quite the contrary. I am convinced, with Myers and Freud, that the hidden mind of the unconscious is as much a Gothic basement filled with the haunting ghosts of suppressed desires, unspeakable aggressions, and gullible nonsense as it is a potential window into the supernormal and the sublime, "a rubbish-heap as well as a treasure-house," as Myers called it with his usual verve (HP1:73).[31]

What I do mean to suggest is that the task of critical theory has something terribly important to learn before the spectacles of Mr. Harding's lost head, Taylor's stroke of insight, and Beauregard's personal experience of Cosmic Consciousness. To take the most obvious and simple of observations, Taylor shows us definitively that the Human as Two is not just an ancient mystical doctrine. *It is a universal neuroanatomical fact*. In essence (really, *in essence*), we all have two brains in one skull, and they work far more similarly than differently across cultures. This does not, of course, answer the question of the ultimate origins and nature of consciousness, but it at least gives us a very solid base from which to theorize. Actually, it gives us *two* solid bases.

Which, I suppose, is the main point that I want to make here. After all, all of our contextual, materialist, and historical methods are left-brain methods. They emphasize difference and division, not sameness and equality. They only recognize the clock-time of the brain and of the calendar, not the Now of consciousness. They focus on the ego's chatter, not on the Clear Light of Mind. In Victoria Nelson's terms, they thrive on our Aristotleanism and try their best to ignore our Platonism. In more modern terms, they focus on cognition, that is, on all those cultural grids and processes of the computer-brain, not on consciousness as consciousness, on the Sun outside the Cave. They focus on class, race, and gender, even as they ignore our shared DNA and the fundamental, undeniable biological unity of the species. They thus represent, literally, only half the picture, and, with respect to the phenomenology of revelation and religious experience, probably the least important half at that.

So what are we doing here? Do we really think that we can explain what Jill Bolte Taylor refers to as a species-wide, mutating life-force beaming through the portal of the right brain with the local cultural and linguistic equipment of the left brain? Do we really think that we can get to the "alien" presence mediated through (or as) the right brain through methods like social constructivism, discourse analysis, and historical criticism?

I find such assumptions deeply problematic. Recall my earlier point that what we have in the academy are theories *about* religion that attempt to explain the encounter with the sacred in terms of something else, that we have no real theories *of* religion. Translated now into neuroscientific terms, I would say that what we have are some very fine left-brain methods, but no accepted and significantly developed right-brain methods. The field, then, is like a two-engine prop plane that is running on only one engine. It can't even get off the ground. It just goes around and around on the runway. Hence we have a really good view of the pavement, but almost no understanding of the sky and the principles of flight.

Which is not to demean or deny the analytic and linguistic capacities of the left brain. Quite the contrary, ignoring these critical capacities and their attending theoretical categories would be just as problematic, and probably even more dangerous. Biological fiction or no, we cannot stop analyzing the real-world, physical, and profound social effects that a category like "race" has on countless human beings, really on all of us. So too with gender, sexual orientation, and class. This is why I have spent most of my intellectual career tracing, comparing, and analyzing the comparative erotics of Hindu, Catholic, Islamic, Jewish, and New Age mystical literature with the rational and ethical tools of psychoanalysis, feminist theory, queer theory, and historical-criticism.[32]

So please do not misread me here. I am *not* proposing that we surrender the powers of reason and critical theory. I am not antireason or antiscience. I am not proposing that we shut down the engines of our left brains. We'd just go in circles again, now in circles of faith and belief, but in circles nonetheless. I am simply suggesting that, if we are ever going to understand something as doubly complex and as two-brained as the human being, we need *both* sides of ourselves. We need both engines to fly.

As another way of getting at the same point, consider science fiction, fantasy, and fantastic literature again, that is, the great genres of the "What if?" that have engaged us so in the present volume. What if we were to read Philip K. Dick's pink beams of Valis or Charles Fort's alien projection mythology symbolically, and then translate them back into the language of contemporary neuroscience and psychical research? Would we not have an extremely powerful literary expression of the nature of mental reality as an alien projection "from somewhere else," that is, a virtual reality projected through the neurological galaxy of the brain from the Mind via something like Taylor's hemispheric model? It's probably worth mentioning here that the brain really is a galaxy of sorts. With hundreds of billions of neurons and glia, there are as many cells in the human brain as there are stars in a typical galaxy, including our own Milky Way. And this is before we even get to the possible connections between them, which number into . . . into the what? Before such a vast neurological cosmos, Dick's Valis or Fort's X looks *way* more accurate and adequate than the typical abstractions and computer-talk of "modules" and "cognitive grids," which now appear almost obscenely simplistic and naive.

An author of the impossible like Philip K. Dick was extremely sophisticated about all of this. He did not "believe" everything that was happening to him, but neither did he conflate Mind with brain. Indeed, he had been zapped by a form of Cosmic Consciousness and was a self-confessed gnostic on precisely this point, namely, that he had been transformed, reprogrammed by the paranormal encounter. Valis had inspired a new writing practice in him, one dominated by the radical intuition that consciousness is filtered through the brain, not produced by it. Essentially, Dick had had his own stroke of insight (and, perhaps not accidentally, he would soon die after multiple strokes).

Similarly, Charles Fort never confused the alien Mind, or what he called X, with the human brain, for, as he put it, "the way of a brain is only the way of a belly" (LO 560). That is to say, the brain is finally a material reality, whereas Mind is something else, something alien, something really, really weird.

Materialism, Fort's "way of a belly," is the dominant model in neuroscience now. I understand this. I also recognize, with Victoria Nelson, that the greatest taboo among serious intellectuals is "the heresy of challenging a materialist worldview."[33] I am issuing just such a challenge here. In doing so, I have no illusions about trying to go back to any premodern answers. I am simply pointing out that our present Dominant can only be maintained by damning, through willed or benign neglect, what Edward Kelly and his colleagues have called the "rogue" phenomena of the history of animal magnetism, psychical research, and paranormal experience.[34] I am proposing the filter thesis here not to "believe" anything (including the filter thesis, which I would be happy to toss aside before something better), but because whereas the materialist models cannot even recognize the existence of the rogue data, much less explain them, the filter thesis can do both. Moreover, the filter thesis has the inestimable advantage of being capable of embracing both the findings of modern neuroscience (as applicable to the brain) and the most astonishing data of the psychical research tradition (as applicable to Mind). Mine is thus finally a reasonable, *rational* choice, not a decision to "believe" anything at all.

Happily, this same bimodal psychology also helps explain why the literature of the fantastic is "fantastic." That is to say, it explains why the fascinated reader (of a text or of an actual life event) cannot determine whether the occult event is real or not. Recall Todorov's defining discussion of the fantastic, with which we opened our journey:

> The person who experiences the [fantastic] event must opt for one of two possible solutions: either he is the victim of an illusion of the senses, of a product of the imagination—and laws of the world then remain what they are; or else the event has indeed taken place, it is an integral part of reality—but then his reality is controlled by laws unknown to us. . . . The fantastic occupies the duration of this uncertainty.[35]

The filter or transmission thesis explains this "duration of uncertainty" by pointing out that a paranormal event can be *both* real *and* unreal, *both* fiction *and* fact. It can be real and factual to the extent that it is a genuine expression of Mind beyond brain. It can be unreal and fictional to the extent that it is a filtered, translated, or imagined expression of Mind in and through the linguistic, identity, and cultural capacities of the (left) brain. The reader's moment of hesitation, the moment of the fantastic, which of course happens in the reader's head, then, finds its resolution in the very structure of that head, that is, in the fact that there are not one but *two* brains in there, and that one of them is filtering pure consciousness, while the other is translating and projecting that pure consciousness into multiple social, cultural, and religious fictions. Hence my dialectic of consciousness and culture, which can now be seen as an ideal theoretical reflection of the dialectical neuroanatomy of the human brain itself.

From Realization to Authorization: Toward a Hermeneutics of the Impossible

Our four authors of the impossible realized through their radical reading and writing practices that they were caught in a world they did not write, that they were being written, literally, as they spoke, and *especially* when they spoke, language being what it is—the ultimate magical spell, the most powerful hypnotic inducer of the consensual trance of social reality. What begins to make such individuals authors of the impossible is their radical reflexivity. What finally makes them authors of the impossible, however, is their metadecision to stop reading the paranormal writing us, step back "on the page," and begin *writing* the paranormal writing us.

There are at least two stages in this writing practice. In the first stage, what I would like to call Realization, the individual begins to suspect that paranormal processes are real. Realization is finally achieved when one comes to understand that such events are not only real, but also inherently *participatory*, that is, paranormal events often behave very much like texts: they appear for us but rely on our active engagement or "reading" to appear at all and achieve meaning.[36] In some fundamental way that we do not yet understand, paranormal phenomena *are* us, projected into the objective world of events and things, usually through some story, symbol, or sign. Realization is the insight that we are caught in such a story, that we are embedded in a myth expressing itself through matter, a myth, alas, over which we have little control. Realization is finally the insight that we are being written.

The second stage, what I want to call Authorization, begins when we decide to step out of the script or story we find ourselves caught in (call it culture, society, or religion) and write ourselves. If Realization is the insight that we are being written, Authorization is the decision to do something about it. If Realization involves the act of reading the paranormal writing us, Authorization involves the act of writing the paranormal writing us. Which is another way of saying that what finally makes an author of the impossible is the insight that *because paranormal processes can replicate literary processes and literary processes can replicate paranormal processes, writing can become a paranormal practice.*

If we were to translate all of this back into our concluding thought experiment or "What if?" and its neuroscientific terms, we might say that what this impossible writing practice involves is the consciousness of the author figuring out that what the left brain is up to is eminently practical and necessary but not really real, that consciousness is not the ego or the person-as-mask (*persona*), and that the rules of the social game or religious theatre are just that: rules of a game, roles on a stage.

To author one's world, however, whether literally or metaphorically, implies the use of language, which is a left-brain capacity. So an author of the impossible is not someone who has shut down the left brain with all its critical and linguistic powers and tender sense of individual identity. I do not mean to be so simply dualistic. Rather, an author of the impossible is someone who has ceased to live, think, and imagine *only* in the left brain, who has worked hard and long to synchronize the two forms of consciousness and identity and bring them both online *together*. Finally, an author of the impossible is someone who has gone beyond all of these dualisms of right and left, mystical and rational, faith and reason, self and other, mind and matter, consciousness and energy, and so on. An author of the impossible is someone who knows that the Human is Two *and* One.

I find such an (im)possibility incredibly empowering. If, after all, we can begin to understand and act on these insights, we might at least begin to take back the book of our lives from those who wrote us long ago, for their own good reasons, no doubt, and begin writing ourselves anew, for our own good reasons now. Our ancestors and their deities were completely ignorant of such new good reasons, just as we are completely ignorant of the good reasons and concerns of two thousand years from now. Our system must damn the old ones, and ours will be damned in turn. This, in the end, is all I have tried to say in the present book. It is also what I tried to say, in different ways and with different authors, in all my other books.

Maybe that is all I have to say.

In any case, I do not pretend for a moment that such an (im)possibility explains everything about what we have come to call, for our own reasons and ends, the psychical and the paranormal. I have argued here that such phenomena are profoundly involved with the production of human intention and cultural narrative, that is to say, I have focused on the why-questions of *meaning and story* and not on the how-questions of *explanation and cause*. The simple truth is that I have no idea how a table floats off the floor and taps out messages for a young philosophy graduate student, or how dying loved ones appear in dreams and rooms at the precise time of their passing. I haven't the slightest clue how curtains and tablecloths burst into flames around pubescent girls and boys, or how authors encounter in "real life" scenes that they have imagined in their fiction or dreams. Most of all, I have no idea how dreamlike UFOs appear on radar screens, stop cars, and burn people. What I *do* know is that to the extent that these events involve symbols, myths, stories, and altered states, the literary critic, the anthropologist, and the historian of religions will have as much to say about them as the physicist, the neuroscientist, and the fighter-jet pilot.

Impossible (Dis)Closings

TWO YOUTHFUL ENCOUNTERS

All that we saw was owing to your metaphysics.
—William Blake to an epistemologically challenged angel in *The Marriage of Heaven and Hell*

We want you to believe in us, but not too much.
—An alien to Nebraska law officer Herbert Schirmer

When I decided to write this book, I had nothing invested in the strangest and most troubling of the material, the UFO material. I originally treated these phenomena because I realized that I would never understand the American superhero mythologies, toward which I was then writing, without taking into account the mythology of the alien, the UFO encounter, and the abduction narrative. I was simply trying to understand this mythical material as a responsible historian of religions. I was being a good boy. I had certainly never seen a UFO.

Turns out I was wrong about that. Turns out I had seen one as a boy, and a quite big one at fairly close range, although I have absolutely no memory of this encounter. I only learned of it recently from my mother. She was visiting Houston (the city of spaceships, the Rockets, the Astros, and, as we like to brag, one of the first words uttered on the moon: "Houston, the *Eagle* has landed"). We were watching television together when a quite silly automobile commercial came on screen. It featured a typical disc-shaped UFO. Mom casually asked me if I remembered the day that we saw one. "What?!" I replied in so many eloquent words. She went on to explain how when I was about six and my brother Jerry five, the four of us were on our way to South Dakota for a family event. It was 1969 or so. It was night. As we drove down the dark highway somewhere in northern Nebraska, a very large, rectangular-shaped object appeared in the sky. It had lots of colored lights on it. "So could it have been a military plane or something?" I asked. This was a reasonable question. SAC, or Strategic Airforce Command, is in Omaha, a few hundred miles to the east. "No," Mom replied just as casually and surely. "It was not shaped like a plane of any sort. It was *rectangular*. And it was very large. And it seemed to be following us. We all watched it for quite awhile. It was scary."

So there is another damned fact, so damned I still have absolutely no memory of it. As far as I am concerned, it never happened. But apparently it did. The clear sense of the uncanny with which Mom spoke of it was matched by Dad's calm confirmation of it all when I asked him about Mom's memories, and this despite his usual skepticism of all such claims (I was with him once when he discovered the likely source of some ghostly music allegedly heard in a local abandoned graveyard—a crumbling schoolhouse tucked away in the trees with an old piano in it, whose exposed strings could have easily hummed in the wind). Jerry was less helpful but equally to the point when he wrote back in answer to my brotherly request for his own precise memories: "Dude, I was *five*." Not that age helps much here. Neither Mom nor Dad has the slightest idea what it was. Only that we all saw it, that it was real.

So there is a story, a story I didn't even know I had. Here is another, again from my own life, but now from my adolescence and youth and in a distant, buffered, unconscious mode that can be read in many ways, including in very traditional orthodox ways (that is, through the eyes of Catholic piety, whose reading I once fully accepted).[1] The simple truth is that nothing is really very clear here, that nothing is either really simple or clearly true. And *that* is my point.

We've already encountered this impossible story before, many times, but we have never had the chance to tell it and so make it seem possible. It would do us well now to return to it here at the very end, not to reach any final closure of meaning, much less to give the "correct" reading, but to perform and finalize our own fantastic uncertainty. The story involves the events of Fátima, Portugal, in the second decade of the last century. It has usually been read, with some justification, within the mythological system of Roman Catholicism. I am now going to read it, with some justification, within the mythological system of the ufological literature.

"Here comes a whopper," as Charles Fort would say. . . .

Three little shepherds. Jacinta was just seven years old, her older brother, Francisco, nine. Their cousin, Lucia, was ten. Within a few years both Francisco and Jacinta would be dead, and Lucia, at the tender age of fourteen, would be secretly whisked off to a private boarding school in Porto, far from her home town. She was instructed not to tell anyone where she was going, nor to tell anyone who she was. She was also not to speak of the extraordinary events that transpired for six consecutive months between May 13 and October 13, 1917. She would have to leave all of her loved ones. She could write only to her mother, and this only after the letters from the child or the mother were passed through a vicar of the church. Poor Lucia's immediate response to such a traumatic demand was very clear: she compared her fate to being "buried alive in a sepulcher." She refused to go. But then she later allowed herself to be persuaded, to be buried. She would later enter a cloistered convent, where she would spend the rest of her life in silence and solitude. All that she wrote had to be passed through a bishop's hand, and the Holy Congregation for the Doctrine of the Faith (what was once the Holy Inquisition) reserved the right to grant or deny authorization for any visitor.[2]

What sort of secret knowledge could possibly justify this kind of lifelong vigilance and control? What on earth did Lucia witness?

"What in the heavens" would be more accurate. There are some who believe that what the three children experienced, with literally tens of thousands of corroborating witnesses spread out over exactly half a year, was the most spectacular religious event of the twentieth century. They may be right. What it all *means*, however, is an entirely different question, and perhaps in the end an impossible one.

Here are some of the facts, at least as they can be gleaned from the historical record, from the newspapers of the time, which widely covered the clockwork-like events, and from archival documents. It began on Sunday, May 13, 1917, in a rocky, desolate cove in the district of Fátima, Portugal.[3] There, while tending their sheep, the three children witnessed flashes of lightning (without thunder) and then saw a small young woman standing on top of an oak tree. Lucia conversed with her, in Portuguese. The children returned home and, of course, immediately told the fantastic story to their family.

"If the kids saw a woman dressed in white, who else could she be but Our Lady?" Lucia's father, António, asked with some reason. But his ten-year-old daughter was not so sure. Nor was his wife, Maria Rosa. More skeptical by nature, she asked Lucia to specify exactly what she had seen. The girl made herself quite clear: "I never said that it was Our Lady—rather, a small, pretty lady. . . . She told me that we should continue to go there for six consecutive months, on the 13th of each month, and that at the end of that time, she would tell us who she was and what she wanted of us."[4] Maria Rosa would remain circumspect and careful about what her daughter had seen. In *The Official Interrogations of 1923*, she is recorded as testifying that her daughter had "said that she saw a small, pretty lady; that her dress was completely white; and that to the question, 'Where are you from?' she had pointed to the sky, saying she was from there."[5]

Originally, little Lucia was even more uncertain. In her *Memoirs*, she relates how she considered not returning in July for the third encounter, since she feared that the apparitions might be the work of the Devil—hardly a ringing endorsement of a transparent and unproblematic Marian reading.[6] Later, in the convent and under the watchful eyes of the bishop and her ecclesial superiors now, Lucia would adopt, no doubt sincerely, the orthodox interpretations and write about the events accordingly. The little woman dressed in white from the heavens had indeed become "Our Lady of Fátima" from Heaven. It was an easy transformation. Lucia's father had been right all along.

Maybe. Memories, much less memoirs, are famously malleable, and differing details and alternative interpretations in the newspapers and the historical records abound—so many glitches in the Matrix of Roman Catholicism. The Lady was said to be a little over one meter tall and fourteen to fifteen years of age. She did not look like the images of the Blessed Virgin known in the devotional iconography of the local churches. She was enveloped in a kind of light that was more beautiful than the sun and very bright. Her dress, which appears to have hugged her body somewhat, covered her from the neck to the feet and emitted a similar white light. Some descriptions have her wearing a robe or cape extending to her knees, something on her head (it is not at all clear what), and a chain with a golden ball attached to it at about the level of her waist. She had black eyes and looked serious. Her mouth did not move when she spoke. She did not use her feet when she moved. Rather, she glided or floated.

The children obediently returned every month as instructed, each time with more people in tow. In June there were about 40; in July over 4,000; in August 18,000;[7] in September 30,000; in October, between 50,000 and 70,000, depending upon which account you accept. But, really, who could count them all now? Interestingly, not everyone could see the apparitions, and those who did often saw quite different things. And then there was the weird but beautiful "buzzing." When the Being of Fátima spoke to the children, the witnesses often heard a distinct insectoid buzzing, like a bee or cicada or, as another had it, "like that which is heard next to a hive, but altogether more harmonious, even though words were not heard."[8]

Some also spoke of how the ground shook and described hearing thunder or a rumbling as the Being approached and departed from the tree. The tree moved, as in a wind or suction effect, when the little lady left. There were other technological allusions too, or at least descriptions that could easily be read in this way. "[W]hen our Lady withdrew from the tree, it was like a distant gust from a rocket when it lifts off." Or again, in a more natural register: "When Lucia said, 'There She goes,' I heard a roaring in the air that seemed like the beginning of thunder."[9] Some thought that the globe that brought the Being down in September was shaped like an airplane. Others described it as oval-shaped, with the bottom side being larger than the top side. Others thought it was taller than it was wide. One man saw "a cross of great size exit the sun" and fly toward the east.[10] In October, Gilberto dos Santos saw a "ramp of light," even a "street" in the sky.[11] Today, one might say a "beam."

Then there were the bizarre cloud formations. Witnesses commonly saw a cloud, haze, or fog envelop the tree where the Being apparently stood. They also saw colored clouds in the sky moving in strange, unnatural ways. At least one man, Manuel Marto, saw "a type of luminous globe gyrating within the clouds."[12] In June, as the Being departed, Lucia clearly saw her leave, but all that the people saw was a little cloud: "But it was apparent that Lucia was still seeing something, because she paid no attention to us, until, at last, she said: 'There! Now it can't be seen. It has just now entered the sky and the doors have closed.'"[13] Doors.

There were also sometimes strange perfume-like odors in the air, and the atmosphere would either cool down or heat up considerably at different points of the apparitions. Even stranger, on some occasions, the entire landscape would light up with weird kaleidoscopic effects: "The ground was divided into squares, each one a different color."[14] There were also "rains of flowers" in September of that year, and then again on May 13 of 1918, 1923, and 1924, as if to mark the anniversary of the Lady's first appearance, and then again on October 17, 1957, the latter event "missing" by four days the anniversary of the final and most famous apparition. Described as "angel hair," as petals of flowers, as white balls, or as snow, the material would dematerialize just over the heads of the witnesses, or disappear into nothing when they tried to pick it up. One newspaper account wrote of "white flakes" that seemed like silk, some of which made it to the ground where it could be photographed: "The flakes made a slight sound, like a buzzing, when they were stretched between the hands, and they came apart as if by magic," reported another newspaper.[15]

As extraordinary as this all might sound, it paled before what happened on October 13, 1917, exactly as the Being had promised six months earlier. The Miracle of the Sun. Some reports have as many as seventy thousand people in the cove that day, including numerous intellectuals, journalists, clerics, skeptics, and atheists. As the crowd gathered in the morning, it poured down heavy rain, soaking everyone. Except the oak tree. Alas, it was no more. A victim of devotion and faith, it had been stripped and stripped until there was nothing left but a stump sticking a few inches out of the ground.

As it turned out, the little lady had something far more dramatic than a landing pad on top of an oak tree in mind. A dark cloud approached from the east. The rain stopped, "and a very white and brilliant little cloud raced across the sky, and all the people who [had] surrounded the oak trees fell to their knees without concern for the mud."[16] According to some, black clouds and some lovely pink clouds now appeared. George Barroinski saw a glowing green cloud, which changed colors rapidly, after which "an oval object appeared and left the area, followed by some type of flame."[17] Others saw alternating chromatic effects illuminating the entire landscape, people and all. Then the clouds seemed to part and a shining sun was revealed in full splendor.

It did a good deal more than shine, however. It spun. And then it fell to the earth with a terrifying zigzag motion. People were screaming in horror and praying in sheer terror. The End was not near. It had arrived. Different reports described the Day of Judgment in different ways. To some, the sun was not spherical, and it shone very much unlike the sun, more like a conch shell or a moon. Others were a bit more specific, describing it rather bluntly as "a metallic disk as if of silver," or as "a very clear, silvery blue disk."[18] Apparently, something "stood out" from the sun that could be looked at, that could be seen, that was not the sun. And this is what fell to the earth. The chromatic colors returned: lilac, blue, red, orange, yellow, "that ultra-special electric blue"—everything, including the people, were caught in the cosmic kaleidoscope once again.[19]

The "sun" continued to fall until it almost touched the ground, until it got to the height of a pine tree, as one report had it. It seemed that close. And then it went back up, with the same weird zigzag motion, until it was its old stable self again. Some people now found themselves completely dry, while others, oddly, were still soaking wet. Some went home to find themselves cured of various ailments and chronic illnesses. The papers went wild.

The general outline of these events and their orthodox interpretation are widely known in Catholic devotional circles. My own home church in Nebraska, for example, displayed a classical Our Lady of Fátima statue to the right of the altar, in clear view of any and all. Except for her height (about one meter tall), the statue looked nothing like the Being of Fátima, the little pretty lady whom the children originally described with such wonder and puzzlement. As a pious adolescent and young man, I used to pray the rosary before this image, always with elderly women, before Mass. We all knew the story.

At least we thought we did. I was unaware of all the glitches. I did not know that the children had not originally identified the Being as the Blessed Virgin Mary. Nor did I realize how eerily similar many of the details of the story are to the phenomenology of UFO encounters both before and after the events of 1917. As Paul Misraki, one of the inspirations for Vallee's work, pointed out some time ago, such parallels are not simply imaginative or general. They are precise and exact. We are not dealing with a vague analogy here; we are dealing with an identity.[20]

Consider the following comparative facts. UFO encounters have often been accompanied by the sound of "buzzing bees," by small humanoid figures approximately one meter tall, and by a classic zigzag descent pattern known in ufological circles as "the falling leaf." UFO encounters are also often associated with lightning and/or thunder, strange cloud formations, bizarre chromatic effects, cooling and heating effects, perfume-like odors, and spontaneous healings and cures. The oval, spherical, vertical oblong, and cross shapes reported at Fátima are also well known, indeed they are classic in the ufological literature. As are the ramps of light and the angel hair (known as "fibralvina" in ufology and already reported by Fort in *The Book of the Damned* in 1919).[21] And this, of course, is before we even get to the silvery spinning disks seen in the clouds above the cove.

And there is more. On the humorous side, the Lady's skirt in some reports was all wrong for the Catholic Virgin. It stopped at her knees, not her toes. This sounds tame enough now, but it would have been truly scandalous at a time when not even prostitutes wore such things.[22] A later church official would pick up on this little detail of "Our Lady," who "obviously could not have appeared other than dressed with the utmost decency and modesty," in order to suggest that such obvious indecency was proof that the vision was "prepared by the Prince of Darkness" himself.[23] I don't know about the Prince of Darkness, but just how many Madonna statues *have* you seen showing leg?

There is also the curious scene during which an angel gives the children "Communion," or at least some kind of liquid and solid that were meant to look like the Catholic sacrament. Interestingly, the main visionary, Lucia, received a solid "host," whereas the two other children received a strange liquid. Francisco at least could not identify whatever it was he drank from the chalice. Joaquim Fernandes and Fina D'Armada make comparative sense of this scene by describing multiple UFO encounters in which the contactee is given a strange substance to eat or liquid to drink and then has a mystical vision or is made to understand a message. Their conclusion is clear enough: "The recurring theme in all of these types of cases involves the access to communication and dialogue *requiring* the ingestion of drugs as a means of entering into an extra-human plane."[24]

On the tragic side, Michael Persinger points out that whereas little Francisco died during the influenza epidemic of 1918, Jacinta's premature death displayed symptoms strongly suggestive of lung cancer, which he relates to radiation emitted around the tree before, during, and after the visions. This, after all, was also the children's common playground.

Persinger has written extensively on paranormal phenomena. He is well known in ufological circles for his lab research on the "alien visitation" phenomenon, a humble analog of which he is able to induce in the lab with electromagnetic fields mathematically calibrated to "entrain" specific altered states in the temporal lobes of a human brain via a helmet fitted with solenoids. He is also well known for his tectonic strain hypothesis, which interprets the balls of light common in UFO encounters as temporary spikes of electromagnetic energy created by stressed tectonic plates in the earth, which then interact with the subtle magnetic fields of the human neural net to create the various local illusions and religious visions of the typical UFO encounter (or Marian apparition). Persinger has also suggested a correlation between high geomagnetic activity and poltergeist activity and hauntings, a suggestion that recalls Jung's earlier comparison of UFOs to planetary poltergeists.[25] Also, for what it is worth (quite a bit, I think, in this context), Fort repeatedly suggested that all those "superconstructions" in the sky appear during or around earthquakes.[26]

In this haunting reading, the Virgin, or the energy spike that produced her, at least, actually killed little Jacinta. To support such an interpretation, Persinger points out that the Fátima area is well known as a tectonic strain hotspot, and that the strongest earthquake on record was the Lisbon earthquake of 1755 (Fátima is about eighty-six miles north of the city). Fernandes and D'Armada make the same point, citing an earthquake that measured an astonishing 9.0 on the Richter scale that once ripped through Fátima itself.[27] The seismic activity could have created immense geomagnetic fields, which would then collect and discharge on tall structures, like the tree on which the apparition appeared. As for the regular periodic nature of the six monthly events, Persinger relates these to a lunar phase, that is, another supermagnetic phenomenon with a strong, predictable, periodic nature. The same magnetic discharges, he speculates, would have powerfully stimulated the children's temporal lobes, resulting in the visions.

The specifics and, of course, the later interpretation of the apparitions were shaped "by their obsession with religious themes, their lack of education [all three children were illiterate], and their behavior at the time of the experience . . . If they had grown up in a world of *Star Wars*, they would have seen and heard some variant of Luke Skywalker."[28] Not that the visions were entirely consonant with the children's Catholicism. As we have seen, they were not. Francisco, for example, did not hear the little lady speak and remembered seeing a haze that he interpreted as a headless angel!

There is more than a little justification for such a literally radioactive reading. Numerous individuals reported intense heat and the almost instant drying of both their clothes and the previously soaked soil during "the Miracle of the Sun," features entirely consistent with immense bursts of electromagnetic radiation. The "buzzing" noises can be fit in here as well, as individuals exposed to microwave radiation between 200 and 3,000 MHz commonly experience buzzing noises inside their heads. Raul Berenguel goes even further, pointing out that hearing voices in the interior of the cranium and the phenomenon of buzzing "is *identical* to what is felt by individuals subjected to mind control technologies that use microwaves."[29] We are back to an eerie and potentially troubling scene reminiscent of Vallee's alien-control hypothesis.

Fernandes and D'Armada add one more truly fascinating suggestion that seems particularly impossible. Curiously, the shape of a rosary laid flat on a table (a circle with a line and a cross jutting out) forms the astrological sign of the planet Venus (which is also known as the Morning Star, a common epithet of the Virgin), the goddess Venus, and now the female chromosome.[30] They speculate that we are dealing here with an ancient pagan symbolism rendered Christian by local context and elaborate processes of interpretation, devotion, and official spinning spread out over centuries. The cultural context of rural Catholic Portugal, of course, more or less guaranteed the traditional Marian reading. By the sixth visitation in October, everyone "knew" who the little lady was. Who else *could* she be? Certainly not Venus, the pagan goddess of sex and love. She was "Our Lady," the Catholic Virgin. In this way, "[t]he paranormal became the supernatural, and the supernatural became the religious."[31]

A Venus-Virgin with a knee-high skirt, alien insectoid buzzing, and spinning metallic disks in the sky above Fátima. In effect, a Marialien. Now *that* would have changed how I prayed my rosary. I might even still be praying it.

Required Reading (That Is Never Read)

A SELECT ANNOTATED BIBLIOGRAPHY

> In the midst of all the nonsense and excessive silliness proclaimed in the name of psychic phenomena, the misinformed use of the term "parapsychology" by self-proclaimed "paranormal investigators," the perennial laughingstock of magicians and conjurers . . . this is for real?
>
> The short answer is, Yes.
>
> —DEAN RADIN, *The Conscious Universe*

Most discussions of psychical and paranormal phenomena take place in a near total ignorance of the nature, extent, and quality of the ethnographic and empirical data collected over the last two centuries. I am reminded here of something Major General Edmund R. Thompson, the U.S. Army assistant chief of staff for intelligence between 1977 and 1981, once said about the occasional stunning efficacy of the remote-viewing programs that he oversaw and sponsored: "I never liked to get into debates with the skeptics, because if you didn't believe that remote viewing was real, you hadn't done your homework."[1] The same is true, I fear, of the paranormal and the modern study of religion. We simply have not done our homework.

The same conclusion can be drawn from more mundane methods. In 1977, Stanford astrophysicist Peter Sturrock performed a poll of over one thousand members of the American Astronomical Society about UFOs. He discovered that the more they had read, the more likely they were to think that the subject deserved more attention, and, conversely, that the less they had read about the subject, the less they thought about it. Such a conclusion is not rocket science, even with rocket scientists.[2]

It is in this academic context of near total ignorance that I list below, in rough chronological order, what I consider to be some of the most important studies that need to be read if one is truly serious about inquiring into these matters. I, of course, have not read all of this material either.

Edmund Gurney, Frederic W. H. Myers, and Frank Podmore, *Phantasms of the Living*, 2 vols. (London, 1886). Treating 702 cases, this work constitutes the first major publication of the S.P.R. and stands to this day as one of the most impressive works of psychical research ever published. Read before and alongside Myers's *Human Personality and Its Survival of Bodily Death*, these four volumes constitute a single masterwork composed by many lives and, more to the point, many deaths. A searchable online version of all four volumes can be found at: http://www.esalenctr.org.

George Devereux, ed., *Psycho-analysis and the Occult* (New York: International Universities Press, 1953). A marvelous collection of essays by seventeen authors, including six by Freud himself, published at the high watermark of psychoanalytic interest in these topics at midcentury. The authors show through a blitz of case studies that, because psychical effects are often mediated by unconscious processes (repression, distortion, displacement, symbolization, and so on), observers unfamiliar with psychoanalytic methods often miss the presence of such phenomena altogether, whereas those trained in the psychoanalytic hermeneutic recognize them as important dimensions of dreams, intuitions, and the "parapsychology of everyday life." Far from being a materialist bludgeon, then, psychoanalysis becomes a method of interpretation that reveals *more* psychical connections and communications.

C. D. Broad, *Lectures on Psychical Research: Incorporating the Perrott Lectures Given in Cambridge University in 1959 and 1960*, International Library of Philosophy and Scientific Method, ed. A. J. Ayer (London: Routledge & Kegan Paul, 1962). A series of lectures given at Trinity College, Cambridge University, over a two-year period, this book is one of the finest examples that we have of a trained philosopher engaging the data fairly and thoroughly.

Jule Eisenbud, *The World of Ted Serios: "Thoughtographic" Studies of an Extraordinary Mind* (New York: William & Morrow Company, 1967). Eisenbud was a prominent Denver psychiatrist, Serios a struggling alcoholic who could barely stay off the street but who could also imprint detailed images on camera film with his mind under carefully controlled conditions. Eisenbud generally interprets these images as dreamlike projections from the psyche of Serios. They often included buildings in the real world or, in one really eerie case, Russian Vostok rockets, "apparently in space," Eisenbud calmly notes (226). My favorite section is chapter 14, "The Anatomy of Resistance," in which Eisenbud uses the history of religions and psychoanalysis to explain the dissonance between the data and the denials. The anatomy of resistance boils down for him to an attempt to keep in check "a demonic side of man of almost limitless potency" (324). Not for the metaphysically timid.

Thomas E. Bullard, *UFO Abductions: The Measure of a Mystery*, vol. 1, *Comparative Study of Abduction Reports*; and vol. 2, *Catalogue of Cases* (Mount Ranier, Maryland: Fund for UFO Research, 1987). A folklorist by training (Ph.D., University of Indiana), Bullard is widely cited in the ufological literature as one of the most respected and gifted writers, and for good reason. This is an absolutely massive comparative study of abduction reports by a trained intellectual, who comes to the careful conclusion that whereas many such experiences are probably psychological in origin, some also contain objective, physical evidence whose overall coherency suggests that they cannot be reduced either to the individual psyche or to the oral traditions of folklore. In my own terms, Bullard is an author of the impossible who is comfortable in that "place of hesitation" that defines the fantastic.

Ian Stevenson, *Reincarnation and Biology: A Contribution to the Etiology of Birthmarks and Birth Defects* (Westport, Connecticut: Praeger Publishers, 1997). Twenty-three hundred pages of mind-blowing data from around the world speculatively linking odd birthmarks to a previous life's violent death by gunshot, knife wound, and so on. Because such violent deaths are often surrounded by both traumatic memories on the part of the families and excessive paperwork and field investigations by law officers, Stevenson's studies are often unusually rich (and grisly) in empirical detail. In the end, Stevenson resists identifying the causal or acausal mechanisms of such phenomena, choosing instead to concentrate on documenting the impossible evidence.

Joaquim Fernandes and Fina D'Armada, *Heavenly Lights: The Apparitions of Fátima and the UFO Phenomenon*; Joaquim Fernandes and Fina D'Armada, *Celestial Secrets: The Hidden History of the Fátima Incident*; and Fernando Fernandes, Joaquim Fernandes, and Raul Berenguel, *Fátima Revisited: The Apparition Phenomenon in Ufology, Psychology, and Science* (San Antonio: Anomalist Books, 2005, 2006, 2008). Although highly uneven in places, this trilogy—based on over one hundred firsthand testimonies and the original records of the children's interrogations held at the Sanctuary of Fátima—constitutes the premiere ufological reading of the events of Fátima, Portugal, from May 13 to October 13, 1917. The second volume is particularly insightful, devastating really, in its exploration of the way the church manipulated the paranormal events for its own pious control of the people through the famous "three secrets" and its institutional support of the right-wing, dictator-style politics in Portugal from 1926 to 1974. "Without Fátima, Salazar would not be possible," as one brave Belgian priest put it (199–201).

Salvador Freixedo, *Visionaries, Mystics and Contactees*, trans. Scott Corrales (Avondale Estates, Georgia: IllumiNet Press, 1992). This is another radical attempt to come to terms with ufology and parapsychology from a dissident Roman Catholic perspective. Although again uneven, this text sparkles with a certain comparative courage and ends with the striking (and strikingly gnostic) conclusion that the history of religions is a long series of false prophets, pseudoenlightenments, and manmade scriptures controlled by occult forces that pose as divine but are no such thing. We now "realize that whoever dictates the messages, whoever gives the demurrage [demiurge] his power, whoever breaks the natural laws, is not God but energy entities, intelligent and evolved to a greater or lesser degree, who interfere with human lives. . . . They have appeared and demanded to be worshipped as God. But they are not God. None of them is the Creator-God, the First Cause of the Universe" (151).

Dean Radin, *The Conscious Universe: The Scientific Truth of Psychic Phenomena* (New York: HarperEdge, 1997); *Entangled Minds: Extrasensory Experiences in a Quantum Reality* (New York: Paraview, 2006). As a historian of religions who works with texts, symbols, and myths, I have consciously steered away from the extensive literature on the laboratory and statistical evidence for psychical phenomena. This does not mean, in any way, that I think this data is inconsequential. My favorite author here is Dean Radin. Besides effectively summarizing a vast evidential literature (and being very, very funny), Radin also happens to understand that "quantum theory says nothing about higher-level concepts such as *meaning* and *purpose*, yet real-world 'raw' psi phenomena seem to be intimately related to these concepts" (*Conscious Universe*, 287). The present book can be read as one long commentary on that single line.

Mark Fox, *Spiritual Encounters with Unusual Light Phenomena: Lightforms* (Cardiff: University of Wales Press, 2008). This very recent work, based on almost four hundred contemporary accounts, comes out of the Religious Experience Research Centre founded by Sir Alister Hardy at the University of Wales, Lampeter. Now numbering up to six thousand case studies, this archive represents one of our richest, and virtually untapped, sources of real-world data on mystical experience. Fox demonstrates any number of strong comparative patterns that go directly against the present contextualist dogmas of the field, namely, that paranormal encounters with lightforms are cross-cultural, transhistorical, and manifest a certain "core" phenomenology around their crisis-timing, their benign or loving aspects, and their creative impact on the visionary.

Some More Damned Anecnotes

AN IMPOSSIBLE OPENING

1. There is a debate about whether there was ever a live broadcast of the events immediately surrounding RFK's assassination, as opposed to a report aired soon after the event from a previous audio recording. Adam believes that what he heard was the famous audio broadcast of Andrew West on KDKR AM 1150, which is easily available online. The assassination occurred at about 12:16 a.m. PSD, which (pending any daylight savings complications) would have been 3:16 a.m. ETD in Toronto. If Adam in fact awoke at 3:00 a.m., this strongly suggests that he heard a live broadcast, hence Adam's memory of waking up at 3:00 a.m. may be incorrect. In any case, whereas the apparent precognitive element of Adam's experience hinges on the historical questions of whether there was a live broadcast and when he awoke, its otherwise "impossible" nature does not. Whether read as an example of precognition or some kind of occult connection, Adam's mind was interacting with history as it was presenting itself on the radio, be it live or recorded. My thanks to Jason Edwards for bringing my attention to these historical problems.

2. Stanley Krippner, "Introduction to Third Edition," in *Dream Telepathy*, ed. Montague Ullman, Stanley Krippner, with Alan Vaughan (Charlottesville: Hampton Roads, 2002), xxi. As I explain below shortly, the subject of precognitive and telepathic dreams goes back to the very founding of psychoanalysis. Indeed, the Master himself wrote no less than six papers on the subject.

INTRODUCTION

1. Jule Eisenbud, *The World of Ted Serios: "Thoughtographic" Studies of an Extraordinary Mind* (New York: William & Morrow Company, 1967), 313.

2. See, for example, Ann Taves, "Religious Experience and the Divisible Self: William James (and Frederic Myers) as Theorist(s) of Religion," *Journal of the American Academy of Religion* 71, no. 2 (2003).

3. I am relying here on the entries "Crookes, Sir William" and "Psychic Force" in Nandor Fodor's wonderfully eccentric *Encyclopaedia of Psychic Science* (University Books, 1966/1934). Where else can you find entries on "Copyright" (on the legal issues surrounding the intellectual rights to a channeled publication or spirit communication); on "Poltergeists," those haunted people (as opposed to haunted houses) whose noisy and destructive externalized vital forces Fodor, as a paranormally oriented psychoanalyst now, would later interpret as "projected repressions"; or, most impossibly of all, on "Apports," a five-page essay in which Fodor calmly offers two explanations for how things like scissors, flowers, metals, rocks, even a tree branch fall into a séance room out of nowhere: (1) interdimensional travel; or (2) "the disintegration and reintegration of the apported objects."

4. I spoke to the general editor of the second edition of the *Encyclopedia of Religion*, Lindsay Jones, about this omission. He was not the least bit defensive, and he was entirely open about the reason: no one on his editorial board expressed any concerted interest in the subject.

5. James H. Leuba, "Psychical Research," in *Encyclopaedia of Religion and Ethics*, ed. James Hastings (Edinburgh: T & T Clark, 1918), 10:423.

6. E. R. Dodds, *The Ancient Concept of Progress and Other Essays on Greek Literature and Belief* (New York: Oxford, 1973), 176–77.

7. My sincere thanks to Fritz Graf and Sarah Iles Johnston for two animated tellings of this anecdote.

8. For the fire story, which is told in numerous places, see, for example, Dean Radin, *Entangled Minds: Extrasensory Experiences in a Quantum World* (New York: Paraview, 2006), 59–60.

9. For Hegel's engagement with the Hermetic tradition and various occult streams, see Glenn Alexander Magee, *Hegel and the Hermetic Tradition* (Ithaca: Cornell University Press, 2001).

10. I am indebted here to Glenn Alexander Magee's unpublished paper, "On the Will in Nature: Schopenhauer, Animal Magnetism and Magic."

11. See Stephen E. Braude, *Immortal Remains: The Evidence for Life after Death* (Lanham, Maryland: Rowman & Littlefield, 2003), ix–x.

12. Stephen E. Braude, *ESP and Psychokinesis: A Philosophical Examination* (Philadelphia: Temple University Press, 1979); *The Limits of Influence: Psychokinesis and the Philosophy of Science* (New York: Routledge & Kegan Paul, 1986); *First Person Plural: Multiple Personality and the Philosophy of Mind* (Lanham, Maryland: Rowman & Littlefield, 1995); *Immortal Remains*; and *The Gold Leaf Lady and Other Parapsychological Investigations* (Chicago: University of Chicago Press, 2007). Braude's work easily constitutes one of the most reliable and philosophically astute oeuvres on psychical phenomena we possess. It also happens to be very funny in places.

13. For the material in this paragraph, I am relying on Roger Luckhurst's wonderful book, *The Invention of Telepathy: 1870–1901* (Oxford: Oxford University Press, 2002), 160–67.

14. Ernesto De Martino, *The World of Magic* (New York: Pyramid Communications, 1972), 63.

15. For Turner's encounters, see Edith Turner, "The Reality of Spirits: A Tabooed or Permitted Field of Study?" *Anthropology of Consciousness* 4, no. 1: 9–12. For an example of Mead's endorsement of the subject matter, see her appreciative introduction to what appears to be the first book on remote viewing, Russell Targ and Harold E. Puthoff, *Mind-Reach: Scientists Look at Psychic Ability* (Delacorte Press, 1977). For an astute anthropology of the cultural wars around the paranormal in America, see David J. Hess, *Science in the New Age: The Paranormal, Its Defenders and Debunkers, and American Culture* (Madison: University of Wisconsin Press, 1993).

16. Michael Winkelman, "Magic: A Theoretical Reassessment," *Current Anthropology* 23, no. 1 (February 1982): 44.

17. Alex Owen, *The Place of Enchantment: British Occultism and the Culture of the Modern* (Chicago: University of Chicago Press, 2004), 141.

18. Gardner Murphy and Robert O. Ballou, eds., *William James on Psychical Research* (New York: Viking Press, 1960). See also Deborah Blum, *Ghost Hunters: William James and the Search for Scientific Proof of Life after Death* (New York: Penguin, 2006).

19. For much more on this, see F. X. Charet, *Spiritualism and the Foundations of C. G. Jung's Psychology* (Albany: SUNY, 1993).

20. Dean Radin, *The Conscious Universe: Scientific Evidence for Psi Phenomena* (New York: HarperSanFrancisco, 1997), 131. For more on Pauli and Jung from some rigorous philosophical and scientific perspectives, see Harald Atmanspacher and Hans Primas, eds., *Recasting Reality: Wolfgang Pauli's Philosophical Ideas and Contemporary Science* (Berlin: Springer, 2009).

21. Cross-cultural surveys have shown that "about half of all spontaneous psi experiences occur in the dream state" (Radin, *Conscious Universe*, 68).

22. Ernest Jones, *The Life and Work of Sigmund Freud* (New York: Basic Books, 1957), 3:380.

23. Ibid., 394.

24. I am indebted to Sudhir Kakar for this line of thought concerning Freud's late skepticism and his linking of analytic empathy and telepathy: "The Resurgence of Imagination," paper delivered at the Breuninger Foundation's Symposium on Spirituality and Depth Psychology, August 4–8, 2008, Wasan Island, Ontario, Canada.

25. Elizabeth Lloyd Mayer, *Extraordinary Knowing: Science, Skepticism, and the Inexplicable Powers of the Human Mind* (New York: Bantam, 2007), 3.

26. Ibid., xii.

27. Owen, *Place of Enchantment*, 139; Bruce Mills, *Poe, Fuller, and the Mesmeric Arts: Transition States in the American Renaissance* (Columbia: University of Missouri Press, 2006). For the British scene, particularly around Sir Edward Bulwer-Lytton, see Robert Lee Wolff, *Strange Stories: Explorations in Victorian Fiction—The Occult and the Neurotic* (Boston: Gambit, 1971).

28. Quoted in Owen, *Place of Enchantment*, 41.

29. Jacques Derrida, "Telepathy," trans. Nicholas Royle, *Oxford Literary Review* 10, nos. 1–2 (1988): 3–41 (originally published in 1981); and *Specters of Marx: The State of the Debt, the Work of Mourning, and the New International*, trans. Peggy Kamuf (London: Routledge, 1994), 11. See also Nicholas Royle, *Telepathy and Literature: Essays on the Reading Mind* (Oxford: Basil Blackwell, 2000).

30. Turner, "Reality of Spirits."

31. George P. Hansen, *The Trickster and the Paranormal* (XLibris, 2001), 366, 367. Hansen's work stands virtually alone among parapsychological writings for its deep engagement with the humanities and social sciences.

32. Mircea Eliade, "Folklore as an Instrument of Knowledge," trans. Mac Linscott Ricketts, in *Mircea Eliade: A Critical Reader*, ed. Bryan Rennie (London: Equinox, 2006).

33. Mircea Eliade, *Occultism, Witchcraft, and Cultural Fashions: Essays in Comparative Religion* (Chicago: University of Chicago Press, 1976), 55.

34. Mircea Eliade, *Ordeal by Labyrinth: Conversations with Claude-Henri Rocquet* (Chicago: University of Chicago Press, 1982), 49.

35. Eliade, *Autobiography*, vol. 1, *1907–1937: Journey East, Journey West* (San Francisco: Harper and Row, 1981), 190.

36. Eliade, *Ordeal by Labyrinth*, 49.

37. Mircea Eliade, *Two Strange Tales* (Boston: Shambala, 1986), x–xii.

38. Eliade, *Ordeal by Labyrinth*, 147.

39. Eliade, "Occult and the Modern World," 56.

40. Ibid., 54. Along very similar psychoanalytic-gnostic lines, it is probably no accident that Eliade chose to conclude this same volume on occultism and witchcraft with his "Spirit, Light, and Seed," an essay that advances a strong comparative case for the symbolic equation of divine light and sperm in the history of religions.

41. See especially Wendy Doniger O'Flaherty, *Dreams, Illusion and Other Realities* (Chicago: University of Chicago Press, 1984).

42. Ted Anton, *Eros, Magic, and the Murder of Professor Culianu* (Evanston: Northwestern University Press, 1996).

43. I. P. Couliano, *Out of This World: A History of Otherworldly Journeys, from Gilgamesh to Albert Einstein* (Boston: Shambalah, 1991).

44. Ioan P. Couliano, *The Tree of Gnosis: Gnostic Mythology from Early Christianity to Modern Nihilism* (New York: HarperSanFrancisco, 1992).

45. Ioan P. Couliano, "System and History," *Incognita*, 6. See also his "A Historian's Kit to the Fourth Dimension," *Incognita* 1 (1990), 113–29, and his *Out of This World*.

46. Couliano, "System and History," 9.

47. To my limited knowledge, other than Couliano, the only other scholar of religion who has recognized the mind-blowing implications of Einstein's physics for the practice of historiography is Elliot R. Wolfson. In his magisterial *Language, Eros, Being: Kabbalistic Hermeneutics and Poetic Imagination* (New York: Fordham University Press, 2005), Wolfson explores the curvature of spacetime and the possibility of time loops in order to entertain the idea that "the past is as much determined by the present as the present by the past" (ibid., xvii–xix).

48. John E. Mack, as quoted in Christopher Partridge, "Understanding UFO Religions and Abduction Spiritualities," in *UFO Religions*, ed. Partridge (London: Routledge, 2003), 35–36.

49. I am adopting this expression from Michael A. Sells, *Mystical Languages of Unsaying* (Chicago: University of Chicago Press, 1994). I am using it, however, in a different way. A "meaning event" for Sells is the moment in a piece of mystical literature in which "the meaning has become identical or fused with the act of predication" (9), that is to say, a meaning event is a literary mode that attempts to replicate in human language the structure of the original state of consciousness that inspired it. Sells was writing about Neoplatonic, Christian, and Islamic literature, and his main concern was the nature and structure of something called apophatic theology, that is, ways of "saying away" (*apo-phasis*) our normal ways of speaking and writing about the divine. This was traditionally accomplished through elaborate poetic and philosophical flourishes of affirmation and negation that express the impossibility of understanding "God" as an experience *of* something. Here is one, from the fourteenth-century Dominican priest and heretical theologian Meister Eckhart: "The eye with which I see God is the same eye with which God sees me." Paranormal events, as we shall see, often function in remarkably similar ways. They appear to be designed to confuse. They act like an Eckhartian sermon or a Zen koan. They at once mirror and boggle the human consciousness in which they appear.

50. Owen, *Place of Enchantment*, 19. This, by the way, is true in a literal scientific sense, as our senses can pick up only a miniscule fraction of the electromagnetic spectrum that buzzes and burns all around us at every moment. Reality really is almost entirely "occult" to our normal sensory capacities.

51. Ibid., 22.

52. Ibid., 6.

53. Ibid., 182.

54. Gauri Viswanathan, "Secularism in the Framework of Heterodoxy," *PMLA* 123, no. 2 (March 2008), 469.

55. Owen, *Place of Enchantment*, 237.

56. Christopher Partridge, *The Re-Enchantment of the West*, vol. 1, *Alternative Spiritualities, Sacralization, Popular Culture, and Occulture* (London: T & T Clark, 2004), 68.

57. Ibid., 4.

58. I am influenced in my thinking here by Richard Shweder, *Thinking Through Cultures: Expeditions in Cultural Psychology* (Cambridge, Massachusetts: Harvard University Press, 1991). For more on this, see chapter 4.

59. Victoria Nelson, *The Secret Life of Puppets* (Cambridge, Massachusetts: Harvard University Press, 2001), 288.

60. Ibid., vii.

61. Ibid., 174.

62. Philip K. Dick, "If You Find This World Bad, You Should See Some of the Others" (1977), in *The Shifting Realities of Philip K. Dick: Selected Literary and Philosophical Writings*, ed. Lawrence Sutin (New York: Harmony 1995), 251.

63. Philip K. Dick, "How to Build a Universe That Doesn't Fall Apart Two Days Later" (1978), in ibid.

64. Lawrence Sutin, *Divine Invasions: A Life of Philip K. Dick* (New York: Citadel, 1991), 208–9, 233.

65. Lawrence Sutin, ed., *In Pursuit of Valis: Selections from the Exegesis* (Underwood Miller, 1991), 175–76.

66. Thomas M. Disch suggests the epilepsy diagnosis in his *The Dreams Our Stuff Is Made Of: How Science Fiction Conquered the World* (New York: Simon & Schuster, 1998). Sutin, however, although he finds such diagnoses possible enough, is not finally impressed with either the adequacy or the wisdom of such easy labels. Both authors are sensitive and fair to Dick. For my part, I am not questioning the diagnosis qua diagnosis. I am simply pointing out how little it explains with respect to Dick's place in the general history of religions.

67. Nelson, *Secret Life of Puppets*, 174.

68. This event occurred on November 5, 1989, in Calcutta, my own 11-89, I suppose. I have written extensively about the magnetic-plasmic energies of "that Night" and their reprogramming of my writing practices in *Roads of Excess, Palaces of Wisdom*. That Night, in fact, constitutes the impossible, paranormal subtext of all my books, including this one.

69. This is actually Roger Caillois, approvingly cited by Tzvetan Todorov in *The Fantastic: A Structural Approach to a Literary Genre* (Ithaca: Cornell University Press, 1975), 26. I recognize that Todorov tilts away from the metaphysical, but I am using him for my own purposes here.

70. Ibid., 25.

71. Ibid., 32; italics mine.

CHAPTER ONE

1. Stephen King, *On Writing: A Memoir of the Craft* (New York: Scribner, 2000).

2. Frederic W. H. Myers, *Fragments of Prose and Poetry*, edited by his wife Eveleen Myers (London: Longmans, Green, and Co., 1904), 1.

3. Ibid., 17.

4. Frederic W. H. Myers, "Science and the Future Life," in *Science and the Future Life with Other Essays* (London: Macmillan and Co., 1901/1893), 16.

5. Ibid., 18.

6. Myers, *Fragments*, 46.

7. Quoted in Alan Gauld, *The Founders of Psychical Research* (New York: Schocken Books, 1968), 45. I have relied heavily on Gauld for my historical understanding of the S.P.R. For my understanding of Myers's psychology and numerous key quotes from his scattered essays, I am deeply indebted to Emily Williams Kelly's definitive essay, "F. W. H. Myers and the Empirical Study of the Mind-Body Problem," in *Irreducible Mind: Toward a Psychology for the 21st Century*,

by Edward F. Kelly, Emily Williams Kelly, Adam Crabtree, Alan Gauld, Michael Grosso, and Bruce Greyson (Lanham: Rowman & Littlefield, 2007).

8. Quoted in Gauld, *Founders*, 64.

9. Hence Edmund Gurney, one of the leading authors of the S.P.R., went so far as to entitle his two-volume study *Tertium Quid: Chapters on Various Disputed Questions* (London, 1887). The Latin appears to be related in turn to the Pythagorean *triton genon* or "third race," which was a term used "to describe the unique position of Pythagoras and other kings and sages as neither gods nor men" (Jonathan Z. Smith, *Imagining Religion: From Babylon to Jonestown* [Chicago: University of Chicago Press, 1982], 11).

10. F. W. H. Myers, correspondence, *Journal of the Society for Psychical Research* 4 (1890): 248.

11. Myers, *Science and a Future Life*, 4.

12. Ibid., 7.

13. Frederic W. H. Myers, *Human Personality and Its Survival of Bodily Death*, 2 vols. (London: Longmans, Green, and Co., 1904/1903), 2:307 (compare also 309); henceforth HP, followed by volume and page number.

14. As such authors as Leigh Eric Schmidt and Michael Robertson have recently demonstrated, the distinction is probably first found in Emerson's early essays, after which it blooms in Whitman's ecstatic poem-prophecy, *Leaves of Grass* (1855). See Leigh Eric Schmidt, *Restless Souls: The Making of American Spirituality* (New York: Harper Collins, 2005); and Michael Robertson, *Worshipping Walt: The Whitman Disciples* (Princeton: Princeton University Press, 2008).

15. The category of the spiritual was swamped at this point by the related category of the "spiritualistic," that is, the phenomena of Spiritualism. The category of the mystical was somewhat more fluid. For negative uses, see Myers's reference to "any hollow mysticism, any half-conscious deceit" (Gauld, *Founders*, 143). For neutral uses, consider his rhyming description of the Census of Hallucinations as "not mystical but statistical" (Myers, *Science and a Future Life*, 29) or his use of the phrase "mystic sentiment" as a gloss for "aesthetic emotion" (ibid., 69).

16. See "Appendix C: Correspondence between Myers and Lord Acton on the Canons of Evidence to be Applied to Reports of 'Miraculous' Occurrences," in Gauld, *Founders*, 364–67.

17. Thus Myers describes death as the "complete dissociation from the brain itself" (HP 1:xliii).

18. Myers claims his mother's family was among Wordsworth's "most appreciative friends" (Myers, *Fragments*, 4).

19. Ibid., 6–7.

20. Ibid., 45.

21. Ibid., 16.

22. Gauld, *Founders*, 135.

23. Myers, *Fragments*, 17–18.

24. Ibid., 22.

25. Gauld, *Founders*, 95–96.

26. Myers, *Fragments*, 28.

27. Myers, *Science and a Future Life*, 51.

28. Ibid., 52.

29. Ibid., 56.

30. Ibid., 56–57.

31. Myers, *Fragments*, 41.

32. Ibid., 45.

33. Humanists are generally very suspicious of evolutionary theologies like Myers's, mostly because similar philosophies were used in the nineteenth and twentieth centuries for some truly horrendous political ideologies, including fascist and colonial ones. Much, I suspect, depends upon one's temporal perspective. It may be dubious indeed to make evolutionary

comparisons between contemporary cultures and religions, generations, or even centuries, but it seems difficult to deny that the species and its forms of consciousness have evolved over the last few hundred thousand years, much less the last few million. It also remains true that innumerable expressions of metaphysical religion are simply incomprehensible outside an evolutionary frame. In the end, I would make three simple observations: (1) from a historical perspective, every metaphysical or mystical system employs some version of its era's understanding of the natural world, hence it would be surprising indeed if this were not also the case for modern movements; (2) a badly used idea is not the same thing as a bad idea; and (3) there are in actual fact hundreds of evolutionary spiritualities in the modern world, including multiple examples from India, each with its own nuances and political histories. Basically, I think we need significantly less moral righteousness here and far more historical consciousness, philosophical nuance, moral balance, and, above all, imagination.

34. Ibid., 40, 46–47.

35. Ibid., 47–48. As we shall see, the Sargasso Sea was central to Charles Fort's metaphorical armory as well.

36. F. W. H. Myers, *Essays: Classical* (London: Macmillan and Co., 1883); *Essays: Modern* (London: Macmillan and Co., 1901/1897); and *Science and a Future Life*.

37. F. W. H. Myers, *Wordsworth* (London: Macmillan and Co., 1881).

38. Myers, "Fragments of Inner Life," 6.

39. Quoted in Gauld, *Founders*, 333.

40. Quoted in ibid., 54.

41. Ibid., 53.

42. Ibid., 234.

43. Ibid., 239.

44. Ibid., 318

45. For Lincoln, I am relying on Marcia Brennan, "Tragic Dreams and Spectral Doubles: The Metaphysical Lincoln," in *Poetry Nation Review* (Manchester, UK: Carcanet Press, 2009). For Twain's remarkable story about an eerily detailed and deadly accurate precognitive dream about his brother's death in a riverboat accident, see Deborah Blum, *Ghost Hunters: William James and the Search for Scientific Proof of Life after Death* (New York: Penguin, 2006), 73–74. In another twist in our developing story, it is worth pointing out that Twain went so far as to suggest in an essay for *Harper's* (December 1891) that authors sometimes pick up ideas from one another telepathically. He proposed, Blum explains, "that telepathy could even account for scientists such as Darwin and Wallace developing their insights into evolution during a similar time period" (173).

46. Quoted in Gauld, *Founders*, 18.

47. Ibid.

48. For late nineteenth- and early twentieth-century expressions of the mystical as the erotic, see Wouter J. Hanegraaff and Jeffrey J. Kripal, eds., *Hidden Intercourse: Eros and Sexuality in the History of Western Estoericism* (Leiden: E. J. Brill, 2008). For the sexual magic and occult material, see also Hugh B. Urban, *Magia Sexualis: Sex, Magic, and Liberation in Western Esotericism* (Berkeley: University of California Press, 2006), and Alex Owen, *The Place of Enchantment: British Occultism and the Culture of the Modern* (Chicago: University of Chicago Press, 2004), especially chapter 3, "Sexual Politics," and chapter 6, "Aleister Crowley in the Desert."

49. Blum, *Ghost Hunters*, 201.

50. Ingo Swann, *Psychic Sexuality: The Bio-Psychic "Anatomy" of Sexual Energies* (Rapid City, North Dakota: Ingo Swann Books, 1996), 107–8. Swann is a remarkable figure whose books, a few of them, like this one, already collector's items, deserve a careful study of their own. We will encounter him again below, in chapter 3.

51. Anne Braude's is the classic study of this side of the Atlantic. See her *Radical Spirits: Spiritualism and Women's Rights in Nineteenth-Century America* (Boston: Beacon Press, 1989). For

the other side (of the pond), see especially Alex Owen, *The Darkened Room: Women, Power, and Spiritualism in Late Victorian England* (Chicago: University of Chicago Press, 1989).

52. Targ shared this anecdote with a group of us during the proceedings of a symposium that I codirected with Michael Murphy at the Esalen Institute, "On the Supernormal and the Superpower," June 1–4, 2008.

53. Gauld dedicates an entire chapter to Palladino. See also Hereward Carrington, *Eusapia Palladino and Her Phenomena* (New York: B. W. Dodge, 1909). Carrington, by the way, was an expert on stage magic, so he was hardly one to be easily fooled.

54. Gauld, *Founders*, 236.

55. Ibid., 241.

56. William James, "Address by the President," in *William James on Psychical Research*, ed. Gardner Murphy and Robert O. Ballou (New York: Viking Press, 1960), 61; the original text first appeared in *Proceedings of the Society for Psychical Research*, pt. 20, vol. 12 (1896).

57. Myers, *Fragments*, 32–33.

58. Gauld, *Founders*, 103n3. Sidgwick, by the way, would also confess that "John King is an old friend," even if "he always came into the dark and talked at random" and "our friendship refrigerated" (ibid., 103–4).

59. Karl von Reichenbach, *The Odic Force: Letters on Od and Magnetism*, trans. F. D. O'Byrne (London: Hutchinson & Co., 1926). Reichenbach's work is an unmistakable forerunner of the radical psychoanalyst Wilhelm Reich and his "orgone." And what would have become of psychoanalysis if it had followed the od instead of the id?

60. Gauld, *Founders*, 153.

61. Ibid., 234.

62. The exact scenario was never conclusive, since Gurney was known to suffer from headaches and could have easily been administering a painkiller, but even close friends suspected suicide.

63. Blum, *Ghost Hunters*, 80.

64. Ibid., 91.

65. *Proceedings of the Society for Psychical Research* 3 (1885): 207–380.

66. They quoted him, of course, in the *Proceedings* 19 (1907): 365–66; quoted in Gauld, *Founders*, 336.

67. Gauld, *Founders*, 251.

68. Ibid., 346.

69. Blum, *Ghost Hunters*, 186.

70. Ibid., 259.

71. See Murphy and Ballou, *William James on Psychical Research*, sect. 4.

72. André Breton, *The Automatic Message* (London: Atlas Press, 1997/1933).

73. William James, "Frederic Myers's Service to Psychology," in Murphy and Ballou, *William James on Psychical Research*, 223.

74. Kelly, "F. W. H. Myers," 67.

75. F. W. H. Myers, "The Work of Edmund Gurney in Experimental Psychology," *Proceedings* 5 (1888): 43.

76. Aldous Huxley, *The Perennial Philosophy* (Cleveland: The World Publishing Company, 1962), v–vi. Huxley shared the metaphor of the chemical compound with C. D. Broad, who used it in his own writing on psychical phenomena.

77. F. W. H. Myers, "On Telepathic Hypnotism, and Its Relations to Other Forms of Hypnotic Suggestion," *Proceedings* 4 (1886): 178–79.

78. Kelly, "F. W. H. Myers," 90.

79. F. W. H. Myers, "Automatic Writing, or the Rationale of Planchette," *Contemporary Review* 47 (1885): 234.

80. Myers discussed Freud and Breuer's early studies of hysteria (in chapter 2) and helped introduce Freud's writings to the English-reading public. Indeed, he was the first to publish Freud in English.

81. William James, "Final Impressions of a Psychical Researcher" (originally "Confidences of a Psychical Researcher," *American Magazine*, October 1909).

82. The phrase "cosmic consciousness" James almost certainly borrowed from Richard Maurice Bucke, *Cosmic Consciousness: A Study in the Evolution of the Human Mind* (Innes & Sons, 1901).

83. Gauld, *Founders*, 278–79.

84. F. W. H. Myers, "The Subliminal Consciousness. Chapter 1: General Characteristics and Subliminal Messages," *Proceedings* 7 (1892): 305.

85. Frederic W. H. Myers, "Automatic Writing—II," *Proceedings* 3 (1885): 30.

86. Edward F. Kelly, "Toward a Psychology for the 21st Century," in *Irreducible Mind*, 585.

87. F. W. H. Myers, "The Drift of Psychical Research," *National Review* 24 (1894–95): 197.

88. F. W. H. Myers, "Professor Janet's 'Atomatisme Psychologique,'" *Proceedings* 6 (1889): 195.

89. F. W. H. Myers, "Note on a Suggested Mode of Psychical Interaction," in *Phantasms of the Living*, by Edmund Gurney, F. W. H. Myers, and Frank Podmore (London: Trübner,1886), 285.

90. Myers, "Professor Janet's," 190.

91. F. W. H. Myers, "Obituary: Robert Louis Stevenson," *Journal of the Society for Psychical Research* 7 (1895): 6.

92. Myers, "Subliminal Consciousness," 318.

93. Gauld, *Founders*, 83, 137, 214–15

94. Blum, *Ghost Hunters*, 44, 55.

95. For an analysis of Wallace's views, see especially Janet Oppenheim, *The Other World: Spiritualism and Psychical Research in England, 1850–1914* (Cambridge: Cambridge University Press, 1985), 296–325.

96. Myers, *Science and a Future Life*, 55.

97. Ibid., 37.

98. Quoted in M. H. Abrams, *Natural Supernaturalism: Tradition and Revolution in Romantic Literature* (New York: W.W. Norton, 1971), 223, 269.

99. Ibid., 186.

100. Ibid., 231.

101. Glenn Alexander Magee, *Hegel and the Hermetic Tradition* (Ithaca: Cornell University Press, 2001).

102. See Dana Sawyer, *Aldous Huxley: A Biography* (New York: Crossroad, 2002), 188.

103. Kelly et al., *Irreducible Mind*, xxx.

104. Myers, *Science and a Future Life*, 35.

105. Jonathan Z. Smith has famously suggested that the act of making connections between patterns, actions, and ideas that are otherwise not causally connected is a common human activity in both traditional magical practices and contemporary academic method ("In Comparison a Magic Dwells," in *Imagining Religion: From Babylon to Jonestown* [Chicago: University of Chicago Press, 1982], 19–35). More recently, Christopher I. Lehrich has argued for a similar "magical" structure of critical theory, this time in conversation with modern forms of occultism (*The Occult Mind: Magic in Theory and Practice* [Syracuse: Cornell University Press, 2007]). As a trained scientist who became a historian of religions, Smith wants us to move away from the magical to the scientific. Fair enough. But it seems to me that comparative insights can also sometimes participate in the magical and mystical structures of consciousness, with which we also must deal. In other words, there really *is* a magic in comparison.

106. "Phantasm" was chosen over "phantom," because the latter term implied a visual component, whereas the cases could involve any of the senses, or even what was called a "diffused sensibility" (HP 1:xix).

107. Gauld, *Founders*, 290.

108. For a full, and balanced, early intellectual history of the term, see Roger Luckhurst, *The Invention of Telepathy: 1870–1901* (New York: Oxford University Press, 2002).

109. Gauld, *Founders*, 18.

110. Bertrand Méheust, *Somnambulisme et médiumnité (1784–1930)* (Le Plessis-Robinson: Institut Synthélabo Pour Le Progrés de la Connaissance, 1999), 2:320.

111. Ibid., 2:426.

112. Upton Sinclair, *Mental Radio*, preface by Albert Einstein (Charlottesville: Hampton Roads, 2001).

113. Telepathy as a reduction to the irreducible nature of human consciousness is a lovely example of the kind of mystical humanism or gnostic methodology I proposed in *The Serpent's Gift*.

114. I cannot help pondering the potential connections between Myers's metaphor of the imaginal as an adult insect and the imaginal realm of later UFO encounters, which often involve psychical, evolutionary, and insectoid themes, from the beelike "buzzing" of the craft, through the evolutionary intentions of the interventions, to the insectlike appearance of the telepathic aliens. I don't know what to make of this, but there it is.

115. Myers, *Science and a Future Life*, 37–38.

116. Ibid., 39–40. Myers invokes the same larval/imaginal language at HP 1:97.

117. For an excellent discussion of the evolutionary mysticisms of both Carpenter and Bucke and their correspondence, see Paul Marshall, *Mystical Encounters with the Natural World: Experiences and Explanations* (New York: Oxford University Press, 2005).

118. Henri Bergson, *The Two Sources of Morality and Religion* (London: Macmillan, 1935), 275.

119. See, for example, Myers, *Science and a Future Life*, 40.

120. Myers, however, recognized that telaesthesia merges into telepathy, since it is always possible that a perception at a distance is being picked up from another mind there (HP 1:xv).

121. HP 1:112. This is another place where Myers and Freud are very close. Freud, after all, turned to the exact same Greek classic in order to gloss his own understanding of sexuality as an omnipresent force capable of genital, cultural, literary, and philosophical expression, that is, Plato's *Symposium* and its fundamentally mystical notion of eros. "In its origin, function, and relation to sexual love," Freud wrote, "the 'Eros' of the philosopher Plato coincides exactly with the love-force, the libido of psycho-analysis" (*Group Psychology and the Analysis of the Ego*, in *The Standard Edition of the Complete Psychological Works of Sigmund Freud*, ed. James Strachey [London: Hogarth Press, 1975], 18:91).

122. Blum, *Ghost Hunters*, 264.

123. Myers, *Fragments*, 35.

124. Blum, *Ghost Hunters*, 258–59.

125. Eveleen Myers, preface to Myers, *Fragments*, v–vi.

126. From *Fragments*, quoted in Gauld, *Founders*, 119.

CHAPTER TWO

1. The standard source for Fort's writings is the Omnibus volume, first published as *The Books of Charles Fort*, with an introduction by Tiffany Thayer (New York: Henry Holt and Company, 1941), and later reissued as *The Complete Books of Charles Fort*, with a new introduction by Damon Knight (New York: Dover, 1974). Most recently, the Omnibus volume has been reissued again as *The Books of the Damned*, with a new introduction by Jim Steinmeyer (New York: Jeremy Tarcher, 2008). My page references (which are in fact consistent throughout the three editions) are to the second volume and are preceded in the text by BD (*The Book of the Damned*), NL (*New Lands*), LO (*Lo!*), and WT (*Wild Talents*).

2. Fort made all of this quite clear in a May 1926 letter to the science-fiction writer Edmund Hamilton, as quoted in Damon Knight, *Charles Fort: Prophet of the Unexplained* (New York: Doubleday, 1970), 171–72.

3. Colin Bennett, *The Politics of the Imagination: The Life, Work and Ideas of Charles Fort* (Manchester: Headpress, 2002), 120.

4. Quoted in Jim Steinmeyer, *Charles Fort: The Man Who Invented the Supernatural* (New York: Tarcher/Penguin, 2008), xv.

5. I am indebted for this quote and line of thought to Steinmeyer, ibid.

6. Knight, *Charles Fort*, 65.

7. The phrase "intellectually promiscuous" is mine, but it is entirely faithful to Fort's sexual-intellectual sense of his comparative sins. "I am a pioneer and no purist," he wrote, "and some of these stud-stunts of introducing vagabond ideas to each other may have about the eugenic value of some of the romances in houses of ill fame. I cannot expect to be both promiscuous and respectable. Later, most likely, some of these unions will be properly licensed" (LO 572).

8. Tiffany Thayer, quoted in Knight, *Charles Fort*, 180.

9. Quoted in Steinmeyer, *Charles Fort*, 237.

10. Quoted in Knight, *Charles Fort*, 70,

11. Quoted in Louis Kaplan, *The Damned Universe of Charles Fort* (Brooklyn: Autonomedia, 1993), 125, without reference.

12. Cited and contextualized in Steinmeyer, *Charles Fort*, 75.

13. Quoted in ibid, 143. Dreiser wrote a play inspired by *X* entitled *The Dream*.

14. Steinmeyer, *Charles Fort*, 155, 192.

15. As early as 1879, the Italian astronomer Schiaparelli had claimed something similar, and the great French astronomer Camille Flammarion (1842–1925), who had his own spiritualist and occult interests, enthusiastically endorsed a version of the same idea. For more on this, see R. A. S. Hennessey, *Worlds Without End: The Historic Search for Extraterrestrial Life* (Charleston: Tempus Publishing, 1999), chapter 9, "To the Canals of Mars—and after, 1880–1920."

16. Quoted without reference in Damon Knight's introduction to *The Complete Books of Charles Fort*, xiii.

17. Cited without reference in Kaplan, *Damned Universe*, 124.

18. Steinmeyer, *Charles Fort*, 158.

19. Knight, *Charles Fort*, 5.

20. Quoted in Knight, *Charles Fort*, 12–13. Knight is quoting from Fort's unpublished and partial biography, *Many Parts*.

21. My discussion of *X* relies almost entirely on Steinmeyer, *Charles Fort*, 137–44.

22. Quoted in Kaplan, *Damned Universe*, 121.

23. The source is anonymous. Quoted in David Christian, *Maps of Time: An Introduction to Big History* (Berkeley: University of California Press, 2004), 27.

24. Steinmeyer, *Charles Fort*, 156–57.

25. Quoted in Kaplan, *Damned Universe*, 126, without reference.

26. An important exception here is Colin Bennett's *Politics of the Imagination*. More on Bennett's postmodern reading of Fort below.

27. This is actually Roger Caillois, approvingly cited by Tzvetan Todorov in *The Fantastic: A Structural Approach to a Literary Genre* (Ithaca: Cornell University Press, 1975), 26.

28. Ibid., 25.

29. Quoted in Todorov, *Fantastic*, 25–26.

30. David Ray Griffin, *Parapsychology, Philosophy, and Spirituality: A Postmodern Exploration* (Albany: State University of New York Press, 1997). The parapsychological use of the metaphor of the white crow originates with William James, who used it to point out that only one genuine

psychical case, only one white crow, is sufficient to conclude that the easy assumptions of scientific materialism are false, that not all crows are black. Fort apparently read his James, as he makes a transparent reference to this same Jamesian logic early in *The Book of the Damned* (BD 43).

31. Fort's constant use of "hypnotics" and "somnambulists" to describe those duped by religion *or* science is a case in point. He employs these terms not to affirm the data of psychical research, but to explain the psychology of plausibility within these two Dominants (NL 424).

32. See the letters quoted in Steinmeyer, *Charles Fort*, 210.

33. Letter to Maynard Shipley, quoted in Knight, *Charles Fort*, 182.

34. I explored the later history of this American metaphysical trajectory in my *Esalen* as "the science of mysticism" literature, which came to the fore in the mid-1970s through books like Fritjof Capra's *The Tao of Physics* (1975) and Gary Zukav's *The Dancing Wu Li Masters* (1979). Here I am changing my terms to reflect both a change of mind and a subsequent realization that this literature has its deepest roots in the psychical-research, science-fiction, and Fortean narratives of the nineteenth and early twentieth centuries. The quantum mystical movement, I see now, did not begin in 1975, with the appearance of Capra's *The Tao of Physics*. It began in 1932, with the appearance of Fort's *Wild Talents*, a book that in turn draws inspiration from the earlier psychical researchers' desire to create a true "science of religion."

35. Quoted in Steinmeyer, *Charles Fort*, 47.

36. Brian Stableford, introduction to *H. G. Wells: Seven Novels* (New York: Barnes and Noble, 2006), ix.

37. No doubt, to the horror of Wells, who hated *The Book of the Damned* and its author, calling the latter in a review "one of the most damnable bores who ever cut scraps from out-of-the-way newspapers" (cited in Steinmeyer, *Charles Fort*, 11). So much for easy lineages.

38. Fort explains that *New Lands* is divided into two parts: (1) the neoastronomic, in which he asserts that astronomy and its mathematics are about 50 percent correct (this section is almost all total nonsense); and (2) the extrageographic, which develops the Super-Story of intergalactic or multidimensional colonialism. These break down into chapters 1–12 and chapters 13–38, respectively. Given that the first part covers pages 313–89, we can calculate Fort's "gross and stupid errors" to be around 77 pages. But the theory appears throughout the corpus, hence my playful estimation of 130 pages.

39. This idea would take on a dark history in the late 1980s and '90s, with the rise of assorted right-wing forms of political paranoia in the U.S. that linked UFOs and various supposed government conspiracies, often of an outrageous nature. For more on this, see below, chapter 3, note 49.

40. This series of events and Fort's handling of them bear an uncanny resemblance to the 1967–68 winter events of Point Pleasantville, West Virginia, as novelized by John A. Keel in *The Mothman Prophecies*. Keel was a fan of Fort's and certainly would have known of the 1904–5 events. Both stories even feature what Fort calls an "occult police force" (Keel's "men in black") whose job it is to "kill off mysteries with bogus explanations," "to divert suspicion from themselves, because they, too, may be exploiting life upon this earth" (LO 661).

41. William James, "What Psychical Research Has Accomplished," in *William James on Psychical Research*, ed. Gardner Murphy and Robert O. Ballou (New York: Viking Press, 1960), 25–26.

42. The title finally chosen is a jab at the astronomers, who were good at calculating where a new planet should be and, effectively, declaring "Lo!" that is, "Look there!" only to find nothing at all in the sky. Fort was not very fond of astronomy—one of his real mistakes.

CHAPTER THREE

1. Jacques F. Vallee, *The Magonia Collection (A Reference and Research Library), Annotated Catalogue*, vol. 1, *Paranormal Research* (private publication, July 2002), 3.

2. Jacques Vallee, *Forbidden Science: Journals 1957–1969* (New York: Marlowe & Company, 1996), 44. *Forbidden Science*, vol. 2, *Journals 1970–1979: The Belmont Years*, is privately published, copyright 2007 by Documatica Research, LLC. Both are henceforth cited as FS, followed by the volume and page number.

3. The phrase "Beyond Reason" occurs twice as a section title in Jacques Vallee, *Passport to Magonia: From Folklore to Flying Saucers* (Chicago: Henry Regnery, 1969), 110, henceforth PM; and *Dimensions: A Casebook of Alien Contact* (London: Souvenir Press, 1988), 136.

4. FS 1:147–48. Other significant statements on the category occur at FS 2:42, 61.

5. Jacques Vallee, in collaboration with Tracy Tormé, *Fastwalker (A Novel)* (Berkeley: Frog, Ltd., 1996), 22.

6. For an excellent history of this moment, at least up to the mid-1970s, see David Michael Jacobs, *The UFO Controversy in America* (Bloomington: Indiana University Press, 1975). Jacobs, a professional historian, would later become a major figure in the abduction controversies of the 1980s and '90s through his conclusion that these events are aimed at a sinister alien-human hybrid breeding program. Hence his second book on the subject, *Secret Life: Firsthand Documented Accounts of UFO Abductions* (New York: Fireside, 1992).

7. For Kansas, see FS 2:243–44. For Batman, see PM 71–81. Batman first appeared on the cover of *Detective Comics* #39 in 1939. The earlier paranormal version, of which the comic-book artists and writers appear to have been unaware, was known as Springheel Jack.

8. Ford was deeply disturbed by the way Project Blue Book, and particularly Allen Hynek, had handled the famous Ann Arbor case of March 23, 1966, when sixty witnesses saw four objects float over a farm northwest of Ann Arbor and another land in a swamp in Dexter. The witnesses included four policemen and *an entire dormitory* at Hillsdale College. The case was considered serious enough that the Pentagon got involved. Hynek famously suggested at a press conference a few days later that it may have been "swamp gas," a response that was ridiculed by the press and infuriated Ford, who, as Vallee describes him, was outraged "at the suggestion that his constituents couldn't tell marsh gas from spaceships" (FS 1:182). Ford wrote a letter to the Armed Services Committee of the House of Representatives and demanded immediate hearings.

9. Michael D. Swords, "Donald E. Keyhoe and the Pentagon," in *UFOs, 1947–1997: From Arnold to the Abductees: Fifty Years of Flying Saucers*, ed. Hilary Evans and Dennis Stacy (London: John Brown Publishing, 1997), 89.

10. For stories of psychical researchers or psychics who died in suspicious circumstances, see FS 2:150, 330, 373, 396, 428–30, 443.

11. FS 1:21–22. I once heard Vallee describe this event at a private symposium: "I'm sorry, but it was a UFO," he said to us. The transparency, honesty, and frustration of the aside were palpable. I hope this book as a whole communicates the same intellectual and emotional message: "I'm sorry, but these things are real. Deal with it."

12. Kenneth Arnold, "I *Did* See the Flying Discs," *Fate* 1, no. 1 (Spring 1948): 6, 7, 8.

13. Timothy Good, *Need to Know: UFOs, the Military and Intelligence* (New York: Pegasus Books, 2007), 103.

14. Donald E. Keyhoe, *Flying Saucers from Outer Space* (New York: Henry Holt, 1953), 209.

15. See above, note 8.

16. Jacques Vallee, *Anatomy of a Phenomenon: Unidentified Objects in Space—A Scientific Appraisal* (New York: Ballantine Books, 1965), 1.

17. Ibid.

18. Ezekiel himself never refers to the vision as a chariot. For this, and many other reasons, the Ezekiel vision functions as a key proof-text in ufology. Probably the best treatment of it is Michael Lieb's gorgeous and haunting study of the modern technologization of the sacred, an approach that resonates deeply with my own hermeneutical understanding of the paranormal.

Lieb traces this back to the vision of Ezekiel and its fiery, spinning wheels. Here he mines the apparent psychopathology of Ezekiel, rabbinic fears around studying this particular text, the subsequent chariot (*merkabah*) mysticisms of Kabbalah and their "riders of the chariot," and the rare Hebrew word (*hashmal*) of the prophetic book that points to the original vision's "amber," "glowing metal" or *electrum*-like qualities (the "mysterium of *hashmal*," as Lieb puts it). For Lieb, the "children of Ezekiel," that is, the new UFO visionary of the New Age, is the "new *merkabah* mystic," the new rider of the chariot. The visionary *sign*, moreover, has now become the machinelike *thing*. See Michael Lieb, *Children of Ezekiel: Aliens, UFOs, the Crisis of Race, and the Advent of End Time* (Durham: Duke University Press, 1998).

19. Vallee, *Anatomy*, 27.

20. Like so many other assumed impossibilities, such alien-human contact remains a very real possibility for those in the know. Consider Michael A. G. Michaud's recent *Contact with Alien Civilizations: Our Hopes and Fears about Encountering Extraterrestrials* (New York: Copernicus Books, 2007). Michaud is no naive enthusiast. He served as director of the U.S. State Department's Office of Advanced Technology and as counselor for Science, Technology, and Environment at the American embassies in Paris and Tokyo, and he played an active role in U.S.-Soviet talks on outer-space arms control. And unlike so many other writers, he understands well that many of the deepest challenges here are philosophical, symbolic, and religious, that is, the problems of translation, communication, and worldview that such contact would inevitably involve. He understands, in my own terms now, that any contact team would have to include more anthropologists than rocket scientists.

21. Vallee, *Anatomy*, 39–42.

22. Quoted in ibid., 40

23. "Cloud-shaped" UFOs again blur the line between fraud and reality. Are these just clouds? Or some kind of stealth technology or mimicry technique, as one constantly sees in the natural world, particularly with insects? Much of the literature clearly suggests the latter, although of course there are many sightings that seem to be nothing more than misidentified cloud formations.

24. Vallee, *Anatomy*, 112.

25. By 1992, there were twenty major categories in Vallee's mature classification system. See Jacques Vallee, in collaboration with Martine Castello, *UFO Chronicles of the Soviet Union: A Cosmic Samizdat* (New York: Ballantine Books, 1992), appendix 2: Case Index.

26. Jacques and Janine Vallee, *Challenge to Science: The UFO Enigma* (New York: Ballantine Books, 1966), vi.

27. I. S. Shklovskii and Carl Sagan, *Intelligent Life in the Universe* (San Francisco: Holden-Day, 1966), 448–62. This is Sagan's expansion on Shklovskii's original Russian book, a remarkable cold war accomplishment in a geopolitical context in which, as Shklovskii wryly observed with some dash of hope, "the probability of our meeting is unlikely to be smaller than the probability of a visit to the Earth by an extraterrestrial cosmonaut" (vii).

28. Thomas E. Bullard, "UFOs: Lost in the Myths," in *UFOs and Abductions: Challenging the Borders of Knowledge*, ed. David M. Jacobs (Lawrence: University Press of Kansas, 2000), 145. This is a marvelous essay, and this volume as a whole is probably the best starting point for the historian of religions looking for a succinct and subtle introduction to the problems and promises the subject holds for the field.

29. William Irwin Thompson, *Evil and the World Order* (New York: Harper and Row, 1980), 81. Quoted in Jacques Vallee, "Consciousness, Culture, and UFOs," in *Alien Worlds: Social and Religious Dimensions of Extraterrestrial Contact*, ed. Diane G. Tumminia (Syracuse: Syracuse University Press, 2007), 209.

30. Hence the book ends with a long appendix entitled "A Century of UFO Landings (1868–1968)," which lists 200 press references and 923 reported cases.

31. Vallee had earlier treated the Agobard case in *Anatomy*, 6–8.

32. Agobard, *De Grandine et Tonitruis*, quoted in PM 9–10.

33. *Le Comte de Gabalis: Entretiens sur les Sciences Secretes* (Paris: Claude Barbin, 1670), 304–7. Quoted and translated by Vallee in PM 12. My thanks to Vallee for scanning the relevant pages of the original French edition for me.

34. IC 162. Evans-Wentz also helped him see connections between UFO lore and Joseph Smith, the founder of Mormonism. Both the Tibetan and Mormon traditions emphasize "treasure-books" hidden in the ground, waiting for the proper time to be revealed.

35. PM 35. This telepathic signaling became the major plotline of Spielberg's movie.

36. This material was later significantly expanded upon in light of a photostat of the original Portuguese medical report, psychological testing, and cross-examination of this case (dated February 22, 1958) and published as Gordon Creighton, "The Amazing Case of Antonio Villas Boas," in *The Humanoids: A Survey of Worldwide Reports of Landings of Unconventional Aerial Objects and Their Occupants*, ed. Charles Bowen (Chicago: Henry Regnery, 1969).

37. Ibid., 216.

38. Ibid., 218.

39. John G. Fuller, *The Interrupted Journey* (1966). Vallee revisits and adds to the case in PM 89–95. Vallee discusses his meeting with Fuller and the Hills in June of 1967 in FS 1:277–82.

40. Creighton, "Amazing Case," 200.

41. The title of the novel is taken from the intelligence term for a "source of electromagnetic radiation moving at high speed in the outer layers of the atmosphere, which triggers the sensors of spy satellites."

42. The culture of NASA, for example, is informed by science fiction, particularly that of Star Trek and of Robert A. Heinlein. See C. Penley, *NASA/Trek: Popular Science and Sex in America* (New York: Verso, 1997). One must also mention here that incredible mix of sexual magic, occultism, and science fiction that informed the early subculture of the Jet Propulsion Laboratory in Pasadena, California, via its cofounder, John Whiteside "Jack" Parsons. Heinlein was again part of the mix, as was science-fiction writer and Scientology founder Ron Hubbard. See John Carter, *Sex and Rockets: The Occult World of Jack Parsons* (Los Angeles: Feral House, 2004).

43. Hynek had originally, in early 1965, proposed "the Little Society," a playful spin on Lyndon B. Johnson's "Great Society" (FS 1:134). By the spring of 1967, he had switched the name to "the Invisible College" (FS 1:270). By August of the same year, Vallee had bound seven volumes of the *Archives of the Invisible College*, which included letters, confidential sighting reports, and the very best material from the air force files (FS 1:310).

44. J. Allen Hynek, "The UFO Mystery," in *FBI Bulletin* 44, no. 2 (February 1975), as quoted in IC 4.

45. Vallee had hinted at this control thesis already in PM 48–49. He returned to it again in his most recent essay, "Consciousness, Culture, and UFOs," where he wrote the following, presumably against those authors who see benevolent forces at work in the UFO phenomenon: "*We are not dealing with spiritual transformation here, but with social trance-formations*" (in Tumminia, *Alien Worlds*, 208; italics in original).

46. Vallee discusses the Puppet Master in relationship to Philip K. Dick's *Valis* at FS 2:278. "The Manufacturer of Unavoidable Events" ("Le fabricant d'événements inéluctables") is the title of the short story that Vallee considers to be his most important piece of fiction.

47. Personal communication, 13 October 2008.

48. FS 1:2. Vallee, however, had proposed to Hynek as early as 1963 that the saucer question "plunges deep into mystical and psychic theories" (FS 1:88).

49. IC 117, 120–22. As political scientist Michael Barkun has convincingly shown, this UFO/"secret society" connection—which, as we demonstrated in chapter 1, goes all the way back to Charles Fort—will be picked up by any number of paranoid, racist, and anti-Semitic

political movements in the late 1980s and '90s (see his *A Culture of Conspiracy: Apocalyptic Visions in Contemporary America* [Berkeley: University of California Press, 2003]). This period and its troubling developments fall well after Vallee had formed his own opinions and theories. It is also worth noting in this context that Vallee, although certainly suspicious of government intelligence and official manipulation and their grossly distorting effects on the scientific study of UFOs, generally resists radical forms of conspiracy thinking, as Barkun himself notes with reference to the infamous MJ-12 document and likely hoax (ibid., 143).

50. Later, scholars of new religious movements will expand on this list, adding observations about the clear historical links that exist between the early contactee literature and esoteric movements like Theosophy and the I AM movement, the use of channeling practices to contact various alien entities, and the different ways this material challenges the dominant scientific and religious paradigms. This literature is large, but the state of the art is probably best represented by two books: Brenda Denzler, *The Lure of the Edge: Scientific Passions, Religious Beliefs, and the Pursuit of UFOs* (Berkeley: University of California Press, 2001); and Christopher Partridge, ed., *UFO Religions* (London: Routledge, 2003). Denzler focuses on the tension between science and religion as competing or complementary explanatory frameworks within the UFO community. Partridge identifies the later abduction spiritualities as developments of an earlier theosophical esotericism within a New Age matrix, tracing, for example, the transformation of the "ascended masters" of Theosophy into the "descended masters" of the UFO religions.

51. IC 137–138. Later researchers will pick up on this comparative phenomenology and add near-death experiences (NDE) to the mix. See especially Kenneth Ring, *The Omega Project: Near-Death Experiences, UFO Encounters, and Mind at Large* (New York: William Morrow, 1992).

52. As far as I can tell, Vallee first suggests this in a journal entry of January 26, 1964 (FS 1:95).

53. Quoted in Vallee, *Fastwalker*, 159.

54. Vallee engages in a similar thought experiment in FS 1:161–62.

55. This is a good example of Vallee's resistance to grand conspiracy thinking, as noted above, in note 49.

56. The Arpanet was named after its funding source, ARPA, the Advanced Research Projects Agency of the Pentagon, now called DARPA (the D is for Defense).

57. FS 2:503. The two men would write a book together based on this early work: Russell Targ and Harold Puthoff, *Mind-Reach: Scientists Look at Psychic Ability* (Delacorte Press, 1977). For Swann's perspective, see his remarkable autobiography, *To Kiss Earth Good-Bye* (New York: Hawthorn Books, 1975), especially 52–61. For two technical descriptions, complete with magnometer readings, of this initial experiment and Swann's remote-viewing forays, see Harold Puthoff and Russell Targ, "Physics, Entropy, and Psychokinesis" and "Remote Viewing of Targets," in *Quantum Physics and Parapsychology: Proceedings of an International Conference Held in Geneva, Switzerland, August 26–27, 1974*, ed. Laura Oteri (New York: Parapsychology Foundation, 1975).

58. Targ and Puthoff, *Mind-Reach*, 19.

59. Ibid., 21.

60. Ibid., 27.

61. Targ and Puthoff describe this same event, I gather, in *Mind-Reach*, 47–48. It appears that it was Price, not Swann, who performed this particular remote viewing.

62. Russell Targ and Harold E. Puthoff, "Information Transfer under Conditions of Sensory Shielding," in *Nature* 252 (October 18, 1974): 602–7.

63. FS 2:122. For the language of the techgnostic, I am indebted to Erik Davis, *TechGnosis: Myth, Magic and Mysticism in the Age of Information* (New York: Three Rivers Press, 1998).

64. Targ and Puthoff, *Mind-Reach*, 42. Puthoff, Swann, and Price all had connections to Scientology in the early 1970s. For a balanced discussion of the Scientology piece and Puthoff's break with the religion in the mid-1970s, see Jim Schnabel, *Remote Viewers: The Secret History of America's Psychic Spies* (New York: Dell, 1997), 198–200.

65. FS 2:196, 504–5. Vallee felt that the SRI group never really followed through on a systematic implementation and testing of this address approach (FS 2:289, 480).

66. For a precise description of what became known as Coordinate Remote Viewing (or CRV) that privileges the metaphysics of nonlocal mind and humorously preserves the apparent impossibility of using a randomly generated number as a global address, see Paul H. Smith's *Reading the Enemy's Mind: Inside Star Gate, America's Psychic Espionage Program* (New York: Forge, 2005), 277–79.

67. For Mitchell's positive assessment of Geller, and much else relevant to our present concerns, see his remarkable autobiography, with Dwight Williams, *The Way of the Explorer: An Apollo Astronaut's Journey through the Material and Mystical Worlds* (New York: Putnam, 1996).

68. Jonathan Margolis, *Uri Geller: Magician or Mystic?* (New York: Welcome Rain Publishers, 1999), 11.

69. See Jeffrey J. Kripal, *Esalen: America and the Religion of No Religion* (Chicago: University of Chicago Press, 2007), chapter 14, "Superpowers: Cold War Psychics and Citizen Diplomats," and chapter 15, "Sex with the Angels: Nonlocal Mind, UFOs, and *An End to Ordinary History*."

70. For emblematic histories written by insiders, see: Dale E. Graff, *Tracks in the Psychic Wilderness: An Exploration of ESP, Remote Viewing, Precognitive Dreaming and Synchronicity* (Boston: Element, 1998); Joseph McMoneagle, *The Stargate Chronicles: Memoirs of a Psychic Spy* (Charlottesville: Hampton Roads, 2002); F. Holmes Atwater, *Captain of My Ship, Master of My Soul: Living with Guidance* (Charlottesville: Hampton Roads, 2001); and Smith, *Reading the Enemy's Mind.* For a science writer's balanced account, see Schnabel, *Remote Viewers.*

71. Joseph McMoneagle, *Mind Trek: Exploring Consciousness, Time, and Space through Remote Viewing* (Charlottesville: Hampton Roads, 1997), 27–34.

72. Personal communication, April 29, 2009. May, an accomplished and broadly published expert on low-energy, experimental nuclear physics, joined the SRI team in 1975. He directed the research program there from 1985 until 1991, after which he shifted his affiliation to another U.S. Defense contractor, where he continued his involvement with government-sponsored parapsychology until 1995, when the Stargate program out at Fort Meade was finally shut down. May's importance is signaled by the fact that he presided over an astonishing 70 percent of the total funding and a full 85 percent of the data collection for the government's twenty-two-year involvement in parapsychological research. This and the fact that he has since worked closely with his counterparts in Russia and is a coauthor of a forthcoming work that will no doubt become the definitive study of the remote viewing story on both the American and Russian sides: Edwin C. May, Alexei Yurievich Savin, Boris Ratnikov, Joseph W. McMoneagle, and Victor Rubel, *ESP Wars from Both Sides of the Iron Curtain* (forthcoming).

73. "About the Author," in Joseph McMoneagle, *The Ultimate Time Machine: A Remote Viewer's Perception of Time, and Predictions for the New Millennium* (Charlottesville: Hampton Roads, 1999).

74. "Heretic among Heretics: Jacques Vallee Interview," http://www.ufoevidence.org. Similarly, Targ and Puthoff began their *Mind-Reach* with a definition of "heresy" that described the history of science as "paradoxes becoming commonplaces and heresies becoming orthodoxies" (*Mind-Reach*, 1), in other words, Fort's historical cycles of the Dominants and the damned.

75. FS 2:480. Vallee likes to quote Churchill on this key point: "In wartime, truth is so precious that she must always be protected by a bodyguard of lies."

76. Whitley Strieber, foreword to Vallee, *Dimensions*, vii.

77. Ibid., 291.

78. Ibid., 128; italicized in original.

79. See, for example, Michio Kaku, *Hyperspace: A Scientific Odyssey through Parallel Universes, Time Warps, and the 10th Dimension* (New York: Anchor Books, 1994).

80. Vallee, *Dimensions*, 136; italicized in original.

81. Ibid., 284–85.

82. Ibid. 288–89; italics in original.

83. Jacques Vallee, *Confrontations: A Scientist's Search for Alien Contact* (New York: Ballantine Books, 1990), 217–18.

84. Ibid., 221.

85. Ibid., 224.

86. Ibid., 225.

87. Ibid., 129.

88. Ibid., 133.

89. Ibid., 122.

90. Vallee, *UFO Chronicles*, 141.

91. Ibid., 115. Gerald Heard, the British-American visionary who helped inspire the founding of Esalen (and also wrote an early book on UFOs), had speculated along almost identical X-Men or evolutionary lines. See Kripal, *Esalen*, 92.

92. Vallee, *UFO Chronicles*, 5.

93. For a lovely treatment of this history, "from Plato to NATO," see R. A. S. Hennessey, *Worlds Without End: The Historic Search for Extraterrestrial Life* (Charleston: Tempus Publishing, 1999).

94. For a powerful personal synchronicity or "intersign" that Vallee read in the light of Dick's *Valis*, see FS 2:212–13.

95. "Dr. Jacques Vallee Reveals What Is Behind *Forbidden Science*," 4. http://www.21stcenturyradio.com/ForbiddenScience.htm, accessed on January 8, 2008.

96. Murphy adopted the phrase from the scientists who attended the two UFO symposia sponsored by Esalen in 1975 and 1986. The first was held offsite and in secret, partly to protect the reputations of some of the elite scientists who attended. Another invisible college.

97. For examples of Vallee's precognitive dreams, see FS 2:131, 221, 353, 409–10, 441, and 466. For his experience of "intersigns," see FS 2:212–13, 330–31, 343, 442, and 491. Freud wrote of dream symbolism as "overdetermined."

98. Penciled inscription by Hynek in his personal copy. Both Hynek and Vallee knew Hall, whom they visited at his Philosophical Research Center in Los Angeles (FS 2:64). Indeed, Vallee begins the second volume of his journals with a quote from Manly Hall, whom he describes as an "admirable friend" (FS 2:7).

99. FS 1:233. According to Vallee, Hynek was also especially fond of Aldous Huxley's *The Perennial Philosophy*. A comparison of Huxley's neo-Vedantic perennialism with Manly Hall's Western esoteric perennialism would be interesting and useful here.

100. FS 1:206. There are clear allusions here to the science-fiction writer H. P. Lovecraft, whose fictional universe is structured along similar lines.

101. "Consciousness, Culture, and UFOs," in Tumminia *Alien Worlds*, 206.

CHAPTER FOUR

1. Jim Schnabel, *Remote Viewers: The Secret History of America's Psychic Spies* (New York: Dell, 1997), 35–36. For this opening story, I am relying on two communications I had with Méheust: one a personal conversation on May 25, 2008; the other an e-mail communication dated June 12, 2008. He has also read and corrected the present retelling.

2. This is the sort of thing I was referring to above, in chapter 1, note 105.

3. The counterculture was counter to culture to the extent that it insisted on the primacy of consciousness as metaphysically prior to culture and, subsequently, as the most effective creator of new culture. This was the thesis of the man who invented and first theorized the term anyway. See Theodore Roszak, *The Making of a Counter Culture: Reflections on the Technocratic Society and Its Youthful Opposition* (New York: Anchor Books, 1969).

4. I am indebted here to Richard Shweder, who has written eloquently of a certain "ontological polytheism," of "reality posits," and of a cultural psychology whose goal is to show how psyche and culture "make each other up." See his *Thinking Through Cultures: Expeditions in Cultural Psychology* (Cambridge, Massachusetts: Harvard University Press, 1991).

5. Since 2004, Méheust has also produced a number of works of cultural criticism around the paranormal, including *Devenez savants: Découvres les sorciers: Lettre à Georges Charpak* (Paris: Éditions Dervy, 2004), and a few "popular" works for his publishers, including *100 mots pour comprendre la voyance* (Paris: Les Empecheurs de Penser en Rond, 2005) and *Histoires paranormales du Titanic* (Paris: J'ai Lu, 2006). Space and time (not always absolute in the present pages!) prevent me from treating all of these works here.

6. For a one-hundred-page essay by Méheust on Michel's life and thought and an unedited collection of this correspondence, see Aimé Michel, *L'Apocalypse molle: Correspondance addressée à Bertrand Méheust de 1978 à 1990 (texts inédits)* (Cointrin, Switzerland: Aldane editions, 2008). For a collection of Michel's essays edited and annotated by Jean-Pierre Rospars, see Aimé Michel, *La clarté au coeur du laybyrinthe: Chroniques sur la science et la religion* (Cointrin, Switzerland: Aldane editions, 2008). See also Michel Picard, *Aimé Michel: Ou la Quête du Surhumain* (Agnieres: JMG, 2000).

7. Bertrand Méheust, "Le veilleur d'Ar Men," in Michel, *L'Apocalypse molle*, 12.

8. For the fullest statement of Michel's understanding of the physical phenomena of mysticism and what they portend about the future of the body, see his *Metanoia: Les phénomènes physique du mysticisme* (Paris: Albin Michel, 1986).

9. Méheust, "Le veilleur d'Ar Men," 15, 18.

10. Louis Pauwels and Jacques Bergier, *The Morning of the Magicians* (New York: Stein and Day, 1964). Pauwels was the primary author here. The text is written in his voice, with the clear acknowledgment that the ideas were the product of a five-year study and friendship with Bergier. The constant focus of the text on physics as a kind of modern mysticism is one of many features of the text that point to Bergier.

11. Picard, *Aimé Michel*, ix.

12. Pauwels and Bergier, *Morning of the Magicians*, 96.

13. Ibid., ix, 96, 95.

14. Ibid., 95.

15. Here cited as SF in its recent second edition, Bertrand Méheust, *Science-fiction et soucoupes volantes: Une réalité mythico-physique* (Rennes, France: Terre de Brume, 2007).

16. See also Hilary Evans, *Intrusions: Society and the Paranormal* (London: Routledge & Kegan Paul, 1982), an excellent meditation on the dysfunctional abyss that separates Western society's general acceptance of the paranormal and the intellectual establishment's dismissal of the same.

17. Herbert Thurston, S.J., *The Physical Phenomena of Mysticism*, ed. J. H. Crehan, S.J. (London: Burns Oates, 1952).

18. This esoteric expression involved a literally esoteric author. Méheust derives the expression from an essay in the *Revue métaphysique* signed by "Xodarap" (SF 307).

19. This idea, sometimes called "neutral monism," is a fairly common one, even in the natural sciences. The physicist John Wheeler wrote of reality as "it" and "bit," that is, as composed of both matter and information, and the evolutionary biologist Julian Huxley thought that there is "one world stuff" that manifests both material and mental properties depending upon whether it is viewed from the outside (matter) or from the inside (mind). I am not sure, however, what either author would have thought about reality manifesting itself as physical-mythical. An electron as a bit of information is one thing. A myth in the sky chased by F-94s is quite another. My thanks to Dean Radin for the Wheeler reference.

20. Related to Méheust's technologized Hermeticism is his notion that the origins of American and British science fiction in the earlier French genre of *le merveilleux scientifique*

display the same sacred-to-science patterns. What we have here is the return of the marvelous, but now coded in terms of the scientific discovery. The marvel is no longer the supernatural but the technological. In essence, a new form of the sacred, a "technological sacred," was born under the mask of science and technology (SF 14, 21).

21. This is also why Méheust rejects the ever-popular ancient astronaut theory, whereby the evolution of human beings and their cultures are seen to have been guided for millennia by space-faring aliens (SF 255–56).

22. It is also worth mentioning here that Méheust's work on UFOs became the basis of at least two sci-fi novels: former Oxford linguist Ian Watson's *Miracle Visitors* and Michel Jeury's *Les yeux geants*.

23. This is not quite true, as the biological function of sex is present in and indeed often central to the encounter stories, as Méheust himself notes. Still, the general point stands.

24. Bertrand Méheust, *En soucoupes volantes: Vers une ethnologie des récits d'enlèvements* (Paris: Imago, 1992).

25. Thomas E. Bullard, "UFOs: Lost in the Myths," in *UFOs and Abductions: Challenging the Borders of Knowledge*, ed. David M. Jacobs (Lawrence: University Press of Kansas, 2000), 143.

26. Bertrand Méheust, *Somnambulisme et médiumnité (1784–1930)* (Le Plessis-Robinson: Institut Synthélabo Pour Le Progrés de la Connaissance, 1999); henceforth SM.

27. I am indebted to David Hufford for reminding me here of this particular feature of Berger's thought (personal communication, April 20, 2008).

28. A. M. J. Chastenet de Puységur, *Mémoires pour servir a l'histoire et a l'établissement du magnétisme animal* (Londres, 1786), 29; italics as underlining in the original; quoted in SM 1:15.

29. Consider the case of CSICOPS, the organization ideologically dedicated to criticizing, humiliating, or otherwise shouting down all paranormal claims, and its dubious handling of the alleged findings of Michel Gauquelin that the position of Mars at an individual's birth is correlated with athletic ability (George P. Hansen, *The Trickster and the Paranormal* [XLibris, 2001], 150).

30. Bertrand Méheust, *Un voyant prodigieux: Alexis Didier, 1826–1886* (Paris: Les Empecheurs de Penser en Rond, 2003), 24; henceforth VP.

31. Henri F. Ellenberger, *The Discovery of the Unconscious: The History and Evolution of Dynamic Psychiatry* (New York: Basic Books, 1970).

32. Adam Crabtree, *From Mesmer to Freud: Magnetic Sleep and the Roots of Psychological Healing* (New Haven: Yale University Press, 1993).

33. This comes out especially clearly in Méheust's treatment of Durkheim and the latter's appreciative reading of William James's pragmatism (SM 2:271–73).

34. As such, Méheust's hermeneutic displays strong resemblances to Colin Bennett's reading of the semireal status and interactional nature of the various "imp-happenings," "rejected design-solutions," and "half-realized, undernourished systems-doodles" in the data of Charles Fort's shoeboxes. See his "Charles Fort's Degrees of Reality," in *Anomalist* 7 (1998): 95–96.

35. This "fear of psi" theme is a very strong one in the literature. One of the most insightful treatments occurs in the historical speculations and psychoanalytic analyses of Jules Eisenbud, *The World of Ted Serios: "Thoughtographic" Studies of an Extraordinary Mind* (New York: William Morrow & Company, 1967), chapter 14, "The Anatomy of Resistance."

36. Quoted in Bruce Mills, *Poe, Fuller, and the Mesmeric Arts: Transition States in the American Renaissance* (Columbia: University of Missouri Press, 2006), xiv. For another treatment of the mystical roots of American literature, see Arthur Versluis, *The Esoteric Origins of the American Renaissance* (New York: Oxford, 2001).

37. Mills, *Poe, Fuller, and the Mesmeric Arts*, xiv.

38. Ibid., 39.

39. Ibid., back cover.

40. I am fully aware of how loaded, problematic, and undefined a word like "real" is in this context. I will address some of these issues below, but I hope it goes without saying that I have been problematizing this term all along through my criticisms of subjectivist and objectivist epistemologies.

41. Chancey Hare Townshend, *Facts in Mesmerism, with Reasons for a Dispassionate Inquiry into it* (London, 1840).

42. Chauncey Hare Townshend, "Recent Clairvoyance of Alexis Didier," *Zoist* 9 (1851): 402–14. All citations from this scene are from the original *Zoist* letter.

43. See Jeffrey J. Kripal, *The Serpent's Gift: Gnostic Reflections on the Study of Religion* (Chicago: University of Chicago Press, 2007), especially chapter 2, "Restoring the Adam of Light."

44. Peter L. Berger, *A Rumor of Angels: Modern Society and the Rediscovery of the Supernatural* (New York: Doubleday, 1969), 59. This is a red thread in Berger's early corpus. He makes a similar case at the end of his classic study, *The Sacred Canopy: Elements of a Sociological Theory of Religion* (Garden City: Doubleday, 1967); and he makes a related argument again in *The Heretical Imperative: Contemporary Possibilities of Religious Affirmation* (New York: Anchor Books, 1980).

45. Alison Winter, *Mesmerized: Powers of Mind in Victorian Britain* (Chicago: University of Chicago Press, 1998).

46. Henri Delaage, *Le Sommeil magnétique expliqué par le somnambule Alexis en état de lucidité* (Paris, 1857), 16, quoted in SF 244, my translation. Didier's articulation here is faithful to the Catholic tradition of relic use, which distinguishes between first-, second-, and third-class relics. First-class relics are body parts. Second-class relics are objects that the saint owned or used in his or her own life. Third-class relics are objects, cloth for example, ritually brought into contact with first-class relics and then distributed among the faithful. Didier is basically addressing second-class relics here.

47. For a balanced and fair summary of this phenomenon, see Arthur Lyons and Marcello Truzzi, *The Blue Sense: Psychic Detectives and Crime* (New York: The Mysterious Press, 1991).

48. This story was summarized in a newspaper, *Le Pays*, and then reprinted in the *Zoist* essay cited in note 42. Méheust cites another at VP 247.

49. Méheust discusses Vallee, and particularly his *Passport to Magonia*, at SF 266–70.

50. Chris Aubeck and Jacques Vallee, *Prodigies: Unexplained Aerial Phenomena from Antiquity to Modern Times and Their Impact on Human Culture, History and Beliefs* (unpublished manuscript).

51. See Gregory Bateson, *Mind and Nature: A Necessary Unity* (New York: E. P. Dutton, 1979); and *Steps to an Ecology of Mind* (Chicago: University of Chicago Press, 2000).

52. Ernesto De Martino, *The World of Magic* (New York: Pyramid Communications, 1972), 77.

53. These texts are available in the *Collected Works* (in volumes 10 and 18), but a helpful collection of them with attending material, commentary, and historical contextualization is available in C. G. Jung, *Flying Saucers: Saucers: A Modern Myth of Things Seen in the Sky*, trans. R. F. C. Hull (New York: MJF, 1978). The present quote occurs on page 135 of this text.

54. Bullard, "Lost in the Myths," 165.

55. Ibid., 6.

56. Méheust cites this text at SF 269 in French. The English can be found in C. G. Jung, *Memories, Dreams, Reflections*, ed. Aniela Jaffé, trans. Richard and Clara Winston (New York: Vintage, 1989), 323. Other comments on UFOs can be found in *C. G. Jung Speaking: Interviews and Encounters*, ed. William McGuire and R. F. C. Hull (Princeton: Princeton University Press, 1977).

57. This again is the same dialectical move that lies at the core of my own "gnostic" methodology, cited above in note 43.

CONCLUSION

1. Edward F. Kelly, Emily Williams Kelly, Adam Crabtree, Alan Gauld, Michael Grosso, and Bruce Greyson, *Irreducible Mind: Toward a Psychology for the 21st Century* (Lanham, Maryland: Rowman & Littlefield, 2006), xix.

2. Mircea Eliade, *A History of Religious Ideas*, trans. Willard R. Trask (Chicago: University of Chicago Press, 1978), 1:xiii.

3. On one level, my metamethod here with respect to cognitive science is *interactionist* in the sense that E. Thomas Lawson and Robert N. NcCauley define the term, that is, I seek to put explanatory or reductive and interpretive or hermeneutical methods in a dynamic complementary relationship ("Interpretation and Explanation: Problems and Promise in the Study of Religion," in *Religion and Cognition: A Reader*, ed. D. Jason Slone [London: Equinox, 2006]). On another level, my approach in this book has been more *inclusivistic* in the sense that I have privileged the semiotic nature of paranormal events over their presumed causal structure (but primarily to redress a perceived imbalance). On still another level, I am not so sure either term fits, as my interactionist and inclusivistic moves are reflections of a deeper conviction about how *neither* the humanities *nor* the sciences can explain this stuff, about how the paranormal event is simultaneously subjective *and* objective and so falls somewhere between (or, more likely, beyond) both epistemological Dominants. In this two-way skepticism toward religious literalism *and* scientific materialism, my method is deeply Fortean.

4. For two impressive contemporary statements of the thesis, see: Paul Marshall, *Mystical Encounters with the Natural World: Experiences and Explanations* (New York: Oxford University Press, 2005), especially chapter 8, "Mind Beyond the Brain: Reducing Valves and Metaphysics"; and Kelly et al., *Irreducible Mind*.

5. A personal note. Looking back, I am struck by how this ontological thread runs throughout all my books, from the first pages of *Kali's Child*, where it was expressed mythically through the mystico-erotic union of Kali (as occult energy or maternal matter) on top of Siva (as pure consciousness), through my various comparative studies of sex and spirit (read: matter and mind) in the history of religions in *Roads of Excess* and *The Serpent's Gift*, to the last pages of *Esalen*, where it was rearticulated as the modal metaphysics (the unity of Consciousness and Energy) realized in the human potential movement and expressed in the American counterculture's selective turn to Tantric Asia. Apparently, whether I am aware of it or not, this is what I think. In the terms of professional philosophy, I am probably closest to David Ray Griffin's "nondualist interactionism" (see especially his *Parapsychology, Philosophy, and Spirituality: A Postmodern Exploration* [Albany: SUNY, 1997], chapter 3), although my thought also bears very strong resemblances to what Edward Kelly, following Alfred North Whitehead and the quantum theorist Henry Stapp, calls "neutral monism" (Kelly, "Toward a Psychology for the 21st Century," in *Irreducible Mind*, 630–38). I certainly do not think that the cognitive, binary, computational structure of the human brain is up to understanding the nondual nature of reality, although of course human beings experience, intuit, and know such states of being all the time. That is, after all, what they *are*. For more on these ontological questions, see my "Mind Matters: Esalen's Sursem Group and the Ethnography of Consciousness," in *What Matters: Ethnographies of Value in a (Not So) Secular Age*, eds. Courtney Bender and Ann Taves (forthcoming).

6. Kelly, "Toward a Psychology for the 21st Century," 606–7.

7. I am thinking here of works like Steven Pinker's *How the Mind Works* (New York: W. W. Norton, 1997) and Pascal Boyer's *Religion Explained: The Evolutionary Origins of Religious Thought* (New York: Basic Books, 2001). An interesting exception is Sam Harris, whose otherwise famous ideological reductionism generously leaves open the possibility that psychical phenomena may have something to teach contemporary neuroscience. He even writes of "some

credible evidence for reincarnation," citing Ian Stevenson's work (*The End of Faith: Religion, Terror, and the Future of Reason* [New York: Norton, 2005], 232n18).

8. D. E. Harding, "On Having No Head," in *The Mind's I: Fantasies and Reflections on Self and Soul*, ed. Douglas R. Hofstadter and Daniel C. Dennett (New York: Basic Books, 1981), 23. Or did Hofstadter and Dennet understand Harding's essay under the "Fantasies" of their subtitle?

9. Ibid., 24, 25.

10. Ibid., 28–29. Hence the symbolic importance of decapitation and severed heads in Indo-Tibetan Buddhist and Hindu Tantra. Harding, after all, was hiking in the Himalayas.

11. Jill Bolte Taylor, *My Stroke of Insight: A Brain Scientist's Personal Journey* (New York: Viking, 2008), cover flap.

12. Ibid., 3.

13. Ibid., 66.

14. Ibid., 38.

15. Ibid., 41.

16. Ibid., 45–46.

17. Ibid., 45.

18. Ibid., 13.

19. Ibid., 42.

20. Ibid., 30.

21. Ibid., 31.

22. Ibid., 43.

23. Ibid., 70

24. Taylor even gives us a bit of historical context for one of my central terms. She identifies the first person to suggest that each hemisphere possesses its own form of mind: Meinard Simon Du Pui. "In 1780," she tells us, "Du Pui claimed that mankind was *Homo Duplex*—meaning that he had a double brain with a double mind" (ibid., 27).

25. Ibid., 71. I recognize that, as a brain anatomist, Taylor often presents her case as a physicalist or materialist thinker. That makes good sense, at least to the extent that she wishes to stay within the good graces of professional science as it is presently configured. But I can only observe that her constant invocation of mystical language works strongly against this very materialism and physicalism. In the end, in my reading now, her text is a "fantastic" one capable of being read either way.

26. Mario Beauregard and Denyse O'Leary, *The Spiritual Brain: A Neuroscientist's Case for the Existence of the Soul* (New York: HarperCollins, 2007), 150. Although I am in broad and deep agreement with this work, I am troubled that its use of the scholarly literature on mysticism, spirituality, and religious experience is a *half century* behind the times, that is, the authors rely heavily on authors like William James, Richard Maurice Bucke, Evelyn Underhill, and William Stace (fair enough), but show little or no awareness of the vast literature that historians and philosophers of religion have been working on since the 1960s. I mention this not so much to criticize as to call for some truly reciprocal collaboration between the sciences and the humanities, a collaboration that mirrors the very subjective/objective or mind/matter dialectic that authors like Beauregard propose. I would suggest that such a collaboration is possible only if the historical and hermeneutical complexities are engaged at the same depth and at the same level as the neuroscience.

27. Ibid., 152.

28. Ibid., 293. I am supplying the year 1987 after Beauregard's description of the event as occurring "twenty years ago."

29. Ibid., 294.

30. Ibid., 295.

31. A case can be made for the confluence of psychoanalytic and neuroscientific models of the unconscious. See especially Frank Tallis, *Hidden Minds: A History of the Unconscious* (New York: Arcade, 2002).

32. Beauregard and O'Leary, *Spiritual Brain*, 132.

33. Victoria Nelson, *The Secret Life of Puppets* (Cambridge: Harvard University Press, 2001), 16.

34. Kelly et al., *Irreducible Mind.*

35. Tzvetan Todorov, *The Fantastic: A Structural Approach to a Literary Genre* (Ithaca: Cornell University Press, 1975), 25.

36. I am indebted here to Jorge N. Ferrer and Jacob H. Sherman, eds., *The Participatory Turn: Spirituality, Mysticism, Religious Studies* (Albany: SUNY, 2008).

IMPOSSIBLE (DIS)CLOSINGS

1. There are numerous sources for what follows, ranging from the orthodox Catholic devotional accounts to the highly heterodox ufological revisionings. I pretend no exhaustive study here, much less a definitive position, but I am relating the story in a way that is reflective of my present subjects, hence my privileging of the Portuguese trilogy discussed below in "Required Reading (That Is Never Read)": Joaquim Fernandes and Fina D'Armada, *Heavenly Lights: The Apparitions of Fátima and the UFO Phenomenon*; Joaquim Fernandes and Fina D'Armada, *Celestial Secrets: The Hidden History of the Fátima Incident*; and Fernando Fernandes, Joaquim Fernandes, and Raul Berenguel, *Fátima Revisited: The Apparition Phenomenon in Ufology, Psychology, and Science* (San Antonio: Anomalist Books, 2005, 2006, 2008).

2. Fernandes and D'Armada, *Heavenly Lights*, 8–9; and *Celestial Secrets*, 148–49.

3. This is actually not the beginning. There were a number of preapparitions around 1916, including some very confused accounts of an unidentified figure dressed in a white sheet hovering over a holm oak tree that becomes a crystalline, white, angelic being in the later interpretations, a being that, in one account, has no head, in others switches genders, and in still another is accompanied by a shower of rocks from nowhere (*Celestial Secrets*, 44–72). During the months of the visions, a "fourth witness," Carolina Carreira, also saw a luminous, childlike humanoid with blonde hair in the same vicinity (ibid., 73–84). Fernandes and D'Armada further point out that on March 10, 1917, a group of spiritualists published a mathematical cipher (135197) in a Lisbon newspaper that can be read as a prediction of a coming event on 13-5-19[1]7. More convincingly, and truly impossibly, they discuss another group of psychics in Porto who claimed to be receiving a prediction that "something transcendental" was about to happen on May 13, 1917. So certain were they that they published their (correct) prediction in the *Journal de Notícias* that same day, thus effectively describing an event in a newspaper as it happened. For the relevant historical documents and a full discussion, see *Celestial Secrets*, 3–28.

4. Ibid., 3–4. I have removed all use of italics when quoting from these two authors.

5. Ibid., 11.

6. Ibid., 20.

7. The children were not present in August. They were in jail, imprisoned in an attempt to put an end to the embarrassing spectacle. The apparition acted, at first, as if it did not know the kids were absent. Witnesses reported the usual thunder and bright flash followed by the familiar little cloud over the tree. It quickly rose and melted away this time, however.

8. Ibid., 36–37.

9. Ibid., 41–43.

10. Ibid., 65–68.

11. Ibid., 76.

12. Ibid., 63.

13. Ibid., 47.

14. Ibid., 57.

15. Ibid., 91. For a newspaper photo, see ibid., 92.

16. Ibid., 137.

17. Ibid., 140.

18. Ibid., 143–45.

19. Ibid., 156.

20. Paul Misraki, *Les Extraterrestres* (Paris: Plon, 1962). On September 18, 1962, Vallee visited Misraki in his Paris apartment just as this book was coming out (FS 1:66–67; see also 1:155–62).

21. Fernandes and D'Armada dedicate over twenty pages to this substance and the various theories used to explain it (*Heavenly Lights*, 83–104).

22. Fernandes and D'Armada, *Celestial Secrets*, 151–52.

23. Ibid., 153.

24. Ibid., 94. The fullest treatment of this psychotropic reading of aliens, now focused on DMT and ayahuasca, is Rick Strassman, Slawek Wojtowicz, Luis Eduardo Luna, and Ede Frescka, *Inner Paths to Outer Space: Journeys to Alien Worlds through Psychedelics and Other Spiritual Technologies* (Rochester, Vermont: Park Street Press, 2008). The authors sum up their thesis thus: "that the secret gateway to alien worlds may be hidden inside our own minds and that humans already have been traveling in space and time and making contact with alien species," via the chemical triggers or brain-filter suppressors of nature's psychotropic plants (3).

25. Stanley Krippner and Michael Persinger, "Evidence for Enhanced Congruence between Dreams and Distant Target Material during Periods of Decreased Geomagnetic Activity," in Fernandes, Fernandes, and Berenguel, *Fátima Revisited*.

26. Persinger's readings also bear obvious parallels to the earlier work of John E. Keel, a Fortean writer who advanced a very similar set of electromagnetic or "superspectrum" readings of occult phenomena in his many books, including and especially *The Eighth Tower: The Cosmic Force Behind All Religious, Occult and UFO Phenomena* (New York: Saturday Review Press, 1975).

27. Fernandes and D'Armada, *Celestial Secrets*, 42. They give no date.

28. Michael A. Persinger, "The Fátima Phenomenon," in Fernandes, Fernandes, and Berenguel, *Fátima Revisited*, 7.

29. Raul Berenguel, "Mind Control and Marian Visions—A Theoretical and Experimental Approach," in ibid., 63. Indeed, there is other research to suggest that exposure to high levels of electromagnetic radiation can produce many of the classical UFO (and Marian) phenomena: paralysis, loss of consciousness, visual impairment, and amnesia among them (*Celestial Secrets*, 89).

30. Fernandes and D'Armada, *Heavenly Lights*, 22. Similarly, Vallee notes that the Arabic astrological sign for Venus was seen on the unidentified flying object witnessed at Socorro, New Mexico, on April 24, 1964 (IC 134–35). The witness, a patrolman named Lonnie Zamora, insisted on seeing a priest before he spoke of what he saw, "because he thought he might have seen something diabolical" (FS 1:110).

31. Fernandes and D'Armada, *Heavenly Lights*, 21. See also *Celestial Secrets*, 237.

REQUIRED READING

1. Jim Schnabel, *Remote Viewers: The Secret History of America's Psychic Spies* (New York: Dell, 1997), back cover blurb.

2. David M. Jacobs, ed., *UFOs and Abductions: Challenging the Borders of Knowledge* (Lawrence: University Press, of Kansas, 2000), 2.

Index